Teaching Elementary
Social Studies

Teaching Elementary Social Studies

Principles and Applications

FOURTH EDITION

James J. Zarrillo

California State University, East Bay

Boston   Columbus   Indianapolis   New York   San Francisco   Upper Saddle River
Amsterdam   Cape Town   Dubai   London   Madrid   Milan   Munich   Paris   Montreal   Toronto
Delhi   Mexico City   Sao Paulo   Sydney   Hong Kong   Seoul   Singapore   Taipei   Tokyo

KH

Editor in Chief: Paul Smith
Senior Acquisitions Editor: Kelly Villella Canton
Editorial Assistant: Annalea Manalili
Senior Marketing Manager: Darcy Betts
Project Manager: Renata Butera
Operations Specialist: Renata Butera
Photo Researcher: Annie Pickert
Full-Service Project Management: Sudeshna Nandy
Composition: Aptara®, Inc.
Cover Designer: Karen Noferi
Cover Image: © Katrina Brown/Shutterstock
Printer/Binder: R.R. Donnelley/Harrisonburg
Cover Printer: R.R. Donnelley/Harrisonburg
Text Font: 10/12 Minion

Credits and acknowledgments borrowed from other sources and reproduced, with permission, in this textbook also appear on appropriate page within text.

Photo Credits: Shutterstock, pp. 2, 69, 94, 151, 275; Ann Vega/Merrill, p. 26; Tom Williams/Roll Call/Newscom, p. 120; David Duprey/AP Images, p. 167; Annie Pickert/Pearson, pp. 195, 224; Scott Cunningham/Merrill, p. 251; Jeff Greenberg/PhotoEdit, p. 298

Library of Congress Cataloging-in-Publication Data

Zarrillo, James.
  Teaching elementary social studies : principles and applications / James J. Zarrillo. — 4th ed.
     p. cm.
Includes bibliographical references and index.
ISBN-13: 978-0-13-256551-6
ISBN-10: 0-13-256551-X
1. Social sciences—Study and teaching (Elementary)—United States.
2. Multicultural education—United States. I. Title.

LB1584.Z27 2012
372.83′044—dc22   2011004812

10 9 8 7 6 5 4 3 2 1 RRD 15 14 13 12 11

www.pearsonhighered.com

ISBN 10:   0-13-256551-X
ISBN 13: 978-0-13-256551-6

10/17/11

About the Author
Dr. James J. Zarrillo

Dr. James Zarrillo currently serves as the Associate Dean of the College of Education and Allied Studies at California State University, East Bay in Hayward, California. He is also a Professor in the Department of Teacher Education. In addition to this fourth edition of *Teaching Elementary Social Studies: Principles and Applications,* Dr. Zarrillo is the author of four other books. His area of professional interest is the elementary school curriculum; specifically social studies instruction, the role of children's literature in the elementary school curriculum, and reading instruction.

Prior to coming to California State University, East Bay, Dr. Zarrillo was a member of the faculty at California State University, Long Beach (1988–1995). From 1976 to 1986 he was an elementary school teacher in the Burbank (California) Unified School District, where he taught grades 2, 3, 4, 5, and 6. Dr. Zarrillo earned his bachelor's degree from the University of Redlands; his master's degree from California State University, Northridge; and his doctoral degree from the Claremont Graduate University.

Brief Contents

Contents

Note: Every effort has been made to provide accurate and current Internet information in this book. However, the Internet and information posted on it are constantly changing, and it is inevitable that some of the Internet addresses listed in this textbook will change.

Lesson Plans and Instructional Activities

More than 150 instructional activities appear in this book in a variety of formats. Many are described briefly, usually as examples of instructional strategies discussed in the text. Following is a list of the lessons, projects, units, and other activities presented in detail:

Preface

The fourth edition of *Teaching Elementary Social Studies: Principles and Applications* continues to reflect the reality of a standards-based social studies curriculum and the need to differentiate instruction to meet the needs of a diverse student population. In the fourth edition you will find the opening vignettes of classroom practice, the lesson plans, and the unit plans appearing in the first three editions. Likewise, the discussions of social studies teaching and learning remain, although they have been updated. It must be noted, however, there are *significant new features* in the fourth edition that should make it a stronger text.

Reorganization of the Chapters

The third edition Chapter 4, on units and lesson plans, has been moved forward and is now Chapter 2 in the fourth edition.

The third edition Chapter 8, covering assessment, has been moved forward and is now Chapter 3.

These structural changes were a response to feedback from reviewers of the third edition, who suggested that content on unit plans, lesson plans, and assessment should precede all chapters other than the introductory first chapter.

The third edition Chapter 9, addressing an integrated curriculum, the language arts, the visual arts, and the performing arts, has been split and moved to two others, Chapters 5 and 8.

Reflecting the importance of reading and writing in content-area learning, there is now a new chapter (8) on developing literacy through social studies.

The third edition Chapter 11, which looked at history and geography, is now two separate chapters, one on history (Chapter 10), and one on geography (Chapter 11). This allows for greater coverage of geographic education in the elementary school.

The third edition Chapter 7, on technology, has disappeared. Instead, coverage of the use of technology to teach social studies appears in every chapter.

New to This Edition

Chapter 1: There is a discussion of "21st Century Skills," based on the joint effort of the National Council for the Social Studies and the Partnership for 21st Century Skills.

Chapter 2: I have added a section on unit planning based on the concept of "Backward Design" advocated by Wiggins and McTighe.

Chapter 3: There is less emphasis on creating portfolios for assessment and more emphasis on standards-based assessment.

Chapter 8: There is a new opening vignette on creating an electronic big book. You will also find a discussion of academic language in the section on teaching vocabulary.

Chapter 9: Coverage of service learning has been expanded.

Chapter 10: I added a section on how teachers can adapt primary sources so they can be read by elementary school children. In addition, I included a set of guidelines for teachers who want to plan successful field trips.

Chapter 11: You will find a new section on how to teach geography by using computer-based Geographic Information Systems (GIS).

Chapter 12: Many new teaching ideas for economics and global education were added.

Other New Features

In every chapter, there is expanded coverage of teaching social studies in the Information Age. There are over 40 new teaching ideas using computer-based resources.

The referenced Websites have been brought up to date.

Over 50 new children's books are referenced.

Over 100 new professional references have been added and over 60 have been deleted.

Conceptual Framework

The conceptual framework for the book is unchanged. The field of social studies has a rich history. Driven by the dynamic nature of human society, social studies has evolved into a lively and challenging pursuit, drawing concepts and ideas from history, geography, political science, economics, sociology, and anthropology. Thus, the possibilities to create meaningful, engaging, and stimulating experiences in social studies are endless. The dilemma for many educators, however, remains how to teach such a vast and expanding bed of knowledge. Fortunately, researchers in education, psychology, and linguistics provide some answers. How we teach should be dictated by how children learn, and research tells us children learn best when teachers do the following:

Allow children to construct knowledge as they become active participants in a wide range of learning experiences

Give all children a variety of materials to manipulate, question, and puzzle over

Encourage children to think critically about the content they learn

Plan opportunities for children to interact with one another on a regular basis

Recognize the cultural and linguistic diversity in their classroom and build enriched learning experiences around that diversity

Diversity: The Unifying Theme for This Text

Diversity continues to be the unifying theme for this text. It is impossible to discuss current social studies teaching and learning without acknowledging the importance of understanding diversity. Teachers in the United States now face two extraordinary challenges. They must teach students about those values that unite us, but must also help them accept disparate perspectives, understand different cultures, and avoid stereotypical and biased views of other people. These challenges, it seems, reinforce the power of a text based on understanding diversity.

Diversity has several dimensions. First, our student population continues to be increasingly pluralistic. Data gathered by the U.S. Census Bureau confirms a trend that has been constant for the past four decades. The percentage of Americans identifying themselves as "white" is steadily decreasing, while the percentage of African American, Asian American, or Hispanic American heritage, is steadily on the rise. In 2000, the non-Hispanic, white population was 69% of the total; projections are this percentage will shrink to 52% by 2050. African American, Asian American, and Hispanic American students currently represent over one-third of the K–12 population. They already are the majority in the nation's 25 largest school districts. The 2010 census was being conducted while I was writing this fourth edition—there seems to be little question that the results will verify the United States is becoming increasingly diverse.

A second dimension of diversity is that our teaching should use a variety of instructional strategies and resources to meet the needs of students from various cultural backgrounds and experiences. Third, we need to adapt how we teach to provide meaningful instruction to students with special needs. This book focuses on gifted children as well as those with mild learning disabilities. Fourth, the content of the social studies curriculum should be diverse because social studies is the study of people, and the curriculum should introduce our students to a wide array of individuals and groups. Finally, teachers need to prepare students to live in a democracy where citizens celebrate divergent beliefs and perspectives, no matter how great the pressure is to adhere to a single point of view. Diversity is a theme that unifies social studies teaching and learning: We must acknowledge it in our students, present it as our curriculum, and build on it as a civic value.

To accomplish these goals, we need to infuse lessons with pluralistic, multidimensional resources. For example, children's literature provides authentic accounts of the experiences of people from many cultural heritages. Of particular note are books sharing diaries, journals, and oral histories of people who are "distant," either by time or place, from our students. The authentic nature of this literature helps children better understand the difficult decisions other people have made. In this book, many lessons model how to incorporate children's literature in the social studies curriculum. At the end of each of these lessons are ideas for providing additional multicultural experiences. In addition, a reference list of children's literature that can be used to develop elementary social studies lessons is provided at the end of this text.

Increasingly, teachers are relying on computer-based resources to teach social studies. This text illustrates the use of video, audio, visual images, and texts available on the Web. Indeed, the Internet has changed the nature of social studies teaching and has immense potential, especially as a resource for students as they engage in the process of inquiry. Finally, the work products students create should reflect the technology available to teachers. While there will always be a place for projects created with traditional classroom resources, more and more teachers help their students create digital products like podcasts, PowerPoint displays, and digital movies. Applying a variety of instructional strategies and resources will increase the chances that every child in your classroom will be successful and prepared for a productive life in the 21st century.

Supplements

An **instructor's manual with test questions** has been developed to help use the text as effectively as possible. The manual is organized by chapters each containing a summary listing key points in the chapter; online portfolio assignments, which may be used to facilitate group discussions and activities; and multiple choice and essay questions with an answer key.

PowerPoint® slides for this book can aid in presenting and elaborating on chapter content.

Both of these instructor resources are downloadable from the password-protected Pearson Instructor Resource Center: www.pearsonhighered.com/irc. Please visit the site or contact your local Pearson representative for access to the Instructor Resource Center if you do not yet have a password.

Acknowledgments

I wish to thank the elementary school teachers from whom I borrowed ideas for this book: the teachers I worked with in elementary schools in Burbank, California; the teachers I observed during research projects in school districts in Los Angeles County; the cooperating teachers in the ABC, Castro Valley, Dublin, Hayward, Long Beach, and Pleasanton Unified School Districts who guided my student teachers; and my students at California State University, East Bay.

Thanks also to the reviewers of this edition: Paula J. Arvedson, California State University, Los Angeles; Alison Black, State University of New York at Oneonta; Don Falls, University of South Florida; Ted D.R. Green, Webster University; Margaret Harris, Southern New Hampshire University; Chrystal S. Johnson, Purdue University; Evelyn Kassouf Spratt, The College of Notre Dame of Maryland; Francie Keller Shafer, Southern Illinois University; Louise Stearns, Southern Illinois University; Reese H. Todd, Texas Tech University.

In the first edition of this book, I mentioned my mother, Lois Zarrillo, who taught junior and senior high school social studies from 1937 to 1981, basing her teaching on the belief that every student could succeed. In the second edition, I wrote about my father, Joseph Zarrillo, who had an unquenchable thirst for knowledge about people from every corner of the globe. Sadly, both my parents are gone now. On a happier note, my first grandchild, Hannah, was born while I was working on the third edition, and as I began working on this fourth edition, a second granddaughter, Sydney, burst upon the scene! I hope this book will help the teachers who teach Hannah, Sydney, and the other children who are part of their generation.

James J. Zarrillo

An Introduction to the Social Studies

Chapter 1   The Past, Present, and Future of Social Studies Teaching and Learning

The Past, Present, and Future of Social Studies Teaching and Learning

In this chapter, you will read about

- Perspectives that currently define social studies
- Two historical, influential movements that still characterize the discipline of social studies—Progressive Education and the New Social Studies
- The future of social studies, focusing on 21st Century Skills
- Three components that frame a responsible social studies curriculum: content, processes, and values

In a kindergarten classroom, the teacher reads aloud the picture book *A Chair for My Mother*. Afterward, the children discuss how characters in the story cooperated to solve a problem. Then the children help their teacher make a list of ways they can work together to make their classroom a happier, more productive place.

A first-grade teacher wants his students to engage in a simple form of critical thinking, comparing and contrasting, so he has gathered one set of photographs of people doing things in the winter and another set showing people doing things in the summer. His first graders will work in small groups to identify how weather affects the way people live.

Twenty-three second graders follow their teacher on a "walking" field trip around the playground of their school and the adjoining streets. They look at signs that state rules people must follow. Afterward, the children will be asked to provide a rationale for each rule they observed. Then a group of five students will devise a set of new signs that will make their school safer. They will present their suggestions to the school principal and the Parent-Teacher Association (PTA).

As part of their yearlong study of their community, six third graders undertake a bold project: to compile an oral history of their school. During this project, they will interview former students, teachers, and community leaders.

In a fourth-grade classroom, one Chinese American girl is working with her mother to learn to write in Chinese. She shares some examples of her writing, and her classmates want to learn more. Her teacher finds an excellent Website developed by "China the Beautiful" to use as a resource (www.chinapage.com). She prepares a 4-day "mini-unit" that will allow all the students in the room to learn about the logographic Chinese system and write a few Chinese characters.

Working in small groups, fifth graders read the first-person narratives of former enslaved people found in the book *To Be a Slave* and online from "American Slave Narratives: An Online Anthology" (xroads.virginia.edu/~hyper/wpa/wpahome.html). Later each group will share what they have learned about American slavery with their classmates.

A sixth-grade classroom is alive with many activities as the children learn about ancient Greece. Some students rehearse a play on the myth of Daedalus that will be videotaped. The students plan to post the video on the Internet site TeacherTube (www.teachertube.com). Others paint a mural of the Acropolis, a third group works on a CD presentation on Athenian democracy, while three students explore an Internet Website with photographs of the Parthenon (www.sacred-destinations.com/greece/parthenon-pictures).

■ ■ ■

Social studies in the elementary school involves all this and much more. During social studies, children learn about people—those who lived long ago and those who live today. It is when they become more proficient as thinkers, researchers, readers, writers, speakers, listeners, artists, and technologists, and it is the time when students use what they have learned to become good citizens in our democratic society.

Definitions of Social Studies

In 1992, the National Council for the Social Studies (NCSS) adopted the following definition of "social studies":

> Social studies is the integrated study of the social sciences and humanities to promote civic competence. Within the school program, social studies provides coordinated, systematic study drawing upon such disciplines as anthropology, archaeology, economics, geography, history, law, philosophy, political science, psychology, religion, and sociology, as well as appropriate content from the

humanities, mathematics, and natural sciences. The primary purpose of social studies is to help young people develop the ability to make informed and reasoned decisions for the public good as citizens of a culturally diverse, democratic society in an interdependent world. (NCSS Task Force on Standards for Teaching and Learning in the Social Studies, 1993, p. 213)

The NCSS, the professional organization of social studies educators, has played an essential role since 1921 (www.ncss.org). The NCSS definition seems to be a good place to start our discussion of how to teach social studies in an elementary school classroom. The NCSS definition states the topics covered in social studies and clarifies the purposes of social studies teaching and learning. I have a definition, too:

Social studies is the study of people. Social studies should help students acquire knowledge, master the processes of learning, and become active citizens.

A closer look at my definition may help us bring social studies into sharper focus.

Social Studies Is the Study of People.   People are the domain of social studies. This includes people as nearby as family and as far away as those who live in the most distant nations. It includes people living now, those who lived long ago, and those who will live in the future. Social studies has the potential to be the best part of the school day because it is when children connect with other people. As children learn about others, they will be fascinated by differences among cultural groups, while at the same time they will find the commonalities that create a shared sense of humanity. It is a complex task to teach students about people, and information must come from many fields of study. The NCSS definition points out that it is the various disciplines of the social sciences and humanities that provide the content for what is taught during social studies. While history and geography should serve as the core of social studies, it is imperative that the other social sciences are not neglected; rather, they should be a significant part of every social studies program. The other social sciences are anthropology, economics, philosophy, political science, psychology, religion, and sociology.

The humanities—literature, the performing arts, and the visual arts—are an important part of social studies, too (Simpson, 2009b). The arts serve two functions. First, they help children better understand the people, places, and ideas they study. Stories, songs, dances, plays, paintings, statues, and other works of art allow students to become acquainted with the people who created them. Second, children can show us what they know by expressing themselves through the arts. Social studies involves *integration* of the social sciences and the humanities. A good social studies unit of study should pull information and ideas from several different fields.

Social Studies Should Help Students Acquire Knowledge, Master the Processes of Learning, and Become Active Citizens.   The knowledge children acquire as part of the social studies curriculum tends to be the highest priority for teachers, parents, and children. The common perception is that this is what social studies is all about—knowing things like the location of the Rocky Mountains, the conditions aboard a slave ship, and the purpose of a mailbox. This is too limited a view because social studies must be a vehicle for children to become better communicators, thinkers, researchers, computer users, and artists. Finally, all three definitions state that the ultimate goal of social studies is active citizenship in our society, as our students *use* the knowledge they have acquired and the processes they have mastered to make communities, the nation, and the world better places (Golston, 2010; Parker, 2008). This is the position of the NCSS, that the "core mission of social studies education is to help students develop the knowledge, skills, and values that will enable them to become effective citizens" (NCSS Task Force on Revitalizing Citizenship Education, 2001, p. 319).

In the end, there will never be one universally accepted definition of social studies. This lack of consensus reflects fundamental disagreements on the primary purpose of social studies. Some educators think the emphasis should be on teaching the various social sciences, such as economics and anthropology, while others would emphasize a curriculum based on issues relating to social interaction among people. Another view is that social studies should focus on cultural diversity and pluralism. Others argue that social studies should teach the major events and important individuals in American history and seek to transmit to young people the American concepts of liberty and equality. Finally, some educators advocate a social studies curriculum that develops democratic citizens who are more than loyal and patriotic, but also are critics of their government (Levstik & Tyson, 2008; Thornton, 2008).

Perhaps a good way to conclude our discussion of the definition of social studies is through example. At the end of this chapter, you will find the field notes I took while visiting Mrs. Denise Winslow's sixth-grade classroom one Tuesday afternoon. Her class was studying ancient Greece.

A Brief History of Social Studies Teaching

Now that we have some sense of what social studies is, let's turn to another topic that will help establish a foundation for our teaching. Over the past 150 years, some of the greatest educational thinkers have turned their attention to social studies. Indeed, the history of social studies, in regard to both *what* should be taught and *how* to teach it, makes fascinating reading for anyone interested in teaching and learning. This is too large a topic for a thorough discussion in a methods text, however, so I suggest you read other sources for a more comprehensive treatment: Cremin (1961), Douglass (1967, 1998), Evans (2004, 2006), Hertzberg (1981), Lybarger (1991), Saxe (1991, 1992), and Thornton (2008). I first focus briefly on two "educational movements" from which we can learn a great deal: Progressive Education and the New Social Studies. Our discussion of the history of social studies continues by looking at contemporary issues in the field and then concludes by examining what social studies may look like in the future.

The Influence of Progressive Education and the New Social Studies

Progressive Education.   From colonial times to the end of the 19th century, social studies was a dreary, unimaginative business. The phrase *social studies* was not used regarding what was taught in elementary schools until 1897. In place of the integrated social studies, time was devoted to the separate topics of history, geography, and "civics"—the study of how federal, state, and local governments work. Until the 20th century, students were expected to memorize information in their textbooks and then recite it in front of their classmates. The textbooks were organized around questions, and teachers called on a student who stood and recited the answer (Douglass, 1967).

Fortunately, in the late 19th century great changes occurred in the social studies curriculum and instruction. This was the period of Progressivism, the social and political movement that reformed American life between 1880 and 1920. Profoundly influenced by the educational philosophy of John Dewey (1900, 1902) and the innovations of Francis W. Parker (1883, 1894), social studies was born during this period. Parker boldly

Barbara Schwartz/Merrill

Children are interested in how other people live. This class obviously enjoyed their study of Greece.

asserted that "we learn to do by doing, to hear by hearing, and to think by thinking" (1883, p. 115). He introduced teacher-made materials, field trips, and what we would call today "hands-on experiences." Study in geography began with trips to the surrounding countryside. Children observed and described what they saw. Following this firsthand experience, children made maps by molding sand. Later they would draw their own maps. When studying history, Parker believed that students should learn different points of view and not rely on the textbook as the sole source of information. Parker sought to develop each child's "power of organized inference" (1894, p. 269). Children should compare and contrast, speculate, and find generalizations. Teachers should lead this process by planning activities, asking questions, and suggesting places where answers could be found. Francis Parker's reforms were among the most significant in the history of American education.

It was John Dewey, however, who gave Progressive Education a unifying, underlying philosophy. One of the key elements of Dewey's philosophy was the importance of "child-centered" education. Children, he argued, will receive the best education if they are given choices over what they learn and when they learn it. Dewey also stressed the importance of "activity-based" learning, calling for a challenging curriculum that provided children with many opportunities to build things, manipulate things, and create things. During the first 20 years of the 20th century, the influence of Progressive Education was considerable. There were, however, problems with some Progressive ideas. Some Progressive schools were too permissive—any activity children decided to pursue was viewed as worthwhile. Between 1920 and 1960, the influence of the Progressives steadily weakened. Today's teachers should remember four ideas from Progressive Education:

1. Social studies is more than the memorization of facts. It is a discipline in which students learn to think, to make hypotheses, and to find answers.

2. Social studies should be activity based. Learning requires firsthand experiences. Children need to act, sing, build, dance, take field trips, and have hands-on activities.

3. Social studies requires the use of many instructional materials. Textbooks can play an important role in social studies teaching, but many other learning resources must be used.

4. Social studies instruction should incorporate the interests of children. To put this in practical terms, every instructional unit should be structured so that children select some of their learning activities.

Bruner and the New Social Studies.   In the 1960s, social studies was reexamined. In 1959, the National Academy of Sciences sponsored a summer study group of scientists, scholars from other fields, and educators. Their purpose was to discuss how the study of science could be improved in elementary and secondary education. The results of this meeting, however, would play an influential role not just in science education but in social studies as well. Jerome Bruner, a psychologist from Harvard, wrote *The Process of Education* (1960), a little book reporting on the conference that sounded the keynote for considerable reform in elementary education. *The Process of Education* provided the theory for instructional programs that became known as the "New Social Studies" (and the "New Math" as well). The federal government provided millions of dollars for reform-oriented social studies projects during the 1960s (Hertzberg, 1981).

Bruner believed that the subject matter for social studies should be organized around two concepts: the "structure of the disciplines" and "the spiral curriculum." He thought that what students learn about any subject "should be determined by the most fundamental understanding that can be achieved of the underlying principles that give structure to that subject" (1960, p. 31). Thus, if we wanted elementary students to learn from the field of economics, we would first define the most important principles of economics and then develop materials and activities to teach them. Bruner also asserted the curriculum should "spiral." That is, these important concepts or principles would be taught at several grade levels; as the children grow older, the principles would be covered with greater sophistication. And Bruner believed *any* concept could be simplified and taught to a child at *any* age. The task for authors of social studies textbooks and curriculum guides and for the teachers who used them was to take big ideas and present them so that small children would understand them.

The instructional programs developed as part of the New Social Studies attempted to teach children the fundamental principles from many social science disciplines, especially anthropology and sociology. Bruner had strong ideas about what learning activities should dominate social studies. He felt social studies should be based on inquiry learning. *Inquiry* is a process of solving problems and answering questions. He wrote that one of the purposes of social studies was "the development of an attitude toward learning and inquiry, toward guessing and hunches, toward the possibility of solving problems on one's own" (Bruner, 1960, p. 96). He believed the best way for students to learn how to solve problems was for them to do the same type of activities as grown-up practitioners. If children were studying history, they should go about answering questions the same way real historians do. The programs created as part of the New Social Studies were popular during the 1960s and 1970s. For several reasons, however, they were abandoned in favor of traditional, textbook-oriented approaches (Engle, 1986; Evans, 1989; Fenton, 1991). Nonetheless, today's teachers should remember three ideas from Jerome Bruner and the New Social Studies:

1. Social studies should introduce students to the important principles of several social science disciplines, especially anthropology, economics, and sociology. Teaching these principles requires children to learn more than bits of information. For example, second graders who are learning about how food moves from farms to markets should be introduced to the concept of *economic interdependence*—how people rely on others for their basic needs.

2. Social studies should include the *doing* of social science; that is, children should do the same things that historians, geographers, anthropologists, and political scientists do. For example, children can examine primary sources, such as diary entries and old newspapers, just like historians.

3. Social studies should involve many opportunities for children to solve problems and answer complex questions. This is one factor that distinguishes effective teachers: They challenge their students to use the facts they have learned to complete tasks requiring critical thinking. For example, a group of second graders could use what they have learned about their community to propose a location for a new park.

The Role of History, Standards, Diversity, and Technology

Controversy Over History.   During the past 50 years, there has been considerable debate regarding the role of history in elementary social studies. Should it be the dominating center of the curriculum, or should the fields of anthropology, economics, geography, political science, sociology, the arts, and the humanities play significant roles (Brophy & Van Sledright, 1997; Evans, 2004; Evans & Passe, 2007; Levstik, 2008)? Currently, most state social studies curricula emphasize historical content at the expense of the other disciplines. On the other hand, the NCSS standards for social studies have been sharply criticized because of an alleged lack of historical content (Phipps & Adler, 2003). In addition to arguments over the relevant importance of historical study, the historical content students will be expected to learn has also been controversial. Once the decision is made to focus on history, conflicting viewpoints immediately emerge. Whose history will be examined? Which view of the past will be presented? It is impossible to please everyone across the political spectrum, and it seems that any historical scope and sequence becomes a political document, subject to criticism from either the Left or the Right, or both (Grant, 1997; Leming, Ellington, & Porter-Magee; 2003; Nash & Dunn, 1995; Saxe, 1996; Spies et al., 2004; Symcox, 2002). As I was writing this fourth edition, there was considerable controversy about the social studies and history standards adopted in Texas in May of 2010.

Standards and the "Squeezing Out" of Social Studies.   Another trend of great importance is the movement to standards-based instructional programs. Standards define what students should know and be able to do, and define at what age those goals should be accomplished. Standards have been created by school districts, by state departments of education, and by national organizations. For you, the standards adopted by your state department of education will determine the social studies curriculum you teach. The George W. Bush administration's "No Child Left Behind" legislation of January 2002 provided funds for each state to create standards, but only in the areas of reading, math, and science, not in social studies. Nonetheless, almost all states have adopted standards for elementary social studies. To view the social studies standard for any state, go to the NCSS Website (www.ncss.org) and click on "Standards and Position Statements."

The emphasis on having every child achieve state standards in reading and math has led to less time for teaching and learning social studies in many elementary classrooms (Levstik, 2008). While almost all states have social studies standards, not all states have mandatory *assessments* of those standards. The No Child Left Behind legislation requires tests only of math and reading and, as a result, many states have mandated that children be assessed only in reading, writing, and mathematics. Thus, the time devoted to teaching social studies in some elementary schools has shrunk considerably over the past 10 years (Hinde & Ekiss, 2005; Neill & Guisbond, 2005; O'Connor, Heafner, & Groce, 2007). One writer considers this to be a crisis that has created a situation in which "youngsters are growing up with little or no knowledge of their own and their neighbors' histories, ironically when the nation is debating many foreign policy issues" (Pascopella, 2005, p. 30). Further, fewer and fewer teachers teach social studies during a separate, dedicated part of the day. In a national survey, about half of second- and fifth-grade teachers stated that what little social studies they taught, contained in fewer than 4 hours a week, was taught in an integrated fashion with language arts or science (Leming, Ellington, & Schug, 2006).

Standards in social studies written for national audiences influenced state-adopted standards and are also important because they reflect the perspectives of experts in many different subject areas. The development of national standards started in 1994 when President Clinton signed into law the Goals 2000: Educate America Act, which enabled the federal Department of Education to fund the development of curriculum standards in several areas, including the specific social studies disciplines of civics and government, economics, geography, and history. The NCSS created a task force to write national standards for social studies.

All the national standards projects, those funded by Goals 2000 and the independent initiative of the NCSS, have now been in place for over 15 years:

Standards for social studies in general: *National Curriculum Standards for Social Studies: A Framework for Teaching, Learning, and Assessment* (www.ncss.org, NCSS, 2010)

Standards for civics and government: *National Standards for Civics and Government* (www.civiced.org, Center for Civic Education, 1994)

Standards for economics: *National Content Standards in Economics* (www.ncee.net, National Council on Economic Education, 1997)

Standards for geography: *Geography for Life* (www.ncge.org, Geography Education Standards Project, 1994)

Standards for history: *National Standards for History* (www.sscnet.ucla.edu/nchs, National Center for History in the Schools, 1996)

Again, in your teaching assignment, standards adopted by your state department of education will be the ones you are expected to follow. Because this book is written for a national audience, I will use examples from each of these national sets of standards as the basis for sample lessons and units.

A brief look at the *National Curriculum Standards for Social Studies* would seem to be in order since these standards represent the vision of the NCSS (NCSS, 2010; www.ncss.org). Remember, standards are statements of what students should know and when they should know it. Rather than proposing topics for each grade level, K–12, the NCSS standards are organized under 10 themes. For each theme, there are "learning expectations" for the early grades, the middle grades, and high school. The national social studies

Table 1.1 Ten Organizational Themes for Social Studies

Themes	Theme Description
1. Culture	Social studies programs should include experiences that provide for the study of culture and cultural diversity.
2. Time, Continuity, and Change	Social studies programs should include experiences that provide for the study of the past and its legacy.
3. People, Places, and Environments	Social studies programs should include experiences that provide for the study of people, places, and environments.
4. Individual Development and Identity	Social studies programs should include experiences that provide for the study of individual development and identity.
5. Individuals, Groups, and Institutions	Social studies programs should include experiences that provide for the study of the interactions among individuals and groups.
6. Power, Authority, and Governance	Social studies programs should include experiences that provide for the study of how people create, interact with, and change the structures of power, authority, and governance.
7. Production, Distribution, and Consumption	Social studies programs should include experiences that provide for the study of how people organize for the production, distribution, and consumption of goods and services.
8. Science, Technology, and Society	Social studies programs should include experiences that provide for the study of relationships among science, technology, and society.
9. Global Connections	Social studies programs should include experiences that provide for the study of global connections and interdependence.
10. Civic Ideals and Practices	Social studies programs should include experiences that provide for the study of the ideals, principles, and practices of citizenship in a democratic society.

standards also include examples of exemplary instructional activities. The 10 themes are shown in Table 1.1.

For example, for the theme of "culture," there are five knowledge learning expectations for the early grades. Two of them are:

Learners will understand:
"Culture" refers to the behaviors, beliefs, values, traditions, institutions, and ways of living together of a group of people
Concepts such as similarities, differences, beliefs, values, cohesion, and diversity
(NCSS, 2010, p. 68)

Diversity.　Beyond the controversy over history and the "standards movement," two other phenomena will shape the future of social studies: diversity and technology. In the 21st century, teachers will work with students who are highly diverse, especially regarding language, culture, and exceptionality (Banks & Nguyen, 2008). As this book was being written, data collection for the 2010 census was just beginning, leaving us to rely on the data from the 2000 census. The results of the 2000 census confirmed a trend that has been constant for the past four decades (www.census.gov). The percentage of Americans who identify themselves as "white" is steadily decreasing, as the percentage who are either African American, Asian American, or Hispanic American is steadily on the rise. In 2000, the non-Hispanic, white population was 69% of the total; projections are that this percentage will shrink to 63% in 2020 and to 52% in 2050. In California, by far the most populous state, the 2000 census revealed that "minorities" are now the majority! There, the non-Hispanic, white population is just 46.7%.

There are two paramount issues regarding diversity. First, more and more of our students are acquiring English as a second language and in this book they will be called "English learners," or "ELs." These children face the challenge of learning social studies content at the same time they are learning English. Effective teachers must know how to "shelter" instruction so that English learners acquire the same content as their English-only peers (Cruz & Thornton, 2009; Echevarria & Graves, 2010; Echevarria, Vogt, & Short, 2003). Second, teachers face the challenge of educating their students about different cultural groups, including, of course, those who make up an increasingly large percentage of the U.S. population. All this requires considerable skill as we seek to provide information that is at the same time comprehensible and free of bias (Alvi, 2001; Au, 2009; Seikaly, 2001). Finally, almost every classroom will include students with special needs, and good teachers will successfully "differentiate" or modify how they teach to meet the needs of both students with learning disabilities and those who are gifted (Tomlinson, 2001; 2003).

Technology.　Technology has transformed all aspects of contemporary life, and the elementary classroom is no exception. The explosion of easily available information has resulted in new challenges for both students and teachers (Swan & Hofer, 2008; VanFossen & Berson, 2008). Ten years ago, Fitzpatrick (2000) made a point that is valid today—the irony that students born and raised in the era of the computer and the Internet are better prepared to work in information-age classrooms than their teachers, many of whom are more comfortable with television, newspapers, and encyclopedias. He concluded that "the greatest challenge of the new millennium is therefore not the one facing *students,* but the one facing *teachers* as they work to help fresh, young minds grow toward their fullest potential" (p. 33, emphasis added). While only 35% of schools had Internet access in 1994, now all public schools are connected (Swan & Hofer, 2008). Computer-based resources are replacing more traditional, hard-copy sources, such as pull-down classroom maps, multivolume encyclopedias, and films. The NCSS journals *Social Education* and *Social Studies and the Young Learner* regularly publish articles about the advantages and potential problems with Internet resources. Also, the computer allows students to reveal what they have learned in exciting new ways as children create digital products stored in a variety of formats: on CDs, school Websites, or on Internet sites like TeacherTube and VoiceThread (www.teachertube.com; www.voicethread.com; Nabel, Jamison, & Bennett, 2009; Simpson, 2009a).

21st Century Skills

While staying true to the goals of promoting democratic citizenship and teaching content in several social sciences, the future social studies curricula should help children achieve "21st century skills" (Partnership for 21st Century Skills & NCSS, 2008; Yell, 2008; Yell & Box, 2008; www.21stcenturyskills.org). There seems to a growing consensus that our elementary school students must be adaptable to change. They must be both critical thinkers and effective communicators. The social studies curriculum should have a global focus, stressing the interconnectivity of people who share a planet. The Partnership for 21st Century Skills, a unique collaborative effort among business leaders, educators, and policy makers, has taken the lead in defining what skills our children need to acquire to thrive in the future. The Partnership defined three categories of 21st century skills: (1) Learning and Innovation Skills; (2) Information, Media and Technology Skills; and (3) Life and Career Skills. The specific skills within each category are:

> Learning and Innovation Skills
> > Creativity and Innovation
> > Critical Thinking and Problem Solving
> > Communication
> > Collaboration
>
> Information, Media and Technology Skills
> > Information Literacy
> > Media Literacy
> > Information, Communication, Technology (ICT) Literacy
>
> Life and Career Skills
> > Flexibility and Adaptability
> > Initiative and Self Direction
> > Social and Cross-Cultural Skills
> > Productivity and Accountability
> > Leadership and Responsibility

The NCSS began working with the Partnership in 2007 to define how these 21st century skills could be integrated into the social studies curriculum. The result was a "Skills Map" that provides specific illustrations of the intersection of 21st century skills and social studies (Partnership for 21st Century Skills & NCSS, 2008). The *21st Century Skills Social Studies Map* offers a vision of what elementary social studies teaching and learning should look like to prepare our children for the challenges they will face in the near future. The map provides social studies learning outcomes and learning experiences for each skill at grades four, eight, and twelve. Let's look at three fourth-grade learning outcomes and their corresponding learning activities for the skill of Information Literacy, in the category of Information, Media and Technology Skills:

Examples of Student Learning Outcomes and Learning Experiences from the *21st Century Skills Social Studies Map*. The first outcome is that fourth graders "access information about communities around the world from a variety of information sources" (Partnership for 21st Century Skills & NCSS, 2008, p. 8). The learning activity proposed is that fourth graders are organized in small groups. Each group selects a nation and focuses on daily life in that nation. The students use online encyclopedias, electronic databases, and other Websites. They organize the information they have gathered and share what they have learned with their classmates using presentation software. Later, the children create a Venn diagram to compare and contrast daily life in two geographically diverse communities.

The second outcome is that fourth graders "access information from the expertise of people inside or outside of their own community" (p. 8). Students would participate in an online discussion or videoconference with a local museum director in the local community. They would then analyze an artifact from the local community and speculate on the owner and purpose of the object.

The third outcome is that fourth graders "gather original data from various information sources and create graphs or charts to display the information" (p. 8). For this outcome, students would use an online survey tool to determine what local attractions their families prefer to visit. The data would be organized in a spreadsheet. Their findings would ultimately be displayed with some graphing tool.

These examples are typical of the 26 learning outcomes and corresponding learning experiences in the Skills Map. The content is both local *and global*—and this is rare in elementary social studies curricula—as you will see in the next section. Currently, at different grade levels, the curriculum tends to focus on the local community, the state, the United States, or some part of the rest of world. Rarely is there a mixture, as there is in the Skills Map. And, of course, there is the emphasis on the use of technology to gather, analyze, and share information. In the three examples I selected, students gather information by using online encyclopedias, online databases, online discussions, videoconferences, and online survey tools. The information the fourth graders gather is shared through presentation software, spreadsheets, and computer-based graphing tools.

Social Studies: The Curriculum

Whatever set of standards you follow as a teacher, the structure of the social studies curriculum will have three organizational components: content, processes, and values.

Shutterstock

Expert teaching, collaboration among students, and, in this case, technology, can help children understand even the most challenging social studies concepts.

Content

Scope and Sequence.   Given the domain of social studies—the study of people—there is far more content than can be presented in the elementary grades. Therefore, anyone planning a social studies curriculum must design a *scope and sequence*. A scope and sequence is an outline of the content studied at each grade level. *Scope* refers to the topics covered, and *sequence* to the order of their presentation. The scope and sequence of any curriculum is organized around grade levels. The topics chosen and the concepts related to those topics should be dependent on the developmental level of students. Thus, simpler concepts are usually chosen for earlier grade levels.

One scope and sequence has dominated elementary social studies, namely, the *expanding environments* approach (also called *expanding communities* or *expanding horizons*). Some authorities question when this framework was first implemented; social studies programs from as far back as 1900 in some ways resemble it (LeRiche, 1987). Paul Hanna (1963, 1987a, 1987b) first advocated it as a distinct theory in 1956. The essence of expanding environments is that children should learn about what is nearest to them first and then, as they grow older, about people and places progressively more remote. A scope and sequence following the expanding environments model would be as follows:

Kindergarten: Self, Family, School

First Grade: Family and School

Second Grade: Neighborhood and Community

Third Grade: Our Community and Other Communities

Fourth Grade: Our State

Fifth Grade: United States History

Sixth Grade: World Studies

The expanding environments scope and sequence has been criticized for its lack of substance in the primary grades and for its narrow scope (Akenson, 1989; Duplass, 2007; Larkins & Hawkins, 1990). The NCSS position statement titled "Powerful and Purposeful Teaching and Learning in Elementary School Social Studies" went so far as to state "The 'expanding horizons' curriculum model of self, family, community, state, and nation is insufficient for today's young learners" (NCSS, 2009, p. 31). Opponents of the model claim that devoting four grades to family, school, and community provides children with too limited a view. Certainly, in a time of increased cultural diversity in the United States and of interdependence internationally, the expanding environments concept needs to include cross-cultural and global perspectives whenever possible. On the other hand, Brophy and Alleman (2008) argue that the expanding environments curriculum can be as effective as any other framework. They note this scope and sequence is a way of allowing children to analyze topics that they call "cultural universals," such as food, clothing, shelter, communication, transportation, and government (Alleman & Brophy, 2001b, 2002b, 2002c). If young children are going to learn about government, then it seems to make sense to have them learn about how rules are made and enforced in the contexts they know best—family, school, and community. As children grow older, they can study rule making and governing in the broader contexts of states, the nation, and the world. In this sense, the expanded environments model provides a means for the "spiral curriculum" proposed by Bruner.

The expanding environments concept remains a strong influence on curriculum planners. Alternative outlines, while emphasizing other themes and presenting new topics, generally reflect the self–family–school–neighborhood–community–state–nation–world sequence of expanding environments. For example, California's content standards for history and social science introduced new topics in the primary grades. Otherwise, planners followed the expanded environments scope and sequence, especially in the upper grades with study of the local community in grade 3, state history in grade 4, U.S. history in grade 5, and world history in grade 6 (California Department of Education, 1998; www.cde.ca.gov). I took a quick look at 15 state social studies curriculum standards while writing this edition, and all that I looked at conformed to a large degree to the expanding environments scope and sequence. To see the social studies standards for any state, go to the NCSS Website (www.ncss.org) and click on "Standards and Position Statements."

In most schools, teachers are expected to follow the scope and sequence adopted by the school district, and in almost every case that scope and sequence has been established by the state social studies standards. You may have a personal interest in the American Civil War, for example, but that does not mean you are free to make it a part of your social studies curriculum unless, of course, the standards you are following make it a topic you are supposed to teach. At the same time, teachers and students should have the freedom to pursue topics of interest within their grade-level curriculum. For example, a third-grade class is studying community workers. A child who shows a keen interest in firefighters should be encouraged to complete unique activities relating to fighting fires while other students do other things.

Another point related to scope and sequence: The elementary school is the ideal place for teachers to plan cross-curricular units of instruction (NCSS, 2008a, 2009). These units combine one or more of the following: social studies, science, math, literature, language arts, the performing arts, and the visual arts. One factor that has stimulated the development of cross-curricular units of study has been the reorganization of junior high schools into middle schools, where sixth and seventh graders frequently are taught in "humanities blocks," or 2-hour periods with an integrated curriculum of social studies and language arts (Field et al., 2001; Kellough, 1995; Young, 1994).

Concepts, Generalizations, and Facts.   A scope and sequence will define what is to be covered, though there still remains the large question of what specific content children will be expected to acquire. If fourth graders study their state, what should they learn about it? Again, the relevant set of standards your school district has adopted will determine the content your children are expected to master. The content students learn should consist of concepts, generalizations, and facts. This three-level categorization of the content component of social studies is based on the work of Hilda Taba (Bernard-Powers, 2002; Fraenkel, 1992; Taba, 1967). Note that other authorities in the social studies offer different definitions for generalizations and concepts. Here, though, we will use Taba's system:

- *Concepts* are ideas. They may be stated in a variety of ways. They tend to be broad and somewhat fuzzy. Conflict, justice, and family are all concepts. Perhaps the easiest way to think of concepts is as the big ideas that we want students to understand.

- *Generalizations* are content-specific statements. They are more specific than concepts and are based on the factual content of the social studies curriculum.

- *Facts* support concepts and generalizations.

It is essential that we understand the relationship between concepts, generalizations, and facts. Children learn facts so they can make generalizations. Several generalizations, when understood in concert, explain a concept. Generalizations and concepts enable children to make sense of what they study because facts, if unconnected to larger ideas, are of little value. Taba (1967) points out that the purpose of teaching facts "is to explain, illustrate, and develop main ideas" (p. 19). Figure 1.1 shows the hierarchical relationship among concepts, generalizations, and facts for one part of a third-grade social studies curriculum.

Figure 1.1

Concepts, Generalizations, and Facts for "Coming to Our City" in a
Third-Grade Curriculum

Concept: Movement: A geographic concept—that people, products, and ideas move across political and natural borders.

Generalization: People have come to our city throughout its history.

Facts:
- In about A.D. 1000, Native Americans first settled in what was to become our city.
- In 1792, the Franciscan missionaries built a mission near our city.
- During the 10 years after World War II (1945–1955), the population of our city doubled, from 40,000 to 80,000 people.
- From 1975 to 1990, 9,500 immigrants from Southeast Asia moved to our city.

Processes

In addition to teaching children concepts, generalizations, and facts, social studies programs also should improve students' ability in several processes. A *process* involves doing—it usually can be stated in a single word ending with *-ing.* Sets of social studies standards, whether produced at the national, state, or local level, will have a list of the processes students should master as they learn the content of the curriculum. The processes related to social studies can be categorized as follows:

- *Inquiry processes,* in which children formulate questions, gather data, analyze what they have found, and share what they learned
- *Thinking processes,* in which children develop the ability to apply, analyze, synthesize, and evaluate information
- *Language arts processes,* especially as they relate to the social science disciplines, as students read, write, speak, and listen
- *Visual and performing arts processes,* which are of two kinds, as students learn to *appreciate* the arts and learn to *use* the arts for expression
- *Technology processes,* in which children manipulate computer-based resources
- *Participation processes,* as children express personal views, work cooperatively with others toward common goals, and become active citizens

Values

Content is the *what* of social studies, and processes are the *how to.* That is not all there is to social studies. Recall from the definitions of the first part of this chapter that an important part of social studies is teaching values. The NCSS provided this definition of *values:*

> Values constitute the standards or criteria against which individual behavior and group behavior are judged. Beliefs represent commitments to those values. (NCSS Task Force on Scope and Sequence, 1989, p. 378)

Honesty, for example, is a value. If we are honest, then we will adopt a certain way of living and expect others to behave in a way that reflects that value. The set of values social studies emphasizes involves *civic values,* beliefs that lead to active citizenship. It is not enough that students acquire content and become skillful in a variety of processes. Children should *use* what they know to make their family, school, community, state, nation, and world a better place. This part of the elementary curriculum has existed since colonial times and is fundamental to public schooling in a democratic society. Democracies must have citizens who are knowledgeable and active. Other than civic values, social studies should teach children to value themselves by nurturing positive self-concepts. Along with the rest of the elementary curriculum, social studies programs should help children adopt healthy values toward school and learning (NCSS, 2008b; NCSS Task Force on Early Childhood/Elementary Social Studies, 1989).

It should be stressed, however, that values education should not be a process of indoctrination. Rather, children should adopt civic values because they understand the importance of them in a free society. As children learn to treasure our democratic system, they must concurrently learn of the differences in all aspects of life in a democratic society. In other words, diversity is inevitable in a democracy. The values component of the social studies curriculum can be difficult to teach, but we should not shy away from it. Engle and Ochoa (1988) stated it nicely:

> It is much easier and more straightforward to ask what are the facts than to ask what value or values should we subscribe to in a given instance. Despite the difficulty, a social studies program that neglects to deal with value problems stops far short of teaching students how to think intelligently about the real world. (p. 120)

At the end of this chapter, there is a lesson plan for a kindergarten classroom that is standards based and has objectives from each component of the social studies curriculum: content, processes, and values.

Summary of Key Points

- Social studies is integrated and interdisciplinary in that ideas and information come from many fields of study.
- Social studies goes beyond the textbook and rote memorization of facts.
- Social studies adopts the best ideas from the period of Progressive Education, including hands-on experiences, student selection of activities, thematic units, and the integration of social studies with the arts.

- Social studies continues the innovations of the New Social Studies, such as teaching children the fundamental concepts of the social sciences through inquiry learning.

- Social studies teaching and learning has become standards based.

- The NCSS/Partnership for 21st Century Skills Map defines skills that our students will need to acquire to be successful in the future.

- Social studies content includes concepts, generalizations, and facts.

- Social studies processes fall under the following categories: inquiry, thinking, language arts, visual arts, performing arts, technology, and participatory.

- Social studies emphasizes acquisition of civic values, the set of beliefs that leads to active citizenship.

Lesson Plans and Instructional Activities

At the end of each chapter you will find sample instructional plans in several formats. Most will be *lesson plans,* a teacher's written plan for a social studies lesson of 20 to 40 minutes. Others will be *mini-units,* a series of three or four lessons on a single topic. Some will be *projects,* an activity that takes more than 1 day to complete. Finally, at the end of Chapter 2, you will find a fully developed *unit of study,* a set of lesson plans and instructional activities, all related to a single topic, spanning several days. Each chapter will begin with a *vignette,* a description of a social studies activity in an elementary classroom. At the end of this chapter you will find: (a) a classroom vignette describing a sixth-grade class immersed in a unit on ancient Greece; and (b) a lesson plan for a kindergarten activity on cooperation.

Classroom Vignette/Grade Six: Multiple Activities During a Unit on Ancient Greece

There is a lot going on here! Some students rehearse a play they have written on the myth of Daedalus. This group is excited because a video of their play will be posted on the Internet site, TeacherTube (www.teachertube.com). Another group is busy painting the Acropolis for a large mural on the ancient Greeks. Some kids are in their seats reading books. Mrs. Winslow has brought several books to class from the local library. Matt reads Margaret Hodges's *The Arrow and the Lamp,* a retelling of the myth of Eros and Psyche. Julie examines an information book, *The Parthenon: The Height of Greek Civilization.* Ricardo and Thuy, working on a computer, are looking at photographs of the Parthenon through an Internet Website (www.sacred-destinations.com/greece/parthenon-pictures). Mrs. Winslow works with a group of students who are producing a CD on ancient Greece. This electronic encyclopedia will have photographs, maps, charts, and written text. Ouch! The students know much more about this technology than I do!

I also copied a page from Mrs. Winslow's plan book. This is what she wrote for the day I observed:

1:05–2:00 Social Studies

Ancient Greek unit, Day 10, Multiple Activities:

1. "Daedalus" play group—read through second part of script—first walkthrough tomorrow
2. Mural group—paint Acropolis
3. CD encyclopedia group—I will spend most of my time with this group—edit rough drafts of text, answer questions
4. Computer/Internet—view photographs of the Parthenon available on the Web
5. Other students—read independently

Let's consider these activities in the context of the definitions presented earlier. Both the NCSS definition and Barth's definition stress that social studies must integrate the social sciences and humanities. The focus of the unit was historical, but Mrs. Winslow did a good job of integrating the arts with the historical content of the unit. The play on Daedalus and books such as *The Arrow and the Lamp* were just a few of the ways she introduced her students to the Greek myths. Development of the mural helped students understand Greek architecture and would be followed with lessons showing the Greek influence on American architecture. The arts were also a means for student expression. Rather than limit her students to written assignments, Mrs. Winslow provided opportunities for expression through both the visual and performing arts. My definition stresses that social studies should help students master several processes; in this one day, I saw students reading, writing, acting, talking, cooperating, drawing, painting, and using the computer to gather and present information. Remember, too, that each definition stated that the ultimate purpose of social studies is good citizenship. Mrs. Winslow's unit on the ancient Greeks provided her students with knowledge of the link between ancient Greece and contemporary America and the influence of their democratic governments on society.

 Effective Teaching in Today's Diverse Classroom: It is important to note that the multiple-activity approach used by Mrs. Winslow is essential in a classroom with diverse students. While engaging in different types of experiences, each student in her room was learning more about the ancient Greeks. Some students will learn more through the visual arts, others through reading and writing, and others through the performing arts. Howard Gardner (2006) describes the "multiple intelligences" that people possess, and our teaching should allow children to learn social studies content in a variety of ways. This is especially important for children with learning disabilities. Also, the multiple activities Mrs. Winslow planned provided for both group and individual work. Even though all students need to work with their classmates in small-group formats, it was good to see that she provided an opportunity for students to choose to work individually or with their peers.

Lesson Plan
Kindergarten: Cooperation and *A Chair for My Mother*

Overview: This is a lesson for kindergarten. It is part of a unit titled "Happy Together—Family and Friends." It is planned for 25 students.

Resources and Materials: (a) One copy of *A Chair for My Mother* by Vera B. Williams, (b) paint and paper for bulletin board illustrations, (c) 25 sheets of primary-level drawing/writing paper.

Standard: One of the themes in the *National Curriculum Standards for Social Studies* is "Individuals, Groups, and Institutions." One learning expectation for the early grades is that learners will be able to "show how groups and institutions work to meet individual needs, and promote or fail to promote the common good" (NCSS, 2010, p. 78).

Content Objectives: This lesson will help children see how members of a family and their friends help each other in a time of need. They will consider how they can cooperate in our classroom. It will help children build their understanding of the concepts of cooperation and family.

Process Objectives: The students will (a) *listen* to the book read aloud, (b) *respond* orally to the teacher's questions, (c) *identify* how several characters help Rosa and her family, and (d) complete one of three postreading optional activities.

Value Objectives: This activity should help students acquire the value of "Consideration for Others"—that we should help people who have suffered from an unforeseen circumstance.

Teaching Sequence:

1. Before the lesson begins, be sure all materials and resources are ready; on the blackboard, write the names of the following characters: Rosa, Grandmother, Aunt Ida and Uncle Sandy, neighbors.

2. On a sheet of chart paper, write the following postreading options: (a) Go with Ms. Sanchez (the instructional aide). Draw pictures for *A Chair for My Mother* section of "Our Favorite Books" bulletin board. (b) Go to your seat. Draw and write anything you want about *A Chair for My Mother*. (c) Stay with Mr. Wong (the teacher). Talk about what makes working together difficult and what makes it easy.

3. Ask the children to sit on the carpet and read aloud *A Chair for My Mother.*

4. Ask the children if there is anything they would like to say about the book (use what the children say as a basis for further discussion).

5. Discuss with the children how Rosa, Grandmother, Aunt Ida and Uncle Sandy, and the neighbors helped. Refer back to illustrations in the book.

6. Lead a discussion on how class members can work together and help each other. Begin by making a list of all the classroom chores that are easier to complete if members of the class work together. Other than classroom tasks, ask what other things members of the class can do for each other (many things should come to mind, such as sharing supplies or cheering up class-mates who are sad). Use a piece of chart paper to record the ideas of the students.

7. Explain the options to the children (see item 2).

8. Be sure all the children are either working with Ms. Sanchez, in their seats, or are still on the carpet.

9. Later, bring the group together. Have the children share their pictures, dictated narratives, and the results of the discussion.

Evaluation: At the kindergarten level, evaluation is often informal. The pictures the children draw and the texts they write or dictate can be saved in student portfolios.

Effective Teaching in Today's Diverse Classroom: Mr. Wong's class included several Spanish-speaking English learners. These children spoke some English. The excellent illustrations in the book allowed the English learners to understand the story, even though they did not know the meaning of every word in the text. Like most kindergarten teachers, Mr. Wong modified his speech when talking to his 5-year-old students. He slowed down, repeated things, and avoided large words. This, too, helped the English learners understand what he was saying. If the class had included English learners who spoke almost no English, then the activity would need the assistance of a bilingual person (the teacher, an instructional aide, a parent volunteer, or an older student). Each of the following adjustments could be added: (a) Someone should explain the plot of the story in the native language of the English learners (in this case, Spanish), and (b) the postreading discussion could be conducted in the English learners' native language. We want children to understand the concepts of cooperation and to see their importance in the story and in the classroom. To achieve this objective, it might be necessary to conduct all or part of the lesson in a language other than English.

The Fundamentals of Social Studies Teaching

Social Studies Lesson and Unit Plans

In this chapter, you will read about

- Simple guidelines to help in planning effective social studies lessons

- Instructions on writing instructional objectives

- Perspectives on using two kinds of lesson sequences—direct instruction and the concept attainment model

- Six principles to consider when planning units of study

- A third-grade sample unit on boats

The students in Donna Richard's fifth-grade classroom took part in a 6-week instructional unit on Native Americans. They studied the cultures of five tribes before the arrival of Europeans to North America: the Mohawk, the Seminole, the Oglala Sioux, the Tlingit, and the Navajo. Mrs. Richard wanted her students to learn about the diversity of Native Americans and to see for themselves the problems caused by stereotyping a cultural group. By allowing students to compare the historical diversity of multiple Native American groups, they would find out that not all Native Americans lived in tipis, hunted buffalo, or wore feathers. Further, students would learn where and how "Indians" live in the United States today.

To initiate this unit, Mrs. Richard started with a study of the Sioux of the mid-19th century. Using an LCD (liquid crystal display) overhead projector, Mrs. Richard projected an image of a painting by George Catlin, *Buffalo Chase, Upper Missouri,* onto a movie screen positioned at the front of the classroom. The painting, also called *Buffalo Chase, Bulls Making Battle with Men and Horses,* is part of a collection stored at the Smithsonian Institution. It is also on the Smithsonian's Website, www.si.edu. A copy of the painting can be found at the end of this chapter as Figure 2.6. (For more on teaching about the artist, George Catlin, see Rosenbaum, Potter, and Eder, 2008.) Providing black-and-white copies of the painting to student groups, Mrs. Richard asked students to study the painting and to answer a series of eight guided-response directives. The next-to-last query was, "Pretend you are one of the Sioux. Write down what you are thinking, feeling, hearing, or seeing." Answers to this request led to several lively discussions. In one group, Darlene started off by saying that if she were a Sioux in the painting, she would be scared. She wanted to know why one Sioux was jumping on a buffalo. In response, Jerome speculated that the Sioux wanted to pull one of his arrows out of the buffalo and use it again. Mrs. Richard noted that Jerome's guess was a good one because the book *Buffalo Hunt,* by Russell Freedman (1988), related how sometimes arrows would barely penetrate the buffalo's hide and the Natives would try to pull them out to use again.

Dontray said he was going to write about shooting the buffalo with arrows. Mrs. Richard asked about things the Sioux might have heard during the hunt. Andrew stated it must have been loud. Darlene added one thing the Sioux would have heard was the horse screaming. Mrs. Richard asked whether anybody had anything else to say or if anyone had a question, before she left the group to allow them to start writing, No hands went up, so the five students started writing their responses. After about 10 minutes, members of each group shared their work.

The final query in the study guide led to the second half of the lesson. That directive was, "Think back to what we learned about the Mohawk. Think what the Mohawk ate and how they got their food. Think about what we have learned about the Sioux. All people need some way of getting food. What is the same and what is different about these two tribes?" Mrs. Richard encouraged each group to make a simple comparison chart by folding a sheet of paper in half lengthwise and on one side writing details they remembered about the Mohawk and on the other side writing what they learned about the Sioux. Mrs. Richard had information books, encyclopedias, and online resources ready for students who could not recall information about the Mohawk. Fortunately, though, at least one member of each group noted that the Mohawk had fields and raised crops of squash, corn, and beans. After all the groups reconvened, Darlene stated an accurate conclusion: "The Mohawk had a lot more ways of getting food. They farmed, they fished, and they gathered berries. The Sioux just hunted and gathered." Matt added that both groups hunted but they hunted different things. The Sioux hunted buffalo, whereas the Mohawk hunted deer and turkeys and other birds. Jerome made another comparison: The Sioux hunted while riding horses, whereas the Mohawk hunted on foot. Mrs. Richard then asked the class why the food-getting practices of the two groups were different. Students first considered this question in their groups. All the groups quickly stated that the Mohawk could not hunt buffalo because no buffalo lived where the Mohawk lived and that the Sioux could not fish because the Plains did not have enough rivers and streams. By the time the lesson ended, most students could not come up with a good explanation of why the Mohawk farmed and the Sioux did not, so Mrs. Richard decided to plan a lesson on that topic.

This lesson is noteworthy for two reasons. First, the lesson was an important component in Mrs. Richard's attempt to help her students take a comprehensive look at Native Americans. The final directive, comparing the food-getting practices of the Sioux and the Mohawk, helped students understand that before the coming of European Americans, there were significant cultural differences between the Native American tribes of North America. The diversity among Native American tribes, unfortunately, is rarely taught in elementary schools (Field & Finchum, 2006; Finchum, 2006; Brophy, 1999). Second, the success of this lesson, like almost all lessons that go well, was the product of Mrs. Richard's thoughtful and thorough planning. This chapter is about planning lessons and instructional units. It will introduce a variety of formats for preparing exciting, challenging, and effective social studies lessons and units.

■ ■ ■

General Guidelines for Planning Social Studies Lessons

The concept of "lesson" should be broad and include each of the following:

- Lessons that are teacher directed and involve the entire class (often called "whole-group" lessons)
- Lessons designed for small groups or individuals
- Lessons placing the teacher in a less central role, serving as facilitator, tutor, and provider of resources

Regardless of the specific lesson format we use, we should follow two guidelines when planning an effective lesson. These two guidelines are:

1. *Decide precisely what we expect students to do.*   The teacher must have a clear idea of what the students are supposed to do *from the beginning of the activity to the end.* Some lessons go poorly because the teacher knows exactly what the students are to do at the *end* of the lesson but has not really thought about what they should do before then. This does not mean that we should choreograph every step so that all our students behave like members of a chorus line. Many lessons will have some students do one thing while their classmates do another. Other lessons will have time for students to be creative. The point is that before we teach a lesson, we should be sure we know what we expect the student(s) to do. Make a list! For example, for her lesson on *Buffalo Chase, Upper Missouri,* Mrs. Richard wrote:

1. I want the students to look closely at the painting.
2. I want them to answer questions about the painting while working in small groups.
3. I want them to compare and contrast the food-getting practices of the Sioux and the Mohawk.

2. *Decide what the teacher must do for students to achieve what is expected of them.* After we have a clear idea of what we expect our students to do during the lesson, we must think of ourselves. If our students are to be successful, what must the teacher do? There is much to consider here: What materials must be gathered? Will the classroom furniture need to be rearranged? What visual aids will be needed? What must the teacher say and when? What problems should be anticipated? Make a list! Mrs. Richard wrote:

1. Get the LCD projector.
2. Write the study guide and run 32 copies.
3. Make sure the timeline and the map are ready.

Lesson Plan Formats

I distinguish two general formats for lesson planning: *comprehensive* and *abbreviated*. Comprehensive lesson plans are detailed and quite time consuming to prepare. The lesson plan at the end of Chapter 1 was comprehensive (for *A Chair for My Mother*). Abbreviated lesson plans are much less detailed and take less time to prepare, but still require care and thought in their preparation.

The Comprehensive Lesson Plan

The comprehensive type of thorough lesson planning has several forms. As you have no doubt discovered, it seems as if each person who teaches a methods course has a preferred form. Relatively few times during their careers do teachers prepare comprehensive plans. Teacher credential candidates write them during their methods courses and field experiences. Teachers write them in two instances: (a) when they are being evaluated by a principal, and (b) when they are doing a complex or innovative activity—then it is a good idea to write a comprehensive plan. It would be impossible for teachers to write a comprehensive plan for each instructional activity they teach because there simply is not enough time to do so. These lengthy, detailed plans are important, though, because their preparation is part of learning to teach. They require attention to each aspect of a lesson and ensure that lessons are logically sequenced. Figure 2.1 is an outline of the comprehensive lesson plan format I use throughout this book.

Let's take a closer look at each part of this format.

1. *Overview.* The overview places the lesson in context. In this section, state the grade level and number of students who will participate in the activity. In most cases, the lesson will be part of an instructional unit—provide the title of the unit.

2. *Resources and materials.* Instructional resources include Websites on the Internet, textbooks, CDs and DVDs, and children's books. Materials are things like paint, glue, and construction paper.

Figure 2.1

Comprehensive Lesson Plan
Format

1. Overview
2. Resources and materials
3. Standards
4. Content objectives
5. Process objectives
6. Values objectives
7. Teaching sequence
8. Evaluation

3. *Standards.*   Our comprehensive lesson plans should clearly state which standard(s) the lesson addresses.

4. *Content objectives.*   I prefer a simple form for writing objectives. This section is a list of the content—the subject matter we expect our students to learn in our lesson.

5. *Process objectives.*   This is a list of what we expect our students to accomplish during the lesson. Whereas content objectives list the "what" of the lesson, process objectives focus on the activity of *students,* both mental and physical.

6. *Values objectives.*   Not all lessons will include this section. Here we list any values the lesson will help our students acquire.

7. *Teaching sequence.*   At this point in preparing a comprehensive lesson plan, teachers should shift their focus to what they will do. Considerable controversy surrounds the topic of teaching sequences. Many authorities have advocated sets of teaching steps that are usually called teaching "models" (Joyce & Weil, 2008). Some teaching models are discussed in a subsequent section of this chapter. My approach is pragmatic and situation specific, because what teachers do and the order in which they are done, depend on what we expect our students to do. Teachers should tailor their teaching sequence to fit the needs of students, the resources available, and the objectives of the lesson. The teaching sequence should start with the things the teacher will do before he or she begins teaching, such as preparing materials and gathering resources.

8. *Evaluation.*   You can collect several types of data to help you determine whether students achieved the lesson's objectives. In Chapter 3, you will read about the many ways you can evaluate your students.

Figure 2.2

Teacher's Plan Book: *Buffalo Chase, Upper Missouri*

12:45 to 1:50

SOCIAL STUDIES
   Day 3 of mini-unit on Sioux
   ▶ *View Buffalo Chase, Upper Missouri*
   ▶ *Complete study guide in groups*
   ▶ *Introduce follow-up projects*

Resources Smithsonian Website, LCD projector, time line, map, 32 copies of study guide, related books, books on Mohawk

At the end of this chapter you will find an example of a comprehensive plan, this one for Mrs. Richard's lesson with *Buffalo Chase, Missouri*.

The Abbreviated Lesson Plan

When you assume responsibility for teaching all day, either as a student teacher or as a first-year teacher, you will not have time to prepare comprehensive lesson plans for each activity that takes place. Then, you should use an *abbreviated* form and save comprehensive planning for those lessons requiring extra attention. You should, of course, continue to think about all the elements that are part of a good lesson.

The Plan Book Grid.   The most common form of abbreviated planning is done in a planning book. Several companies produce these plan books, although each is in a unique format. Most, however, are spiral bound. A week is spread across two pages; along the left side are the days of the week, and along the top are blocks of time. In each square, about 2 inches on each side, we write what we will do that day in that block of time (usually representing 1 hour). Figure 2.2 shows what Donna Richard wrote in her plan book for the lesson with the painting *Buffalo Chase, Upper Missouri*.

Three-Column, Single-Sheet.   Another form of an abbreviated plan is completed on a sheet of paper with three columns. The useful outline format requires a separate sheet of paper for each lesson. Table 2.1 provides an example of this format, again with the *Buffalo Chase* lesson.

Table 2.1 Three-Column, Single-Sheet Lesson Plan
Lesson: Painting—*Buffalo Chase, Upper Missouri*
Date: Tuesday, October 11
Time: 12:45–1:50

Objectives	Teaching Sequence	Materials/Resources
CONCEPT: Human–environment interaction	(1) Use LCD projector to show the painting	(1) Smithsonian Website, www.si.edu
	(2) Timeline, map	(2) LCD projector
GENERALIZATIONS—	(3) Show the painting again, students comment	(3) 32 copies of the study guide
(1) The buffalo was the essential resource for the Sioux	(4) Work in groups on study guide, questions 1–7	(4) Timeline
(2) The Sioux and the Mohawk had different food-getting practices	(5) Reconvene as a whole group, discuss questions 1–7	(5) Map
	(6) In groups, discuss question 8 (Mohawk–Sioux comparison)	(6) Related books
FACTS—	(7) Reconvene as a whole group—question 8	
(1) Use of bows, arrows, and lances to hunt	(8) Introduce related projects and books	
(2) Sioux hunted in groups		
(3) Horses increased efficiency		
(4) Danger		

Writing Lesson Objectives

An essential element of lesson planning is the writing of instructional objectives, which delineate the expectations we have for our students in any given lesson. In Chapter 1, I shared with you that social studies lessons can be broken down into content, process, and values objectives. The state-adopted social studies standards will help you determine content objectives. To establish how to write more meaningful objectives, consider the following topics.

Making Objectives More Meaningful

One key to making objectives more meaningful is to write objectives identifying specific and observable performances by students. According to Ralph Mager, author of *Preparing Instructional Objectives* (1997), written objectives must identify what students are expected to do and demonstrate how they do it. Using Mager's standards, we can differentiate a poor objective from richer ones with these examples. "To be able to develop an appreciation of music" is an inadequate statement of performance. It does not tell what the student is to do, and it is not observable. However, both "To build a model of the Parthenon" or "To list three reasons why the American Colonists declared independence from Great Britain" can provide more meaningful structure to lesson planning. Instructional objectives that provide focus and direction for both teachers and learners are essential to planning more effective lessons.

One simple component of objectives that can help focus expectations for students is the verb that describes the desired performance. Action verbs, as discreet as possible, can better pinpoint what we want students to do. For example, if, after watching a film on the economy of Mexico, students are expected to identify the correct answers to questions on a worksheet, then the instructional objective could be "Students will circle each product that is exported from the Republic of Mexico."

Raising the Levels of Performance: Objectives in the Cognitive Domain

In his *Taxonomy of Educational Objectives* (Bloom, 1956; Gronlund & Brookhart, 2008), Benjamin Bloom created a framework for writing objectives at many cognitive levels. Bloom's taxonomy remains a useful tool for teachers, especially because it provides a basis for planning activities requiring complex, critical thinking. In his taxonomy, Bloom categorizes mental activities into six sequential levels: knowledge, comprehension, application, analysis, synthesis, and evaluation. Social studies activities should include objectives in each level, especially the last three, which require students to use higher-level thinking processes.

1. *Knowledge.* Bloom (1956) stated the following definition for the knowledge category: "Knowledge involves the recall of specifics and universals, the recall of methods and processes, or the recall of a pattern, structure, or setting" (p. 201). This is the mental process of remembering. As conceived by Bloom and his associates, this is a broad category involving knowledge of facts, terminology, sequences, categories, processes, principles, and theories.

2. *Comprehension.* To Bloom (1956), comprehension "refers to a type of understanding . . . such that the individual knows what is being communicated and can make use of the material . . . without necessarily relating to other material or seeing its fullest implications" (p. 204). The ability to restate or summarize is evidence of comprehension, as is the ability to state the main idea in something.

3. *Application.* At the application level, the student begins to use what he or she knows and understands. Application is "the use of abstractions in particular and concrete situations" (p. 205). An objective in this category would ask a student to apply a law or theory. Another example is the ability to apply a process learned in one context to another context.

4. *Analysis.* The analysis category refers to the ability to identify the component parts of something and to describe their relationship. It includes distinguishing one thing that is closely related to another and comparing and contrasting them. Bloom noted that distinguishing fact from hypothesis is an analytic operation.

5. *Synthesis.* In the synthesis category, the learner creates something new as the parts of something are rearranged into an original configuration. This category includes

the activities of speculating and hypothesizing. Students who develop a plan to solve a current social problem are engaged in this category of cognitive activity.

6. *Evaluation.*   The last category of the cognitive domain involves "making judgments" (Bloom, 1956, p. 207). This includes rating a list of things in priority order or judging things according to a set of criteria.

Objectives for the lesson with *Buffalo Chase, Upper Missouri* could be written using Bloom's taxonomy. Notice that, to have objectives in each of the six categories of the cognitive domain, some activities would have to be added to the lesson:

1. *Knowledge.*   List the weapons the Sioux used to kill buffalo.

2. *Comprehension.*   Describe the dangers to the Natives' horses during a buffalo hunt.

3. *Application.*   Dramatize the buffalo hunt by pretending you are a hunter who is telling his children about the day's hunt.

4. *Analysis.*   Compare the food-getting practices of the Sioux and the Mohawk.

5. *Synthesis.*   Speculate on the sounds of the buffalo hunt and write about what the Sioux would have heard.

6. *Evaluation.*   Make a list ranking the most important qualities and characteristics of an effective buffalo hunter.

Figure 2.3 provides a list of verbs, arranged by category within the cognitive domain, that could be used in writing objectives.

Figure 2.3

Taxonomy of Educational Objectives: Cognitive Domain—Suggested Verbs to Use When Writing Objectives

1. Knowledge	3. Application	5. Synthesis
define	demonstrate	compose
identify	dramatize	design
list	illustrate	hypothesize
match	sequence	invent
recall	show how to	speculate
2. Comprehension	4. Analysis	6. Evaluation
describe	compare	criticize
explain	classify	judge
paraphrase	diagram	justify
restate	distinguish	prioritize
summarize	verify	rate

Perspectives on the Teaching Sequence

As I noted earlier, many authorities have developed step-by-step teaching sequences. In this section, I describe two of these teaching models.

Lessons often begin with a whole class activity to motivate learning or provide procedural directions.

Some lessons require planning for small-group work, guiding concept development, or teaching students how to review what they have learned.

Direct Instruction

For some lessons, teachers should choose a teaching sequence that fits under the model of "direct instruction" (Hollingsworth & Ybarra, 2008; Joyce & Weil, 2008; Marchand-Martella, Slocum, & Martella, 2003). This approach was championed 30 years ago by the influential Madeline Hunter (1984), former principal of the University Elementary School at UCLA. Hunter developed a generic, seven-step teaching sequence she believed could be applied to any subject at any grade level. Other forms of direct instruction feature similar step-by-step teaching sequences with the teacher directing the lesson. The Hunter model is a direct instruction sequence of seven steps:

1. *Anticipatory set.*   During the first step, the teacher directs the students' attention to the lesson. The goal here is to get students who will participate in the activity to stop thinking about other things and start thinking about the lesson. For example, Mrs. Richard began by asking students to look at the projected image of the painting. This focused students' attention on the task at hand.

2. *Objective and purpose.*   Next, the teacher states the purpose of the lesson. Hunter (1984) suggests that this include "what will be learned and how it will be useful" (p. 175). For example, "Today we are going to look at a painting of the buffalo hunt, an important aspect in the lives of the Plains tribes. This will help us better understand how these Native Americans lived."

3. *Input.*   Hunter (1984) states that "students must acquire new information about the knowledge, process, or skill they are to achieve . . . from discovery, discussion, reading, listening, observing, or being told" (p. 176). This can be a selection from a textbook, a demonstration, a film, or a lecture.

4. *Modeling.*   In the fourth step, the teacher, another adult, an older student, or a member of the class demonstrates what all the students will be expected to do. This may involve showing a range of options and then having students choose one to complete.

5. *Check for understanding.*   Before allowing students to work independently, Hunter suggests, teachers should find out whether the students know what is expected of them. This can be determined by asking questions or by taking a quick look at the initial efforts of a few of the students.

6. *Guided practice.*   The students work while the teacher circulates. The teacher gives help on request and looks for students who are having difficulty.

7. *Independent practice.*   The final step does not appear in every lesson. This is a time when students complete tasks without help from the teacher.

At the end of the chapter, you will find an example of how the lesson on *Buffalo Chase, Upper Missouri* could be written using the Hunter format.

From my perspective, no one teaching sequence can be applied to every teaching situation. *How* we teach should depend on *what* and *whom* we teach. One problem with models of direct instruction is that some educators think this type of teaching works for all subjects and at all grades. Rather, direct instruction is one of the many models we can use in social studies; it should never be the only teaching sequence we follow.

The Concept Attainment Model

Authorities recommend other teaching sequences, and I use many of them in this book (e.g., in Chapter 6, the Three-Step Interview and Jigsaw). These teaching sequences are designed for specific purposes, not as generic models, such as direct instruction. To provide one example for comparison, here I describe the teaching sequence developed by Joyce and Weil (2008) to help children acquire concepts. It is based on the research of Jerome Bruner and his colleagues (Bruner, Goodnow, & Austin, 1956). It is called the *concept attainment model,* which is frequently used in social studies. I have found it works better with older children than with younger ones and that it should be used at the end of an instructional unit. The concept attainment model has three variations. I describe the reception form, which has the greatest level of teacher direction. It has three phases, each with three parts:

1. *Presentation of Data and Identification of Concept.*
   1.1 The concept attainment model is like a game. It begins with the teacher explaining the purpose of the activity, which is to help students better understand a concept. The first phase starts with the teacher presenting students with examples and nonexamples of a concept. The examples and nonexamples can be the names of people or places, things, or events. The teacher tells the students whether each item is an example or a nonexample of the concept.
   1.2 Next, the teacher encourages students to compare the examples and nonexamples: What makes them different? What do they all have in common?
   1.3 At this point, students should be ready to state a definition for the concept. The definition is a hypothesis that will be refined in the second and third phases.
2. *Testing Attainment of Concept.*
   2.1 In the second phase, the teacher presents items that are *not* labeled as "examples" or "nonexamples." Students state whether each item is an example of the concept. The definition may be revised because of the characteristics of the items.
   2.2 The teacher now comments on the definition the students have developed. If necessary, the teacher may restate the definition of the concept.
   2.3 The final part of this phase is a challenge. Now the teacher asks students to generate examples of the concept. This will test whether they can apply the definition they have learned.

3. *Analysis of Thinking Strategy.*   The third phase need not be included each time the concept attainment model is used. This phase asks students to reflect on the first two phases of the model.

    3.1 Students describe how they reached their conclusions about the status of each item. What were they thinking when they decided that something was or was not an example?

    3.2 Students then talk about how they changed their definitions. Why did they have to change their early definitions?

    3.3 Finally, students talk about the characteristics of the concept and consider the process of hypothesis testing.

At the end of the chapter you will find an example of how the concept attainment model could be used at the conclusion of the unit "19th-Century Native Americans."

Principles for Planning Instructional Units

Social studies lessons should be organized into well-designed units of instruction. An *instructional unit* is a set of related activities with a unifying element, something serving as a focus for the unit. Too often, elementary social studies is nothing more than a discon- nected series of isolated activities. The NCSS position paper titled "Powerful and Purpose- ful Teaching and Learning in Elementary School Social Studies" stresses this point, that elementary school social studies be "more than a collection of enjoyable experiences. A piecemeal approach to social studies can result in a disconnected conglomeration of activ- ities that lack focus, coherence, and comprehensiveness" (NCSS, 2009, p. 32). Well- planned units of study, then, are the starting point for powerful and purposeful social studies teaching and learning. Some units are brief and include only three or four lessons—I refer to these as "mini-units." Most social studies units, however, are more ambitious and run for several days. The idea of the unit is an old one. In fact, some of the finest instructional units in social studies are almost 100 years old and were developed during the era of Progressive Education at places like the Laboratory School of the Univer- sity of Chicago and the Lincoln School in New York City (Cremin, 1961; Mayhew & Edwards, 1936). A good place to start our discussion is with six principles for planning instructional units in the social studies:

1. Plan units using the principles of "backwards design."

2. Units should be integrated.

3. The scope of each unit should be clearly defined.

4. Activities in a unit should follow a logical sequence.

5. Units should feature a variety of instructional resources.

6. Units should include whole-group, small-group, and individual activities.

All children are special, wonderfully unique, and capable of thriving under your guidance. As you create instructional units, be sure to include activities that allow each child to be successful.

Plan Units Using the Principles of Backward Design

Wiggins and McTighe (2006) provide an excellent framework for creating instructional units in elementary social studies—what they call "backward design." The authors claim that much teaching is ineffective because teachers develop unit plans based on getting through the textbook or keeping kids busy. Rather, their framework requires teachers to consider first the relevant social studies standards their students are expected to achieve. Once the standards for a unit are defined, then teachers ask how they will know if their students have achieved the desired results. This early focus on assessment is essential in effective unit planning. Finally, teachers create the instructional activities that will "enable students to achieve the desired results" (p. 22). More specifically, the three stages of unit planning using backward design are:

1. Stage One: Desired Results
   Teachers make choices here, and define what social studies standard or standards the unit will address. Then, teachers state the unit's knowledge, process, and values objectives.

2. Stage Two: Assessment Evidence
   Once the desired results are defined, teachers then develop an assessment plan clearly stating what sources of evidence will determine if students have achieved the desired

results. Wiggins and McTighe are advocates for "performance-based" assessment, which we will discuss in Chapter 3.

   3. Stage Three: Learning Plan

      In the last stage, teachers create learning experiences that lead to achievement of the unit's desired results. Important here is that teachers plan activities to "hook" and "hold" student interest, and are "tailored" to the "different needs, interests, and abilities of learners" (Wiggins & McTighe, 2006, p. 22).

Units Should Be Integrated

It is the position of the NCSS that "social studies is integrative by nature" (NCSS, 2009). How true! Social studies units can be integrated through content or by process; in fact, *content integration* occurs when a unit goes beyond history and geography to include concepts from other social sciences (political science, anthropology, economics, and sociology), the arts (literature, the visual arts, and the performing arts), science, mathematics, and physical education. *Process integration* is the result of planning activities that make a social studies unit a vehicle for teaching the language arts (speaking, reading, listening, and writing), the performing arts, the visual arts, and technology skills (see Chapter 5, which discusses the integrated curriculum).

Standards-Based Units Should Have a Clearly Defined Scope

All units, of course, should be designed to teach one or more state-adopted social studies standard. It is important that every unit have a clearly defined "scope." In the jargon of curriculum development, *scope* refers to the limits of the content covered in a lesson, unit, or academic year. Generally, most social studies units attempt to cover too much material. The NCSS Task Force on Standards for Teaching and Learning in the Social Studies (1993) noted that "the most effective teachers do not diffuse their efforts by covering too many topics superficially" (p. 216). The point is that some social standards are best taught through more than one instructional unit. On the other hand, it is possible for some units to address more than one standard.

      For example, one of the National Standards for History, for grades K–4 is that the "student understands the history of his or her local community" (National Center for History in the Schools, 1996, p. 27). This standard is quite broad, and might be addressed in four units such as "Native Americans Who Lived Where We Do Today," "Mission and Rancho Days in the East Bay," "Hayward's First Century," and "Hayward Today" (Hayward, California is where my university is located). On the other hand, two national standards for history for fifth graders are "the student understands how the debates over slavery influenced politics and sectionalism" and the "student understands the abolitionist movement" (National Center for History in the Schools, 1996, pp. 96 and 97). These two standards could be the target of a single unit titled "The Debate over Slavery."

      Standards define the unit's scope, but there are no shortage of topics that can serve as the unifying elements for social studies units. Following are some possibilities:

   ■ *Historical focus (when).*   With the current emphasis on history in the social studies curriculum, units that focus on a particular time and place are very popular. Examples are

"Life in the Young Republic: The United States from 1790 to 1850," "The Early Days of Our City," or "Ancient China."

■ *Person or people (who).*　　It is also possible to develop units that examine a cultural group—for example, "The Navajo: Yesterday and Today." Excellent units can be constructed around one person—for example, "Dr. Martin Luther King, Jr."

■ *Location (where).*　　Sometimes called "area studies," location units have as a unifying element a place—for example, "Japan" or "Hawaii." Units that look at places should also be limited by time. For example, the unit on Japan could avoid superficial coverage by being redesigned to become "Modern Japan: 1945 to the Present."

■ *Question or problem.*　　Some of the most intriguing social studies units have questions as their unifying elements. Activities in a unit help students develop a complete answer to the unit's unifying question. Examples are "How Does a Person Become President of the United States?" or "Why Is Gold Valuable?"

■ *Things.*　　Things, both human made and natural, can be the focus of a social studies unit. The unit on boats in this chapter is an example of this type of unit. Other examples are "Rivers" or "Calendars." The idea here is to show how different people in different times and places developed or used the object.

■ *Concept or theme.*　　An example of a unit based on a concept is "Immigration: Coming to the United States." Broad concepts can be the unifying elements of units. I have seen units on "Change," "Conflict," and "Shelter" that were fascinating. One advantage of conceptual and thematic units is that they allow us to take a global perspective and incorporate content covering several times, places, and peoples.

The process of developing units varies from school district to school district. The ideal scenario is one in which the development of instructional units utilizes the talents of many teachers to create "curriculum guides." The best guides have units that are fully developed, aligned with standards, and are complete with clear learning objectives, assessment plans, lists of available resources, and practical lesson plans.

Activities in a Unit Should Follow a Logical Sequence

Planning effective units of instruction in social studies requires us to think about the sequence of activities in each unit. Which lessons should be planned for the first few days of the unit? Which activities should serve as a culmination to the unit? As I explain later in this chapter, a unit should consist of activities involving all students in the classroom (whole group), activities that are completed by only some students in the room and are cooperative efforts (small group), and activities completed individually (individual). As a general rule, the unit should begin with whole-group activities. As the unit progresses, more and more small-group and individual projects get started, and by the last third of the unit, few whole-group activities may take place as the concluding days of the unit are devoted to small-group and individual projects.

We should meet two goals at the start of a unit: (a) determine what our students know about the topic we will be studying and (b) find out whether our students would like to investigate anything in particular. Here are some techniques for accomplishing these goals:

- *The K–W–L chart.* An example of a K–W–L chart (Ogle, 1986) appears later in this chapter in the unit on boats. K–W–L charts can be used to assess student's knowledge of a topic and to discover special areas of student's interest (see Chapter 9 for a description of this instructional strategy).

- *Open-ended journal prompts.* A simple way to find out what students know about a topic is to have them write a response to "Write what you know about _____." A simple way to learn what is of special interest to them is to say to them, "Write any questions you have about _____." The advantage of open-ended prompts is that they provide information from each student in the classroom. Many of us have our students write responses in journals, which are used throughout the unit.

- *Discussion.* An informal discussion on the first day of the unit can be used to assess student knowledge and interest. We can take notes, or we can record on chart paper what our students say.

It is usually best to start a unit with activities establishing time and place because students need to know the context of what they will be studying. Timelines and chronologies are good ways to establish time, and maps and globes of many kinds can be used to give students a sense of place (see Chapter 11). Also, at the beginning of a unit, it is a good idea to use resources that provide an overview of what students will be studying. I suggest starting the unit with videos, films, and the chapter from the textbook. Constructivist learning theory states that it is best to move from the whole to the parts, and I think this is essential in social studies. These initial activities will help students acquire essential "core" understandings, content we expect all students to know.

For the middle of a unit, we should plan a mixture of whole-group, small-group, and individual activities. We should devote the social studies period on some days to small-group and individual work. Students should have begun to study topics of personal interest. Cooperative learning is important as small groups work on projects that involve writing, the visual and performing arts. The content students acquire will be more detailed and will vary from student to student.

For the conclusion of a unit, it is a good idea to plan activities that introduce the next unit of study. I call these "segue" activities. Alleman, Brophy, and Knighton (2008) called this "foreshadowing upcoming content" (p. 30). A *segue activity* shows students the relationship between one unit and the next one that will take place. For example, chronology is a frequent source for segue activities. If we were studying the history of our state, then a unit on the Native Americans who inhabited our state would be followed by a unit on the first European settlers. The link between the two units can be shown with a timeline, revealing how one set of events follows the other.

Many units end with culminating activities. Such activities can take many forms, but they usually involve the performing arts. Students act in plays, produce films, and present material they have written. Other culminating activities can be simulations. For example, "A Day with the Ingalls" could be the culminating activity for the unit "The Prairie Pioneers." Several Websites in the popular Think Quest library, prepared by students, would provide essential information, such as "Pioneer Games, Toys, and Songs," and "Pioneer Life in America" (www.thinkquest.org). Teachers could also use children's books as resources: Wilder's *Little House* books, of course; *Prairie Girl: The Life of Laura Ingalls Wilder* (Anderson, 2008); *The Laura Ingalls Wilder Songbook* (Garson, 1968); *Skillet Bread, Sourdough, and Vinegar Pie: Cooking in Pioneer Days* (Ichord, 2003); *Frontier Living* (Tunis, 1961); and *My Prairie Year: Based on the Diary of Elinor Plaisted* (Harvey, 1986). Students would sing, play, eat, study, and work in historically authentic ways. Part of the day could be devoted to a simulation of the one-room schoolhouse of the late 19th century. In any case, the culminating activity should be a project that students have worked on for some time.

Figure 2.4 presents a summary of the principles for the sequence of activities in a unit.

Units Should Feature a Variety of Instructional Resources

There are two good reasons for using a variety of instructional resources in each social studies unit we teach: (a) The units will be enriched and more appealing to students in our classrooms, and (b) we will have a better chance of meeting the needs of our highly

Figure 2.4

Sequence of Activities in a Social Studies Unit

Beginning (First one-third)	• Assess student knowledge and Interest • Establish context (time and place) • Whole-group activities: Provide overview and core content • Begin small-group projects, individual activities
Middle (Middle one-third)	• Students learn more specific information • Fewer whole-group activities, more small-group and individual activities
End (Last one-third)	• Small-group, individual projects completed • Culminating activity • Segue activities

diverse students. Although many students do quite well with units relying on the social studies textbook, other students will need films, photographs, and other visual media to learn the content we present. In addition to the social studies textbook, we can choose from both hard-copy and CD reference materials (encyclopedias, atlases, and almanacs); children's literature (fiction and information books); charts, graphs, and maps; videos and films; filmstrips, study prints, and listening media (audiotapes and compact discs); realia (real things); community resources (people who visit our classes, places we visit); and computer-based resources (software programs, hypermedia, and the Internet).

Units Should Include Whole-Group, Small-Group, and Individual Activities

Good social studies units of instruction include activities that require students to work in several grouping formats. All three types of grouping should be a part of a social studies unit. A unit that relies heavily on lessons during which all students are expected to do the same thing at the same time will not meet the needs of a diverse student population. Differences in ability, language status, and cultural identity require frequent use of small-group work and individualized activities.

I distinguish whole-group, small-group, and individual activities as follows:

■ *Whole group.*   A whole-group activity is an activity that involves participation by all students in the classroom. During some whole-group activities, such as watching a film or listening to a guest speaker, all students participate in the activity at the same time and in the same place. Other whole-group activities include a teacher making a presentation and then students completing an assignment while working in small groups. In others, the teacher may pose a question, and then the students break into groups to discuss the question. Another format for a whole-group activity is a learning center. Students might visit the center in groups of six, one group a day. Again, from my perspective, a whole-group activity is assigned to all students in the room.

■ *Small group.*   A small-group activity has two characteristics: (a) Only a part of the class takes part, and (b) the participants work together. Small-group activities are projects, usually in writing, the visual or performing arts. Many of these small-group activities use a cooperative learning structure.

■ *Individual.*   Individual activities may be voluntary or assigned. Like small-group activities, they do not involve the whole class; rather, a student works independently, typically on a project of personal interest.

Many different formats can be used in planning instructional units in social studies. Elsewhere in the book are examples of shorter "mini-units," which can be completed in less than a week. At the end of this chapter is a longer unit on boats, designed for a highly diverse group of 25 to 30 third graders.

Summary of Key Points

- Lesson plans are of two general types. Comprehensive lesson plans are detailed and lengthy. Abbreviated plans are written in outline form.

- Instructional objectives focus on the direction and expectations of teachers. When they are well written, these objectives provide specific and observable expectations of student performance.

- Bloom's taxonomy of cognitive objectives describes levels of thinking processes. Instructional objectives can be written to require students to use higher-level mental activities.

- Direct instruction models, like Madeline Hunter's seven-step lesson plan, follow a teacher-directed format. The concept attainment model is less well-known.

- Units should be planned following the principles of backward design.

- Units should be cross curricular and integrate the social science disciplines, language arts, the visual and performing arts, science, mathematics, and physical education.

- Units should have a clearly defined scope. Each unit has a unifying element, which may be a period of history, a person or group of people, a location, a question, a thing, or a concept.

- Activities in a unit should follow a logical sequence. Activities at the beginning of a unit determine what your students know about the topic you will be covering and establish what subtopics they would like to investigate. Segue activities at the end of a unit introduce the next unit of study.

- Units should use a variety of instructional resources and feature whole-group, small-group, and individual activities.

- You may use many different formats for planning units, including detailed (comprehensive) unit plans and mini-units.

Lesson Plans and Instructional Activities

At the end of this chapter, you will find three lesson plans, all for fifth graders. The first two lessons are based on the same instructional resource, George Catlin's painting, *Buffalo Chase, Upper Missouri*. The purpose here is to show how one resource can be used for lessons following different formats. The third lesson, also focusing on the Sioux of the Plains, is an example of the Concept Attainment Model. Finally, you have an example of a lengthy, complete instructional unit for third graders on "Boats." Presented here are:

1. A lesson plan in the "comprehensive format" for fifth graders based on the painting, *Buffalo Chase, Upper Missouri;*

2. A lesson plan using the same painting, *Buffalo Chase, Upper Missouri,* but this time using the "Hunter format;"

3. A third lesson plan based on *Buffalo Chase, Upper Missouri,* in this case based on the "Concept Attainment Model format;" and

4. A comprehensive unit plan for a third-grade unit on "Boats."

Lesson Plan
Grade Five: Comprehensive Format:
Buffalo Chase, Upper Missouri

Overview: For a lesson in a mini-unit on the Oglala Sioux, a part of a unit on 19th-century Native Americans, students will work in groups to discuss a historical painting depicting a buffalo hunt, an important aspect of Sioux life.

Resources and Materials: (a) study guide, one per student (see Figure 4.5); (b) time-line for the unit; (c) map of the United States; (d) children's books: *Buffalo Hunt* (Freedman, 1988), *Buffalo Woman* (Goble, 1984), *Indians of the Plains* (Rachlis, 1960), and *Where the Buffaloes Begin* (Baker, 1981); (e) sources to help students recall what they learned about the Mohawk (e.g., information books, encyclopedias, and charts the students completed).

The essential resource for the lesson is a copy of George Catlin's painting *Buffalo Chase, Upper Missouri* (also called *Buffalo Chase, Bulls Making Battle With Men and Horses*). You could use either of two formats:

1. *With a computer.* A copy of the painting is available on the Smithsonian Institution's Website, www.si.edu. The painting is part of the collection of the National Museum of American Art in the Smithsonian.

2. *Without a computer.* A copy of the painting can be found in most books on the work of George Catlin, such as *George Catlin and the Old Frontier* (McCracken, 1959, p. 146).

Standard: From *Geography for Life,* the national geography standards, Standard 15, Knowledge Statement 2: The student knows and understand how the characteristics of different physical environments provide opportunities or place constraints on human activities (Geography Education Standards Project, 1994, p. 173).

Content Objectives: Students will grasp the concept of human–environment inter-action as they see an example of how resources influence the food-getting practices of a cultural group. They will learn that the buffalo (American bison) was the essential resource of the Sioux and other Natives of the Plains. Specifically, the lesson teaches that the Sioux used bows, arrows, and lances to hunt buffalo; the Sioux hunted in groups; the use of horses increased the Sioux's efficiency; and the buffalo hunt was dangerous to both the Sioux and their horses. The comparison of the Sioux and the Mohawk will help students understand two concepts: (a) There were great differences in how Native Americans lived prior to the coming of Europeans, and (b) the resources of a region play a central role in determining how groups of people obtain food.

Process Objectives: Students will (a) *observe* the painting; (b) *respond* to the teacher's open-ended question; (c) *describe* the physical setting and the action taking place in the setting; (d) *speculate* on why one hunter is not riding a horse; (e) *compare* hunting buffalo with and without horses; (f) *speculate* on what the hunters thought, felt, heard, and saw; (g) *compare and contrast* the food-getting practices of the Sioux and the Mohawk; and (h) *state* why the practices of the two groups differed.

Values Objectives: Students will acquire the values of cultural understanding and respect as they learn more about the Sioux.

Teaching Sequence:

1. Prepare the resources for the lesson: Website, projector, books, study guide, timeline, map, and materials for review of the Mohawk.

2. Ask the students to look at the painting. Show it for a brief time and identify your expectations for the lesson: Ask students to examine the painting to learn more about how the Sioux hunted buffalo.

3. Point to the relevant dates on the timeline: (a) 1680, the earliest probable date that Natives of the southern Plains had horses; (b) 1730, the date the Blackfoot, a northern Plains tribe, had horses; and (c) 1885, the approximate date by which buffalo had virtually disappeared from the Plains.

4. Use the map to show the region of the United States where Natives hunted buffalo.

5. Again, show the slide. Ask an open-ended question: "Would anyone like to say anything about this painting?" Use students' responses as a basis for discussion.

6. Divide the class into groups of four to work on the study guide. Distribute the study guides. Tell students that before they write, they should discuss each question. Circulate among the groups and help students share ideas.

7. Call the groups together and have the students return to their seats. Ask for volunteers to share their answers.

8. Use the last query in the study guide to stimulate a comparison of the food-getting practices of the Sioux and the Mohawk. Have students answer the query in groups and then share conclusions with the whole group. Finally, ask each group to explain what factors caused the two tribes to use different ways to get food.

9. Introduce related books to the class. Discuss each one and encourage the students to read them.

Evaluation: Collect the study guides. This would be a good source of information to place in the students' portfolios. You could also take notes as you circulate among the groups.

 Effective Teaching in Today's Diverse Classroom: In the 21st century, all our students will need to know how to use resources on the Internet. This lesson could be extended so students use the Internet. The National Museum of American Art in the Smithsonian Institution has an extensive collection of George Catlin's paintings, including 10 depicting Natives of the Great Plains hunting buffalo. A small group of students could complete a project using the Smithsonian's Website as an instructional resource (www.si.edu). I was particularly interested in his two paintings of Natives hunting buffalo in deep snow. One other point: As I noted in the description of the lesson, it is important that students learn about the great diversity among Native American tribes. That is why lessons about the Natives of the Great Plains must be part of a broader study of other tribes. It is also important to have students learn about how Native Americans live today.

It is absolutely essential that all our students learn how to access information on the Internet. Children with mild disabilities need to meet these challenges, and teachers would be wise to consider a modification in curricular content to assist them by breaking the task *into small manageable units.* For example, the task of locating information on a Website could include lessons on each of the following: (a) typing in the URL, (b) using the links on the site's main page, often displayed in a vertical or horizontal "bar," (c) finding information using the site's internal search system, and (d) scanning a location for the specific information you need.

Also, in this lesson, children with learning disabilities may need help in completing the study guide (Figure 2.5). One intervention a teacher could consider here is to *change the task criteria.* A teacher might well ask the more able students to complete their responses to the eight questions in 20 minutes. Children with disabilities could be given extra time.

Finally, an important intervention to meet the needs of our more advanced students is to pose tasks requiring complex thinking, such as making inferences. After students understand that not all Native tribes hunted buffalo and that some, like the

Figure 2.5

Study Guide: *Buffalo Chase, Upper Missouri*

Name _____

Date _____

Look closely at the painting. Talk about each question with the members of your group. Then write your answer. You do not have to write the same answer as the other members of your group.

1. How would you describe the land where the action takes place?

2. How many Sioux can you see?

3. What weapons are the Sioux using to kill the buffalo?

4. What is happening to the horses in the painting?

5. In the middle of the painting, we see one hunter who is not on a horse. Why?

6. Imagine hunting buffalo without horses. Why would it be more difficult?

7. Pretend you are one of the Sioux. Write down what you are thinking, feeling, hearing, and seeing.

8. Think back to what we learned about the Mohawk. Think what the Mohawk ate and how they got their food. Think what we have learned about the Sioux. All people need some way of getting food. What is the same and what is different about these two tribes?

Mohawk, had agriculture, more advanced students could be asked to speculate on the implications for a Native tribe that depended on migrating buffalo as a primary food source. More advanced children could be asked what this meant for the tribe's shelter, which had to be portable, like a tipi; the implications for what tools and animals would be valuable, because the Sioux needed accurate bows and arrows and swift horses; and what talents would be prized by members of the tribe, such as the ability to find and kill buffalos.

Figure 2.5 is the study guide Mrs. Richard developed for the lesson; Figure 2.6 shows the painting *Buffalo Chase, Upper Missouri.*

Figure 2.6

George Catlin toured the American Great Plains in the 1830s. He painted what he saw. This painting, completed in 1833, is known by two descriptive titles: *Buffalo Chase, Upper Missouri,* and *Buffalo Chase, Bulls Making Battle With Men and Horses.*

Smithsonian American Art Museum, Washington, DC/Art Resource, NY

Lesson Plan
Grade Five: Direct Instruction: *Buffalo Chase, Upper Missouri*

1. *Anticipatory set.*   Show the painting. Ask students to look at it closely.

2. *Objective and purpose.*   Say, "Today, we are going to learn about how the Sioux and other Native Americans who lived on the Great Plains hunted buffalo. We will look closely at this painting, and then you will work in groups to answer some questions about it. Then I will ask you to think about the similarities and differences between the Sioux and the Mohawk."

3. *Input.*   Use a timeline to show students the historical period when Natives hunted buffalo on horseback. Use a map to show them the region of the United States where buffalo roamed and the location where the artist George Catlin observed the buffalo hunt depicted in the painting. Then ask the class to break into groups. Distribute the study guides and explain how the students are to work in groups. Turn the projector on again so that everyone can see the painting.

4. *Modeling.*   Read aloud the first query and work with one group on the response. Stress the importance of listening to what each member of the group has to say before writing a response. Also point out that students should talk just loudly enough so other members of their own group can hear them but not the other groups in the room.

5. *Check for understanding.*   Ask each student to write a response for the first query and then to work on the second query. Move from group to group to be sure that students write responses in the appropriate places and that each group discusses them before writing.

6. *Guided practice.*   As the groups work on queries 3, 4, 5, 6, and 7, circulate among them. Try to maximize the number of students who talk in each group. Help groups fully explore queries 6 and 7. After discussing the first seven queries, have each group respond to the last query, which asks students to compare the Sioux and the Mohawk.

7. *Independent practice.*   Ask for volunteers for projects. One group of students could use the Smithsonian Website to create a CD scrapbook on George Catlin's paintings. Another group could look at other books, especially *Buffalo Hunt* (Freedman, 1988) and *Indians of the Plains* (Rachlis, 1960), for pictures showing other techniques used to hunt buffalo; then that group can write their own book, *How to Hunt a Buffalo*. A third group could make a large chart comparing the cultures of the Sioux and the Mohawk.

Lesson Plan
Grade Five: The Concept Attainment Model: The Sioux of the Plains

Concept: The Sioux (Dakota); more specifically, the culture of this tribal group of Native Americans who lived on the Great Plains (sometimes called the "Western Sioux")

1. Explain to students that you will present some sentences to them. Each sentence will be either an example of something or a nonexample. (You might have to use other words to explain this distinction, like "This fits but this does not fit.") Here each sentence will be labeled as a "Yes" or a "No." Write the following sentences on sentence strips, number them, and display them on a pocket chart:

    a. No: They made boats out of driftwood and tar.

    b. Yes: They hunted buffalo for food, clothing, and shelter.

    c. Yes: They lived in tipis.

    d. No: They lived in longhouses in villages surrounded by a fence.

    e. Yes: The most important ceremony was the Sun Dance.

    f. No: They trapped beaver.

    g. Yes: The men wore their hair long.

    h. Yes: Men paid for desirable things with horses.

    i. No: They farmed corn.

    j. No: For the most part, they lived peacefully and did not fight with other tribes.

2. Ask students to compare the two groups of sentences. What do the "Yes" sentences have in common? What makes the "No" sentences different from the "Yes" sentences?

3. Ask students to write a definition or description for all the "Yes" sentences. They should come up with something like "Things we know about the Sioux."

4. Now you present five more sentences to the students (see the following numbered list). This time, the sentences are not labelled "Yes" or "No." The students must decide whether each is a "Yes" or a "No":

    a. They communicated with a written language.

    b. Women owned property; daughters inherited it.

    c. The goal of a warrior was to "count coup" by touching an enemy.

    d. The wealthy were expected to give feasts and offer presents to the poor.

    e. They made beautiful clay pottery.

5. Comment on the definition the students have developed. If necessary, restate the definition of the concept.

6. Finally, ask the students whether they can generate examples of the concept. Ask, "Who can say something else about the Sioux that would be a 'Yes' sentence?"

Unit

Grade Three: Boats

Part I: Organizing Framework

This unit is organized by the learning expectations for the early grades taken from the NCSS *National Curriculum Standards for Social Studies* (2010). Your instruction will be standards-based, but all teachers must clearly communicate their expectations to the children. To achieve this purpose, this unit uses a simple format: a set of four questions phrased in words third graders can understand. The questions, are, in fact, the knowledge objectives for the unit. This is the first stage of the backward design process: defining and narrowing the focus of the unit. The unit takes about 3 weeks to complete.

Unit Question 1: What are the different types of boats, and why are they different?

Standard: Thematic Strand 1, Culture. Learning Expectation—Processes (b): Learners will be able to explore and describe similarities and differences in the ways various cultural groups meet similar needs and concerns.

In this unit of study, children will learn all people share certain needs that boats help them meet: finding food, exchanging goods, traveling to achieve personal goals, and defending themselves. The focus in this unit is on the different designs and functions of boats.

Unit Question 2: Where in our state, country, and world would you find people using boats?

Standard: Thematic Strand 3, People, Places, and Environments. Learning Expectation—Processes (c): Learners will be able to gather and interpret information from various representations of Earth, such as maps, globes, geospatial technologies and other geographic tools to inform the study of people, places, and environments, both past and present.

The unit of study on boats will require children to interpret several maps as they learn about the commercial, recreational, and military uses of boats.

Unit Question 3: What types of jobs do people perform on boats, and how have those jobs changed over time?

Standard: Thematic Strand 7, Production, Distribution, and Consumption. Learning Expectation—Processes (a): Learners will be able to ask and find answers to questions about the production, distribution, and consumption of goods and services in the school and community.

In this unit, students will learn about the division of labor on a boat. They will understand the goods or services provided by the people working on the boat require that jobs become specialized.

Unit Question 4: How have boats changed over time?

Standard: Thematic Strand 8, Science, Technology, and Society. Learning Expectation—Processes (a): Learners will be able to ask and find answers to questions about the ways in which science and technology affect our lives.

Technology has changed the design of boats, especially regarding propulsion, to make them more efficient. These changes have modified both the lives of people who work on boats and the lives of people who use them.

Part II: Assessment Plan for the Unit

The assessment plan for this unit is presented as Figure 3.5 in Chapter 3. While all activities in the unit will generate behaviors and products that can be used for assessment; certain unit activities are essential for assessment purposes. You need to know to what extent each child has mastered the objectives for the unit and met the standards the unit addresses. Here, again, is a summary of the assessment plan for the unit:

Objective 1: What are the different types of boats, and why are they different? Activities used for assessment:

■ Field trip to harbor
■ Concept attainment lesson
■ Unit test

Objective 2: Where in our state, country, and world would you find people using boats? Activities used for assessment:

■ Map reading
■ Inquiry—"Voyage to Hawaii"
■ Unit test

Objective 3: What types of jobs do people perform on boats, and how have those jobs changed over time? Activities used for assessment:

■ Bulletin board display
■ Videocassette—*Ships*
■ Unit test

Objective 4: How have boats changed over time? Activities used for assessment:

■ Bulletin board display

■ History of boats lesson

■ Unit test

Part III: Instructional Activities

(1) Introductory Activities

Please note that the instructional activities in the unit will be presented in two formats. In the first, you will find both content and process objectives, which provide a full description of the activity. In the second, briefer format, the activity is described in a few sentences.

Unit Introduction: K–W–L Chart

Content Objectives: Children will be presented with the four questions they will be expected to answer during the unit—the unit questions. Because it is impossible to predict what any group of children will say when asked, "What do you know about boats?" other content objectives cannot really be listed.

Process Objectives: Children will *recall* what they know about boats, *ask* questions they would like to have answered, and *discuss* the unit's four questions.

1. With the children, start a K–W–L chart on boats. Divide a sheet of chart paper into three columns, one with the heading "What We *K*now About Boats," the second with the heading "What We *W*ant to Learn About Boats," and the third with the heading "What We *L*earned About Boats." The first two columns will be completed on the first day of the unit. The third column will be filled in as the unit progresses. Items under the "W" column should be written as questions. If the children do not ask questions covering the subtopics you planned to cover, add them (in this unit, the four unit questions must be written down). If members of the class show an interest in something you were not planning to include, I suggest you modify your unit plan. Add resources and activities to fit the children's interests.

2. Begin by asking, "What do you know about boats?" Record what the children say under the "K" column. I like to have the four unit questions written on strips of paper so that they can be placed under the "W" column along with the questions the children ask. Be sure to have a brief discussion about each question so the children have a clear understanding of what they are expected to learn. See Figure 2.7 for an example of a K–W–L chart for this unit.

Field Trip to Los Angeles Harbor

Everyone loves a field trip. The class will travel to the harbor to observe first hand several types of boats, including fishing boats, tugboats, oil tankers, freighters, cruise

Figure 2.7

K–W–L Chart for a Unit on Boats: First Day of Unit

K What we <u>K</u>now about boats	W What we <u>W</u>ant to learn about boats	L What we <u>L</u>earned about boats
• Lots of us have visited the <u>Queen Mary</u> • Some boats have sails, others don't • Pedro, Leshana, Juan– their dads work at the harbor, and so does Donna's mom • <u>Titanic</u> was a movie about a boat that sank	*Our Questions* A. How much does it cost to buy a boat? B. How fast can boats go? C. How can a big boat like the <u>Queen Mary</u> move? *Unit questions* 1. What are the different types of boats, and why are they different? 2. Where in our state, country, and world would you find people using boats? 3. What types of jobs do people perform on boats, and how have those jobs changed over time? 4. How have boats changed over time?	

ships, and the fireboat. The children will complete data retrieval charts summarizing what they have learned about each type of boat.

(2) Unit Question 1: What are the different types of boats, and why are they different?

Teacher Read-Aloud: Boats on the River

Content Objectives: Children will expand their knowledge of the different types of boats and focus on the different designs and functions of the following: ferryboat, paddlewheel, ocean liner, tugboat, motorboat, sailboat, rowboat, freighter, submarine, and battleship.

Process Objectives: Children will *listen* to the book being read aloud, *share* their personal responses, *identify* and *differentiate* the design and function of each boat, and *classify* the boats by function.

1. Read aloud the wonderful book *Boats on the River* (Flack, 1946). Afterward, ask the children if they would like to say anything about the book.

2. Write the following words on the chalkboard: *ferryboat, paddlewheel, ocean liner,* *tugboat, motorboat, sailboat, rowboat, freighter, submarine,* and *battleship.* Go through the book a second time and discuss with the class Jay Barnum's paintings of the boats, focusing on what each boat is used for (its function or purpose). Focus on the following principle: that design serves function. Organize the boats under the following categories on the chalkboard: "Used to Move People," "Used to Move Products," "Used for War," "Used for Fishing," and "Used for Fun" (Note: Some boats should be placed under more than one category).

To adapt this activity for a group of English learners, you might consider photocopying the illustrations of the boats so that there is one, large image of each boat. Then, label the illustrations so there is both a written and a visual connection for each type of boat. This will help remind students of what each type of boat looks like.

Jigsaw: Modern Warships

Children will learn about the design and military function of five types of modern warships: aircraft carriers, battleships, submarines, transport ships, and search-and-rescue ships. For each type of warship, the teacher will prepare an online data file on a CD, with descriptions and illustrations. The class will be divided into five groups. Have each member of one group pick a different type of warship; he or she will become an "expert" about that warship and share his or her expertise with the remaining members of the group.

Bulletin Board Display: Voyages

This display will reveal what one group of children learned about the different types of boats used to transport people, both historical and contemporary. The bulletin board display will include images of (1) Chumash canoes—the Chumash were a tribe of Native Americans in California who built oceangoing canoes; (2) the Pilgrims' *Mayflower;* (3) a modern commercial cruise ship; and (4) a dozen other boats used to transport people (e.g., ferries, ocean liners, recreational craft). The group will use CD encyclopedias, Internet resources, hard-copy encyclopedias, and information books as resources. Each of their paintings will have a caption listing the type of boat and, if the boat has a name, the boat's name. Children will make oral reports about what they learned.

This should be an activity that will work for your students with learning disabilities. The students could, of course, be asked to write a report of their findings. Instead, here the final product has two parts: (1) the paintings of the boats displayed on the bulletin board and (2) the oral reports. Other than the brief captions, there is no written product. This is an example of *changing the task modality* to allow children with disabilities to show what they know.

Inquiry: The Voyage to Hawaii

Content Objectives: Children will learn about the migration of people from Tahiti to Hawaii in about C.E. 1200. They will understand that the Polynesians accomplished incredible feats of navigation, sailing with the resources they possessed. They will locate Tahiti and Hawaii on a world map. The inquiry will ask them to decide what supplies the Tahitians should take on their canoes as they prepare for their voyage to Hawaii.

Process Objectives: Children will *listen* to the historical overview provided by their teacher, *view* pictures of Polynesian catamarans, *locate* Tahiti and Hawaii on a world map, *examine* a list of resources available to the Tahitians, and *identify* the items they would take with them if they were making the voyage.

1. All the information you need for this lesson is available on the Website of the Polynesian Voyaging Society (www.pvs.hawaii.org). The site has excellent illustrations of the double-hulled canoes the Polynesians used, maps of the journey from Tahiti to Hawaii, and background information on all aspects of Polynesian shipbuilding, navigation, and migration. Present the background information the children will need to complete this inquiry activity. Explain that historians think a group of people from Tahiti emigrated to Hawaii in C.E. 1200. Display illustrations of the Polynesian canoes the Tahitians used for the voyage. You may want to take the class onto the playground and draw an outline of a Polynesian double-hulled canoe so the children have some idea of the size of these boats. Share that the catamarans could hold as many as 50 people. Show that storage space would be limited.

2. Use the maps to show the distance from Tahiti to Hawaii. Members of the Polynesian Voyaging Society built a replica of a 13th-century canoe and sailed from Hawaii to Tahiti and back in 1976. The journey from Tahiti to Hawaii took 25 days. Explain the problem the sailors must solve: what should be taken on the voyage? Point out that the Tahitians did not know what they would find when they arrived in Hawaii, so they had to pack for both a long ocean voyage and an uncertain future. Present the children with a list of things the Tahitians could have taken with them: taro, coconuts, breadfruit, pigs, dogs, tools to repair the ship, weapons, extra sails, extra paddles, extra clothes, water, line and hooks for fishing, buckets, and shell jewelry. Have each group of five children generate a prioritized list of the items they would take with them if they were on the first voyage to Hawaii.

Your English learners will need some "sheltering" on the task requiring them to prioritize the items the Polynesians would select for an exploratory voyage. Working with your English learners in a small group, take some extra time to analyze each possible item, first being sure they understand the purpose of the item (e.g., for *sails,* be sure they understand that wind powered the catamarans). Then, talk about the possible consequences of including or not including the item on the voyage.

(3) Unit Question 2: Where in our state, nation, and world would you find people using boats?

Map-Reading Activity

The children will identify port cities on coasts, rivers, and lakes. They will understand that not all port cities are located on ocean or gulf coasts; some are far inland (like Duluth, Cincinnati, and Kansas City). Speaking of Duluth, this lesson will provide an opportunity for the students to learn about Lake Superior and the other Great Lakes by taking the "Great Lakes KML Tour available through Google Earth (www.earth.google.com; for more on using Google Earth, see Britt & La Fontaine, 2009).

Teacher Read-Aloud: Freighters

The teacher reads aloud the book, *Freighters: Cargo Ships and the People Who Work Them* (Ancona, 1985). The children will listen to their teacher read aloud, compare and contrast the design and function of a freighter with an ocean liner and a fishing boat, recognize the purpose of a canal, identify the locations of the Suez and Panama Canals, and examine a world map to determine the most direct international trade routes between seven port cities.

(4) Unit Question 3: What types of jobs do people do on boats?

Pantomime: Working on a New England Fishing Boat

Content Objectives: Children will learn the tasks that must be completed by people who live in a New England fishing village.

Process Objectives: Children will *listen* to their teacher read a book aloud, *ask* questions about the content of the book, *identify* the tasks people in the village must complete, and *dramatize* five of those tasks.

1. Read aloud *Surrounded by Sea: Life on a New England Fishing Island* (Gibbons, 1991). Afterward, ask the children if they have questions or comments about the book.

2. Then focus on the different activities taking place on the island from season to season. On the chalkboard, make a list of the work to be done: mending nets, repairing sails, loading equipment, bringing in the catch, and unloading the fish for processing. Have the children pretend to do each job.

Video: Ships

The class will view the video, *Ships*, and learn about the different jobs on an ocean liner, focusing on the responsibilities of the cruise director, the engineer, the captain, the stewards, and the radio officer.

(5) Unit Question 4: How have boats changed over time?

History of Boats Lesson

Content Objectives: Children will learn that although the functions of boats have remained constant, their design and capacity (e.g., speed and size) have changed radically. They will learn about the design and function of seven famous boats.

Process Objectives: Children will *listen* to information presented by the teacher, *examine* illustrations of each boat, *distinguish* the differences between the boats, and *predict* how boats might be different in the future.

The lesson will ask the children to examine each of the following boats:

- An ancient Egyptian boat built for the pharaoh, Cheops
- A Roman trireme
- A Haida canoe (the Haida are a Native tribe living in British Columbia and Alaska)
- The *Constitution* ("Old Ironsides")
- The *Great Eastern* (a ship powered by sail and steam)
- The *Queen Mary* (powered by engines)
- The *Nautilus* (first atomic-powered submarine)

1. Examples of historical boats can be taken from books with excellent illustrations: *Into the Wind: Sailboats Then and Now* (Ofinoski, 1997), *The Book of Fantastic Boats* (Bernard, 1974), *Oars, Sails, and Steam: A Picture Book of Ships* (Tunis, 1952), and *Ships, Sailors, and the Sea* (Humble, 1991). Two books by David Weitzman are excellent resources: *Old Ironsides: Americans Build a Fighting Ship* (2003) and *Pharaoh's Boat* (2009). For an illustration of the Haida canoe, use the Website of the Canadian Museum of Civilization (www.civilization.ca).

2. Prepare a timeline showing when each kind of boat was used; also prepare an illustration of each boat.

3. Display an illustration of each boat and discuss two features: (a) how the boat was powered and (b) how the boat was used. Ask questions that will help children see how each boat is alike and different from the one that preceded it.

4. Finally, have children predict how boats might be different in the future.

For children with learning disabilities, this would be a good opportunity to meet their needs by *dividing material into small, manageable units*. The important thing for teachers in this lesson is to keep focused on the content objective: to learn that although the functions of boats have remained constant, their design and capacity (e.g., speed and size) have changed over time. While this is shown most clearly by examining seven boats used at different chronological points, the objective can be achieved by looking at just the *Constitution,* which was powered by sails, and the *Queen Mary,* powered by powerful engines. This narrowed focus should help children with learning disabilities.

Song: "The Erie Canal"

Time for a song! Teach the class the American folk song "The Erie Canal." First, read aloud Peter Spier's picture book about the song, *The Erie Canal* (1970). Spier's illustrations show the horse- and mule-drawn barges that were used on the canal.

(6) Concluding Activities

Suchman Inquiry: What Makes Things Float?

Content Objectives: Children will learn why some things float and others do not. They will see that almost anything will float, regardless of weight, if it is supported by a large enough platform.

Process Objectives: Children will *observe* items of various weights placed in a tank of water, *predict* which items from a second set will float, *ask* questions attempting to resolve the paradox of why some heavy things float and some light things do not, and *propose* a rule that defines why things float.

1. This inquiry activity provides a cross-curricular link to science. Fill an aquarium with water. Then present this puzzler to the class: "Explain why incredibly heavy ships like ocean liners and aircraft carriers float."

2. First, show the class a lightweight item that will float in the tank—a paper clip. Ask the children whether the paper clip will float. They typically think it will. Then place the item into the tank. The paper clip should float if you set it on top of the water horizontally rather than put it in vertically. Next, show a heavier item that will sink, like a large nail. Ask the children whether the item will float. Usually, the children will predict it will sink. Then place the large nail into the tank. It will sink. Ask the class if they can state a rule explaining why some things float and others sink. Usually, children will conclude that heavy things sink and light things float. Ask, "Okay, then explain how can heavy ships like an ocean liner or an aircraft carrier stay afloat?" Tell the class to ask you yes/no questions as you continue the demonstration. Float plastic plates and trays in the tank as supports under items of differing weights. The children will eventually see that heavy items can float if the surface area of water underneath them is expanded. A heavy wrench will float in the tank if it is placed on a cafeteria-style tray.

Concept Attainment/Assessment

This activity will assess and reinforce children's understanding of the different functions of boats. The children will classify 10 boats into four functional categories:

(a) Used to Move People, (b) Used to Move Things, (c) Used for Fishing, and (d) Used for War. The students will examine copies of illustrations of 10 boats (found from Websites, books, and encyclopedias).

Unit Test

The third graders will take a simple end-of-unit test. It is important to remember that any test designed for third graders must be brief and should fit the abilities of the children. This test should ask the children to respond to the following: Choose one boat we have learned about during the past few weeks. Answer each of the following questions:

a. Which boat did you choose?

b. What makes the boat go?

c. What is the boat used for?

d. Is the boat a modern boat or an old boat?

e. Where does the boat go?

f. What jobs do people perform on this boat?

To help children choose, allow them to look at the illustrations of boats you used for the concept attainment lesson. Answer questions the children ask about how to complete the assignment. Give children plenty of time to finish writing their answers.

Permit your English-language learners to complete the test orally in either English or their first language if they cannot write simple phrases or sentences in English. For children with learning disabilities, this might be an opportunity to challenge them to expand their abilities to write sentences. The "test" will be difficult for a student with a disability. You might let such students respond first orally, allow them to write their answers, and then guide them to more correct form (spelling, sentence structure), This would be an example of *changing the criteria for success on a task*.

Segue Activity: Think-Pair-Share on Boats and Planes

Let's suppose the next unit for this class of third graders will be on airplanes. A simple segue activity is for you to pose these questions: "How are ships and airplanes alike? How are they different?" The children will learn that despite the obvious differences between airplanes and boats, these serve the same functions (transport people, transport goods, or warfare). They will understand the significant differences between airplanes and boats (speed, size, and utility). Have each child work with a partner. First, each child thinks about the questions. Then the partners discuss their responses. Finally, the children share their responses with their classmates.

(7) Enrichment Activities

In Chapter 4, I will write about several instructional modifications that could be used to meet the needs of more advanced students. One technique is called *tiering assignments*. In such an approach, each unit has certain "core" assignments that all children complete. Every unit, however, should include opportunities for all children to explore topics of personal interest. Gifted students need chances to either examine additional topics (*breadth approach*) or examine topics previously covered at a deeper level (*depth approach*). At the same time, enrichment activities will allow you to help children who have special needs. For example, children who are having difficulty using a CD encyclopedia can be assigned to an activity that will give them an opportunity to become more proficient. Each child in the class should choose (or be assigned to) at least one enrichment activity.

Construction: Paper Boats

Using the directions on www.wikihowcom/Make-a-Paper Boat or in *Let's Make a Toy Sailboat* (Stokes, 1978), show the children how to make one of three types of paper boats.

Oral Presentation on Semaphore

Have a group of children teach their classmates some of the semaphore alphabet. Semaphore is a system of visual signaling using two flags, held one in each hand; each flag is a square constructed of one white triangle and one black triangle. The group can construct semaphore flags from black and white construction paper and dowel rods and then teach their classmates the first letters of the semaphore alphabet. This would be an example of a breadth activity in that it introduces a new topic not covered in the unit's core assignments.

Independent Reading

Children may choose to read one of the unit-related books you have brought to class. Each book should be displayed on a table or in a special bookshelf. Figure 2.10, at the end of this chapter, is a list of books that could be used for this unit. A student choosing to read *Ship* by David Macauley would be an example of a depth activity, allowing the student to learn a great deal more about sailing ships, a topic previously covered in the unit's core assignments.

Design a Fantastic Boat

Allow any child who wants to draw a picture of a fantastic boat to do so. Encourage children to use their imaginations. Each boat should be different and unusual. *The Book of Fantastic Boats* (Bernard, 1974) could serve as inspiration. This would be a good activity for gifted students.

Encyclopedia of Boats

Some children may choose to create a class "encyclopedia" of boats. You will have to provide a booklet that has 10 photocopied pages like the sample in Figure 2.8. Two pieces of 9- by 12-inch construction paper can serve as the cover. Each page has a

Figure 2.8

Form for an Encyclopedia Entry, Grade 3

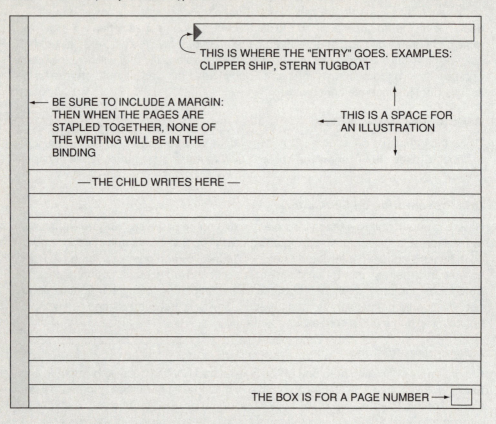

THIS IS WHERE THE "ENTRY" GOES. EXAMPLES: CLIPPER SHIP, STERN TUGBOAT

BE SURE TO INCLUDE A MARGIN: THEN WHEN THE PAGES ARE STAPLED TOGETHER, NONE OF THE WRITING WILL BE IN THE BINDING

THIS IS A SPACE FOR AN ILLUSTRATION

— THE CHILD WRITES HERE —

THE BOX IS FOR A PAGE NUMBER →

place for a title, an illustration, and a brief description. When finished, the children can arrange the entries in alphabetical order and then complete a title page and a table of contents. Help the children bind the booklet together.

Part IV: Outline of Daily Plans—The Unit Grid

The easiest way to make an outline of what will happen each day during the unit is with a unit grid. Figure 2.9 shows a grid for this unit.

Effective Teaching in Today's Diverse Classroom: The unit on boats includes several features that make it appropriate for children with learning disabilities. First, the unit uses a *wide range of resources:* books with excellent illustrations, Websites, children's books, encyclopedias, a video, a field trip, and maps. This will help children

Figure 2.9

Unit Grid for Boats

DAY 1	DAY 2	DAY 3	DAY 4	DAY 5
1. K–W–L chart 2. Field trip	1. Read aloud *Boats on the River* 2. Introduce independent reading	1. Jigsaw: Modern warships	1. Continue Jigsaw: Modern warships 2. Introduce Encyclopedia of Boats Project	1. Map-reading activity 2. Introduce Semaphore Project
DAY 6	DAY 7	DAY 8	DAY 9	DAY 10
1. Read aloud *Freighters* 2. Song: "The Erie Canal"	1. Video: *Ships* 2. Introduce Bulletin Board Project	1. Life on a New England fishing island 2. Introduce "My Voyage" writing	1. Inquiry: The Voyage to Hawaii	1. History of boats lesson 2. Introduce boat construction and design a fantastic boat
DAY 11	DAY 12	DAY 13	DAY 14	DAY 15
1. Sing "The Erie Canal" again 2. What makes things float?	Individual and small-group work	Student presentations on semaphore and the bulletin board	1. Individual and small-group work 2. Concept attainment lesson	1. Unit test 2. Segue-Boats Planes

who are not proficient readers learn the content the unit presents. The K–W–L activity will help children *activate their background knowledge* about boats. As children hear their classmates talk about boats, they will recall things they know. For our English learners, this unit has a great deal of "*comprehensible input.*" The picture books read aloud by the teacher have simple texts and excellent illustrations. Lessons are supported with the use of illustrations. Many activities, like the inquiry on the voyage to Hawaii, feature *cooperative learning.* Group work will push children into their zones of proximal development and provide the *contextual support* English-language learners need to succeed. Many children learn best through *the arts.* This unit provides learning experiences in the performing arts (the pantomime and singing of "The Erie Canal") and the visual arts (bulletin board display and design a fantastic boat). *Firsthand experiences* make it easier for all children to learn new things. Many children will see real boats for the first time on the field trip. The mixture of *whole-group, small-group,* and *individual* activities allows more able children to be challenged and permits children who are particularly interested in boats to satisfy their curiosity.

Figure 2.10

Children's Books: Grade 3 Unit on Boats

INFORMATION BOOKS

Ancona, George. *Freighters: Cargo Ships and the People Who Work Them*.
This book is too difficult for most third graders to read. The photographs, however, are a good source of information.

Barton, Bryon. *Boats*. Illustrated by the author, this is a very easy reading book, within the capabilities of almost every third grader. Barton's illustrations are a problem: They are cartoonlike and lack the realism a good information book requires.

Bernard, Christine. *The Book of Fantastic Boats*. Illustrated by Roy Coombs's brilliant, full-color illustrations of boats through the ages, this book includes novelties such as the first submarine (the *Turtle*, 1776) and the *Popoffka*, a 19th-century Russian warship that was round! More able third-grade readers can understand the text.

Carter, Katherine. *Ships and Seaports*. Illustrated with photographs, this book is very easy reading.

Cook, Nick. *The World's Fastest Boats*. Illustrated with photographs. This book, which can be read by most third graders, shows catamarans, hydrofoils, and several types of jet engines.

Freeman, Marcia. *Fire Boats*. Illustrated with photographs. This is a very easy-to-read book.

Gibbons, Gail. *Surrounded by Sea: Life on a New England Fishing Island*.
This book tells of one year, season by season, on an island off the coast of Maine. Most third graders could read this book.

Hartford, John. *Steamboat in a Cornfield*. Illustrated with historical photographs, this is a picture book about an incident in 1910. The steamboat *Virginia* went aground while traveling on the Ohio River. An excellent book, the period photographs are fascinating. A good choice to read aloud.

Hubbell, Patricia. *Boats: Speeding!Sailing!Cruising!* This book is written for very young readers. The multimedia illustrations are very interesting and include vintage clip art, hand drawn images, and photos from old newspapers.

Humble, Richard. *Ships, Sailors, and the Sea*. Illustrated by several artists, this book is part of the superb "Timelines" series. Although it is difficult for third graders to read, the detailed, full-color illustrations of historical ships are an excellent resource.

Kalman, Maira. *Fireboat: The Heroic Adventures of the John J. Harvey*.
Author/illustrator Kalman tells the story of a New York City fireboat, launched in 1931, retired many years later, and then called into service on September 11, 2001. Almost all third graders can read this book.

Kentley, Eric. *Boat*. Illustrated with photos and drawings. Part of the excellent "Eyewitness Books" series.

Kentley, Eric. *Eyewitness: Boats*. Specially commissioned photographs show how boats have changed over the years.

Lasky, Kathryn. *Born in the Breezes: The Seafaring Life of Joshua Slocum*. Illustrated by Walter Lyon Krudop. This is the story of the 19th century mariner who tried to sail around the world on his own. Able third graders can read it.

Lasky, Kathryn. *Tall Ships*. Illustrated with Christopher G. Knight's photographs, this book is too difficult for third graders to read, but the photographs are a useful teaching resource.

Lasky, Kathryn. *Tugboats Never Sleep*. Illustrated with Christopher G. Knight's photographs, this book can be read by most third graders.

Macauley, David. *Ship*. This is a fascinating book in two parts. In the first, archaeologists discover a 15th-century caravel. In the second, how the caravel was built is described. As with all his books, Macauley's drawings are great. Third graders will need help with the text.

Ofinoski, Steven. *Into the Wind: Sailboats Then and Now*. Illustrated with photographs and drawings. Easy reading, the book shows many boats, including a jangada, a one-sailed Brazilian fishing boat.

Olney, Ross R. *Ocean-Going Giants*. Illustrated with photographs, this book can be read by most third graders.

Rand, Gloria. *Sailing Home: A Story of a Childhood at Sea*. Illustrated by Ted Rand. This book is based on the journal of Captain Masden, who sailed with his four children around the Hawaiian Islands between 1896 and 1910.

Rosenblum, Richard. *Tugboats*. Illustrated with the author's excellent drawings, this book is for more able readers.

Scarry, Huck. *Life on a Barge: A Sketchbook*. Illustrated by the author, this is a wonderful book about the author's trip on a barge in the Netherlands.

Scott, Geoffrey. Egyptian Boats. Illustrated by Nancy L.Carlson, this is a nicely done book that is easy to read.

Stetson, Emily. *Knots to Know: Hitches, Loops, Bends, and Bindings*. Illustrated by Marc Nadel and Sarah Rakitin. Throughout the years, sailors have known how to tie several unique knots in ropes. This excellent book teaches children to tie more than 50 different types of knots, though third graders will need help with the text.

Sullivan, George. *The Civil War at Sea*. Illustrated with photographs. Excellent photos of ships used in the American Civil War.

Tunis, Edwin. *Oars, Sails, and Steam: A Picture Book of Ships*. The text is written for older children, but the author's artwork is one of the best sources on the history of boats.

Van Tol, Robert. *Submarines*. Illustrated with photographs, this is a book that most third graders can read.

Weitzman, David. *Old Ironsides: Americans Build a Fighting Ship*. Author and illustrator Weitzman tells a story about the early American warship. His illustrations are excellent.

Weitzman, David. *Pharaoh's Boat*. A fictional account of a boat built for the ancient Egyptian pharaoh, Cheops.

(*continued*)

Figure 2.10

(*Continued*)

Wormfield, Hope Herman. *Boatbuilder.* Illustrated with photographs, this is a good book to read aloud. It is about Ralph Stanley, a sailboat maker who lives and works in Maine.

Zeck, Pam, and Zeck, Gerry. *Mississippi Steamwheelers.* Some third-grade readers can handle this book, which is illustrated by George Overlie.

FICTION

Brown, Marcia. *Henry-Fisherman.* Illustrated by the author, this book was a Caldecott Honor book in 1950. It is within the reading ability of most third graders and tells the story of a boy living in the Virgin Islands.

Fisher, Leonard Everett. *Sailboat Lost.* This is a wordless picture book with wonderful illustrations by the author. In the story, high tide takes a boat out to sea.

Flack, Marjorie. *Boats on the River.* Illustrated by Jay Hyde Barnum, this 1947 Caldecott Honor Book is a perfect book for this unit. Flack's poetry describes a ferryboat, a paddlewheel riverboat, an ocean liner, a tugboat, a motorboat, a sailboat, a rowboat, a freighter, a submarine, and a battleship. The illustrations are bright and accurate, although the book does show its age.

Kay, Verla. *Tattered Sails.* Illustrated by Dan Adreasen. Kay's verses describe the journey of one family from England to America in the 1600s.

Molloy, Anne Stearns. *Shaun and the Boat: An Irish Story.* Illustrated by Barbara Cooney, this book is for more able third-grade readers.

Spier, Peter. *The Erie Canal.* Illustrator Spier has taken the lyrics to this folk song for his text. His illustrations have accurate historical detail. For the teacher, background on the canal is provided.

Van Allsburg, Chris. *The Wreck of the Zephyr.* Illustrated by the author, this is a picture book fantasy about a sailboat that could fly. Most third graders can read it.

Assessment of Social Studies Learning

In this chapter, you will read about

- The purposes and goals of both formative and summative assessment
- The essentials of effective assessment in elementary social studies
- Gathering data from multiple sources
- Alternatives for keeping records of student performance
- Guidelines for data analysis
- Sharing assessment data with students and parents

In Chapter 6, you will read a description of a Group Project. While one group of students worked on the chronological mural of the city, third-grade teacher Al Braccio entered data on a Group Project Evaluation Form. The form is a kind of rating scale that enabled Mr. Braccio to document his observations of each child's performance during Group Projects. It also allowed him to make anecdotal notes for future group work planning. For example, Brad wrote an excellent caption for his part of the mural but did not complete tasks in a timely manner. Next time, Mr. Braccio will be sure Brad works with someone who provides a good model of staying on task. Sara, an English learner, continued to show excellent work habits and social skills. Mr. Braccio noted that the cooperative nature of the project gave her an opportunity to use her

Figure 3.1

Group Project Evaluation Form

Title of Project: *Chronological mural of our city*
Dates: *May 6–19*
Participants: *Sara, Debbie, Ben, Denise, Cliff, Tina, Dan, Amber, Brad, Claudia*

	Social Skills	Illustration	Caption	Timetable
Sara	1	1	2	1
Debbie	1	2	1	1
Ben	2	1	2	1
Denise	1	1	1	1
Cliff	1	2	2	1
Tina	1	2	2	2
Dan	3	2	2	1
Amber	2	2	1	1
Brad	2	2	1	3
Claudia	1	2	1	3

1: Excellent   2: Good   3: Needs improvement   4: Unacceptable

Notes:
5-11   Good to see Sara & Debbie work together. Sara is making so much progress in her English.
5-12   Had to intervene with Dan and Amber. They argued. Dan has difficulty sharing. He wanted to do all the artwork.
5-13   The drawings look great. Sara and Ben are exceptional artists. Brad and Claudia needed help with their drawings.
5-15   Brad and Claudia haven't used their time wisely. They will finish a couple of days late.
5-16   I am pleased with the way Tina and Cliff helped each other.

improving English skills, an excellent reason to continue to plan Group Projects for the children. All in all, the evaluation form (see Figure 3.1) proved to be a useful device for recording important data about the progress of each child working on the project.

■ ■ ■

Purposes and Goals of Assessment

Assessment is the process of gathering, analyzing, and sharing information on the ability and achievement of students. Although some educators have distinct definitions for *assessment* and *evaluation,* in this book the terms are synonymous. In educational settings, assessments are made for two purposes: *Formative assessment* is the process of helping students achieve more—think of a ball of clay being "formed" into a finished work of art. *Summative assessment* is the process of making judgments. In elementary social studies, summative assessment usually means completing a report card of some sort—think of "summing" things up. Teachers must be able to fulfill both purposes of assessment. Our assessment plans for social studies must provide the data we need to make instructional decisions to increase the achievement of our students. We also need data to summarize the progress of our students and categorize their performance. Given the primary role standards are playing in almost all elementary classrooms, the ultimate goal of the assessment process is to tell us how much progress each student has made toward achieving each of our grade-level standards in social studies. To make this judgment, assessment must first reveal the extent to which students have met the objectives for a lesson or a unit.

Essentials of Effective Assessment

Teachers will develop an assessment plan for each social studies unit they teach. This plan should have the following essential elements: (1) it will define sources of evidence that allow teachers to determine if students have mastered the standard(s) the unit addresses, (2) it will include some performance assessments, (3) it will be developed at an appropriate point in the instructional planning process, and (4) it will allow the teacher to gather evidence from multiple sources.

Standards-Based Assessment

The ultimate goal of the assessment plan is to make judgments about student progress in mastering the relevant social studies standard(s) addressed in the unit. For this example, I will use the *National Standards for History* (National Center for History in the Schools, 1996). Let us assume the social studies standards for fourth graders are the national standards in the category of "The History of Students' Own State or Region." There would then be five standards that all fourth graders would be expected to achieve:

1. Students understand the history of indigenous peoples who first lived in their state or region.

2. Students understand the history of the first European, African, and/or Asian-Pacific explorers and settlers who came to their state or region.

3. Students understand the various other groups from regions throughout the world who came into the state or region over the long-ago and recent past.

4. Students understand the interactions among all these groups throughout the history of their state.

5. Students understand the ideas that were significant in the development of the state and that helped forge its unique identity.

One way to organize standards-based assessment is by creating a social studies portfolio for each student (Adams & Hamm, 1992). A *portfolio* is a place of storage, one for each student, and may be as simple as a manila folder. For social studies, however, the portfolio should be a larger container, maybe a small box or basket. Some teachers I have known use a single portfolio for all school subjects; others have two or more portfolios for each student. Returning to our fourth-grade example, the first standard is that the student understands the history of the indigenous peoples of the state or region. Let us assume the student lives in Ventura, California, and her class has been studying the Chumash tribal group. The teacher will have defined key sources of evidence for this first standard which could be placed in the portfolio behind a divider titled "Social Studies Standard One: Indigenous Peoples." That evidence could include a story the student wrote titled "My Day with the Chumash," a copy of an evaluation checklist completed by the teacher on the student's mini-mural on Chumash food gathering, a map the student completed showing the location of Chumash villages, and the end-of-unit test.

Many teachers are now compiling computer-based storage systems for evidence gathered for social studies assessment. Student work, tests, and other sources of data are stored on CDs or some other computer-based storage device.

Performance Assessment

The plan should include performance assessments. Educational assessment has undergone a revolution in the last four decades (Alleman & Brophy, 2001a; Nickell, 1999; Nitko & Brookhart, 2006). Forty years ago, almost all judgments about student achievement were based on tests. For the most part, these tests were part of the social studies textbook or tests developed by teachers. Assessment was the process of developing, implementing, and interpreting tests. Well-designed, developmentally appropriate tests can provide useful information and should be a part of social studies assessment, but even the best tests do not provide a complete picture of what our students know, are able to do, and value. Tests capture student performance at one point in time, limit ways of expressing knowledge, and require performance in artificial situations divorced from typical social studies activities.

The alternative to tests is generally referred to as *authentic assessment* or *performance assessment* or *performance-based assessment* (Alleman & Brophy, 1998, 2001a; Darling-Hammond, Ancess, & Falk, 1995; Gallavan, 2008; Wiggins, 1993, 1999; Wiggins & McTighe, 2006). In this book I will use the descriptor "performance assessment." Performance assessment has the following characteristics:

■ Some sources of evidence are tasks requiring complex, higher-level thinking, often through inquiry and problem solving.

■ Some sources of evidence assess students' performance on tasks corresponding to the types of things people do in the "real" world, rather than tasks performed only in school.

- Data used for evaluation can come from the everyday assignments students complete, assuming the teacher plans a wide range of challenging social studies activities.

- The process is ongoing and longitudinal, with data gathered, analyzed, and shared throughout the school year.

- Students show what they know and can do in a variety of ways—through writing, speaking, art, and drama.

Assessment in the Planning Process

The assessment plan should be defined at an appropriate point in the planning process. In the previous chapter, I referred to the unit planning system developed by Wiggins and McTighe (2006). They refer to their system as "backwards design." You might recall that in this system of planning the first step is to define what standards the unit will address and then define the objectives for the unit's lessons and activities. These are the unit's "desired results." The second stage is to develop an assessment plan for the unit. Here, teachers define the sources of evidence that will allow them to determine if students have achieved the unit's desired results. Only after the assessment plan has been created, do teachers move to stage three and define the unit's learning activities.

Wiggins and McTighe are correct in stating this process is not what usually happens in instructional planning. Too often, teachers begin the planning process by defining activities because of their appeal. The sources of appeal can be noble—the teacher plans the activity because it is intellectually challenging. Or, the appeal can be less noble—the kids will have fun and stay busy. Or, the appeal can be an external expectation—the teacher needs to cover all the material in the social studies textbook and the activity will get another chapter out of the way. The teacher then scurries to find a standard fitting the activity and only at the end of the planning process, if at all, thinks about assessment. The process described by Wiggins and McTighe makes better sense: define desired results, then define sources of evidence to determine if those results have been achieved, then define activities enabling students to achieve the desired results.

Multiple Sources of Evidence, Key Sources

The assessment plan should allow the teacher to examine data from multiple sources. The next section of the chapter will provide a wide range of sources of evidence that can be used to evaluate student performance in elementary social studies. These include:

- Written products, like captions or reports

- Nonwritten products, like charts or maps

- Oral activities; products that involve several forms of expression, like a video presentation that has a written script, an oral presentation, and charts and diagrams

- Informal observations of students

- Tests

While every activity in a unit will yield evidence that potentially can be gathered and analyzed, the important thing is that the unit has an assessment plan defining key sources of data for determining whether or not students achieved the desired results of the unit.

Gathering Data

All assessment plans will require teachers to participate in a process that parallels social science research, which has three components: (a) gathering data, (b) analyzing data, and (c) sharing data. First, let us take a more detailed look at the possible sources of data that can provide evidence about student progress.

Written Products.   A variety of social studies lessons will generate written products that can serve as sources of data for determining student achievement. In this section, I use examples from the original document presenting the NCSS *Curriculum Standards for the Social Studies* (National Council for the Social Studies [NCSS], 1994).

Stories.   Stories written by students can be used as a means of evaluating what they learned. The NCSS (1994) provides the following example (p. 57): A teacher wanted her class to understand the concept of an "artifact" and how family artifacts can help people learn about how their relatives lived in the past. The teacher asked her second graders to bring something to class their parents or grandparents owned when they were young. The children gathered things like waffle irons, newspapers, old photographs, and kitchen tools. Each child then wrote a story about her or his artifact.

Captions.   To accompany simple illustrations and as a part of bulletin board displays, students write captions. The captions can be used for assessment.

Editorials.   The editorial form of journalistic essay requires the writer to organize facts to persuade the reader and is a good project for older elementary students. Here's another example from the NCSS (1994, p. 83): An eighth-grade class examined different perspectives on the American Revolution (patriot, loyalist, and indifferent). To assess students' understanding of multiple perspectives, the teacher had students work in groups to gather information on contemporary policy issues (e.g., welfare reform). Each student then wrote a newspaper editorial advocating a position on that issue.

This example would be a good one to explore in terms of defining criteria and a scoring rubric for analysis. Although the essay could be evaluated by several criteria, let's assume the teacher decided on only one: the ability to provide factual support for the position adopted in the editorial. The teacher could develop an evaluation chart with the scoring rubric displayed in Figure 3.2. In this example, the teacher decided on three components of providing factual support in the editorial: (a) the number of facts, (b) their relevance to the writer's position, and (c) the degree to which their presentation strengthened the writer's position.

Figure 3.2

Evaluation Rubric for Newspaper Editorial

Unit: "The American Revolution"

Assignment: Newspaper editorial on contemporary policy issue

Student's Name _____

Date _____

Criterion: Ability to provide factual support for the editorial position

_____ 1. Essay cites several facts, each relevant to the topic, presented in a
manner that strengthens the writer's position.

_____ 2. Essay cites few facts, each is relevant to the topic, and they are presented
in a manner that strengthens the writer's position.

_____ 3. Essay cites few facts, and they are not relevant to the topic *or* they are not
presented in a manner that strengthens the writer's position.

_____ 4. Essay failed to cite facts to support the writer's position.

Answers to Questions.   When students read from their social studies textbooks, many
lessons will require them to answer questions. For assessment, the key is to ask a variety of
questions, including those with answers explicitly stated in the text, those that require students to synthesize information from different parts of the text, and those that require
interpretation.

Journals.   Many of us have our students write in journals. Some journals are ongoing
summaries of what students think they have learned; others are change-of-perspective
journals written as if the students were in a different time and place. For example, the NCSS
(1994, p. 60) describes a second-grade classroom where the teacher asked the children to
select a way they could make their community a better place to live. Working in groups, the
children selected an organization in their city that could make their idea happen. The children then sent a proposal to that organization. The teacher required the children to keep
journals during this activity. The teacher evaluated the journals for clarity, thoroughness,
and accuracy.

Scripts.   When our students write scripts for performing arts presentations, we can save
these and place them in the students' portfolios.

Summary Reports. After our students participate in a project, we can ask them to write reports summarizing what they did and learned. The NCSS (1994, p. 65) provides an example of how this form of writing can be used for evaluation: A primary class participated in a unit on economic specialization during production. The class was divided into two groups: One group made their cookies with an assembly line; the other group made their cookies as individuals. Afterward, the class compared the two approaches in terms of productivity, pride, creativity, and quality control. Students prepared written summaries about the production process. Their teacher evaluated the summaries in terms of accuracy of description and extent to which each student used economic concepts to describe what happened.

Notes. As students gather information from reference materials, we can ask them to take notes. Although notes usually are used as a tool to create something else (e.g., an oral presentation or a bulletin board display), the notes themselves provide evidence of the extent of each student's mastery of the process of gathering information.

Letters. Students should write letters as part of social studies. The letters can be "real" correspondence and be mailed to other students, to local newspapers, or to government officials. Others can be hypothetical, written to imaginary or historical people. The NCSS (1994, p. 104) describes an eighth-grade teacher who was concerned about the stereotypes his students held about the Islamic world. The teacher had collected letters to the editor published in the local newspaper showing a lack of respect toward women, social groups, and cultural groups. Students in his class pretended they were members of a slighted group and responded to the published letters. The teacher evaluated the letters based on clarity of purpose, accuracy of information about the target group, and effectiveness of presentation.

E-Mail. Just as we would save letters our students have written, we can save their e-mails. In terms of storage space, it is much more economical to save e-mail electronically on a CD than to save letters written on sheets of paper.

Essays. We should have older students write essays taking a position and supporting that position with evidence. These essays are the written project most closely resembling a traditional test. For essays used for assessment at the elementary level, however, we should require students to work together to gather information, provide opportunities for discussion on what they plan to write, and create a format for us to give them our feedback on preliminary drafts of their essays.

Nonwritten Products. Social studies should never consist solely of paper-and-pencil tasks. Throughout this book, I present many activities in which students create things that are not "written." The collection and analysis of these products are essential as an alternative to written assessments, especially in a classroom with a diverse student population, because many students find it easier to express what they know through speaking, making charts and graphs, or producing art.

Charts. A great deal of social science data are best presented in charts and graphs. The national *Curriculum Standards for Social Studies* provide these examples of how charts and graphs can be placed in a portfolio and used for assessment: In one classroom, students interviewed recent immigrants to the United States. Working in three groups, the students made three charts: one summarizing reasons for coming to the United States, the second problems encountered during immigration, and the third feelings immigrants have about leaving one place for another. Each group had to respond to questions from their classmates using the charts as a data source (NCSS, 1994, p. 53). In another classroom, students compiled charts on Native American tribes by using the following categories: geographic region, life before European contact, life after European contact, and contemporary status (p. 81). Charts are a good evaluative tool to assess our students' ability to both identify and categorize relevant information.

Maps. We can assess our students' knowledge of geographic information by asking them to make maps. We should use "mental maps," those drawn from memory, to assess our students' knowledge of geographic features (Wise & Kon, 1990). An example is offered in the national social studies standards: A second-grade class was studying their city, including the locations of major places. The children used a variety of maps to increase their knowledge and made pop-up maps of different areas. To evaluate what they had learned, their teacher asked them to make mental maps of the city and to include features from the area they studied while making their pop-up maps. The mental (or "sketch") maps were evaluated for accuracy (NCSS, 1994, p. 56).

Visual Arts. We can use a variety of visual arts products for assessment. Visual arts are important because they separate knowledge from the ability to express that knowledge through writing or speaking. Murals, posters, cartoons, constructions, and any other visual art form can be used to determine what students have learned. A good example is provided by the NCSS (1994, p. 52). In a unit on their community, primary-age children each selected a topic from this list: transportation, land use, schools, people, stores, or residences. Each child then drew two illustrations—one depicting the topic as it appears today and the other as it appeared long ago. The teacher used the drawings to assess the children's understanding of the broad concept of change and their specific knowledge of how their city had changed. The checklist in Figure 3.3 could be used to analyze the illustrations.

Oral Activities. We can use a variety of speaking activities to assess our students in social studies, especially mastery of the process of civil discourse. By listening to them, we can also judge their ability to work productively in groups. Whereas we can assess more formal oral reports in the same fashion as a written essay, discussions require us to use one of the following analytic techniques:

■ *Listen to a group and assess only one objective.* For example, we could observe three students discussing a topic and record information on the sole objective "takes turns and allows others to speak." We would assess each student in the group on her or his achievement of the objective.

■ *Listen to a group and record a few observations in anecdotal form.* We could take notes and record only those observed phenomena that "stand out" ("Heidi was able to support her position with evidence," "Vijay was patient and waited politely to speak," or "Shannon wanted to dominate and interrupted others").

Figure 3.3

Evaluation Checklist for Now and Then Illustrations

Unit: "Our Community: Yesterday and Today"

Assignment: Now and then illustrations

Student's Name _____

Date _____

Check all that apply:

_____ Illustrations depict the same topic or place.

_____ "Now" illustration provides three or more clearly distinguishable features.

_____ "Then" illustration provides three or more clearly distinguishable features.

_____ "Then" illustration is historically accurate.

_____ Illustrations were completed on time.

For example, in a fourth-grade classroom, students took part in a simulation on international trade and the relative wealth of nations. Some groups were given considerable resources (school supplies such as glue and tape), whereas other groups were not and were considered "impoverished." After the simulation, the whole class met to discuss the experience in relation to the international economic concepts they were studying. The discussion helped the teacher assess the extent to which the students could apply those concepts to a specific situation (the simulation) (NCSS, 1994, p. 66).

Performing Arts. If we are skilled, we can use drama, dance, and song to learn about our students. They will provide us with much useful information for assessment in social studies prior to their performance—in the writing of the script, the creation of the setting, and the design of the costumes. Each of these components will reveal the depth of a student's knowledge of other people, places, and times. In a class studying the American Revolution, for example, children were placed in groups. Each group selected a person from the period (e.g., Mercy Otis Warren, George Washington, Elizabeth Freeman, or Patrick Henry). The group then produced a scene depicting that person's contributions before, during, or after the war. The scene had to include dialogue and a setting (backdrops and/or props). The teacher evaluated each group for the accuracy and importance of the information they presented in their scene. The teacher asked the class to place the scenes in chronological order. The teacher used this for evaluation as well (NCSS, 1994, p. 53).

Multiple-Form Products. Many social studies activities challenge students to produce something requiring a combination of writing, the arts, charts, and speaking. In many classrooms, these multimedia products are completed with computer-based resources as students produce multimedia reports on CDs or add links to a class Website. The finished products will feature written text, visual images (photographs taken with a digital camera or a video), and charts or graphs. Although it is possible for us to look at just one aspect of the product for evaluation (e.g., just the written part), many products should be evaluated as a whole. For example, a third-grade class was learning how humans change the environment. The children decided to undertake a whole-class project on the effects of the styrofoam cups used in the school cafeteria. The children gathered data on the number of cups used annually and the amount of fluorocarbons released by the cups. They summarized information on the topic they found in hard-copy and computer-based reference materials. They learned about the cost of replacing the styrofoam cups with paper cups. The class prepared a videotaped proposal for their schoolmates and, eventually, the school board.

In another example of a multiple-form product, a seventh-grade class studied international economic interdependence. Teacher and students together constructed a survey to determine the global connections of local businesses. Members of the class used the survey to interview representatives of those businesses. Each student then prepared a poster illustrating the international aspects of the business. Each student was to prepare a short statement, similar to a news story, to use with the poster in a presentation. The teacher evaluated each student, using both the poster and the written statement, in terms of thoroughness, depth of information, and accuracy (NCSS, 1994, p. 102).

Tests. One positive outcome of the move to performance assessment is that tests have become more "authentic"—in fact, some teachers use a writing or an arts project as a test (Gallavan, 2008; Wiggins, 1989, 1992, 1999). For example, a teacher decides that each student will produce an illustrated timeline of the history of South Carolina. This is a test in that all students will be required to complete the task, and the teacher will use the results to evaluate what students have learned about their state. This assignment is more authentic than most tests, however. First, the task is familiar; students have made several timelines during the year. Tests, too, often measure student performance on tasks that are novel. Second, the task, unlike most tests, does not require students to write. Finally, the task has different "correct" versions. Although successful timelines will share common information, they will not be exactly alike (Brandt, 1992; Nitko & Brookhart, 2006).

Well-designed and developmentally appropriate tests should also be a part of our assessment plans. They will provide us with information that cannot be gained from other sources of evidence. Tests will also provide information we can use to support conclusions we have made after we have reviewed the other sources. Social studies tests are part of the resources that come with social studies textbooks. Often there is a test, usually multiple choice questions and some simple essays, for each chapter. Some states have adopted end-of-the-year standardized tests to determine if students have met the state-adopted social studies standards. These state-adopted tests are *standardized* in that the testing procedure must be identical each time the test is given. Though it varies from year to year because some states add mandated tests and others drop them, about 25 states have now mandated standardized tests in social studies (Grant, 2007; Grant & Salinas, 2008).

Some teachers develop their own tests. If teachers were to develop social studies tests, they should be concerned with some key concepts relating to tests. Tests should be *reliable,* which means the results will be consistent when given in similar situations. Tests must be *valid,* which means they measure what they claim to measure, and the inferences teachers make about the results are accurate (Wiggins & McTighe, 2006). With our English language learners (ELLs), test validity is a big issue because some tests do not measure the test taker's knowledge of social studies; rather, they measure the test taker's ability to read and write in English. How do we as teachers transform our social studies tests so they are more authentic? Here are some ways the tests have been modified:

Time. The more traditional tests have strict, uniform time limits. Some projects used for assessment, however, should have flexible time limits; students need to be given ample time to finish the task.

Location. Traditional tests are taken in school at the student's seat. Many of us, however, are developing tests for students to complete at home, on field trips, or in the library.

Collaboration. In a traditional test, students work on their own. Many social studies activities, however, require students to work in groups, and some tests require group work, too. Sometimes the group work is a prelude to the performance that will be assessed. For example, each second-grader must draw a picture of his or her favorite place in the community and write a brief rationale for this decision. Prior to beginning, small groups of children talk about what they will draw. The drawings and accompanying essays will be used for evaluation.

Alternatives to Reading and Writing. Most traditional tests demand a high level of literacy—the test taker reads questions and then writes answers. Some tests, however, ask students to draw, to make maps, or to talk.

We should create tests that provide information on each student's progress toward achieving our grade-level standards. When used with other sources of information and more authentic tests, more traditional tests can provide useful information. *Essay tests* are particularly helpful when they ask students to compare and contrast (remember, though, we should use essay tests only when our students have well-developed writing skills). *Multiple-choice tests* have the advantage of being easy to correct and, if properly constructed, can cover a wide range of content. This type of test, along with *true/false tests,* however, typically fail to assess more than knowledge of facts and reveal little about students' grasp of concepts and generalizations. It takes time to prepare a good multiple-choice test. An item has a "stem" ("The city with the most people in our state is . . .") and then three or more "options" (a. Los Angeles, b. San Francisco, c. San Diego). The options should be plausible, but only one of them should be the correct answer. Other forms of tests include *matching* (students link items in one column with items in another) and *completion* (students "fill in the blank[s]" of a partial sentence). Those of us who use these traditional forms of tests should follow the guidelines listed here:

- Plan activities that help students become familiar with the test format—practice tests or tests completed in groups—but do not devote too much time to test-taking practice.

- Be absolutely sure that the form of the test matches the developmental level of the students who will take it. Be sure tests used with primary-age children are simple and short.

- Teach older students, especially those who will go to a middle school or junior high school in the subsequent year, how to study for tests.

Records Teachers Should Keep

Whether they use a portfolio or some other storage system, teachers will keep some products created by students. For the most part, however, after students' products have been analyzed they will go home with the students to be shared with their families. Teachers will need to keep several types of records providing data on the performance of our students.

Anecdotal Records.   Anecdotal records can be written on sheets of paper, on "sticky" notes, or in computer files. It is not difficult to imagine a time when most teachers will use laptop computers to record their classroom observations. "Kid watching" is an essential part of evaluation, and these anecdotal notes will provide us with a great deal of important information. As we watch our students participate in social studies activities, we should write brief descriptions of noteworthy events. We should include the date, time, and context of the activity. Obviously, we will not be able to write something about each student every day, but over the course of time, our anecdotal records will show patterns. Here are two examples:

May 8, 2009

DeSean and Peyton are drawing a map of the classroom. So far, so good, and this is nice to see because Peyton usually likes "to take over" and boss classmates around. They are working well together and their map is accurate.

May 10, 2009

Normandy is having difficulty with the scale of miles activity. The scale is 100 miles to 1 inch on the map. Instead of multiplying distances by 100, she is adding 100 to the distance.

Evaluation Rubrics and Rating Scales.   An example of a rubric was shown in Figure 3.2. A *rubric* provides a scale with written descriptors to categorize student performance. A rubric should have three or more categories, and the descriptor for each category should be written with enough detail to distinguish it from the others. Reliable and valid rubrics are difficult to develop, the best ones requiring a group effort and testing in several

Figure 3.4

Rating Scale for Assessing an Eighth-Wonder Project

Unit: Europe and the Middle East in ancient days *Assignment:* Group project—Construct an Eighth Wonder					
	Names of Students				
	Roberto	Zella	Ned	Jiri	Winona
Criteria					
1. Helped group reach agreement	4	1	3	2	4
2. Supported other members of the group	4	1	3	2	4
3. Showed knowledge of characteristics of seven ancient wonders	1	1	4	1	4
4. Assisted in the design of the Eighth Wonder	4	1	1	1	4
5. Used art skills to construct Eighth Wonder	4	1	1	1	4
6. Provided a cultural context for defining Eighth Wonder	1	1	4	1	4
1: Excellent *2: Very good* *3: Acceptable* *4: Area of difficulty*					

classrooms so the descriptors are refined. Other forms of *rating scales* may use single-word descriptors (e.g., "outstanding" and "above average"). Figure 3.4 shows an example of a rating scale for assessing a Group Project. After studying the Seven Wonders of the Ancient World, students were placed in groups and given the challenge of constructing a model of an Eighth Wonder (see NCSS, 1994, p. 100).

Checklists.   Checklists allow us to record information about our students (Figures 3.3 and 3.6 are examples). Unlike rubrics or rating scales, checklists do not provide a continuum so we can capture gradations of student performance. They are simple and typically require a yes/no judgment.

Analyzing and Sharing Assessment Data

Next in the process is the analysis of the data that have been gathered and, ultimately, sharing the results of that analysis with children and their families. An important point to emphasize at the start is that we analyze student work to determine if students have met the social studies standards appropriate for the classroom. Thinking back to the first chapter, standards-based curricula should have standards relating to content, processes, and values. Those three elements of the curriculum will serve as the framework for our discussion of the analysis of data.

Verifying Acquisition of Content

For all social studies lessons, we must have some means to assess the extent to which our students achieved the content objectives for the *lesson*. What does the student *know*? As students talk, write, draw, and act, they are providing the evidence necessary for us to judge their level of achievement. For example, Chapter 12 contains a plan for a lesson that took place during a sixth-grade unit on careers. Students completed a variety of tasks based on advertisements for jobs in the local newspaper. The content objective was that students "understand the specialized nature of jobs, how each job has unique responsibilities and

This teacher is evaluating a student's written response to a chapter in the social studies textbook. He will then use his computer to record and save the results

requirements." Groups of students selected ads and answered questions the teacher wrote on a sheet of chart paper. The written responses indicated to what degree each group could identify the unique responsibilities and requirements of the job described in the ad they selected. The teacher also kept notes as she observed each group working.

In addition to assessing student mastery of content in lessons, teachers must have evidence so we can judge to what extent our students have achieved the broader content objectives established for a *unit*. Chapter 2 contains an example of a third-grade social studies unit on boats. The unit is organized around four questions serving as the unit's content objectives. Although every lesson in the unit will produce either behavior or products that can be assessed, some activities are particularly important from an assessment standpoint. The unit assessment plan in Figure 3.5 shows how the unit's activities will be used for assessment purposes.

Figure 3.5

Teacher's Assessment Plan for Unit "Boats"

BOATS

Objective 1: What are the different types of boats, and why are they different?

    Unit activities used for assessment of this objective:
        Field trip to harbor
        Concept attainment lesson
        Unit test

Objective 2: Where in our state, country, and world would you find people using boats?

    Unit activities used for assessment of this objective:
        Map reading activity
        Inquiry—The Voyage to Hawaii
        Unit test

Objective 3: What types of jobs do people perform on boats, and how have those jobs changed over time?

    Unit activities used for assessment of this objective:
        Bulletin board display
        Videocassette, *Ships*
        Unit test

Objective 4: How have boats changed over time?

    Unit activities used for assessment of this objective
        Bulletin board display
        History of boats lesson
        Unit test

Measuring Mastery of Processes

Either checklists or rating scales can be used to record student progress toward mastering the process objectives of social studies lessons and units. Here our concern is with what students can *do.* We need to observe our students, keep good records, and refer frequently to the portfolios to reach conclusions about each student's abilities. Here is an example of use of a checklist: A school district wrote objectives for the use of print encyclopedias in fourth grade. Teachers used the checklist in Figure 3.6 for assessment.

Good checklists can be used effectively, but the achievement of process objectives is a matter of degree, and checklists do not allow us to record different levels of achievement. Rating scales do, though, and are a better tool for recording each student's level of success. For example, if one third-grade social studies objective for the year is that each student

Figure 3.6

Checklist for Assessing Use of Print Encyclopedias

Student's Name _____

School _____

Teacher _____

Date Achieved	Project or Assignment	Objective
_____	_____	1. Uses information in encyclopedia to answer questions
_____	_____	2. Compares information in encyclopedia with other source
_____	_____	3. Uses index to locate an entry
_____	_____	4. Given a topic, locates appropriate entry(ies)
_____	_____	5. Scans for relevant details
_____	_____	6. Records information in a format that facilitates future use

"adjust his or her behavior to fit the dynamic of various groups and various situations," it is unlikely any students will fail to demonstrate this behavior on at least some occasions. Let's look at an example of a rating scale for achievement of process objectives.

The national geography standards established geographic skills to be learned by the end of the fourth grade (Geography Education Standards Project, 1994). These are process objectives, describing what students should be able to do, and are organized in five sets of skills. Figure 3.7 shows a rating scale in the form of a class profile for these geographic skills (for the complete wording of each objective, see Geography Education Standards Project, 1994, pp. 46–49).

Evaluating Development of Values

Values are criteria by which behaviors, beliefs, and attitudes are judged. For example, justice is a value. That those accused of crimes are entitled to a fair trial is a belief, keeping an open mind while serving on a jury is an attitude, and speaking in favor of due process rights of people in totalitarian regimes is a behavior; each is consistent with the value of justice. This aspect of social studies is difficult to evaluate. We can make judgments about people's values, beliefs, and attitudes only by observing their behavior. As teachers, we can take essentially two approaches. In the first approach, we can ask our students to express their attitudes and beliefs through discussion and writing. The content of these discussions and written statements can be judged for consistency with the values of our social studies program. For example, the *National Standards for Civics and Government* (Center for Civic Education, 1994) lists equality of opportunity as a fundamental value of American democracy. We could ask our students to establish criteria for classroom officers, and then we could assess those criteria in terms of how inclusive they are.

In the second approach, we can observe our students' behavior to see to what extent they have adopted the values we are trying to teach. This is somewhat trickier than it might seem because of cultural differences. For example, a teacher wants his students to adopt the value of equality of opportunity. He thinks a behavior demonstrating this value is when his students listen quietly and let others take turns during group discussions. This behavior, however, will be easier for children from some cultural groups than from others. Korean American children, especially those whose parents were born in Korea, have learned at home a set of rules for taking part in a discussion—be quiet and do not talk unless the leader of the group asks you a question. Native Hawaiian children, in contrast, who have participated in traditional "talk story" events, are accustomed to jumping into conversations in a way many European Americans would consider inappropriate and Korean Americans would find shocking (Au, 1993). It is important to consider cultural influences on behavior before we make a judgment about whether a behavior was the result of a commitment to a value.

Standards-Based Analysis

Initially, the teacher's focus is on analyzing data to determine if the objectives for a lesson are achieved. Then, the focus shifts to the broader objectives of the unit. Ultimately, the data

Figure 3.7

Class Profile: Geographic Skills, Grade 4

Names	1.1 Ask geographic questions	1.2 Distinguish geographic/non-geographic	2.1 Locate information	2.2 Record observations	3.1 Prepare maps	3.2 Construct graphs	4.1 Use maps	4.2 Use tables and graphs	4.3 Use texts and photos	4.4 Use simple math	5.1 Present geographic information	5.2 Use geographic inquiry	5.3 Apply geographic generalizations

− Achieves objective partially and only with assistance.
+ Achieves objective partially without assistance.
∗ Achieves objective.
★ Achieves objective at high levels of proficiency.

are analyzed to determine if each student has met the relevant social studies standard(s). This usually involves synthesizing conclusions reached after lesson-level and unit-level analysis. A good approach adopted by some of our school districts is to create individual profiles that show each student's progress toward achieving each grade-level standard (Figure 3.8 is an example). As in our initial example in this chapter, Figure 3.8 assumes that a school district has adopted the five standards in the topic "The History of Students' Own State or Region" from the *National Standards for History*. Features of Figure 3.8 reflect basic principles in standards-based assessment:

■ The evaluation process is longitudinal and ongoing. Most standards are achieved gradually. The individual profile in Figure 3.8 requires the teacher to make an assessment of each student in December, March, and June.

■ The evaluation process acknowledges that there are gradations of achievement. The profile in Figure 3.8 allows the teacher to reach one of four conclusions about each standard at each point in time. Some standards may not yet be addressed. For those that have been covered, some students will have evidence in their portfolios that the standard has been met, other students will have evidence leading to the conclusion that the standard has been partially met, and for some students the evidence will indicate the student has not met the standard.

■ The evaluation process should use several sources of data. Judgments about achievement of standards are most valid if the teacher relies on more than one source of data. Figure 3.8 requires the teacher to use at least three sources of evidence related to the standard. These could be any of the sources of data mentioned in this chapter (i.e., written products like stories or journals, nonwritten products like charts or maps, or tests).

How will teachers know that a student has met a standard? This can be tricky because most standards are phrased with verbs requiring interpretation, such as "understands," "describes," "compares," and "analyzes." There are three possibilities:

1. *Rely on tests.* This option removes, to a large extent, any subjective judgment by teachers and relies on assessment with quantifiable outcomes. For example, for the standard that "The student understands the history of indigenous peoples who first lived in his or her state," a 50-point test could be developed and administered to each student. The criterion for meeting the standard might be 80% (40 points). The problem with this approach is that it excludes many valid sources of evidence, like projects, that are more difficult to quantify. Tests relying on multiple-choice questions cannot effectively measure critical thinking. In many states, however, this option is being implemented as standardized, end-of-the-year tests in social studies are mandated and must be administered to each student.

2. *Rely on the teacher's judgment.* This option leads to a level of subjectivity, of course, but it does allow the teacher to consider a variety of evidence. The teacher would look at several sources of data and decide, on the basis of all the evidence, whether the student understands the history of the indigenous peoples who first lived in his or her state.

Figure 3.8

Individual Profile—Standards Assessment

Individual Profile—Grade 4 Social Studies				
Student's Name _____				
MS = meets standard PM = standard partially met NM = standard not met NO = standard not yet addressed				
December	March	June		Standard
				1. The student understands the history of indigenous peoples who first lived in his or her state.
				Sources of evidence for this standard: (a) (b) (c)
				2. The student understands the history of the first European, African, and/or Asian-Pacific explorers and settlers who came to his or her state.
				Sources of evidence for this standard: (a) (b) (c)
				3. The student understands the various other groups from regions throughout the world who came into his or her own state over the long-ago and recent past.
				Sources of evidence for this standard: (a) (b) (c)
				4. The student understands the interactions among all these groups throughout the history of his or her state.
				Sources of evidence for this standard: (a) (b) (c)
				5. The student understands the ideas that were significant in the development of the state and that helped to forge its unique identity.
				Sources of evidence for this standard: (a) (b) (c)

3. *Combine options 1 and 2 by establishing a criterion for each standard while placing values on several sources of evidence.* For example, for the standard "The student understands the history of indigenous peoples who first lived in his or her state," teachers would use a test, journal entries, a story written from the perspective of a Native American, a study guide, and a readers' theater presentation. Points would be assigned to each source of evidence for a total, say, of 100. Even with well-developed rubrics, there would be some level of subjectivity in assigning points to some sources of evidence (e.g., the story and reader's theater presentation). To meet the standard, each student would need to achieve a preset criterion, such as 80 points.

Sharing What Has Been Learned

We have gathered data from a variety of sources. We have analyzed those data to determine to what extent each student has acquired content, mastered processes, and adopted values. We have considered all the evidence and reached conclusions about the student's achievement of grade-level standards in social studies. The final component of assessment is sharing the results of our analysis. This will take place in a variety of formats, as discussed in the sections that follow.

Informal Conferences with Students.
Conversations with our students about their progress is an essential part of good teaching. These should be private and can address any aspect of the social studies program. For example, "Tony, your drawing of the Iroquois village is very good. I always look forward to your artwork, but this isn't what longhouses looked like. Where could you find more information about them?" In this case, we have commented on Tony's failure to achieve a content objective—the ability to describe accurately Native American dwellings. Our comments could focus on process: "Carmela, I looked at your map of the city, and it really shows you know how to create your own symbols." Here we are informing her that she has achieved a process objective—the ability to construct an accurate map with original symbols. Finally, the purpose of a conference could be to address a need in terms of values and beliefs: "Paul, I noticed today at recess that you called Orlando out when it was clear to everyone else he was safe. Why is it important for all of us to follow the rules when we play softball? How would you feel if you had been Orlando?"

Parent Conferences.
We should communicate with parents in a variety of formats. Schools may schedule formal conferences once or twice a year. In terms of social studies, we should be able to state our conclusions about the achievement of standards to parents *and support those conclusions with items from their child's portfolio.* The focus of the conference should be on the standards. I think it is good practice not to wait until the formal conferences to talk with parents about how their child is doing in social studies. When our students do something great, we should take the time to call their parents. All too often, we contact parents only when something wrong happens.

Report Cards.   All schools have some form for reporting students' progress. These summative reports vary widely in format. "Social Studies" usually appears as a topic on the report card. More and more school districts are basing the report card on *standards.* Each standard is listed, and the teacher must indicate the level of the student's achievement of each standard (by using a rubric similar to the one provided in Figure 3.8). Some school districts use *letter grades* (e.g., A, B, C). Strong arguments can be made against using letter grades in elementary school, especially with our youngest students. If we are in a situation where we give grades, then we should be sure our students understand our criteria for making judgments. We must tell students what activities will be used to determine grades. Many school districts have report cards with *categories* or *scales.* Categories, for example, might be "area of need," "making progress," or "area of strength." Some districts have constructed summative rubrics with categories described in several sentences. Each student is then placed in the appropriate category. Finally, some report cards ask us to make *written comments.* Usually, this format is combined with either grades or a scale. Providing written comments for each student is time consuming, and rarely is there enough space to write all that we want. Whatever the format, we must be able to support our judgments with evidence from our students' portfolios.

Assessment and Diversity: Final Thoughts

Our theme of diversity dictates that we use a variety of data sources to help us determine what our students know and are able to do. Diverse sources allow us to reach accurate conclusions about the achievement of our students. For too long, paper-and-pencil tests were the only assessment tool used in social studies. Both cultural and personal characteristics make it difficult for some students to show what they know on this type of test. When we shift to authentic assessment, especially when we use discussion, visual and performing arts, we create a more equitable and accurate system for evaluation, especially for children with learning disabilities.

For our English learners, it is important that assessment be uncoupled from English literacy tasks. We are on the wrong path if our assessment reveals the student's level of English proficiency rather than what he or she has learned in social studies. Quite simply, we frequently do not know whether low achievement among our English learners is the result of their not knowing social studies content or their not knowing English. To make the distinction, English learners must have the opportunity to show what they know through the performing and visual arts. When possible, assessment should be done in the student's primary language. For example, if one of our standards is that students accurately describe the dwellings of four 15th-century Native American tribal groups, it does not matter if the descriptions are written in English or Spanish (note, too, that the descriptions could be drawn rather than written). Primary language assessment requires a bilingual teacher or a bilingual instructional aide and, of course, this may not be possible in all schools for all children.

Summary of Key Points

- The process of assessing students has undergone great changes in the past 40 years. A shift has occurred toward performance or authentic assessment, an ongoing process in which data are gathered from multiple sources.

- Assessment has three parts: gathering, analyzing, and sharing data.

- Unit assessment plans should provide evidence on student progress toward social studies standards, include performance assessments, be developed at an appropriate place in the planning progress, and gather data from multiple sources.

- In addition to saving student work, teachers should use anecdotal records, evaluation rubrics, rating scales, and checklists.

- We should analyze evidence to determine to what extent each student has acquired content, mastered processes, and adopted values. Our conclusions should be made in reference to our stated objectives for lessons and units.

- Ultimately, the data we have gathered and analyzed should allow teachers to determine whether each student has met each grade-level standard.

- We should share our conclusions with students and parents in a variety of formats including informal discussions, formal conferences, and report cards.

- For a diverse classroom, it is essential that students be allowed to show what they know and can do through discussion and the arts.

PART III

Differentiation, Integration, and the Development of Academic Skills

Differentiated Instruction

In this chapter, you will read about

- The ideas of Stephen Krashen and James Cummins on linguistic diversity and language acquisition—and the instructional implications of their ideas.

- The advantages of planning social studies programs that meet the needs of culturally diverse classrooms.

- Instructional strategies that will help children with learning disabilities and children who are gifted.

att Marcella's second-grade classroom reflected the diversity of his community. Twelve children were Hispanic, five were Vietnamese American, four were African American, and nine were European American. Eight children were immigrants to the United States. Mr. Marcella wanted to start the year with a social studies unit that incorporated the diversity of his students and, at the same time, introduced his students to each other. He planned a unit called "Families and Friends." During the unit, his students listened while he read picture books about friendship and families. The children's favorites were *Abuela,* Arthur Dorris's charming fantasy about a Latina girl and her grandmother who fly above New York; *Peter's Chair,* Ezra Jack Keats's story about an African American boy who runs away from home because of the arrival of his new sister; and *The Lost Lake,* Allen Say's beautifully illustrated tale about a Japanese American father and son who go backpacking.

Mr. Marcella's class sang songs about families and friendship. His favorite was "Five People in My Family," a song he had learned when he was a boy from The *Sesame Street Song Book : 64 Favorite Songs* (Moss, Raposo, & Cerf, 1994). His students liked "I Live in the City" by Malvina Reynolds, a song about how people of many cultural groups build a city. Throughout the unit, the children worked in small groups to define friendship, focusing on a list of things friends do for their friends. During the unit, Mr. Marcella gave the children many opportunities to write about their families, their feelings, and their friends. Then, because Mr. Marcella knew autobiographies would help the children appreciate the diverse backgrounds of their classmates, he made creating autobiographies a culminating activity. Some children were able to bring photographs from home to illustrate their books, while others drew pictures. Mr. Marcella helped the students organize their books around topics such as celebrating holidays, starting school, moving to a new apartment, and enjoying summer vacations. First, the children drew pictures or used their photographs to help recall details. Then they wrote descriptive sentences relating to what was happening in their illustrations. Although most children were able to write a few sentences about each illustrated event, some needed to dictate their text, and three wrote in Spanish. When completed, the autobiographies were shared with the whole group as the children (some with Mr. Marcella's help), read their books aloud.

As a culminating activity, Mr. Marcella and his students created a classroom quilt. Each child was represented on the quilt with either a self-portrait or an illustration showing something the child considered special.

■ ■ ■

Like Mr. Marcella, all elementary school teachers teach social studies in the context of an increasingly diverse society. You will need to adapt your teaching to fit the backgrounds, abilities, interests, and needs of your students. In fact, your success will depend on your ability to plan an instructional program that accounts for the diversity of your students. This is a tall order, so let's take a look at how students in your classrooms might differ.

Dictionary definitions of *diversity* use words such as "different" or "varied" and these are good descriptors of the children we teach. Capitalizing on the diversity of our students will enhance our joy of teaching. As a group of scholars aptly put it, "Diversity in the nation's schools is both an opportunity and a challenge. The nation is enriched by the ethnic, cultural, and language diversity among its citizens and within its schools" (Banks et al., 2005, p. 39). Every year, each teacher works with a group of different individuals, each with unique challenges and gifts.

How will your students differ? Students in all elementary school classrooms vary in a number of ways. Both girls and boys will be assigned to our rooms, and some will be older (or younger) than most of their classmates. Although students usually are assigned to classes by age, a variety of factors can result in a group with significant age differences, and the "higher" the grade you teach (e.g., fourth, fifth, or sixth), the greater the span between your oldest and youngest students. Some of your students will be well adjusted, confident, and happy. Others, however, will struggle with personal issues and the effects of difficult past experiences. Most public elementary schools reflect the concept of the neighborhood school, and the level of homogeneity in family income status among the students will be high. There is a good chance, however, that some of your students will be significantly more affluent (or impoverished) than their classmates.

Students will differ widely in their native talents and abilities, with variation in all areas of mental and physical performance. Good teachers develop an instructional program that allows each child to develop the full limit of his or her ability. Public Law 94–102, the Education for All Handicapped Children Act of 1975 (now called the Individuals with Disabilities Education Act [IDEA]), established the requirements for children with special needs in public schools. Congress reauthorized IDEA in 2004. Among these requirements is that each child is placed in his or her "least restrictive environment." This requires schools to educate students with disabilities with nondisabled students to the maximum extent appropriate for the student with disabilities (Lewis & Doorlag, 2010; Turnbull, Turnbull, & Wehmeyer, 2009). Thus, you might teach children with exceptionalities for part or all of the school day. By the time they reach your classroom, your students will have clearly defined tastes, interests, and preferences. Without any special effort on your part, many of your students will be interested in the topics presented in social studies. Others, though, will become engaged only if the activities you plan and the resources you select are exciting and challenging.

An ever increasing percentage of students first acquire a language other than English. These children face the challenge of learning social studies content, mastering social studies processes, and adopting social studies values *at the same time* they are learning to read, write, speak, and listen in English (Cruz & Thornton, 2009; Rodriguez, Salinas, & Guberman, 2005). The United States is a pluralistic society. Our cultural identity plays a primary role in shaping our values and behaviors. Research shows there are important differences in the way children of different cultural groups communicate, interact, and learn.

The only way to meet the needs of our diverse student populations is to "differentiate" instruction (Tomlinson, 2001, 2003). Differentiated instruction abandons a "one-size-fits-all" mentality in favor of modifying how you teach to meet the needs of your students. Teachers can make three categories of modifications. First, teachers can change the *content* taught, perhaps by breaking an area of study into smaller units or, for your gifted students, by introducing more challenging topics. Second, you can change the *instructional process* through a number of interventions, such as simplifying the way you talk to make your presentations comprehensible to your English learners. Finally, teachers can change the work *products* you expect students to complete; one possibility would be to let students who have difficulty with written tasks present a report orally. This chapter focuses on these three aspects of diversity—language, culture, and exceptionality (children with learning disabilities and gifted children).

Linguistic Diversity

First, let us look at the challenge children face learning social studies at the same time they are learning English as a second language.

English Learners

Children with native languages other than English may be called "language minority students." Those language minority students who have not achieved a level of English language proficiency (reading, writing, and speaking) comparable to a monolingual child of the same age have been classified as "limited English proficient" (LEP) or English learners (ELs). Remember, not all language minority students have EL status; some will come to your classroom fully bilingual. They will astound you with their ability to use their native language and English. There will be a wide range of English competency among your EL students: Some will have virtually no English, whereas others will be on the threshold of becoming fluent in English. The level of each child's English proficiency will be a key factor in designing appropriate social studies instruction (Paul, 2007).

I find the label *limited* English proficient unfortunate and misleading because all of us grow as language users over a lifetime. The extent of our language proficiency is without limits, so all of us are to some degree "limited." The use of *limited,* with its negative connotation, is unfair to the children who are classified as LEP. In this book, I will use the descriptor "English learner" (EL).

The number of English learners in our schools has increased dramatically in the past 40 years. By 2006, the number of English learners in public schools in the United States had increased to about 5 million, up from 3.8 million in 2004. The projection is that by 2015, there will be about 10 million English learners in our classrooms (see the website, of the National Clearinghouse for English Language Acquisition, www. nclea.gwu.edu). The U.S. Census Bureau's 2007 American Community Survey showed 20% of all Americans speak a language other than English in their homes. Since 1960, the pattern of immigration has shifted from Europeans to immigrants from Asia and the Spanish-speaking Americans. Recently, there have been significant increases of immigrants from India and Pakistan, the former Soviet Union, and the Middle East. Thus, many schools now have significant populations of Mandarin, Vietnamese, Arabic, Hindi, Farsi, and Russian-speaking English learners. The 2007 American Community Survey showed immigrants are settling all over the United States. From 2000 to 2007, for example, South Carolina saw the largest increase in foreign-born residents and Arkansas experienced the largest increase in Latino residents (for more sources of data, see the Websites of the U.S. Census Bureau, www.census.gov and the National Center for Education Statistics, www.nces.ed.gov).

Second-Language Acquisition and Learning in Social Studies

The ideas of Stephen Krashen and James Cummins provide a theoretical framework for effective social studies teaching with English language learners.

Krashen: Second-Language Acquisition.   Stephen Krashen is a linguist who has developed a model of second-language acquisition that has been widely adopted in the United States by second-language teachers (Crawford & Krashen, 2007; Krashen, 2003; Krashen & Terrell, 1995). Although his ideas are controversial among linguists, Krashen's perspectives have helped teachers be more effective in teaching their English learners (McLaughlin, 1987). There is no need in a book about social studies teaching and learning to explore all of Krashen's theory of second-language acquisition, but two of his ideas are essential: (a) the concept of *comprehensible input* and (b) the impact of the *affective filter.*

Krashen believes second languages are acquired when a person is exposed to *comprehensible input in a low anxiety environment.* We acquire a second language by listening to spoken language, and reading written language that is slightly more advanced than what we know. The goal of English-speaking teachers is to make the English understandable, and this requires them to modify what they say and how they say it. Also, English learners should read materials with English words, phrases, and ideas just slightly beyond what they know. If you want English learners to understand what you are saying and at the same time acquire English, your goal must be to provide comprehensible input.

For example, teachers working with English learners during a social studies lesson will repeat certain key words and phrases, slow their speech, and refrain from using difficult vocabulary not essential in the lesson. Although their speech will be simplified, it will not change so it seems artificial. The key, of course, is for teachers to communicate with the students. The social studies textbook is often not comprehensible input for English learners. So teachers may read the text aloud to students or present the material through charts and graphs, illustrations, or films. Some teachers rewrite important sections of the textbook in simplified English so the English learners have a version to read and understand.

Krashen argues that an *affective filter* can make it difficult for students to acquire a second language. The affective filter is an attitude or feeling that works as a mental block. Anxiety, fear, and a lack of motivation can operate as affective filters. Put simply, if you want to make it difficult for students to understand something, you should scare or bore them! Even if the teachers or other students are providing comprehensible input, it might not get through if the student is worried, upset, frightened, or disinterested. Worry, anxiety, fear, and boredom work as filters, and the input teachers so carefully offer is wasted. Consider the following examples: In one classroom, most of the social studies "talk" is among children working in small groups. These conversations are among peers, and there are no affective filters; all the comprehensible input an English learner hears will "get through." In another classroom, in contrast, the teacher asks questions from the textbook and randomly calls on children to answer. The affective filter will be "thick," as the fear of being called on blocks the available comprehensible input. The implication for social studies teaching with English learners is quite clear. The teaching must provide comprehensible input in a situation where the students' affective filters have "dropped," and are low enough to allow the input in.

Cummins: Dimensions of Language Proficiency. Canadian linguist James Cummins has had an immense influence on educators in the United States (1979, 1986a, 1986b, 1989, 1992; see also Chapter 1 in Cruz, Nutta, O'Brien, Feyten, & Govoni, 2003). As with Krashen, our discussion of Cummins's ideas must be selective. Most significant to the teaching of social studies is his description of the *dimensions of language proficiency.* His discussion of *cognitive demand* and *contextual support* provides us with a useful framework for planning effective lessons for all students, particularly for those whose first language is not English.

Cognitive demand is the level of thinking a student must achieve to complete a task. Cognitively *undemanding* tasks include writing a description of a new pair of shoes, asking to borrow a yardstick, or reading the television program listings in the entertainment section of a newspaper. At the other end of the continuum are cognitively *demanding* tasks, which require complex thinking, such as discussing the relative merits of capitalism and socialism, reading and understanding information about the Russian monetary system, or writing an essay on comprehensive health care. In social studies, students should be asked to complete tasks at all points along the cognitive demand continuum, from the facile to the most difficult.

Contextual support is the level of help a person has to complete a task. Many language tasks have a great deal of contextual support. The person performing the task can ask questions, seek help from other people, and refer to illustrations or real objects. At the other end of the continuum are tasks a person must perform in isolation. Any task, regardless of its cognitive demand, can either have a great deal of contextual support or very little, depending on how teachers structure the situation. For example, a group of students is asked to compare and contrast a Mohawk longhouse and a Sioux tipi. If the students can work together to write their answer, if they can ask the teacher for help, and if they have accurate illustrations to examine, the task has a high level of contextual support. In contrast, if students must work individually, are given 15 minutes to write their answers, and are not permitted to ask anyone for help, there is no contextual support to complete the task.

Cummins developed a diagram to help educators understand the roles of cognitive demand and contextual support in school-related tasks (1986b, 1992). The diagram, consisting of four quadrants, classifies the way language is used. My students have found it easier to understand and apply these concepts if they are presented in a four-level chart. Figure 4.1 places social studies activities in four categories, explains the level of cognitive demand and contextual support in each of the categories, and provides an example in each category of an activity from a third-grade unit on boats (the full unit appeared in Chapter 2). Following are explanations of the categories.

Category 1: Activities Are Cognitively Undemanding, Completed with Contextual Support.   During the instructional unit, the teacher read aloud an illustrated book titled *Surrounded by the Seas: Life on a New England Fishing Island* (Gibbons, 1991). Before reading the book, the teacher wrote on the chalkboard some of the jobs people on the island perform: repairing sails, loading equipment, bringing in the catch, and unloading the fish for processing. The photographs in the book are excellent and make it easy for all children to see what is involved in each task. Also, the teacher modeled each job through a slow and somewhat exaggerated pantomime. Finally, the children joined their teacher in pretending to do each job through a group pantomime experience. The teacher's objective was simple and appropriate: She wanted her students to have a basic understanding of the work people on the island do as a part of an economy based on fishing.

This activity is a good example of those falling in Category 1 because the information the students were expected to learn—the different jobs related to island fishing—was relatively simple, and the behavior expected of students—to listen and to pantomime—was easy, fun, and performed in a group. The photographs and the modeling supplied by the teacher provided a great deal of support. If, on the other hand, students were expected to complete a chart, answer questions, or work independently, the level of cognitive demand would increase, and the activity would belong in Category 3.

Figure 4.1

Social Studies Activities: Cognitive Demand and Contextual Support

CATEGORY 1

Activities are cognitively undemanding, completed with contextual support.
- The topic is simple and easily understood.
- Students are asked to do things that require relatively simple thinking (e.g., recalling and summarizing).
- Completion of the activity is supported by cooperative learning, visual aids, real things, and hands-on experience. Materials that students read or view are easy to understand.
- These are the "easiest" activities to complete. All students should be successful.
- Example from a third-grade unit on boats: Pantomime—Life on a New England fishing island.

CATEGORY 2

Activities are cognitively undemanding, completed with little, if any, contextual support.
- The topic is simple and easily understood.
- Students are asked to do things that require relatively simple thinking (e.g., recalling and summarizing).
- Students complete the activity individually, with little support of any kind.
- Even though the topic is easy and the required thinking is simple, the lack of contextual support will make it difficult for some students to be successful.
- Example from a third-grade unit on boats: Independent reading of picture books.

CATEGORY 3

Activities are cognitively demanding, completed with contextual support.
- The topic is complicated and difficult to understand.
- Activities in this category require complex thinking (e.g., analyzing, synthesizing, and evaluating).
- Completion of the activity is supported by cooperative learning, visual aids, real things, and hands-on experience. Materials that students read or view are easy to understand.
- The topic and level of thinking will challenge students, but the contextual support will help them be successful.
- Example from a third-grade unit on boats: Lesson on the history of boats.

CATEGORY 4

Activities are cognitively demanding, completed with little, if any, contextual support.
- The topic is complicated and difficult to understand.
- Activities in this category require complex thinking (e.g., analyzing, synthesizing, and evaluating).
- Students complete the activity individually, with little support of any kind.
- These are the most difficult activities to complete successfully.
- Example from a third-grade unit on boats: Student-authored encyclopedia.

Category 2: Activities Are Cognitively Undemanding, Completed with Little, if Any, Contextual Support.   Few instructional activities fall into Category 2. Here, the topic or material requires simple thinking (cognitively undemanding), and little, if any, help is provided for children (which makes it context reduced). During the unit, children read picture books independently. Each story was related to the unit's topic, boats. The stories were simple, so cognitive demand was minimal. Because the children read on their own, the level of contextual support was reduced.

Category 3: Activities Are Cognitively Demanding, Completed with Contextual Support.   In Category 3, I have placed a lesson the teacher presented on the history of boats, emphasizing how methods of propulsion have changed over the years (sails, oars, and engines). The specific learning objective was that "students will learn that although the functions of boats have remained constant, their design and capacity (e.g., speed and size) have changed radically." This was cognitively demanding material, especially because most of the third graders knew very little about boats when the unit began. It was, therefore, important that the teacher provide contextual support for her students. Following is a description of how she designed the lesson to provide the support for her English learners, or in Cummins's words, how the activity became more "contextually embedded":

1. Early in the unit, the students participated in a field trip to a harbor to see boats in action. This gave them a "firsthand" experience. This activity provided a knowledge base for all the lessons that followed.

2. When selecting her materials, the teacher chose books with excellent illustrations: *Boats: Speeding! Sailing! Cruising!* (Hubbell, 2009); *Boat* (Kentley, 1992); *The Book of Fantastic Boats* (Bernard, 1974); *Oars, Sails, and Steam* (Tunis, 1952); and *Ships, Sailors, and the Sea* (Humble, 1991). The English learners in this classroom would not have been able to read any of these books, but it was not necessary because the content could be presented through the illustrations.

3. The teacher made good use of maps and charts. The lesson was supported with a timeline and a map showing when and where the following boats were built and used: a boat built for the Egyptian pharaoh Cheops (powered by sail and oar), a Roman trireme (sail and oar), a Haida canoe (sail and oar), "Old Ironsides" (the *Constitution,* sail), the *Great Eastern* (sail and steam engines), the *Queen Mary* (engines), and the *Nautilus* (first atomic-powered submarine).

4. During the lesson, the teacher modified the way she talked so her presentation was understandable. She slowed down, watched her choice of words, and repeated certain descriptions and explanations. At no time, however, did her speech sound artificial.

5. At the end of the lesson, the teacher and the students completed a large data retrieval chart as a summary of the presented material. The chart listed each boat in the presentation, the source of power for each boat, and when and where each boat was built. It is important to provide clear summaries of essential material for English learners.

6. The children worked in cooperative groups to answer three questions: (a) What are the advantages of ships that have engines? (b) If a ship had oars and sails, what conditions would make it difficult for the ship to move in the water? (c) Many people today buy boats with sails because they enjoy sailing. Why might it be more fun to sail than to go on a boat with an engine? It is unlikely the English learners could complete this task individually. To use Vygotsky's words, working in groups allowed the students to move into a "zone of proximal development."

7. After the lesson was over, the Spanish-speaking aide worked with children who needed primary language support. The aide reviewed the essential information in the lesson and answered any questions the students asked.

Category 4: Activities Are Cognitively Demanding, Completed with Little, if Any, Contextual Support. Activities falling under Category 4 are the most difficult for students to complete successfully. Cummins claims one reason English learners have difficulty in school is that teachers ask them to do Category 4 activities before their level of English proficiency is adequately developed. Category 4 has a high level of cognitive demand because the topic is challenging, the material is new, or the activity requires complex thinking. It is important that English learners be confronted with this type of intellectual challenge. The problem is that in Category 4, the task lacks contextual support. The student is left to do the most difficult type of activity with the least amount of help! In the unit on boats, some students chose to compile a small encyclopedia on boats. They wrote and illustrated several "entries," each summarizing what they knew about the entry (such as "submarine," "clipper," or "starboard"). The task for a third grader was challenging because the students could not simply copy information from an encyclopedia. They had to synthesize and condense what they knew about each item to fit the restricted space available on each page of the homemade "encyclopedia." Most social studies lessons using the textbook, unless they make use of other resources, fall into Category 4 and will be frustrating experiences for your second-language learners.

Effective Instruction with English Learners: A Summary. The perspectives of Krashen and Cummins lead to some simple conclusions: (a) Teachers must present social studies content so it is comprehensible to their English learners; (b) the classroom environment must be as free as possible of anxiety and fear so the comprehensible input can be received; and (c) social studies activities for our English learners should have a great deal of contextual support (those falling into Categories 1 and 3). This type of teaching, where the teacher uses a variety of strategies to help support English learners as they learn social studies, science, and math, is called different things. The most popular descriptor is "sheltered instruction," although in California the phrase "Specially Designed Academic Instruction in English" is used (Diaz-Rico & Weed, 2005; Echevarria & Graves, 2010). Echevarria, Vogt, and Short (2003) developed the SIOP ("Sheltered Instruction Observation Protocol") model as a means of evaluating the effectiveness of content teaching with English learners. Drawing on the ideas of Krashen and Cummins and from the SIOP model, Figure 4.2 summarizes the key things to remember about good social studies teaching with English learners.

Figure 4.2

Effective Social Studies Teaching with English Learners

(1) Clear and Reasonable Objectives
- Content objectives for lessons are well defined
- The amount of material students are expected to learn is reasonable

(2) Materials Supplement the Textbook
- "Visual" resources (graphs, charts, and illustrations)
- Information books written at many reading levels
- Adapted, simplified version of textbook pages
- Materials in the students' first language

(3) Effective Vocabulary Teaching
- In addition to the words taught to all students, those that might confuse English learners are taught

(4) Comprehensible Input
- Teacher modifies his or her speech
- Variety of materials are used
- Instruction takes place in a low-anxiety environment

(5) English Learners Get Help
- Teacher frequently checks for level of understanding and provides corrective feedback
- When possible, introductions and summaries are provided in the English learner's first language (preview/review)
- Extra help provided in one-to-one or small-group tutorials

(6) Multiple Grouping Patterns
- Small group experience utilizes cooperative learning
- English learners work with their monolingual English-speaking peers
- English learners are sometimes grouped together for extra help
- Whole-group, partnerships (two-student groups), and individualized activities are used

(7) Firsthand and Hands-On Experiences
- Field trips are planned
- Hands-on experiences allow students to examine objects and make things

(8) Experiences of Students Used to Enrich Instruction
- When possible, cultural identity of students is incorporated in units
- Everyday experiences of students used as a basis to learn about other people

Cultural Diversity

In addition to differences in native language, our classrooms are culturally diverse. Remember that native language and cultural identity are not synonymous. Among our Spanish-speaking students, we could have Ecuadoran Americans, Nicaraguan Americans, and Mexican Americans. African American, Asian American, and Native American children come to our schools with rich cultural identities. The challenge of educating children from many backgrounds has always been a facet of American public schooling. The fact is schools in the United States have done a poor job of educating Native Americans, African Americans, children of poverty, and immigrant students (e.g., the results of the National Assessment of Educational Progress at the U.S. Department of Education Website, www.nces.ed.gov). All too frequently, culture and native language have been ignored, with the unfortunate results of lower achievement and high dropout rates (Banks & Banks, 2003; Banks & Nguyen, 2008; Garcia, 1994). Our goal should be to practice "culturally responsive pedagogy," which has two aspects. The first is the focus of this section of this chapter, how we align our teaching to the cultural identities of our students. The second aspect will be covered in the next chapter, how we incorporate the cultural identities of our students in our social studies curriculum (Gay, 2000; Hollins & Oliver, 1999).

Teaching a group of diverse children is, at the same time, a great challenge and a great joy.

Definitions of Key Words and Descriptors

It would probably be a good idea to first clarify some terms regarding culture because they will be used throughout this book. I prefer to use an anthropological definition of *culture:* the shared behaviors, beliefs, and values of a group of people (Ember & Ember, 2010). Thus, culture is commonly shared and learned by a group of people. Remember, though, that people are not members of a culture. Each person belongs to a *cultural group;* the group shares a culture.

The NCSS Task Force on Ethnic Studies produced its *Curriculum Guidelines for Multicultural Education* (1992). This document considers an *ethnic group* to be a special kind of cultural group. Authors of the guidelines believe some ethnic groups are defined by different things, like religion (Jewish Americans) or national origin (Polish Americans). James Banks (Banks & Banks, 2003) believes there is a "core" culture in the United States including things almost all Americans share, such as baseball and income taxes. Therefore, every American is a member of a core U.S. cultural group and an ethnic group. This gets even more complicated because each person also identifies with other types of groups (e.g., gender, woman; social class, upper; religion, Lutheran). Finally, every individual adopts certain behaviors, beliefs, and values that are the result of personal decisions, rather than of culture, gender, religion, or social class.

In this book, I will use *cultural group* and always try to be absolutely clear as to the identity of the group (e.g., Vietnamese Americans). I will also use the phrase *minority groups,* which includes African Americans, Asian Americans, Hispanic Americans, and Native Americans. As I have noted previously, the combined total of "minority" groups will constitute the *majority* of the K–12 student population in the United States in the near future, so the use of "minority" and "majority" is problematic. One other point is tricky: I will refer to those of us who are "white" or "Anglo" or "mainstream" or "majority" as European Americans. I acknowledge there are problems with this descriptor, too. (Kleg, 1993).

How Culture Shapes Learning

A great deal of research has been conducted on the different styles of learning, communication, and participation of minority students (Gay, 1991; Ladson-Billings, 1995; Losey, 1995; Stone, 1991). For example, studies have been conducted with African Americans (Boykin, 1982; Ladson-Billings, 1995; Shade, 1986), Native Hawaiians (Au, 1980, 2009; Boggs, Watson-Gegeo, & McMillen, 1985), Mexican Americans (Heath, 1986; Losey, 1995; Ramirez & Castaneda, 1974), the larger Hispanic community (Grossman, 1984), and Native Americans (Greenbaum, 1985; Phillips, 1972). These studies indicate there are differences in the way children of different cultural groups communicate, learn, and interact. Our goal as teachers should be to create a "cultural congruence" between our classroom and the homes of our students (Au, 2009).

Before proceeding, one important caution is in order. Although researchers can describe norms—typical ways of thinking or behaving among the members of a cultural group— these are generalizations. For some individuals within the group, they will not be accurate. Kurtz-Costes and Pungello (2000) stressed this point when providing recommendations for teachers working with immigrant students: "Successful educators recognize that each child deserves to be treated as an individual with his or her own unique gifts" (p. 122). Let me provide an example from an observation I made while supervising two university students who were participating in a second-grade bilingual (Spanish–English) classroom. All the children were Hispanic. Research has shown Hispanic students have a preference for social learning, for working in groups (Losey, 1995). The children in this classroom decided to stay indoors during recess since the temperature had climbed to 100°F. All the children were drawing pictures of the fire station they visited earlier in the week. They were free to work where they wished. Of the 28 children, 20 worked in small groups, chatting happily as they drew. This was consistent with the research. Eight children, however, did not follow the norm, choosing to work individually. My afternoon in that classroom provided a good example of how a cultural norm will not define the behavior of every member of a cultural group.

It would be impossible in a book of this size to summarize all the conclusions reached on each cultural group, but here are some examples of these cultural differences:

- How children understand the history we attempt to teach them will be influenced greatly by their cultural identity. In fact, after reviewing the research on social identity and the teaching and learning of history, Epstein and Shiller (2005) concluded what children will learn from their textbooks and their teachers will be limited when there is a conflict with what they learned at home. Specific studies have shown differences in what African American and European American children "see" in the same photograph and differences in the way Northern Irish and American children explain the events in the past.

- *European American* teachers and parents will expect students to ask questions and express personal opinions. However, many *Korean American* children will be hesitant to demonstrate these classroom behaviors. In traditional Korean culture, student behavior of this sort is considered rude; it shows disrespect for the teacher. In Korea, children refrain from asking questions because it indicates the teacher did a poor job. It is not appropriate for a child to express an opinion to an adult (California Department of Education, 1992).

- *Native Hawaiians* have a strong tradition of group storytelling called "talk-story." It is no wonder, then, that many of these students thrive in activities requiring cooperation and a lot of talking. Many native Hawaiian students become frustrated with activities asking for silence and that are completed individually (Au, 1993, 2009).

- Some teachers claim their *African American* students give no answer, give single-word answers, or give short, flippant answers to questions asked in front of the whole class. The same students on the playground talk in an animated manner and speak at great length when explaining things and describing events. Shade and New (1993) note this is because "in the traditional African American community, children are not usually expected to be information givers and are infrequently asked direct questions" (p. 320). Communication among African Americans is passionate and less formal than among

European Americans. Teachers should expect their African American students to differ from European American children in each of the following aspects of language use: (a) turn taking (when people speak, European Americans follow a more rigid structure during a conversation); (b) tone (European Americans speak in less audible tones); (c) gestures (most European Americans use few gestures); and (d) pace (European American speech is slower). Research shows African American students do better in school when (a) teachers plan participatory learning experiences where students move around, such as dramatic role play; (b) students have many opportunities to talk with classmates in informal, conversational settings; (c) students have a chance to think out loud and work in small groups; and (d) teachers present material auditorily through music, rhymes, and chants (Hollins, Smiler, & Spencer, 1994; Ladson-Billings, 1995).

■ Prior to coming to school, *Native American* children learn by observation and direct experience. This stands in stark contrast to European American children, whose caretakers spent a great deal of time talking to and with children. Native American children have learned not to respond quickly to questions because such a response is disrespectful. This hesitance to respond is often misinterpreted by teachers from other cultural groups (Gilliland, 1992; Stokes, 1997).

■ In the aftermath of the horrific events of September 11, 2001, *Arab American* and *Muslim American* children frequently are stereotyped and find themselves on the receiving end of considerable anger (Alvi, 2001; Seikaly, 2001). Like all students, Arab American and Muslim American children should feel safe and secure in our classrooms. Many American teachers have little accurate information about these two groups and most American students either know little about the Middle East or have inaccurate views influenced only by stereotypes and distortions (Jaffee, 2004). For example, how many of us are aware that some Arab Americans are Christians—typically of the Maronite, Melkite, Chaldean, and Coptic denominations? At the same time, not all Muslim Americans are Arab Americans; in the United States, there are Muslims from many ethnic groups. The nation with the most Muslim citizens is not an Arab nation—it is Indonesia.

■ Teachers should understand the unique challenges faced by Muslim girls in American schools (Elnour & Bahir-Ali, 2003). First, many teachers have a stereotypical image of Muslim girls, especially regarding clothing. In fact, how Muslim girls dress will depend on their families' interpretation of Islam. Some may wear jeans and blouses, typical of many American teenagers, while others will wear clothing covering their entire bodies except for the faces and hands. The authors point out that many Muslim families do not allow their daughters to participate in extracurricular activities (but then again, many do). Conservative Muslim girls follow norms of behavior severely restricting their actions with boys and men. Some Muslim girls will avert their gaze so as not to look directly into the eyes of their male teachers, and some Muslim girls will avoid situations involving direct interaction with males, such as being the only girl in an otherwise all-boy group working together on a project.

Good teachers respect the diversity of their students. We should use the resources of our local community to learn about the cultural identities of our students. We should understand the level of English proficiency of our English learners. We should get to know our students as individuals, and have a good sense of each student's interests and abilities. The methodology for today's classroom must reflect the diversity of our students, must be multidimensional, and must include a wide variety of instructional resources and strategies. This book describes that culturally responsive methodology.

One way to "celebrate" the cultural diversity of our students is to use their experiences as a basis for social studies teaching. At the end of the chapter, you will find that a mini-unit does just that.

Exceptionality

Our discussion on exceptionality will focus on children with mild learning disabilities and children who are gifted. Educators have struggled with how to label children with disabilities, and some choices include "challenging condition," "exceptional," or "special needs." Turnbull and her coauthors make a good point when they argue we should avoid labels unless they are absolutely necessary. If we need to refer to a child we should use her or his name (Turnbull, Turnbull, & Wehmeyer, 2009). The scope of our discussion dictates I use the broad descriptor "exceptionality" and the specific descriptors "learning disability" and "gifted." Note there are many other categories of exceptionality we will not address here, such as emotional/behavioral disorders and communication impairments.

Like all your students, the four children pictured here are different in many ways. Good news! Their teacher has found an activity that all of them find interesting.

Figure 4.3

Effective Social Studies Teaching with Children with Mild Learning Disabilities

(1) Modifications in Curricular Content
- Divide material into small, manageable units
- Present material in a systematic fashion

(2) Modifications in Instructional Processes
- Adapt materials
- Additional presentations and practice
- Increased use of graphs and charts
- Use of instructional prompts and cues
- Active student involvement

(3) Modifications in Student Work Product
- Adapt task characteristics/requirements
- Change task criteria
- Change task modality

Differentiating Instruction for Children with Learning Disabilities

There are a number of instructional interventions to help children with learning disabilities learn social studies content and master social studies processes (Lewis & Doorlag, 2010; Sheehan & Sibit, 2005; Steele, 2005; Tomlinson, 2001, 2003; Turnbull, Turnbull, & Wehmeyer, 2009). Children with learning disabilities have difficulty in basic psychological processes as evidenced by problems with listening, thinking, speaking, reading, writing, spelling, and mathematical calculations. The primary manifestations of a learning disability are problems with reading and any number of other characteristics that may include memory deficits or difficulty with fine motor coordination (Sheehan & Sibit, 2005). Our discussion is limited to children with *mild* disabilities who are able to function in a "general education" classroom along with children who do not have disabilities. As noted previously, differentiated instruction for children with learning disabilities involves three categories of modifications in how we teach: (a) content, (b) instructional processes, and (c) work products (Figure 4.3).

Modifications in Curricular Content.   One option for teachers working with children with learning disabilities is to make changes in the content such students are expected to learn. Caution is in order here. We are not talking about "watering down" the curriculum; rather our goal is to have children with learning disabilities meet the same standards as other students. Two interventions will help:

Divide material into small, manageable units.   Teachers can look at what they expect students to learn and consider presenting it in smaller units or "chunks." In this section, all instructional examples come from a fifth-grade unit on the American Revolution of 1775.

In such a unit, a single lesson could cover the three causes of the Revolution (results of the Seven Years' War, oppressive taxation, and colonial unity). This topic could be broken into small units, and for children with learning disabilities, the teacher could plan additional, separate "mini-lessons" on each cause.

Present material in a systematic fashion.   While teachers should always accomplish this task, it is very important for children with learning disabilities. When starting a unit of study, it is important to present an overview, showing all the topics to be covered. When moving from one topic to another, we should review what has been learned before and highlight the relationship between each day's lesson and what immediately preceded it.

Modifications in Instructional Processes.   Good news! There are several ways to change how we teach to help children with learning disabilities. Note that no teacher would implement every option with every lesson; rather, successful teachers choose wisely from the following menu items.

Adapt materials.   Your goal is to have children learn content. How they acquire that knowledge should vary depending on each child's strengths and needs. In other words, your objective should not be to "get through the textbook"; it is to have children learn the content specified in your state social studies standards. For a unit on the American Revolution of 1775, the textbook could be supplemented or replaced by easier-to-read information books selected from the school or community library. Another useful adaptation is to have audiotapes of chapters in the grade-level social studies textbook. Children who have trouble reading would then have an auditory presentation of the material to supplement the visual. All instructional units and as many lessons as possible should use materials and activities in *multiple modalities:* visual, auditory, kinesthetic, and tactile. Kinesthetic means "bodily movement." A kinesthetic activity would require students to move. A teacher might plan a dramatic role play of the Boston Tea Party and ask students to work in groups of four to throw imaginary chests of tea off a ship and into Boston Harbor. Tactile means "touch." Tactile activities are very important for our youngest students. For our fifth-grade unit on the American Revolution, students hand-mixed flour and water to make "firecakes," a common, but not very tasty, meal for George Washington's soldiers.

Additional presentations and practice.   Children with learning disabilities may need more than one chance to learn content or master a process. After an instructional activity involving the whole class, we could plan an additional presentation for those who need it. We might present content at a slower pace, use simpler materials, or introduce new supporting resources, like photographs, maps, charts, or diagrams. For a process, such as learning to use a scale of miles on a map to calculate the distance between two cities, children with learning disabilities will need additional guided practice with close supervision.

Increased use of graphs and charts.   Teachers should consider using graphs and charts to support both oral presentations and reading assignments. Graphs and charts simultaneously simplify material, highlight the most important words and phrases, and visually reveal the relationships between subtopics. In Chapter 8, you will find examples of several graphs and charts, including a graphic organizer, a semantic map, expository text structures, and a data retrieval chart.

Use of instructional prompts and cues.   A very useful strategy is to emphasize essential bits of information, words, and phrases by prompts and cues. This can be done with written material by highlighting, underlining, or color coding. For example, in a lesson on how the Colonists responded to the taxes imposed by the British Parliament between 1765 and 1773, one of the teacher's content objectives was for the children to understand a *boycott*, a practice used successfully by the Colonists to protest the import taxes known as the Townshend Duties. The teacher prepared a poster with the definition of a boycott, "an organized plan to not buy things." The key words in the definition were *not buy*. The teacher used a red marking pen to write those words; the rest of the definition was written in black. Prompts and cues can be used in oral presentations as well. A common prompt is "remember to." One assignment in the American Revolution unit asked the fifth graders to write newspaper headlines for important events. After giving instructions to the whole group, the teacher might end with "Again, remember to keep your headline short, under six words." Other cues include repeating words and phrases and clapping hands two times before and after an important phrase or sentence. Some teachers use their hands very effectively when they are talking to their students by showing numbers (holding up one finger when stating "first") or pointing to places on maps or charts to focus student attention.

Active student involvement.   It is important that as many social studies lessons as possible keep children actively involved. Elementary school teachers should avoid the lecture/ discussion instructional model—where the teacher makes an oral presentation and, at certain times, students respond to questions. While some material may be presented to children in oral presentations by elementary teachers, these lectures should be brief and supported by other materials, such as charts, diagrams, maps, illustrations, and real objects. For children with learning disabilities, it is very important that instructional activities typically requiring relatively little student involvement, such as oral presentations and silent reading assignments, be modified. At different points in the lesson, students need to be asked to *do* something. One choice is for a mass response using colored cards. Each student has a red card and a blue card. The teacher asks a question and poses two possible answers, one to be signaled by the red card, the other by the blue card. The teacher restates the question and the possible answer and then says, "Without looking at your neighbor, please show me your answer." All students show the teacher one of the cards. This is also an excellent way to check to see if the students understand the material presented. Another good choice is to pose a question and ask the students to discuss possible answers with a partner. This technique is called "Think–Pair–Share" and is described in Chapter 6.

Modifications in Student Work Product.   There are three ways teachers can differentiate instruction for children with learning disabilities by changing the tasks, or work products, they are asked to complete:

Adapt task characteristics/requirements.   An example of adapting task characteristics used for many years for older students is to make an examination "open book," and allow students to refer to a textbook when answering test questions. For elementary school children with learning disabilities, we can modify the characteristics of almost every task we pose to students. For example, if a group of fifth-grade students is asked to answer questions appearing at the end of a chapter in their social studies textbook, some differentiation will be required for children with learning disabilities. After students have tried to answer the questions on their own, the teacher may want to help children by providing two possible page numbers where each answer can be found. Another example: One of the unit projects challenged students to find out what types of food do not spoil easily, a major consideration for both the Colonial and British armies. Children who would be unable to complete this assignment on their own could be helped in several ways. The teacher could provide reference resources, like appropriate volumes of a hard-copy encyclopedia and Websites. Or, the teacher could give a child a list of foods to research. Finally, a very important way to change task characteristics for children with learning disabilities is to allow tasks to be completed while *working in groups* (see Chapter 6 on cooperative learning).

Change task criteria.   Another way to differentiate instruction is to change the criteria for "success" for students. Usually, changes are made in the criteria of speed and accuracy. Teachers have to be careful here because there are some school tasks where speed and accuracy are essential and cannot be compromised, especially in reading and mathematics. For many other tasks, though, the path to successful completion requires adjusting criteria in early efforts. This is common sense; initially all of us took longer to do things we now do in half the time. For example, think how long it takes you to look up a word in a dictionary now, as an adult, and how long it took when you were 10 years old. One activity in the American Revolution unit challenged the fifth graders to make a propaganda poster, which could either encourage Colonists to joint Washington's Colonial army or encourage Colonists to join Loyalist regiments and fight with the British. Although most students had 5 days to complete the project, additional time was given to children who would find the task difficult. Accuracy cannot be sacrificed for "literal comprehension" questions where there is a correct answer (see Chapter 8). On the other hand, open-ended questions with no one correct answer can allow teachers to accept responses that are, at least, partially justifiable. For example, after the lesson on the Colonial boycott of British goods following the imposition of the taxes on goods imported from Britain, the teacher asked students to write a response to the following question: "Some colonists boycotted British goods for several years. What do you think were some of the effects the boycott had on their everyday lives?" A child with learning disabilities answered, "People would have to learn to live without certain things. Maybe they would drink coffee instead of tea." This is a reasonable response, though it mentions only a single effect and neglects two other effects a complete answer would mention: merchants selling those items would suffer losses and the Colonists could start producing their own products and stop importing items from Britain. Although a more able student might be challenged by the teacher to come up with at least one more effect, this child's response should be considered acceptable.

Change task modality. The third modification in task characteristics involves changing the modality of an assignment. In this sense, modality refers to whether the task is written, presented orally, completed through the arts (drawing, singing, acting, etc.), or some combination of modalities. A common modality change is to allow students with difficulty writing, an opportunity to complete the same assignment through an oral presentation. For example, one project in the American Revolution unit was a summary report on how the Revolution changed the lives of children living at the time. A student with a learning disability could be allowed to make an oral presentation to the class rather than write a report. In some cases, students can use the visual arts to show what they have learned (see Chapter 5). Teachers must be cautious here, however. Children will not learn to write if they are never challenged to do so. Thus, on some assignments, children with learning disabilities must be required to produce a written product.

Gifted Children

It is worth pondering the definition of "giftedness" found in federal law:

> [Gifted children] possess demonstrated or potential abilities that give evidence of high performance capability in areas such as intellectual, creative, specific academic or leadership ability or in the performing and visual arts. (Public Law 95-561, Title XIV, section 902)

Perhaps the key words are "high performance capability." Gifted children can have high general intellect; the ability to think creatively and critically; the ability to lead; and extraordinary talent in the visual or performing arts. Currently 29 states have laws or policies requiring "gifted and talented" education (Lewis & Doorlag, 2010; Tomlinson, 2001, 2003; Turnbull, Turnbull, & Wehmeyer, 2009; see also the Website of the National Association for Gifted Children, www.nagc.org). Our concern is differentiating instruction for the gifted children who are in our elementary classrooms. Again, we will organize our discussion by the three categories of modifications teachers can implement: changes in content, changes in instructional processes, and changes in work product.

Modifications in Curricular Content. In many instructional units, gifted students are challenged to learn more social studies content than their peers. This can be done by adding "depth," so students learn more information about a topic; or by "breadth," by adding new topics. Here is an example of a "depth" modification. All students in our American Revolution unit would be expected to know the main ideas Jefferson expressed in the Declaration of Independence. Gifted students, however, might be asked to find out more about the 27 specific "abuses and usurpations" described in the middle part of the Declaration. Jefferson claims the British were guilty of "transporting us beyond Seas to be tried for pretended offenses." What did this mean? What crimes could result in Colonists being taken to Britain for trial? Why did Jefferson label them "pretended"? An example of a "breadth" modification would be: While all students would be expected to know about Paul Revere, some gifted students could learn about two other Colonists, in two different contexts, who rode through the night to warn that the "British were coming," Sybil Ludington and Jack Jouett.

I must share one anecdote here from my own teaching experience. I spent five wonderful years teaching at Joaquin Miller Elementary School in Burbank, California. Our fourth-grade social studies curriculum focused on the history of California. One year, I differentiated instruction for one gifted student by modifying the curriculum through a "breadth" project. I asked this student to write a biography about the man our school was named for, the American poet, Joaquin Miller. Miller had a somewhat nefarious past and when the student finished her biography she told me, "Quite frankly, Mr. Zarrillo, I think it was a big mistake to name our school after that guy!"

Two techniques used to allow gifted children to learn additional content are "compacting the curriculum" and "tiering assignments." Compacting the curriculum is a process in which students are allowed to show what they know at the beginning of a unit. This is typically done with a pretest. Children are not asked to learn what they already know; rather, they are asked to learn extra content while the rest of the class works on the topics they have mastered. Tiering assignments involves creating several activities, all leading to the achievement of a single standard. Some "core" activities are required of all students. There are, however, several other activities at various levels of difficulty. Children with learning disabilities might be asked to complete the simpler ones while gifted students pursue the most difficult. You will see an example of tiered assignments in the unit on boats in Chapter 2.

Modifications in Instructional Processes.   Differentiation in instructional processes involves using more challenging materials, providing more critical thinking activities, and planning more creative activities. Just as children with learning disabilities need simpler, easier-to-read materials, gifted children can be asked to read more difficult books. Also, gifted students can be asked to explore a wider range of reference materials, especially Websites.

Gifted children typically thrive on activities requiring critical and creative thinking. Such activities, fully described in Chapter 7, involve solving open-ended and interdisciplinary problems. Critical thinking activities allow gifted children to enhance their abilities to locate, analyze, and present information. In our unit on the American Revolution, one critical thinking activity planned for gifted students asked them to answer the question, "What would have happened if the British had won the Revolutionary War?" The focus would be on the political, economic, and social history of the American Colonies with this revised scenario. Students would need to study the history of parts of the 18th century British Empire that did not become independent until later, like Canada or Jamaica.

Modifications in Student Work Product.   The most notable modification in this category is the increased autonomy teachers should afford gifted students. Two aspects of autonomy to consider here are *initiative* and *direction*. One way to accomplish this is to allow student initiative. At times, gifted students should be encouraged to choose the extra topics they pursue. For example, a student who is talented in music may want to learn more about and eventually perform the songs of the best-known American composer of the era, William Billings (who, interestingly enough, had one blind eye, a crippled leg, and a crippled arm!). Another student, more interested in the visual arts, may want to analyze Emanuel Leutze's famous painting *Washington Crossing the Delaware* and create a more realistic depiction of the event (perhaps General Washington should be seated, not standing; and did Leutze paint the appropriate American flag?).

Autonomy should also be accomplished by providing less direction to gifted children. On many tasks, gifted children will be impatient to begin and the instructions offered to the rest of the class will be unnecessary for them. One format for "tiering" the directions for a task is to provide a "core" set of instructions for all students. Then allow those students who want to get to work to do so while at the same time asking students who would like more direction to gather with the teacher in a corner of the classroom.

Summary of Key Points

- Students will differ in gender, age, language status, cultural identity, challenging condition, psychosocial status, family income, ability, interest, and physical characteristics.

- English learners will be learning social studies at the same time they are acquiring a second language.

- Social studies teaching should present comprehensible input to students in a low-anxiety environment.

- Most social studies activities, especially those planned for a diverse class, should have a great deal of contextual support.

- Cultural identity shapes learning. Methodology must account for the learning styles, ways of communicating, and participation preferences of several cultural groups.

- To meet the needs of students with learning disabilities and gifted students, teachers should differentiate instruction by modifying curricular content, instructional processes, or work product.

Lesson Plans and Instructional Activities

This chapter concludes with a mini-unit for fourth graders on "Chinese Writing." It is offered as an example of how teachers can use the cultural diversity of their students as a basis for instructional activities.

Mini-Unit

Grade Four: Chinese Writing

This mini-unit was planned for a fourth-grade class in which the majority of students were English learners. One girl in the class, Chimei, was learning to write Chinese. Chimei's mother was teaching her. During a time when students could "show and tell," she talked about what she had learned. Other students expressed interest when Chimei showed them the beautiful examples of Chinese writing she had produced. The teacher saw Chinese writing as an excellent opportunity for a mini-unit and used the NCSS standards for social studies as an organizing framework for unit objectives.

Part I: Organizing Framework

Standard: From the *National Curriculum Standards for Social Studies,* NCSS Thematic Strand I: Culture. Learning Expectation—Processes (b) for the middle grades: "Learners will be able to find, select, organize, and present information to compare various cultures according to specified aspects of culture, such as institutions, language, religion, and the arts" (NCSS, 2010, p. 95). The students will learn about a significant difference between English and Chinese—their writing systems.

This mini-unit answers one question:

Unit Question: How Is Chinese Writing Like English Writing, and How Is It Different?

Part II: Instructional Activities

Resources and Materials: (a) Children's books: *Chinese Writing: An Introduction* (Wolf, 1975); *Lóng Is a Dragon* (Goldstein, 1991); and *Chinese Calligraphy* (Wong & Miran, 2002); (b) "China the Beautiful" Website (www.chinapage.com); (c) a member of the community who can write and speak Chinese (not absolutely necessary but a real plus); (d) blank paper, fine-tipped paintbrushes, and black tempera paint.

Content Objectives: Students will learn that the English system of written language differs from the Chinese system in two ways: form and number of characters. They will also learn the function of the Chinese writing system is the same as English.

Process Objectives: After students *listen* to their teacher read aloud *Lóng Is a Dragon,* they will observe the logographic system of Chinese writing, *compare* the Chinese characters to English letter forms, *reproduce* the basic strokes of Chinese writing, *recognize* the tonal system of Chinese oral language, and *write* five Chinese characters.

Values Objectives: Students will develop an appreciation for the beauty and sophistication of the Chinese system of writing. It is hoped students will abandon ethnocentric attitudes they might have toward languages other than English and see that other languages are neither better nor worse than English, just different.

Day 1

1. Read aloud *Lóng Is a Dragon: Chinese Writing for Children.* Be sure students understand that Chinese writing is logographic. Each character represents something (a thing, a person, a place, or an idea). A good way to do this is to compare the English representation of a word (e.g., *water*) with the single symbol in Chinese. Note the origins of the characters as pictographs (pp. 4–8 of *Lóng Is a Dragon*). Stress the artistic, almost spiritual, side of writing in Chinese.

2. Display computer-based images of certain Chinese characters produced by Chinese grand masters of calligraphy. (You may need to define *calligraphy* for your students.) The Website titled "China the Beautiful" has excellent descriptions and examples of Chinese calligraphy from A.D. 900 to the present (www.chinapage.com). You may want to point out to students that there are really five styles of Chinese calligraphy and that within each style is room for artistic expression. The samples of Chinese writing available on the Website identified here dramatically illustrate the artistry of the calligrapher.

3. Begin instruction in the basic strokes (pp. 9–10 of *Lóng Is a Dragon*). The ideal situation is to have a person who is familiar with writing Chinese demonstrate these strokes for the class. (Chimei's mother could not visit this class, but the mother of another child in the class, Zhou, was able to participate.) Any teacher, however, can demonstrate the basic strokes with practice (true mastery takes time). Stress the importance of moving the brush in the correct direction. The children should begin to understand that drawing the Chinese characters takes considerable skill and practice.

Day 2

1. Read aloud parts of *Chinese Writing: An Introduction* or have a class visit from a person who speaks a Chinese dialect. Although Chinese has many spoken dialects, it has only one written form. This is one advantage of a logographic writing system: Speakers of different dialects are able to understand the same system of writing. Students are fascinated to learn that spoken Northern Chinese has four "tones" (other dialects have as many as nine tones) and that each tone gives an utterance a different meaning. Thus, *tung* can mean "to succeed," "together," "to govern," or "painful," depending on the vocal pitch of the speaker (see p. 13 of *Chinese Writing*).

2. Teach the children how to make five characters (see pp. 11–26 of *Lóng Is a Dragon*). The children should first draw the character in pencil and then, if you think they are ready, trace it with fine-tipped paintbrushes and black tempera paint.

Day 3

1. Stress again the mental state of the calligrapher (pp. 23–24 of *Chinese Writing*).

2. Continue to work on painting the characters. Today try a sentence (p. 27 of *Lóng Is a Dragon;* p. 18 of *Chinese Writing*)!

3. Ask the class the unit question: "How is Chinese writing like English writing, and how is it different?" Place the children with partners to answer the question using the cooperative learning structure called Think–Pair–Share (see Chapter 5). If students have trouble with the question, help them by suggesting two categories of comparison: (a) function—the language serves the same function; it is used to communicate; and (b) form—the written languages look different.

Day 4 and Beyond

The mini-unit will be just the beginning! Depending on students' responses, the entire class might benefit from a longer unit looking at other aspects of China, such as the visual arts, music, and religions of the Chinese people. Perhaps small groups of students will want to learn more about the history, geography, and current political status of China. They could share what they have learned with their classmates.

Evaluation: You can use two sources of data to assess your students. First, keep a record of the Think–Pair–Share activity on day 3. It might be a good idea to make a chart listing each set of partners with space to write comments next to each name. Circulate around the room as students figure out how Chinese writing and English writing are the same and different. Note the level of success students have in answering the question. Another alternative is to have each student write an answer after the Think–Pair–Share experience concludes. These written answers could serve as a simple test.

Second, it is important to keep anecdotal notes during the first 2 days of the unit. The notes should record some of the questions students ask and summarize your assessment of which students seem to grasp the similarities and differences between the two language systems. The comments students make as they work during the unit should give you an idea of whether they have adopted the values you proposed in the objectives sections of the mini-unit. Interestingly enough, the samples of Chinese writing painted by each student would have little value in assessment; this writing experience, though essential to achieve the mini-unit's objectives, provides little evidence to determine whether students understand the differences between the two writing systems (e.g., a student could make an elegant copy of a Chinese character yet not understand the logographic nature of that character).

Effective Teaching in Today's Diverse Classroom: The mini-unit was a great success and a good example of culturally responsive teaching. It was a perfect chance to raise the self-esteem of Chimei and the five other Chinese American students in the classroom. The mini-unit is a good example of what can happen when a teacher chooses to avoid a "deficit" model of teaching in a diverse classroom. Rather than viewing cultural diversity as a hurdle to be overcome, this teacher used the cultural identity of one of her students to enrich the curriculum. Also of note, even though many children were in the beginning stages of acquiring English, all were successful. The unit made strong use of visual aids (the illustrations in the books and the demonstrations by Zhou's mother). Full participation did not require the use of English.

     For children with mild learning disabilities, the intervention of *additional presentations and practice* could be appropriate. It may be necessary to have an extra small group lesson that reteaches the difference between Chinese writing, which is logographic, and English writing, which is alphabetic. This is a difficult difference for children to understand. You would not, of course, use those descriptors. Instead, you might focus on the example of "water," which is represented by a single Chinese symbol, but takes five English letters to spell. Some children, both those with learning disabilities and those without, will need one-on-one help to make the strokes correctly when writing Chinese. This additional practice will be essential for some children. For your gifted students, this mini-unit would be a good opportunity to provide some curricular *breadth.* Gifted students could be challenged to learn about another form of writing, ancient Egyptian hieroglyphics (a good Website is the one created by art teacher and amateur Egyptologist, Mark Milmore, www.eyelid.co.uk).

CHAPTER 5

A Multicultural, Integrated Social Studies Curriculum

In this chapter, you will read about

- Four approaches for incorporating multicultural perspectives into the social studies curriculum

- Three considerations for transforming social studies units of study, including scope, geographic boundaries, and people

- How to use children's books to present multicultural perspectives

- Teaching students to use oral histories to appreciate significant events and to connect more personally to family and community history

- How to incorporate the personal experiences of your students into the social studies curriculum

- An example of how to adapt a traditional social studies unit so it becomes multicultural

- The role of speaking and listening in an integrated social studies unit of study

- The performing arts and the visual arts in elementary social studies

Sara's letter read:
November 22, 1778
Dear Patricia,

My dear cousin, I can't believe your last letter. I don't know how to tell you this, but you are a traitor. Your brother Andrew has made a big mistake by joining Washington's army. When Andrew is caught, he will be hanged. My father has gone to join the British army, and they will win! God save our wonderful King George III.

Your loving cousin,
Sara

P.S. Is it cold in Virginia? It is freezing in South Carolina.

Sara and Patricia were fifth-grade classmates. They were studying the American Revolution, and during one of the unit's projects, they participated in a writing simulation. The class divided into pairs; Sara pretended to be a colonial child whose family remained loyal to the British King George III, and Patricia pretended to be her cousin from Virginia whose family fought for the rebel cause. The girls exchanged letters after participating in multiple lessons that identified the political differences between loyalists and rebels. The letter exchange in Sara and Patricia's classroom was an activity designed to help them see how the same set of events can be viewed from different perspectives.

In the previous chapter our focus was on *how* we teach, specific teaching strategies that differentiate instruction and are culturally responsive. In this chapter, the focus shifts to the curriculum, *what* we teach. Here, our discussion will be on transforming the social studies curriculum by:

1. Modifying the curriculum so it is truly *multicultural*, and
2. Modifying the curriculum so it is thoroughly *integrated*

■ ■ ■

A Multicultural Social Studies Curriculum

As noted in Chapter 1, your social studies curriculum will be defined by your state standards. Almost any topic you study, however, can be "transformed" to include both (a) multiple perspectives on historical and current events, and (b) information on the contributions of women, children, and people from several cultural groups. Thus, a multicultural social studies curriculum is one in which students are made aware that historical events affect more than those people who are traditionally identified as participants. For example, Sara and Patricia's teacher included the letter exchange activity as part of an American Revolution unit developed to include objectives about the roles of colonial women and children, Native Americans, African Americans, common soldiers, and the loyalists, in addition to information about events leading to and during the Revolutionary War. The objectives and activities were designed to capture the interests of students of diverse backgrounds.

First, let us take a closer look at the topic, *multicultural education*. Multicultural education is probably a familiar topic. I would guess you have either taken a course titled "Multicultural Education" or have had discussions of multiculturalism in several of your college courses. Our concern here is how to transform the elementary social studies curriculum so it may accurately be described as multicultural. As so often is the case with school-related words and phrases, *multicultural education* has many aspects and, thus, many definitions (Banks & Banks, 2003). There are really two interrelated dimensions:

1. *The curricular dimension.* In multicultural education, students learn about many cultural groups, both those comprising the pluralistic society in the United States and those who live in other countries. A multicultural social studies curriculum provides children with opportunities to learn about other cultures as they learn about

themselves. Students should study both the current status of cultural groups and the history that led to the present. The personal experiences of each child should be considered valuable and worthy of inclusion in the social studies curriculum. A multicultural curriculum does not limit itself to presenting information about a wide range of people; it provides the perspectives of people who frequently have been silenced or relegated to the margins in traditional social studies programs (Banks et al., 2005; Burstein & Hutton, 2005).

2. *The equity dimension.* Multicultural education is the reform process that creates classrooms where all students have equal educational opportunity. This means teachers take positive steps to ensure students of both genders, of every ethnicity, with non-English native languages, with challenging conditions, and from all social classes, reach their full potential (Banks & Banks, 2003; Gay, 2000).

A Multicultural Curriculum: Four Approaches

James Banks (Banks & Banks, 2003) described the following four approaches for incorporating multicultural perspectives into the curriculum:

The Contributions Approach. The contributions approach is sometimes called the "heroes and holidays" approach. The social studies curriculum remains the same because the only things added are a few lessons on Martin Luther King, Jr. during January, a dance festival for Cinco de Mayo, and a Multicultural Day, on which parents bring to school the foods of their homelands. The key element missing is a lack of depth: No comprehensive study of other cultural groups is undertaken, nor is any attempt made to look at topics from a full range of perspectives.

The Additive Approach. In an additive approach, the units of study change only in that content is added to include multicultural perspectives. For example, in a fifth-grade social studies curriculum on the United States, two units of study are added: "The Civil Rights Movement" and "The Immigrant Experience." The additive approach is an improvement over the contributions approach, but the problem is experiences and perspectives of minority groups in the United States and people in foreign countries appear as an afterthought.

The Transformation Approach. In the transformation approach, the social studies curriculum has undergone a significant revision. The key element of a transformed social studies curriculum is that it allows students to consider more than one perspective on a concept, topic, or issue. An excellent example of a curriculum providing multiple perspectives is "Land and Landscape: Views of America's History and Culture," which was developed by the National Museum of American Art of the Smithsonian Institution (Powe, 1998). Students view a series of historic photos and then compare and contrast the Native American and European American ideas of the ownership of land. A transformed curriculum is essential in a society that values diversity and is part of the foundation on which effective social studies teaching is built.

The Social Action Approach.   The social action approach includes all the elements of the transformation approach but goes further and asks students to make decisions and take action (Ukpokodu, 2006), often in the form of service learning. For example, if a class of elementary students studied their city, they would learn about problems the city faces. If the teacher had adopted the social action approach, students would not only talk about issues but also prepare a simple "position paper" and present it to the city council. Not all units present the possibility for social action, and some actions are appropriate only for middle and high school students. In this chapter, our discussion covers the "how to" process of transforming the curriculum, and in Chapter 9 we provide a more complete examination of social studies service learning and social action projects.

The Transformation Process

Transforming the social studies curriculum to make it multicultural is an evolutionary process and includes the following steps:

1. *Reconsider the scope of the social studies curriculum.*   This task, in most cases, should be undertaken by a committee of teachers. Units of study should be analyzed for their content. Do they reflect only the perspectives of the mainstream, European American majority? Should some units be eliminated? Should new ones be created? For example, most fourth graders study their state—Virginians study Virginia, Californians study California, and so on. The curriculum is almost always chronological. In the study of Virginia, for example, the units of study would be "The Natives," "Colonial Virginia," "Virginia in the New Republic," "Virginia in the Civil War," "Reconstruction in Virginia," "Virginia in the Twentieth Century," and "Virginia Today and Tomorrow." The transformed curriculum would include information on African Americans, Native Americans, immigrants to Virginia, women, and children. Units need not be based on historical periods. Instead, issues or themes could be used as the focus:

   - "People and the Natural Resources of Virginia." What are the resources of Virginia? How have the natives, colonists, and subsequent inhabitants of the state used these resources? What must be done to preserve the natural resources of the state? Throughout the history of the state, why have different groups taken opposing positions on the use of the state's resources? Are the resources recognized to be important to Virginians today the same as in colonial times? How have the resources of Virginia shaped the economy and jobs of the people of Virginia? What natural resources in Virginia are threatened today, and what can be done to save them?

   - "The Struggle to Be Free." At the same time prominent Virginians led the American Revolution, what was the status of Native Americans, African Americans, women, and poor European Americans? How did laws in Virginia maintain a system of slavery and indentured servitude? How might a slave, an indentured servant, a shopkeeper, and a plantation owner have reacted differently to the Declaration of Independence and the adoption of the U.S. Constitution? During the period of segregation (1870–1965), what was life like for African Americans living in Virginia? How did people gain civil rights in Virginia in the 20th century?

■ "Technology and Life in Virginia." How have the tools and machines used by Virginians changed over the years? How did the industrial revolution of the 19th century change the way people lived? What does the information age mean for the citizens of Virginia? Will technology close the gaps between the rich and the poor or exacerbate the differences?

■ "Production, Distribution, and Consumption." What have Virginians produced? How have goods and services been distributed? What has been imported and exported? How did a slave-based economy function? How did the economy of Virginia change after the Civil War? How do Virginians earn their livings today?

2. *Expand the geographic boundaries of your units of study.*   Take a global perspective and look for cross-cultural comparisons. For example, first graders should not only study their school and neighborhood but also compare them to schools and neighborhoods in other states or countries. If third graders are learning about what characterizes a city, they could explore how their city compares to others.

3. *Introduce your students to a mosaic of people.*   This is the *who* of the transformed curriculum. Whatever the topic, consider the contributions of, and the impact on, African Americans, Asian Americans, Native Americans, Hispanic Americans, women, and children. This should be a process of inclusion, not exclusion. For example, the addition of Revolutionary War hero Sybil Ludington, who warned the residents of Danbury, Connecticut, of an impending British raid, does not mean you eliminate coverage of Paul Revere. The transformed curriculum should continue to present information that has traditionally been a part of social studies.

In Their Own Words: Children's Books

To transform the curriculum, children must hear the voices of a wide range of people. It is one thing to read second-hand descriptions of the experiences of other people; it is another to read first-hand accounts, written or dictated by people who were participants in the events. After many years of neglect, there are currently a large number of books that share the perspectives of African Americans, Asian Americans, Hispanic Americans, Native Americans, members of religious minorities, children, and people from outside the United States. Some of the accounts are autobiographical; others are anthologies of oral histories.

For example, in *Voices from the Fields: Children of Migrant Farmworkers Tell Their Stories,* editor Beth Atkin (1993) interviewed and photographed nine children of migrant workers. Perspectives of children usually are overlooked in elementary social studies, so Atkin's book is an important addition to our reservoir of instructional resources. Other edited books can provide your students with the words of enslaved people (*To Be a Slave,* Lester, 1968), teenage civil rights activists (*Freedom's Children: Young Civil Rights Activists Tell Their Own Stories,* Levine, 1993), African Americans throughout U.S. history (*The Black Americans: A History in Their Own Words,* Meltzer, 1984), and Native Americans who came in contact with European Americans (*Native American Testimony: An Anthology of Indian and White Relations,* Nabakov, 1978).

Autobiographical accounts provide an essential level of authenticity to social studies teaching. This transforms your curriculum. For example, students can expand their knowledge of global events by reading about the following topics:

A childhood in Communist Prague (*The Wall: Growing Up Behind the Iron Curtain,* Sis, 2007)

Memories of a family's flight from the Warsaw Blitz and life in a refugee camp during World War II (*How I Learned Geography,* Shulevitz, 2008)

Conditions in North Korea during the 1940s and 1950s (*Year of Impossible Goodbyes,* Choi, 1991)

A childhood in Vietnam (*The Land I Lost: Adventures of a Boy in Vietnam,* Huynh, 1982)

A Chinese girl's immigration to Brooklyn (*In the Year of the Boar and Jackie Robinson,* Lord, 1984)

Life in Japan immediately after World War II (*The Bicycle Man,* Say, 1982)

The internment of Japanese Americans during World War II (*Journey to Topaz,* Uchida, 1971)

Figure 5.1 lists some of the children's books that are first-person accounts. At the end of the chapter is a lesson plan based on the narratives of enslaved people found in *To Be a Slave.*

In Their Own Words: Oral History

Children should never consider social studies to be a dry subject telling the stories only of other people living in other places. Our own families and communities can be rich sources of information. Oral histories collected by your students will help you transform the curriculum. *Oral history* is a method of gathering spoken, first-person accounts of past events (Ritchie, 1995). Oral histories collected by adult historians are tape recorded, carefully indexed, and placed in an accessible archive. Several authors have written about how students can collect and use oral histories (Anand et al., 2002; Haas, 2008; Huerta & Flemmer, 2001; Mehaffy, Sitton, & Davis, 1979; Olmedo, 1996; Walbert, 2004). Oral history projects conducted by students can be relatively simple. For example, Miller (2000) described how fifth-grade students wrote biographies after each fifth grader conducted an interview of a second grader in the same school. On the other hand, some oral history projects will challenge both students and teachers. Alibrandi, Beal, Thompson, and Wilson (2000) provided

Figure 5.1

Books for Children: First-Person Accounts

Atkin, S. Beth (editor). *Voices from the Fields: Children of Migrant Farmworkers Tell Their Stories*. Atkin interviewed and photographed nine children.

Choi, Sook Nyul. *The Year of Impossible Goodbyes*. The author tells of her childhood in North Korea during the 1940s, the Japanese occupation, and escape to South Korea.

Crews, Donald. *Bigmama's*. African American author-illustrator Crews reminisces about summer trips to his grandparents' farm. Easy-to-read picture book.

de Paola, Tomie. *26 Fairmount Avenue*. Popular author/Illustrator recounts his year in kindergarten, 1938.

Frank, Anne. *The Diary of a Young Girl*. More able fifth and sixth graders can read this well-known diary of a Dutch Jewish girl in World War II.

Garza, Carmen Lomas. *Family Pictures*. This Mexican American painter tells of growing up in a small town in Texas. Easy-to-read picture book; the text is in Spanish and English.

Hautzig, Esther. *The Endless Steppe*. The author, who was born to wealthy Jewish parents in Poland, provides an account of growing up in a slave labor camp in Siberia.

Huynh, Quang Nhuoug. *The Land I Lost: Adventures of a Boy in Vietnam*. The author remembers incidents from his childhood in Vietnam.

Lester, Julius (editor). *To Be a Slave*. Anthology of autobiographical narratives told by several former slaves.

Levine, Ellen (editor). *Freedom's Children: Young Civil Rights Activists Tell Their Own Stories*. Thirty African Americans who were children or teenagers during the 1950s and 1960s describe their experiences.

Lord, Bette Bao. *In the Year of the Boar and Jackie Robinson*. Fictionalized account of the author's immigration from China to Brooklyn in 1947.

McKissack, Patricia. *Goin' Someplace Special*. Author of children's books tells her own story of growing up in Nashville.

Meltzer, Milton (editor). *The Black Americans: A History in Their Own Words*. Testimony of African Americans from the early 1600s to the 1970s.

Myers, Walter Dean. *Bad Boy: A Memoir*. Noted author tells of growing up in Harlem in the 1950s.

Nabakov, Peter (editor). *Native American Testimony: An Anthology of Indian and White Relations*. This book contains 200 years of Native American commentary and is an excellent teaching resource. Almost all entries can be read by fourth- or fifth-grade students.

Reiss, Johanna. *The Upstairs Room*. Author's experience when she and her sister were hidden by a farm family during World War II.

Say, Allen. *The Bicycle Man*. Author-illustrator Say, who grew up in Japan, tells the story of the day when two American soldiers visited his school.

Shulevitz, Uri. *How I Learned Geography*. Author-illustrator Shulewitz describes his experiences as a boy when his family fled the Warsaw Blitz and lived in a refugee camp during World War II.

Sis, Peter. *The Wall: Growing Up Behind the Iron Curtain*. Author-illustrator Sis describes his boyhood in Prague during Communist rule.

Uchida, Yoshiko. *Journey to Topaz*. Fictionalized account of the author's family's evacuation and internment during World War II. The sequel is *Journey Home,* where Uchida and her family are released from the camp in Topaz, Utah, and return to California.

a report of a project conducted by middle school students incorporating oral history, field trips, historical maps, and data from the computer-based GIS (geographic information systems).

The Benefits of Oral History.   The process of collecting, analyzing, and reporting oral histories is a wonderful experience for our students for many reasons:

■ Oral history allows students to become historians; they will learn how historians work and will have firsthand knowledge of one important source of historical evidence.

■ Oral history transforms the curriculum in that it inevitably increases the sources of information available to our students. If we limit social studies to sources in print, we ignore the history most immediate, relevant, and comprehensible to our students: their history, the history of their families, and the history of their immediate communities. Hickey and Kolterman (2006) showed how oral history can be used in a social studies unit that helps children learn about the roles of women in history.

■ Oral history is an excellent language arts activity. In the process of gathering, analyzing, and reporting oral histories, students will listen, speak, read, and write.

■ Olmedo (1996) explained why oral history projects work well with English learners. These projects are relevant to their experiences, they teach social science inquiry processes, and allow English learners to use both their languages. Oral histories can be collected in any language, so we can encourage our bilingual students to gather oral histories in their native languages.

■ Oral history makes any subject more interesting. Hirshfield (1991) noted, "Oral history attaches emotion to events that can be provided only by the person who has lived through them; the young interviewer inevitably develops a deeper understanding of the recent past" (p. 111).

Guidelines for Oral History Projects.   Oral history projects require thorough planning. The following guidelines will help us prepare for the use of oral histories and help children successfully complete an oral history project.

1. *Determine the focus of the oral history project.*   Choose the project focus. Oral histories can *supplement* other resources. For example, a group of fourth graders studying the recent history of their state will read about recent immigrants in their textbooks, in children's books, and in resources found on the Web. Add oral histories to the print and other media resources. For some topics, oral histories can be the *sole source* of information for a lesson. A fifth-grade class did a project on how their grandparents met. In this project, the only sources of data for a Website the students created were the oral histories they gathered.

2. *Identify the project's outcomes for students.*   It is important that students understand the entire process of gathering data from interviews, analyzing the data, and creating a final product. They should know about how long each phase of the process will take.

Perhaps most important, they should understand what they will ultimately produce, and there are several possibilities: a Website, a CD, a podcast, a written report, a bulletin board display, or an oral presentation.

3. *Engage students in doing some background work.*   The more your students know about the time, places, people, and events that are the substance of the interview, the better. They will need this knowledge to make sense of what they hear and to ask follow-up questions. This is easier in some projects than in others.

4. *Direct students to plan their interviews.*   After the topic has been defined and students have acquired background knowledge, ask the class to make a list of people they could interview. Discuss with students why thinking carefully about how the person(s) they choose to interview will inform their own knowledge base and contribute to their oral history project. Explain how being a good communicator can help them better reach their goal. Determine as a group that the value of any interview is directly related to the quality of the questions asked.

5. *Create a list of questions to be asked during the interview.*   In some projects, a standardized set of questions should be asked of all interviewees. In other projects, each interviewee will have a different set of questions. Questions should be open ended; questions that can be answered with one word or a short phrase should be avoided. For example, a group of sixth graders compiled an oral history of playground games as part of a large project on "Kids at Play: A History from Ancient Egypt to Today." Rather than ask senior citizens, "Did you play with jump ropes when you were in elementary school?" students should ask, "Tell me about the games you remember playing at recess when you were in elementary school." Generate with your class samples of open-ended questions:

    What do you remember about _____?

    How old were you when _____ happened? How do you know the event happened when you were _____?

    How did this event affect (change) your life?

    What did you do when _____?

    What else was going on during the same time?

6. *Help students understand how to "go beyond" previously determined questions.*   As Gail Hickey (1991) stated, predetermined questions should be "a guide rather than a strict script" (p. 217). Interviewing is difficult for elementary students to master, but the ability to ask a good follow-up question is essential for the oral historian. When students hear something unusual, they should ask additional questions, even though it means deviating from the standardized list of questions. Remember, too, your students should be interested in interviewing people who have *first-hand* knowledge. It is inevitable that some interviewees will repeat things they have heard. Family stories passed down for generations will be told and are interesting to hear; from a historical sense, however, the real value of oral history is in recording eyewitness accounts.

7. *Hold the interviews in a controlled setting.* A significant challenge in an oral history project is the logistics of the interviews. In many cases, the teacher will contact informants and arrange for them to come to school for their interviews. In other projects, the students establish contacts through the use of letters and follow-up telephone calls. If interviews take place outside school, students must be accompanied by their parents. Hirshfield (1991) lists two essential features of the interview setting. First, the interview should be one on one. Second, the interview should be in a quiet place with no distractions. Be sure interviews are conducted only after an appointment has been made and confirmed.

8. *Help your students be good interviewers.* Students should ask one question at a time. If students use a tape recorder, they should know how to operate it. If students write down the answers provided by the interviewee, they should be trained to write fast and accurately. My experience has been that the vast majority of students cannot write fast enough to record what the interviewee is saying. Tape recorders are a much better tool for interviewers to use. Students should be sure they have the correct spelling of names and places. They should ask follow-up questions to be sure that dates, places, and names are stated (and recorded) clearly. It is a good idea to role play oral history interviews beforehand so students become comfortable with the process and efficient in getting information—one student plays the informant, the other the interviewer. To help students while they role play the act of interviewing or to help them feel more confident when they conduct their interviews, consider providing some kind of planning form, such as the one displayed in Figure 5.2. Students can use this form to think critically before they conduct any interviews and to hold them accountable for getting their interview plan in motion.

9. *Request that interviewees sign a release form.* A release form authorizes interviewers to share what they have heard from the interviewee. The form can be simple (a sample is shown in Figure 5.3) and should be approved by the school principal. The important thing is that people who are interviewed know other people will hear or read what they have said and their comments "belong" to the school. In the unlikely event they are published, the copyright and any money generated by the publication in which they appear belong to the school.

10. *Support interviews with documents and artifacts.* Many times, an interview will lead a person to "dig out" old clothing, photographs, letters, souvenirs, gifts, or other items. Usually, these are too valuable to take to class. Under some circumstances, they can be borrowed, photographed, or photocopied. These documents and other artifacts are important historical sources and can provide illustrations for the text of a report based on the interviews.

11. *Analyze interviews.* After students have completed their oral interviews, their work has just begun. First, students should do what real historians do—make an index (list) of the interviews. Second, they should meet in groups and attempt to make sense of what they heard. The simplest form of analysis is to edit out irrelevant comments and compile an anthology of the interviews. This would work if all the interviewees

Figure 5.2

Planning the Interview

Interviewer _____ Date _____
Whom will you interview?
_____
What is the purpose of your interview? _____
_____
_____
When will you conduct the interview? _____
_____
Date _____ Time _____
What questions do you intend to ask and in what order?
1. _____
_____
2. _____
_____
3. _____
_____
4. _____
_____
5. _____
_____

Remember, answers you hear to your questions may change any follow-up
questions you may ask. Be flexible!

responded to one broadly stated question (e.g., "What do you remember about the teachers' strike in 1980?"). Students will learn more if they compare and contrast the interviews. Some projects lend themselves to a chronological review; events described in several interviews can be arranged in the order in which they took place. Typically, though, the analysis will look for similarities and differences.

At the end of the chapter is a description of an oral history project completed by third graders on the history of their elementary school.

Incorporating the Personal Experiences of Your Students

First-hand accounts of events, including both those found in children's books and those recorded as oral history, are two ways to transform the curriculum. Equally essential is using the personal experiences of your students as a basis for social studies teaching and learning (Alleman & Brophy, 1994). Virtually everyone who writes about social studies and

Figure 5.3

Permission Form for Oral History Interviews

Please complete the following before or after your interview. Thank you.

I agree to be interviewed by _____

I understand that what I say will be shared as part of a classroom project. I also understand that my comments may be published for school use and that if the school decides this interview project is important enough to be shared beyond the use of _____ that I will be

School name

contacted for further permission.

_____

Signature of Interviewee   Date

minority students stresses the importance of incorporating the personal experiences of students into the curriculum (e.g., Banks & Banks, 2003; Garcia, 1994; Short et al., 1994). This is a venerable idea, advocated in the late 1800s by Francis Parker, John Dewey, and other Progressive educators (Cremin, 1961). By "personal experience," I mean the daily existence of students outside school. Here are some ways to connect social studies to the personal experiences of students.

Cultural Universals.   All people share basic needs, such as food, clothing, shelter, and transportation. These "cultural universals" can be used to transform social studies teaching and learning by linking the lives of your students to people from other places and times (Alleman & Brophy, 2000, 2004; Brophy & Alleman, 2008; Stevens & Starkey, 2007). Units and lessons can begin by having students consider their own existence, proceed to a middle section where information is presented about people living in other places or in other times, and conclude with cross-cultural comparisons. For example, a unit on the Pilgrims might include an activity on "Lunch with the Pilgrims, Plymouth, 1622." First, the students would answer these questions:

- When do we eat lunch at school?
- Does your family have a "lunch" at home on the weekends? (Many cultural groups eat their main meal at midday.)

- What types of foods do we eat for lunch at school? How are they different from break-fast and dinner?

- With whom do you eat lunch at school? (Do adults eat with children?) With whom do you eat lunch at home?

- How does lunch begin at home? (Some students might begin with a prayer or other ritual.)

- What beverages do we drink with lunch at school? What do you drink with meals at home?

Students would learn that the first Pilgrims ate with their fingers, drank a low-alcohol beer with their midday meal, and consumed incredible amounts of food each day—in good times, a half pound of butter, a half pound of meat, and a pound of bread. Several children's books would serve as resources: *Thanksgiving: The True Story* (Colman, 2008), *The Thanksgiving Book* (Hillstrom, 2007), *Giving Thanks: The 1621 Harvest Feast* (Waters, 2001), *Colonial Living* (Tunis, 1957), *Meet the Real Pilgrims* (Loeb, 1979), *Eating the Plates* (Penner, 1991), and *Sarah Morton's Day* (Waters, 1989). Students could then make comparisons and observe the similarities and differences between lunch today and the midday meal of the Pilgrims. Finally, there should be an examination of how the coming of European Americans changed the food sources and meal customs of the Native Americans living in Massachusetts during the 17th century. A small group of students could prepare a presentation for their classmates.

The Experiences of Childhood.   When we are teaching about another cultural group or about people who lived in the past, one effective way to link the subject matter to the personal experiences of your students is to focus on the experiences of children. All too often in social studies, the curriculum seems to ignore the existence of children. I think the status of children is highly relevant and an interesting avenue to understanding other cultural groups. Today almost all children go to school and participate in some form of recreational activity. School and play are perfect topics to include in any study of another group of people, whether they lived long ago or are living today. Comparisons based on school and play will provide information about many other topics you wish to cover, such as the roles of men, women, and children; the values of the group; and the technology of the group of people being studied.

For example, consider a second-grade unit on "Our Grandparents." The teacher calculated an "average age" for her second graders' grandparents. The year was 2007, so most of her second graders were born in 2000. She figured that their parents were 30 when the children were born: 2000 − 30 = 1970. She then figured the grandparents were 25 years old when the parents were born: 1970 − 25 = 1945. Thus, the grandparents, on average, had been born in 1945 and turned 7 in 1952. What games did the grandparents play when they were in second grade? What books did their teachers read aloud to them in 1952? How did their grandparents dress when they went to second grade? The unit provided answers to all these questions as the class looked at what it was like to be a second grader in 1952.

A Child's Life History.   The life histories of our students can be used in a variety of ways as part of the social studies program:

■ Some students may have participated in events you are studying. For example, in California, the experiences of immigrants are part of the social studies curriculum in grades 2 to 5. Students in our rooms who are immigrants can tell about their immigration; these oral histories can supplement other resources. One important note: Some students may have fled their native countries under horrible conditions; if these students do not want to recount their experiences, that wish should be respected.

■ Students can learn how historians work by writing *documented* histories of themselves (autobiographies) and their families (Czartoski & Hickey, 1999; Schwartz, 2000). There is value in having students write from memory. Memories can be combined with a historical record; however, old photographs, report cards, and birth certificates should be consulted and referenced. Students should interview their parents, siblings, former teachers, and other people who have known them. The addition of the documentation will show students how historians gather data to support their texts.

■ Students should learn about their communities, and as they do, they can combine their personal experiences with field trips, oral history, and the examination of documents, like old newspapers (Hickey, 1999). Many school districts make a study of the local community the focus of third-grade social studies. It is important that your curriculum incorporate the people and places your students know well. For example, children walk and drive by many buildings with historical significance every day. Children can take "walking field trips" to visit these buildings. They can learn when a building was built and who has occupied it.

Current Events.   The events of the day can also be used to provide a link between personal experiences and social studies. Three general strategies come to mind:

■ Of greatest value are events your students experience firsthand. Although the content may not fit with the curriculum guide or the textbook you are following, it makes sense to break away and explore significant events (Passe, 2008). For example, students who have coped with earthquakes and floods should be challenged to consider the social aspects of those natural disasters (e.g., public agencies that address emergencies, private organizations that assist, the role of individual citizens in helping out, and the possible future consequences of the event). An argument can be made that teachers play a key role in helping children cope with the trauma of a natural disaster (Pang et al., 2008).

■ Primarily through television, but also through the Internet, other media, and daily conversation, your students vicariously experience important events as they happen. Students will have considerable curiosity about significant events, and the social studies curriculum should respond to their questions. In the aftermath of September 11, 2001, for example, a great deal was written about how teachers should teach about what transpired on the day itself, what preceded it, and what has happened since (Berson & Berson, 2001; Mehlinger, 2002; Simpson, 2001; Singleton, 2001; Stevens, 2002; Webeck, Black, Davis, & Field, 2002).

■ Students could look at newspapers to find events that parallel those they are study-ing. For example, Diane Short and her colleagues (1994), in their junior high school unit on the American Revolution, ask students to search newspapers for articles about current political unrest in a lesson about colonial protests to British policies.

Consumer Goods.   Articles of clothing, toys, cans of food, and other consumer goods, can be the starting point for lessons in geography and economics. Students will see the goods they use every day come from many countries. For example, several children in a second-grade classroom had shirts made in Sri Lanka (they found this information on the labels sewn into the collars). This led to a mini-unit on that nation. Where is Sri Lanka? What resources does it have? What is life like for the workers who made the shirts? How do the shirts arrive in the United States? Why is it less expensive to make the shirts in Sri Lanka than in the United States?

A Multicultural Curriculum: How to Adapt a Traditional Unit of Study

Almost all fifth graders study the history of the United States. An important unit of study during the year is the American Revolution. How could a standard unit be transformed so the scope of the unit, its geographic boundaries, and the people discussed become more multiculturally focused?

The transformed curriculum connects students with a wide spectrum of cultural groups. Here, a gifted storyteller introduces children to a trickster tale from the Ashanti of West Africa.

First, the activities in the unit should go beyond those suggested in a traditional teacher's edition of a basal social studies textbook series. We need to gather ideas and information from other sources, like a middle school unit on the American Revolution prepared at the Center for Applied Linguistics (Short et al., 1994). Designed for English learners, this material is a good example of a curriculum relating to today's diverse classrooms. This material and others can help fifth graders see the perspectives of people often left out of traditional units of study, such as children and teenagers, women, Native Americans, African Americans, and, in this case, colonial loyalists. Review the following examples:

Expand the Resources Found in Traditional Units.   Additional resources, beyond the textbook, can be added to a traditional unit to enhance information and descriptions of people, events, and ideas. McCormick (2004) showed how primary source material, written in 1776, could be used successfully to teach fifth graders about the Battle of Trenton. Also, earlier in this chapter, I noted a lesson on Paul Revere could be expanded to introduce Sybil Ludington. In 1777, 14-year-old Ludington warned the militia in Danbury, Connecticut, of the movements of a British raiding party. Good sources of information on Ludington are (a) a children's book, *Sybil's Night Ride* (Winnick, 2000); (b) two simple picture books, one by Drollene Brown (1985), *Sybil Rides for Independence,* and the other by Marsha Amster (2000), *Sybil Ludington's Midnight Ride;* (c) a poem by Cindy Mahrer, located in a unit published by the Center for Applied Linguistics (Short et al., 1994); and (d) Internet sites, like the site for the museum of the town of Patterson, New York, www.historicpatterson.org.

The Internet continues to grow as a significant resource for transformed social studies. For example, the best source of information on the experiences of African Americans during the Revolutionary War is "Revolution," a Website created by the Public Broadcasting System as part of the "Africans in America" television series (www.pbs.org/wgbh/aia/tguide). Many fifth graders can read the text on this Website, which also includes reproductions of historical documents. Students could read about Prince Hall and Colonel Tye, African Americans who fought on opposing sides during the war.

Provide More Than One Perspective on Historical Events.   A transformed curriculum can help students understand a wider range of perspectives. Several activities could accomplish this goal. For example, students could use a Venn diagram to compare and contrast the political views of the colonists who remained loyal to the British king (loyalists) with those of the rebels. The students will see that while these two groups differed fundamentally on some issues, there were some areas of agreement (e.g., both groups in the South supported slavery). Otherwise, the class can be divided into two groups of equal number— one group being loyalists, and the other being rebels—and each loyalist can pair up with a rebel. Throughout the unit, the "two cousins" of each pair can write one another—the loyalist urging fidelity to the crown, the rebel advocating revolution. Sara's letter at the beginning of the chapter was completed as part of this unit. A unique children's book showing multiple perspectives on the same events compares the views of King George III and George Washington, *George vs. George: The Revolutionary War as Seen by Both Sides* (Schanzer, 2004).

Most instructional units on the Revolution fail to present the perspectives of the common, ordinary foot soldiers in the colonial army. Some of these soldiers, however, were not much older than today's fifth graders. To provide the perspectives of these young people, use Milton Meltzer's (1987) *The American Revolutionaries: A History in Their Own Words, 1750–1800*. Two passages I suggest for inclusion are those written by 16-year-old colonial soldiers James Collins and Thomas Young. They describe the bloody battle of Kings Mountain, where a rebel army defeated an army of colonial loyalists. A good activity is to have students participate in a readers' theater project, with students reading aloud in dramatic fashion excerpts from the passages dictated by Collins and Young. A more elaborate readers' theater presentation could use a script taken from many of the oral histories and documents preserved in Meltzer's book.

Include a Wider Spectrum of Biographies.   Our students should learn about a wide spectrum of Revolutionary War personalities including:

- Deborah Sampson, who fought in the Revolutionary War disguised as a male soldier. See the children's books *I'm Deborah Sampson: A Soldier in the War of Revolution*, by Clapp (1977); *The Secret Soldier: The Story of Deborah Sampson*, by McGovern (1975); and *Deborah Sampson Goes to War*, by Stephens (1984);

- Prominent colonial women, such as Abigail Adams (see the biographies by St. George, 2001 and Wallner, 2001) and Mercy Otis Warren;

- Margaret Corbin, Molly Pitcher, and Sarah Shattuck, women who participated in Revolutionary War battles (Anderson, 2008; Rockwell, 2002);

- Patience Wright, a spy during the American Revolution (Shea, 2007);

- African Americans such as James Armistead, Austin Dabney, Saul Matthews, and Salem Poor, who all served in the colonial army (see the children's book, *Come All You Brave Soldiers: Blacks in the Revolutionary War*, by Cox, 1999);

- British military leaders, such as John Burgoyne, Charles Cornwallis, and Banastre Tarleton; and

- Native American leader Thayendanegea (Joseph Brant), who sided with the British.

Reveal a Wider Range of Events.   Traditional social studies units on the American Revolution are, for the most part, limited to political and military events. Again, no good unit can ignore the signing of the Declaration of Independence or the impact of the battle of Yorktown. A unit on the American Revolution, however, could also include information most adults, much less elementary children, do not know. How many of us, for example, are aware that the central problem for those who remained at home during the war was runaway inflation, or that women at home assumed new roles, such as running the businesses their husbands left behind when they went to war? To embellish textbook coverage of the home front, I suggest four excellent children's books: Brandon Miller's (2005) *Declaring Independence: Life During the American Revolution;* Kay Moore's (1998) *If You Lived in the Time of the American Revolution;* Barbara Brenner's (1994) *If You Were There in 1776;* and John Loeper's (1973) *Going to School in 1776.*

Encourage the Reading of Juvenile Novels.   Students should be encouraged to read fiction with characters who are young people, loyalists, or African Americans. For example, James Lincoln Collier and Christopher Collier have written a trilogy telling of the wartime and postwar experiences of African Americans in the North (*Jump Ship to Freedom* [1981], *War Comes to Willy Freeman* [1983], and *Who Is Carrie?* [1984]). Another book by the same authors, *My Brother Sam Is Dead* (1974), tells the story of Sam, the only rebel in a family led by a loyalist father. Two juvenile novels written by well-known authors also focus on the tension between loyalists and rebels (*Early Thunder* by Jean Fritz [1967] and *Johnny Treegate's Musket* by Leonard Wibberly [1959]).

Expand the Study of Prominent People and Events.   Even people, events, and ideas covered traditionally in a unit on the American Revolution can be transformed by offering a different perspective. George Washington, for example, is usually presented as a political and military leader. To many children, I suspect, he seems as lifeless as his image on a dollar bill. I suggest two children's books to help students see the "human" side of Washington. Miriam Anne Bourne's (1983) *Uncle George Washington and Harriet's Guitar* is based on the Washington family letters written from 1790 to 1795. We see Washington from the perspective of his nieces and nephews. *George Washington's Teeth* by Deborah Chandra and Madeline Comora (2003) does more than cover his dental problems, it provides insight on the daily routines of his life. Finally, while all units should emphasize Washington's unique contributions to U.S. history and his rightful status as "father of our country," students should also examine Washington's economic interests as a slaveholder and the consistent criticism of his leadership of the Continental army—see the children's books *George Washington: An Illustrated Biography* (Adler, 2004) and *George Washington and the Birth of Our Nation* by Meltzer (1986).

The Integrated Curriculum

Modifying the elementary social studies curriculum so it is multicultural will make your teaching more powerful and relevant. In addition, a social studies curriculum should be integrated so it links several areas of the curriculum. Teachers who plan and implement this type of instruction may describe their teaching as "cross-curricular," "thematic," or "integrated." Although these descriptors are often used as synonyms, I use the term *integrated* in this book. The social studies curriculum becomes integrated when teachers go beyond history and geography to include concepts from the other social sciences—political science, anthropology, economics, psychology, and sociology, as well as mathematics, science, physical education, literature, and the arts. The focus of this chapter is on how to integrate speaking and listening, the performing arts and visual arts with social studies (Hinde, 2005). Please note the following:

■ An integrated social studies curriculum, of course, also involves the other language arts—reading and writing (literacy). I felt the integration of literacy with elementary social

Anthony Magnacca/Merrill

Participation in dramatic presentation can help children develop a strong sense of empathy with people from other times and places.

studies was so important that in this fourth edition, I have devoted a separate chapter to that topic (Chapter 8).

■ Chapter 9 shows how significant ideas from political science can be part of elementary social studies; Chapter 12 discusses the importance of teaching students concepts from anthropology, economics, psychology, and sociology.

■ Teachers do have to be careful regarding curricular integration in social studies. In some instances, integrated units of study focus too heavily on the language and visual arts and the social studies content is watered down. Thus, it is important to remember an integrated social studies unit is a *social studies* unit—and must teach state-adopted social studies standards (Brophy & Alleman, 2008).

Speaking and Listening in the Social Studies Program

Almost every activity described in this book requires students to speak, either to each other or to their teacher. Most talk should be informal and conversational as students work in small-group formats. More formal speaking assignments are appropriate for students in the upper-elementary grades. Students should work together to report the results of an inquiry or a project. One of the best formats is several students sharing the responsibility for an oral presentation. Several things can be done to ensure this is a worthwhile experience for both the students delivering the report and for their classmates who are listening. First, students who are to speak should practice their parts several times. Next, no student should speak for more than a few minutes. Finally, the oral report should be supported by visual aids, such as charts, graphs, maps, and diagrams.

As noted in Chapter 9, an essential part of citizenship education is helping students master the process of "civil discourse." Discussion should be an important part of social studies teaching and learning at every grade level (Hess, 2004; Wilen, 2004). Students should talk about controversial issues and explore multiple perspectives on events in the past. The research in this area, done primarily in high schools but relevant to the elementary school, is contradictory. Although teachers and students frequently report they engage in discussion about controversial issues, "when researchers observe social studies classes they rarely find discussion of any sort and little attention to controversial issues" (Hess, 2008, p. 127). Here I will look at two perspectives on classroom discussions. First, let's review what the research reveals about classroom discussion. Then, let's look at what teachers can do to promote civil, nonthreatening, and nontheatric discussions among their students.

Diana Hess (2004) reviewed the literature on classroom discussion in social studies and identified seven characteristics of effective discussion:

1. The focus is on an *interpretable* topic (an issue or text). To have a good discussion, there must be more than one possible perspective. This is similar to the requirement for a good inquiry; you cannot hope to have a discussion among many participants if you start with a question that has a single, correct answer.

2. The leader of the discussion and the participants have prepared. Depending on the topic, the preparation can be informal and take only a few minutes. Other topics will take days of reading and note-taking. One teacher required students to write something down on the topic to be discussed and these initial, written thoughts became a "ticket" that allowed them to talk.

3. Most of the talk comes from the participants, not the leader. This is so important. If teachers are leading a discussion, they want to say as little as possible. If a student is facilitating a discussion, she or he must understand the limited nature of a facilitator's role.

4. There is enough time spent on a particular topic to explore it thoroughly. This is the same point raised by Newman in Chapter 7 regarding critical thinking. Critical thinking, an important goal of discussion, is possible only if topics are explored in depth.

5. Participants feel comfortable, but disagreement is still possible. Our discussion, based on Rossi's suggestions in the next paragraph, will further explain how these two goals can be met. Teachers need to create an atmosphere that is nonjudgmental. Students need to "depersonalize" their responses by separating the content of a comment from the commentator.

6. Many people talk. This has the best chance of happening if the previous five points are implemented. Many children will talk if there is something stimulating to talk about,

the children have prepared, the leader limits her or his comments, adequate time is devoted to the topic, and the children feel comfortable in expressing their perspectives.

7. Finally, the participants in the discussion ask good questions based on what has been said earlier. Being a good discussant requires students to be good listeners. Teachers should model this behavior by asking their questions in the context of previous commentary (e.g., "One idea we heard was that we should use the PTA money to buy more computers. If we did that, are there costs other than the computers for which we would have to pay?").

Rossi's (1996) article provides guidance for those of us who want to help our students learn how to express their opinions and, at the same time, listen to others in an appropriate fashion. Things haven't changed since the article was published and Rossi continues to be on target when he notes this is a challenge in the age of radio and television talk shows where the goal is to incite, not educate, and that because "these shows demonstrate merely discussing controversial issues is not sufficient to promote civic competence and democratic attitudes" (p. 18). Rossi's five conditions for creating a civil classroom climate can serve as a framework for a description of how to have productive and polite discussions in an elementary classroom.

1. *A cooperative versus a competitive context.* We should model the attitude that when disagreements arise, the goal is not to "win" but rather to learn. We should praise students when they ask clarifying questions and make efforts to understand why their classmates have reached different conclusions. Students should learn that monopolizing the discussion is inappropriate. Personal attacks, of course, should never be tolerated in any civil discussion.

2. *Relevant information.* Discussions should be based on accurate and pertinent information. The leader of a discussion (teacher or student) should help students question in a respectful manner the accuracy of statements made by classmates. Rather than stating, "You're wrong," students should say something like, "I don't think it is accurate to say that . . ." We should record these disputes and help students find information that provides accuracy. It is important that students support their views with facts and explain why they believe the way they do.

3. *Perspective taking.* Role play can help students understand and empathize with someone else's perspective. On some issues, both historical and contemporary, students should assume the role of another person and express that person's views. This activity will help increase the amount of information presented in a discussion and will ensure a range of opinions is presented.

4. *Disagreeing while confirming.* In discussions in which people disagree, it is essential that "somehow, participants need to be able to disagree with each others' ideas while confirming each others' personal competence" (Rossi, 1996, p. 20). This needs to become a part of every student's listening behavior. Our youngest students should understand that interrupting others is inappropriate because they learn less when they listen less. As students grow older, they should learn to say things like, "You have done a lot of work

and you know your stuff, but I don't agree with what you said" or "What you have said is making me think" or "After listening to you, I see we agree on many things."

5. *Inclusion.*   Many students are uncomfortable talking in a group discussion. We must create situations in which many students have a chance to express themselves. The cooperative learning structures discussed in Chapter 6 maximize participation, but they involve very small groups (Think–Pair–Share and Three-Step Interview). Many students who would otherwise remain silent will speak if they have a chance to prepare and practice their comments. We could provide some students with the discussion topic in advance, help them structure their response, allow them a chance to practice, and provide feedback *before* the day of the discussion.

The Performing Arts and the Visual Arts

The *performing arts* are music, dance, and drama. The *visual arts* incorporate a variety of media (e.g., crayon, clay, paint, film, video, and computer-based multimedia). The role of the arts in social studies is multifaceted (Eisner, 1991; Selwyn, 1995; Tibbett, 2004). First, the arts provide alternatives for the presentation of social studies information. Films, paintings, live dramas, and other art forms are particularly important resources for English-language learners. Howard Gardner's (1991, 2006) ideas on multiple intelligences provide a strong rationale for using the arts to help students learn about other people because some students find it difficult to learn from written material. The arts are an alternative. As students view the visual arts and view and listen to the performing arts, they use their senses to learn. These can be powerful experiences because "what all of the arts have in common is their capacity to generate emotion, to stimulate and to express the 'feel' for a situation, individual, or object" (Eisner, 1991, p. 554).

Second, as Selwyn (1995) notes, "the study of the arts is part of the study of history. Music, visual arts, dance, theater, crafts, writing, and other arts are both artifacts of and a means by which to study a culture" (p. 9). As many instructional units as possible should present information through the arts. Many current social studies textbooks include illustrations of paintings, statues, ceramics, and other art forms. Teachers can augment these resources by selecting books displaying the art of a particular culture. When students view another culture's art, they will see intercultural differences and similarities. Although the specific forms of art will vary from culture to culture, students will see certain universal themes are present. For example, forms of dance are wonderfully different among cultural groups; yet, all dance can be classified as essentially social, ritual, or performance.

Third, the arts should also be used to allow students to express what they have learned. Too often, social studies tasks are limited to reading, writing, and speaking. Our students should have opportunities to display their knowledge through the performing and visual arts. In the next two sections, we look at some specific art forms that can be used with elementary students.

The Performing Arts.   In Chapter 10, I describe a lesson in which kindergartners assumed the roles of a 19th-century farm family and pantomimed chores after listening to their teacher read *Ox-Cart Man* (Hall, 1979). This informal type of *role play* can be a powerful teaching tool, and is easy to implement (Barnes, Johnson, & Neff, 2010; Mahood, 1980; Shaftel & Shaftel, 1967). We merely ask students to pretend they are someone or something, and then the make believe begins. A more formal type of role play is the mock trial described in Chapter 9. In that activity, students assumed the roles of judge, attorneys, witnesses, and the jury. Each student performed in his or her new identity without a script. This formal role play required students to learn a great deal about their new identities, to "think on their feet," and to improvise.

Readers' theater is simple, effective, and fun (Laughlin, Black, & Loberg, 1991; Sloyer, 1982; Young & Vardell, 1993). The text of picture books, excerpts from fiction, poetry, and parts of information books all can be presented. In readers' theater, students read their lines during the performance. In *choral reading,* parts of the text are read simultaneously by two or more students. With a *nonedited* form of readers' theater, every word of the text is read. Narrators read the words outside quotation marks, and student actors read the dialogue inside quotation marks. In other presentations, the text of the book is modified for the performance. Three things help make readers' theater experiences positive. First, no student should be asked to read aloud a text that is too difficult. Second, it must be very clear to each reader when she or he is supposed to read. While performing, many students become nervous, and simple things become difficult. We could make copies of the portion of a book being read, provide each reader with a copy, and highlight each student's part with a colored marker. Third, even though readers' theater does not demand students memorize their parts, students need to rehearse several times before they read in front of an audience.

Almost all children enjoy acting in *plays.* Here, of course, actors must memorize their parts. When compared with readers' theater, the production is more elaborate, with costumes, a set, and props. Plays are particularly valuable in social studies because they help students learn about people in different places and times. This assumes, of course, that the script, set, costumes, and props have a reasonable degree of historical and cultural accuracy. The first step is to write a script, which may be done by the teacher, the students, or teacher and students working together. The easiest way to produce a script is to adapt a picture book or an excerpt from a children's novel. The second step is to select the parts, and this should be done carefully. Teachers should ensure the same students are not always the leads, and should guide students to roles they will be able to perform successfully. Plays, of course, require rehearsal. One form of play that has long been a part of social studies is the *historical pageant,* a multiscene play depicting the history of a place, person, idea, or event. For example, *California—Our State* could have the following scenes: (a) a vignette from a Yurok village (Native tribal life), (b) the death of Juan Cabrillo, (c) a California fiesta (during Mexican rule of California), (d) the discovery of gold, (e) the San Francisco earthquake of 1906, (f) a conversation among migrant workers in the 1930s, and (g) the establishment of a "dot com" business in 1995.

Selwyn (1995) suggests an interesting form of tableau vivante for social studies lessons—*human statues.* A group of students is given a scene to portray. The group then discusses how they should position themselves—how each person will kneel, sit, stand, or recline. All the group members come to the front of the class and strike their poses, each a human statue, frozen in position. Unlike true tableau, these statues can speak, and the student-statues can explain how they feel emotionally and physically. The class can ask questions, but this must happen quickly because the statues are human (and can be still for only a limited time).

Students can *dance* as a part of social studies. Some forms of pantomime blur the line between theater and dance as students convey meaning purely through body movements. Performing culturally authentic dances can be a worthwhile experience for students, but it is essential that the dances be treated with respect (such dance is typically referred to as *folk dance*). Students should see the dance performed with authenticity, either by members of the cultural group or by dancers who have studied the dance and understand its cultural context. Also, it is best to avoid sacred dances; these can become trivialized and their religious significance lost as the purpose of the dance, with children, shifts from ritual to social. Rather than have our students perform ritual dances, it would be better to have them observe the dance respectfully, either through a live performance or through film or video.

The Visual Arts.   A group of student teachers I supervised one semester compiled the following list of media that elementary students can use to express themselves through the visual arts: crayon, paint, ink, torn paper, tissue, photography, motion picture film, videotape, clay, chalk, computer graphics, colored pencils, felt and cloth, charcoal, salt and flour, string, potatoes (to make prints), and colored sand. After a day to think about it, we were able to double the list!

Many forms of *murals* can be made as part of social studies units. *Mural* comes from the Latin word for "wall" (*murus*), and all murals are large pictures on walls, typically with several images. Because we cannot paint or draw directly on school walls, our murals are usually bulletin board displays. Even though many murals are made on sheets of "butcher paper," I think it is more practical to draw or paint images on separate sheets of paper and then staple them to the bulletin board. Many murals will involve writing, too, as students write captions to accompany their visual images. One suggestion: Do not worry about scale; it will be fine to have drawings of the Sphinx and Tutankhamen be the same size.

A *diorama* is a three-dimensional display. The simplest ones are completed in shoe boxes, which limit the perspective of the viewer. Larger dioramas, though, are more rewarding and look better. I suggest using a piece of plywood as a base. Dioramas depict scenes from the world around us, both past and present, as they incorporate student-made figures from clay and other materials and manufactured items such as toy houses and people.

Collages are combinations of images. In its simplest form, students construct a collage with cut or torn paper. Pictures from magazines and other materials, like natural objects, textiles, and manufactured items, can be used. A collage should have a clearly stated theme or idea.

Finally, we should be careful as we use the visual arts to teach social studies. Some art projects done as part of social studies actually contribute little, if anything, to student learning of the content of an instructional unit. For example, fourth graders who paint a mural of an Iroquois village will learn very little if they merely follow a prescribed process with no attempt to place the subject of their mural in historical context. In fact, many social studies art projects become nothing more than exercises in mass production. I have seen too many first graders dutifully manufacture paper replicas of the hats the Pilgrims supposedly wore.

When done as part of social studies, visual arts activities should either help students acquire information or allow them to express what they have learned.

At the end of the chapter is an example of a project using the visual arts to increase students' understanding of 19th-century Native Americans living on the Great Plains.

Summary of Key Points

- There are four approaches for incorporating multicultural perspectives into the social studies curriculum: contributions, additive, transformation, and social action.

- There are three considerations for transforming social studies units of study: scope, geographic boundaries, and people.

- Children's books are an important resource for elementary school teachers—they present children with the perspectives of a wide variety of people.

- Oral history projects, while difficult to implement, allow children to appreciate significant events and to connect more personally to family and community history.

- It is important to incorporate the personal experiences of your students into the social studies curriculum.

- To adapt a traditional unit of study to make it more multicultural, a teacher should expand the resources used in the unit, provide more than one perspective on historical events, include a wide range of biographies, and reveal a wider range of events.

- The social studies curriculum should provide many opportunities for students to develop as speakers and listeners through the performing arts and the visual arts in elementary social studies.

- It is essential that students learn the process of civil discourse—to listen and talk in a polite, respectful manner.

- Performing arts activities include role play, readers' theater, plays, and pageants.

- Of all the forms of the visual arts, murals, dioramas, and collages have been popular choices for social studies projects.

Lesson Plans and Instructional Activities

This chapter concludes with lesson plans and group projects that are good examples of a transformed curriculum—a curriculum that is multicultural and integrated: (a) a lesson plan for fifth graders using the narratives of enslaved people found in *To Be A Slave* (Lester, 1968); (b) an oral history project for a third-grade classroom on the history of their elementary school; and (c) a description of a group project completed by fifth graders—a picture history depicting the events in Paul Goble's picture book *Lone Bull's Horse Raid*.

Lesson Plan
Grade Five: From *To Be a Slave*

Overview: This lesson is a part of a fifth-grade unit on the southern colonies and uses a book, *To Be a Slave,* to identify first-person accounts of life as a slave. Working with a modification of Jigsaw (a cooperative learning structure discussed in Chapter 6), all 30 students will take part in reading and responding to narratives dictated by enslaved people in the 19th century.

Resources and Materials: (a) Copy of *To Be a Slave;* (b) copies of the following narratives: (1) Moses Grandy (p. 43), (2) Anonymous (pp. 44–45), (3) Josiah Henson (pp. 48–49), (4) Charles Ball (p. 54), (5) Sis Shackelford (p. 56); (c) timeline for the unit; (d) map of the United States in 1859. Note: This lesson can be done with any collection of narratives from enslaved people. For example, portions of Charles Ball's narrative are included in a Website called "Excerpts from Slave Narratives." (http://xroads.virginia.edu/~hyper/wpa/wpahome.html).

Standard: From the *National Standards for History,* grades 5 to 12, Era 4 (Expansion and Reform, 1801–1861), Standard 2d: "The student understands the rapid growth of the 'peculiar institution' after 1800 and the varied experiences of African Americans under slavery. Therefore, the student is able to describe the plantation system and the roles of their owners, their families, hired white workers, and the enslaved African Americans" (National Center for History in the Schools, 1996, p. 95).

Content Objectives: Students will understand the history and economics of slavery. They should reach the generalization that African American slaves in the United States were bought and sold like other "goods." Facts presented in the lesson will include that (a) slaves were transported from Africa in inhuman conditions; (b) slaves were bought and sold without regard to the status of other members of their families; (c) some slaves were sold privately, from neighbor to neighbor; (d) many slaves were auctioned; and (e) slaveholders would give extra food to slaves about to be auctioned.

Process Objectives: Students will (a) *listen* to their teacher read the background information, (b) work in groups to *analyze* one of the slave narratives, (c) *answer* three questions about the narrative, and (d) *compare and contrast* their answers with those of groups that analyzed different narratives. A member of each group will report to the whole group.

Values Objectives: Your students should believe all people have fundamental human rights, such as liberty. In this lesson, they will learn more about a period in U.S. history when human rights were denied to enslaved African Americans.

Teaching Sequence:

1. Be sure all teaching resources are in place. You will need six copies of each of the five narratives.

2. A few days before the lesson, select one child from each group to be a "reader." The reader will read the narrative to the rest of the group. The readers should have 2 or 3 days to rehearse their oral reading. If you prefer, you can have your readers record their readings of the narratives on audiotape.

3. Start the lesson by referring to the timeline and the map. This lesson should be preceded by others on (a) the cultures of West African tribal groups, and (b) the "middle passage" from Africa to colonial America. Subsequent lessons would cover the working and living conditions of enslaved people in the American South.

4. Tell the class that today they will learn about how slaves were bought and sold. Read to the whole class Lester's explanatory comments from Chapter 2. It is not necessary to read all his commentary, but be sure to include the text on pages 39, 40, 43, 44, and 46. Some of the slave narratives include the defamatory "n" word. Discuss the historical context of this word and emphasize that it is insulting and should never be used today. You might also check to see if your school district has a policy in place regarding the use of that and other inflammatory words.

5. Write the following questions on the chalkboard:
   1. Who dictated the narrative you read? Was the slave a man or a woman, a grown-up or a child?
   2. In your narrative, what happened to the slaves?
   3. If a slave master is mentioned in your narrative, what did he or she do?

   Explain that each group is to answer these three questions for the narrative they have read. Distribute the copies of the narratives to the group. Allow time for the readers to read the narratives to other members of their groups. Then have each group select a reporter to share their answers with the class.

6. For each of the five narratives, first have the reader read the narrative to the whole class, then have the reporter share the group's answers to the three questions.

Evaluation: Take notes as you circulate among the groups, recording the names of students who do a good job of answering the questions. Takes notes as well on the oral reading performance of each of the readers. This type of anecdotal record keeping will provide useful information if you gather data on an ongoing basis over the course of the year.

Effective Teaching in Today's Diverse Classroom: Small-group work is essential in a diverse classroom. Research shows that regular experiences in cooperative learning improve intercultural relations. Students from different cultural groups will get along better if they work together to accomplish common goals (see Chapter 6 for a review of the research). One other note: If the class were homogeneous in reading ability, you could have each student read the narratives on his or her own rather than using a group reader. On the other hand, the use of a "reader," who has practiced reading the narrative aloud in advance, will be of great assistance to children with mild learning disabilities. It is an example of *adapting instructional materials*. This allows students to access the narratives not just by reading, but through the auditory modality as well.

Group Project
Grade Three: An Oral History Project— The History of Our School

Project Description: A third-grade teacher decided to have her class write a history of their school, Theodore Roosevelt Elementary School. The children used old photographs, school records, and newspaper articles as sources, but they needed more information. Oral history seemed essential to provide a more complete story. The class made a list of people who might provide oral histories. When two children showed the list to the principal, she steered them toward specific people with whom they would want to talk. (Note: I have left the dates the same as in the first edition of this book—published in 2000. Alas, some of the people listed in the interview roster might not be with us today!) The roster of interviewees included the following:

- The superintendent of schools at the time the school was built (1965). Although in his 80s, the superintendent still lived in the community.

- Three teachers who were on the first faculty. These teachers could share the memories of the first year of Roosevelt School.

- One teacher who had taught at the school from 1970 to 1992. Her longevity would make her an important source for "longitudinal" data on changes over time at the school.

- A school board member at the time the school was built. In his 80s, he would be a valuable source because there was a heated debate over the naming of the school. One faction wanted to name the school after a former mayor who had just died, and another faction wanted to name the school after a famous baseball player who had grown up in the community. Roosevelt was chosen as a compromise.

- Two principals in the school district, one at a junior high and the other at the local high school. Both had gone to Roosevelt School as children and could offer a "child's-eye view" of Roosevelt in previous decades.

- A member of the school board and her brother, the city attorney. These two prominent members of the community were among the first African American students to attend Roosevelt in 1974.

- A group of current sixth graders. These students at Roosevelt could provide information on the more recent history of the school.

- Five current faculty members, each of whom had taught at the school for at least 10 years. Like the sixth graders, members of the current faculty could comment on recent events at the school, and the interviews would be easy to arrange.

Project Activities

1. The children developed questions for the interviews. Each person was asked a very broad opening question: "What is the first thing that comes to your mind about Roosevelt Elementary School?" Then more specific questions were written for each interviewee.

2. The interviews were scheduled. Some of the interviews took place outside school. These had to be approved by the principal, and each student was accompanied by a parent.

3. The interviews revealed fascinating details. For example, the African American students and the teachers who were at the school at the time remembered both acts of kindness and resentment when the African American students first attended. The superintendent told of how difficult it was to decide on the design of the school. The teacher who taught at Roosevelt commented on how different the students have dressed over the years.

4. In addition to personal interviews, some children researched old newspaper articles that provided more specific historical details. School records revealed the number of students who had attended the school at various times and the number of classrooms.

5. The children gathered all this information and wrote a book about their school, illustrated with copies of old photographs. The oral histories brought the book to life through the stories people told.

Effective Teaching in Today's Diverse Classroom: This project is a good example of a transformed social studies curriculum. In learning about their school, the students learned a great deal about the social history of their city and our nation, and they learned it by listening to voices that would never be included in a textbook. Although some members of the community would have preferred to ignore the racism that greeted the first African American residents of this city, the book written by this group of students tackled the issue head on.

This would be a difficult project for children with mild learning disabilities. It would help them if the interviews were conducted by a small group of students.

Redesigning tasks that might otherwise be completed individually so they are completed in *small groups* is an important strategy to help students with challenging conditions. The children would definitely need to tape record the interview, and children with disabilities might well need to listen to the interview more than once. Then, the members of the group can work together to analyze the results.

Group Project
Grade Five: A Picture History of *Lone Bull's Horse Raid*

A fifth-grade class was studying Native Americans prior to the coming of the Europeans. They would learn about five tribes. The class had many English learners and others who found it difficult to read grade-level material. While the class was learning about the Sioux, the teacher asked for volunteers who wanted to complete a project that would "require a lot of artwork." This group of students read Goble and Goble's (1973) picture book *Lone Bull's Horse Raid.* The story is told from 14-year-old Lone Bull's perspective. Lone Bull is an Oglala Sioux who steals horses from the Crow. A day-by-day plan for the project follows:

Day 1

After discussing the book, explain the idea of a "picture history." Describe how the Natives of the Great Plains used picture histories, painted on their tipis or on buffalo robes, to record significant events. You can find good illustrations of picture histories painted on buffalo robes on the Website of the Glenbow Museum in Calgary, Canada (www.glenbow.org). You also might share illustrations of Grecian urns and Roman columns, cross-cultural examples of other forms of picture histories. Help the group make a list of the scenes from the book to illustrate (e.g., Lone Bull and his friend, Charging Bear, riding with Lone Bull's father; stalking the Crow camp; stealing the horses; fighting the Crow; and giving away the stolen horses).

Day 2

Have the group decide who will illustrate each scene. Students may work together or individually. Decide on a form for the picture history. If you are ambitious, you could construct a model tipi 4 to 5 feet high. Edwin Tunis's (1979) book *Indians* has a good set of directions on pages 90 to 94. If you decide to make a tipi, the scenes should be painted on the outside of the tipi. A simple picture history could be painted on a strip of paper approximately 2×6 square feet. Students should complete a sketch of their scenes.

Days 3 and 4

Bring several copies of Paul Goble's other books to class for group members to examine. They should try to use the same colors and style as Goble. If you can find books with photographs of decorated tipis, by all means bring them to class. Each scene should be blocked out so each artist knows the space she or he has. If you are making a tipi, the scenes from the book should be painted before the tipi is assembled.

Days 5 to 8

Once the art is done, have group members decide whether they want to tell or read the story to their classmates. The picture history, rather than the book's illustrations, should be used during the performance. Be sure the group has plenty of time to rehearse.

 Effective Teaching in Today's Diverse Classroom: As I noted in Chapter 4, it is important that we help our students develop accurate knowledge about Native Americans rather than reinforce stereotypical images. This lesson supports the stereotype that all Indians lived in tipis, committed acts European Americans considered criminal, and thrived on violence. Fortunately, this lesson was part of an in-depth study of Native Americans, with separate units of study on diverse tribes. Goble's books are historically and culturally accurate and are excellent teaching resources. The lesson is ideal for a diverse classroom because it allows students to express what they know through both the visual and performing arts.

CHAPTER 6

Cooperative Learning

In this chapter, you will read about

- The fundamental reasons cooperative learning is a powerful instructional tool for teaching social studies

- Several cooperative learning structures, including Group Projects, Jigsaw, Think–Pair–Share, Three-Step Interview, and Student Teams–Achievement Divisions (STAD)

- Factors affecting the success of cooperative group learning; the development of group goals, individual accountability, social skills, and effective planning

- Decisions teachers make to organize cooperative groups; how to place students in groups, when to use ability and interclass grouping, how long members of groups should work together, and when to change group dynamics

This was the last day of Rosa Navarro's third-grade social studies unit on boats. For 13 days, the children had participated in a variety of activities. The third-grade teachers at Ms. Navarro's school chose transportation as an organizing theme for the first half of the school year—the second half would be devoted to the history of their community. After the unit on boats, Ms. Navarro planned on teaching a unit on airplanes. Today, the final lesson on boats would be a "segue" activity, one that led the class to the unit on airplanes. This simple activity would use a cooperative learning structure called *Think–Pair–Share.*

On a sheet of chart paper, Ms. Navarro had written the following questions:

- How are boats and airplanes alike?
- How are they different?

In the first phase of the activity, she asked the children to think quietly about each question. She encouraged them to write down any answers they had to either question. She then asked the children to sit next to their "buddies." Ms. Navarro assigned each child a different buddy each week so that, during the year, every child in the room would get a chance to work with every other child. After each set of buddies was "paired up" and ready to share their answers, Ms. Navarro asked one member of each duo to give an answer and then the other. She allowed time for partners to chat casually about the similarities and differences of their responses. Finally, Ms. Navarro called the class back to their seats. It was time to share responses with the whole class. Tiffany and Maria volunteered to go first. Tiffany stated they made a list of the many ways boats and airplanes were alike ("They carry people around," "They go faster than walking," "They come in many sizes"). Roger noted two differences: Boats only travel on water, but airplanes travel in the air, and the fastest airplanes were "a lot faster than the fastest boats." The sharing continued for another 10 minutes.

This was a good social studies activity for two reasons. First, it accomplished the goal of forming a bridge from one unit of study to another as Ms. Navarro's class started thinking about the content of their next unit—airplanes. Second, every child in the room had the opportunity to express his or her ideas. In most class discussions, only a few children talk; most children spend their time listening. In Think–Pair–Share, all 28 children in the room had an opportunity to express their perspectives.

■ ■ ■

Introduction to Cooperative Learning

Collaboration and cooperation among students have been essential parts of social studies for more than 100 years. During the Progressive era (about 1890–1940), students in elementary schools frequently worked on projects with their classmates. One of the greatest Progressive thinkers, William H. Kilpatrick (1918, 1925), proposed that social studies consist almost entirely of students working on projects they selected and planned. Although students could work on projects individually, Kilpatrick encouraged group work. His three characteristics of a successful project are worth remembering in the broader context of cooperative learning: Children should be involved in "purposeful activity" conducted in a "hearty fashion" in a "social surrounding" (1918, p. 321). There has long been a broad consensus that group work is essential in elementary classrooms, especially in social studies (Gillies, 2007; Stahl, Van Sickle, & Stahl, 2009; Sunal & Ridgway, 2007). An important focus in this chapter will be on instructional formats, or structures, for group work developed by Spencer Kagan, Robert Slavin, David Johnson, and Roger Johnson.

Let's look at two definitions of cooperative learning consistent with these structures:

It involves students working together as equals to accomplish something of importance to all of them. (Slavin, 1990, p. 34)

Cooperative learning means instructionally using small groups so students work together to maximize their own and each other's learning. (Johnson & Johnson, 1992, p. 45)

Spencer Kagan (1989–1990, 1997) has written about several cooperative learning *structures*. These structures are "content-free ways of organizing social interaction in the classroom" (1989–1990, p. 12). Kagan distinguishes cooperative "structures" and "activities":

> Teachers can design many excellent cooperative *activities,* such as making a team mural or a quilt . . . In contrast *structures* may be used repeatedly with almost any subject matter, at a wide range of grade levels, and at various points in a lesson plan. (1989–1990, p. 12)

Robert Slavin (1990) prefers to call these structures "systematic and practical cooperative learning methods" (p. 21). I refer to them as either "models" or "structures" and describe five models of cooperative learning. First, though, let's take a look at the research supporting the use of cooperative learning.

An Overview of the Research and Descriptions of Cooperative Learning Structures

Research on cooperative learning shows it can have positive results (Johnson & Johnson, 1998; Johnson & F. P. Johnson, 2005; Johnson, Maruyama, Johnson, Nelson, & Skon, 1981; Slavin, 1980, 1994a). Cooperative learning can boost student achievement, but we must keep two things in mind. First, almost all the studies have focused on learning basic skills in reading and mathematics. Second, to be effective, cooperative learning must involve *group goals* and *individual accountability* (Slavin, 1992). Group goals exist when students work toward some reward for their group. Individual accountability means each member of the group must demonstrate what she or he has accomplished. After reviewing 46 studies, Qin, Johnson, and Johnson (1995) concluded that cooperative effort produces higher-quality problem solving than does individual effort. This is an important finding because problem solving is an essential part of social studies. When confronted with a problem, students working in groups are able to exchange information, share insights, and compare the worth of various solutions.

Unfortunately, virtually none of the best research on cooperative learning has looked at elementary social studies (Slavin, 1989–1990, 1994a). It seems safe to say that on the basis of research on cooperative learning in other areas of the curriculum and with older students, cooperative learning should be a part of our social studies program. Remember, too, the social studies curriculum is concerned with more than content. We also teach processes and values. A good K–6 social studies program emphasizes social processes, which include working cooperatively toward a common goal.

A classroom of diverse students should have many opportunities for cooperative learning because research shows the use of cooperative learning improves intergroup relations. Cooperative learning helps students of different cultural groups respect each other. It promotes positive feelings toward students with disabilities. Slavin (1989–1990) summarized the results of several studies:

> When students of different racial or ethnic backgrounds work together toward a common goal, they gain in liking and respect for one another. Cooperative learning also improves the social acceptance of mainstreamed academically handicapped students by their classmates . . . as well as increasing friendships among students in general. (pp. 53–54)

In addition to the research base, a theoretical argument can be made for using cooperative learning. Our common sense would tell us "two heads are better than one." Interaction with other people exposes us to different perspectives and helps clarify what we know. A compelling theoretical argument for cooperative learning was presented by the Russian psychologist Lev Vygotsky. He believed a gap exists between what children can learn and do independently and what they *could* learn and do if they had help. This assistance could be collaboration with an adult or peers—Vygotsky considered the best situation to be one where a child works with more capable peers. Vygotsky's ideas place great emphasis on the social aspects of learning. Fifty years before cooperative learning became part of the conventional wisdom, Vygotsky had already explained why it helps children learn (Vygotsky, 1962).

As with any instructional technique or resource, moderation in cooperative learning seems to be a reasonable attitude. Teachers would make a mistake if they *never* used cooperative learning, and they would make a mistake if they used *only* it and excluded whole-group and individual activity. Let's take a look at five cooperative learning structures particularly well suited for social studies teaching—a sixth structure, Group Investigation, is one of the models of inquiry presented in Chapter 7.

Group Projects

In the Group Projects cooperative learning structure, two or more students work together to produce something. In social studies, Group Projects fall into five categories:

1. *Inquiry projects,* in which students work together to solve a problem—they "produce" an answer

2. *Written projects,* in which students work together to produce a written product, like a book or a script

3. *Visual arts projects,* in which students work together as they paint, draw, sculpt, or use computer-based resources to produce a work of art

4. *Performing arts projects,* in which students work together to act, dance, or sing in a live or recorded performance

5. *"Combination" projects,* in which students are asked to use more than one format (e.g., some projects require students to do things in both the visual and the performing arts and to write something)

Increasingly, the product(s) developed by students in a group project make use of computers and are stored digitally. For example, Waring, Santana, and Robinson (2009) described a fifth-grade project that produced digital biographies of less-well-known Americans who were active during the American Revolution of 1775–1781. The students used Microsoft Movie Maker to create slide shows with still visual images and narration the students had written. Hines (2008) described a project in which her third and fourth graders produced a newspaper with stories about the first wave of the Great Black Migration from the South to the North in the United States between 1916 and 1930. The newspaper was created on computers as students used Pages, part of Apple Computer's iWorks software.

Group Projects work best if students volunteer to participate. Once students volunteer, these become "interest" groups because the members have expressed an interest in the project. Sometimes, though, teachers assign students to work on a project. A teacher might want to create a group that is heterogeneous and has a mixture of genders, ability levels, and ethnicities. Or, a teacher might decide some students need to participate in a project because they have not previously chosen to do so. Some students, for example, never choose to participate in a performing arts project unless it is a requirement.

The big issue in planning a Group Project is what role each student will play in the common task of finishing the project. In some cases, the students themselves will decide what each member of the group will do. In others, the teacher will assign the tasks. On some projects, students work together throughout the project, whereas on others, group members complete tasks individually, and their efforts are reassembled at some later point.

Here is an outline of the steps in a Group Project in the social studies. They are written from the teacher's point of view, but notice how, in each step, student autonomy can be increased:

1. *Form the group.*   For greater student autonomy, teachers should ask for volunteers.

2. *Provide an overview of the project.*   In some situations, students themselves will define precisely what they will produce. In every case, teachers should listen to the interests, ideas, and needs of the group members and make adjustments accordingly.

3. *Decide what each student will do.*   In performing arts projects, this means assigning roles. In writing projects, it means listing what will be written and by whom. If the teacher wishes to increase the level of student control over the project, the teacher should allow students to decide what roles they will play.

4. *Make a list of materials and resources.*   All materials and resources should be available when they are needed.

5. *Establish a timetable.*   The timetable for completing the project should include times when the entire group will meet again. In some projects, it may be best to let members of the student group establish the timetable.

6. *Work with individuals, subgroups, and the full group.*   Teachers should have a schedule indicating when guidance and assistance will be provided to members of the group. To increase student autonomy, they should be encouraged to help each other before they turn to the teachers.

At the end of the chapter is a description of a Group Project that produced a chronological mural.

Student Teams–Achievement Divisions (STAD)

Robert Slavin (1989–1990, 1994a) has been an effective advocate of cooperative learning. He and his colleagues at Johns Hopkins University developed several cooperative learning structures. One of the most popular is Student Teams–Achievement Divisions (STAD; Slavin, 1978, 1994b). According to Slavin, STAD is "most appropriate for teaching well-defined objectives with single right answers, such as specific locational characteristics in geography and some map skills, knowledge of events in history, and principles of economics or government" (1992, p. 21). Thus, STAD should be limited to teaching students basic information; it is not a method of teaching but an *alternative* to independent seat work during which, at the conclusion of a lesson, students work alone on follow-up assignments.

The teacher places students in four-member heterogeneous teams that are a cross section of the whole class—boys and girls, a mix of ethnicities, and high-achieving, mid-achieving, and low-achieving students. The teacher presents a lesson or group of lessons to the whole group, and then the students work together to learn the material. This "team study" may take from a half hour to several days. Slavin recommends the teacher prepare worksheets for the students to complete together. STAD works only if all members of the team accept it is their responsibility to help their teammates learn all the presented material. The teacher then gives a quiz students take individually. The teacher compares each student's quiz score with that student's performance on earlier social studies quizzes and gives each student a score reflecting if, and how much, that student exceeded her or his average previous performance. The four scores for each team are added to create a team score, and the teams with the highest scores are given points, certificates, or some other reward. Following are some examples of instructional objectives lending themselves to units using STAD:

- *Grade 2.*   Explain what role each of the following plays in keeping our community safe: firefighters, police officers, public health inspectors, public works crews, school crossing guards.

- *Grade 3.*   Identify the following places on a map of our city: Miller Elementary School, City Hall, Olive Park, Verdugo Park, McCambridge Park, St. Joseph's Medical Center, Bob Hope Airport, Media City Mall, NBC Studios, Warner Brothers Studios, Golden State Freeway, Ventura Freeway.

- *Grade 5.*   List and describe three examples of "checks and balances" in the U.S. Constitution.

- *Grade 6.*   Compare and contrast the Aztec and Inca systems of government, economic production and distribution, religion, and social organization.

Jigsaw

Jigsaw was developed by Elliott Aronson and his colleagues (Aronson, Blaney, Stephen, Sikes, & Knapp, 1978). Here is how it works: The teacher places students in six-member groups, also called "home teams"; so a class of 30 students would have five home teams. The teacher then breaks down a topic or unit into six subtopics. For example, if a class of students is to do a unit titled "City Workers," the six subtopics might be (a) police officers, (b) firefighters, (c) recreation leaders, (d) sanitation workers, (e) librarians, and (f) animal control officers. Each member of a home team is assigned a subtopic and is expected to become an expert on that subtopic.

Students then learn about their subtopics. Aronson describes Jigsaws in which students would be able to read a section of a text to find out what they needed to know. I think Jigsaw works well when students learn from a variety of sources, including videos, computer-based resources, audiotapes, and lessons taught by the teacher. Once students learn information about their topics, they meet in "expert teams." For example, the six students who all had learned about firefighters would meet together, the six who had learned about recreation leaders would meet, and so on. In these expert team meetings, students can compare what they found out and decide on how they wish to present what they learned to the other members of their home team. Students then return to their home teams. Each student is an expert who has information to share. The students take turns teaching the other members of their home teams all they have learned.

Landorf and Lowenstein (2004) provided an excellent example of how Jigsaw can be used in an elementary school classroom. They described how a third-grade teacher in Florida, Jennifer Morrow, used Jigsaw to help her students investigate the "Rosa Parks Myth." Ms. Morrow followed a classic Jigsaw design, with five home teams. Each member of each home team was assigned to one of five expert teams. Each expert team, with one member from each home team, examined a different children's book about Rosa Parks. Ms. Morrow strictly defined the roles of the members of the expert teams. Each group had a *facilitator,* who made sure each person had a chance to speak; a *scribe,* who recorded the conclusions of the team; a *manager,* who kept the team members on task; a *conductor,* who kept track of time; and a *communicator,* who talked to the teacher if the team had questions.

Think–Pair–Share

Think–Pair–Share is a simple cooperative learning structure that works well in social studies (Lyman, 1992; Lyman, Foyle, & Azwell, 1993). Think–Pair–Share greatly increases the number of students who actually say something during a class discussion. If a teacher leads a discussion in front of the whole class, few students actually make contributions. Rarely does more than a quarter of the class do anything but listen; it is not unusual for three or four students to dominate. In Think–Pair–Share, every student in the class will have an opportunity to express her or his perspective. This cooperative learning structure has three phases:

1. *Think.*   The teacher poses a question that should stimulate a discussion. The question cannot be too difficult or too simple. If the question is too difficult, students will have nothing to say. If the question is too simple, all that can be said will be over quickly. I think the question should be written either on the chalkboard or on a sheet of chart paper. All students think about possible answers. Depending on the complexity of the question, the teacher might want students to write their answers on paper. For a third-grade unit on the future of their city, a teacher could ask her students to answer any of the following questions through Think–Pair–Share:

   - What challenges would our city face if its population increased significantly in the next 20 years?
   - Which of the city's businesses will grow in the next 20 years? Which of the city's businesses might have a difficult time?

■ What will the schools in our city be like in the next 20 years? How might they be different from the way they are today?

2. *Pair.* Each student then works with a partner. The partners explain the rationale that led to their answers. During this phase, each student in the class will have an opportunity to talk.

3. *Share.* Now the whole class reconvenes. The floor is open; students may share their answers with their classmates. If partners have arrived at a shared answer, then each partner may talk a bit about how the duo arrived at their answer.

Three-Step Interview

Like Think–Pair–Share, Three-Step Interview is a cooperative learning structure that maximizes student participation (Kagan, 1989–1990, 1997). Three-Step Interview is simple and can be used repeatedly during a social studies unit:

1. During the first step, the teacher asks a question (or questions). Again, the questions should be written on the board or chart paper, and should be thought provoking. The class then separates into groups of four. Within each group, each student works with a partner. One partner is the interviewer, the other the interviewee. For example, Ahmed, Ashah, Keiko, and Hideo are the members of a group. During this first step, Ahmed asks Ashah questions; Keiko asks Hideo to give his answers to the questions.

2. In the second step, students reverse roles. This time, Ashah interviews Ahmed while Hideo interviews Keiko. The Three-Step Interview works best when students learn how to ask follow-up questions, much like a good newspaper reporter: "Why do you think that is the answer?" "What makes you think that?" Follow-up questions should be asked with respect, but they can be challenging: "Are you sure? What about _____ (some fact or idea the interviewee had not considered)?"

3. In the third and final step, the group of four reconvenes. In round-robin fashion, each student shares her or his answer.

Making Cooperative Learning Work

Four features must be present for cooperative learning to be effective: (a) group goals, (b) individual accountability, (c) social skills, and (d) effective planning.

Group Goals

As Johnson and Johnson (1992) note, "Students must believe they sink or swim together" (p. 47). The Johnsons call this *positive interdependence.* The group must have a clear sense of what they are supposed to accomplish, and this goal must be shared and understood by all members of the group. Sometimes the group goal is simple. For example, in Think–Pair–Share, the partners have the goal of listening to each other and exchanging ideas. In a Group Project, the goal is to produce something. The Johnsons and Slavin believe there must be tangible rewards for groups that accomplish their goals. I am not sure. I have seen many groups work together beautifully, with their only reward being their joy in creating something they were proud of. Tangible rewards include points that can be redeemed for rewards or recognition certificates. I have seen rewards as different as popsicles and the opportunity to be first in line for lunch. If tangible rewards are given, they must be given to each member of the group.

Individual Accountability

As Johnson and Johnson (1992) explain, "Students learn together so they can subsequently perform better as individuals. To ensure each member is strengthened, teachers hold students individually accountable to do their share of the work" (p. 48). It is essential that each student's performance be evaluated. This does not necessarily mean assigning a score or grade to each student. It does mean keeping some sort of record describing two things: (a) the student's performance in the process of working in a group, and (b) the student's level of achievement in the *product* the group created. I described ways of keeping evaluative records in Chapter 3, including an example from the chronological mural project described at the end of this chapter.

Social Skills

Johnson and Johnson (1989–1990, Johnson & F. P. Johnson, 2005) have discussed at great length the social skills students must master to be successful in cooperative learning. Students must "get to know and trust one another, communicate accurately and unambiguously, accept and support one another, and resolve conflicts constructively" (1989–1990, p. 30). Here are the four steps in teaching these social skills:

1. *Students must see the need for the skill.*   For example, we can explain to our students how resolving conflicts quickly and fairly will help a group finish its assignment.

2. *Students must understand the skill.*   Unfortunately, this book does not have enough space to fully describe the social skills of trust, communication, support, and resolution. I recommend the books the Johnsons and their colleagues have written (Johnson & Johnson, 1998; Johnson & F. P. Johnson, 2005; Johnson, Johnson, & Holubec, 1994). One simple method is to describe the words used in the social skill. For example, to support the other members of their group, students can say things such as, "That looks great!" "Tell me more about where you found that out," "Let's be sure that idea is in our report," and "I haven't thought about that; thanks for bringing it up."

3. *Students must have many opportunities to practice these social skills.*   Students must have frequent chances to work in groups, and teachers must monitor and support those students who work well together.

4. *Students must evaluate how well they are doing.*   The Johnsons call this *group processing.* The group needs to talk about their successes and frustrations. Rather than focus on individual behavior, the group processing should bring clarity to the behaviors that make group work easy and pleasant.

Effective Planning

Some cooperative learning structures require minimal planning (Think–Pair–Share, Three-Step Interview). Other structures will work only if they have been thoroughly planned (Jigsaw, Group Project, Group Investigation, and STAD). For all cooperative activities, each of the following must be accomplished:

- *Be sure the goal is clear.*   If a group is to perform a play, the members of the group must know what the play will look like when it is performed. Will costumes be worn? How long will the play be? Where will the performances take place?

- *Be sure the goal is attainable.*   That is, given the best of circumstances, will the group achieve the goal? If a group is given a task beyond their level of ability, expect lots of problems.

- *Be sure that roles are clearly and reasonably defined.*   Students must know what they are expected to do. If some students have to do a great deal of work and others little, this must be decided at the beginning of the activity and accepted by the members of the group.

- *Be sure the group has adequate materials and resources to finish their task.*   Nothing will stop a group from being effective faster than a lack of books, paper, maps, or other essential resources.

- *Be sure that timelines are set and members of the group adhere to them.*   This requires the teacher to regularly monitor the group's performance.

Other Issues in Grouping

What Is the Proper Place of Cooperative Learning in Social Studies?

In their overview of cooperative learning in social studies, Stahl and VanSickle (1992) state "cooperative learning strategies should not replace all other teaching strategies in the social studies classroom" (p. 4). Some activities will involve the whole class. Individual work has its place as children go about exploring topics of personal interest. Cooperative learning, however, helps make social studies social. It provides children with the opportunity to "learn and practice the knowledge, abilities, and attitudes necessary to function effectively within the social group and as part of the social community" (p. 4).

What Criteria Should Be Used to Place Students in Groups?

Most groups should be formed on the basis of either *interest* or *proximity*. Group Projects and Group Investigations work best when students volunteer to take part. Thus, the basis for forming the group is interest in the topic or project. Simple cooperative learning structures, like Think–Pair–Share, lend themselves to proximity grouping; students work with

John Paul Endress/Silver Burdett Ginn

For over 100 years, groups of elementary school students have worked together on social studies projects. One member of a group puts the final touches on a mural.

whomever is seated near them. Almost all groups should be *heterogeneous:* Each group should be a microcosm of the class, with boys and girls from all ethnic groups. Each group should have students at a range of abilities. This is not to say that occasionally a group of girls (or boys) might be the only volunteers for a project. The point is that if segregation gets to be a pattern, the teacher should intervene and modify the composition of the group. For some cooperative learning structures, like Three-Step Interview, Jigsaw, and STAD, the teacher will assign students to groups.

Ability Grouping. The National Council for the Social Studies (NCSS) has issued a policy statement on ability grouping (NCSS Ad Hoc Committee on Ability Grouping, 1992). *Ability grouping* is the practice of placing students in groups on the basis of their level of academic achievement. It tends to happen more in elementary language arts and mathematics than in social studies. The research on ability grouping is voluminous and contradictory (Kerckhoff, 1986; Lou et al., 1996; Oakes, 1985; Slavin, 1987, 1989–1990). Although grouping students by ability can work in some subject areas if done properly (mathematics and reading), educators agree students should not be placed in "permanent" ability-based groups. Ability grouping, unfortunately, often leads to the segregation of the least able, the challenged, the poor, and the linguistically different. Teachers should plan some activities during the year just for their most able or least able students, but for the most part they should design their social studies units so students work in several different groups and with classmates of every ability.

Interclass Grouping. Some schools use a form of interclass grouping for social studies, although this is more prevalent in language arts and mathematics. In a *departmentalized* elementary school, a fifth-grade teacher might teach three 2-hour social studies/language arts blocks each day. Other teachers would teach a mathematics/science block and the arts/PE block.

Team teaching has many forms. For example, two third-grade teachers may decide to rotate their students each day from 12:45 to 3:05 P.M. From 12:45 to 1:50 P.M., Teacher A teaches social studies while Teacher B teaches art. Then students change rooms, and from 2:00 to 3:05 P.M., Teacher A repeats her social studies lesson, and Teacher B repeats her art lesson. In a purer form of team teaching, three second-grade teachers may work together and share responsibility for the 90 second graders in their school. Together, they plan the week's activities for all the second graders. At different times during the year, each teacher would take the lead in planning a social studies unit. The other teachers would play a supporting role, helping fulfill the planning teacher's ideas.

How Long Should Students Stay in a Group?

The amount of time students should spend working in the same group varies. For some models of team learning, the teams should be kept together for several months (Vermette, 1998). Most other groups, however, will not exist for that long. Most groups should be ad hoc; they should exist until they achieve their goal, which may take from a few minutes to 4 or 5 weeks. A Group Project, for example, may take a month to complete, whereas a Think–Pair–Share group activity may last only a few minutes. Ideally, each student in a class should work with every other student in that class in a cooperative group sometime during the school year.

Summary of Key Points

- Group work has a long history in social studies. For more than 100 years, elementary school children have worked together as part of social studies.

- Many cooperative learning structures are perfect for social studies activities. Structures are models for organizing group work.

- Research shows the use of cooperative learning improves intergroup relations.

- Cooperative learning structures include Group Projects, Jigsaw, Think–Pair–Share, Three-Step Interview, and Student Teams–Achievement Divisions.

- The following features increase the chances that cooperative learning experiences will be positive: group goals, individual accountability, social skills, and effective planning.

Lesson Plans and Instructional Activities

Group projects have long been an important part of elementary social studies. Here you will read about one that integrates social studies and the visual arts: a group project for third graders, a chronological mural, revealing 10 periods of time in the history of their community. I have left this project in its original form—as a classic, "hard-copy" mural of large images displayed on a bulletin board. A similar project involving images and descriptions, but displayed on a classroom Website, is described by Edwards and Malloy (2007). In their local history project, second and third graders used a digital camera to take photographs of local history sites —the photos and accompanying written descriptions were then posted on the class Website.

Description of a Group Project
Grade Three: Chronological Mural

Al Braccio's third graders spent the second half of the school year studying their city. Now Mr. Braccio thought it might be worthwhile to have a group of children create a *chronological mural* of the history of their city. A chronological mural shows several scenes in the order in which they took place. Previously, I listed the six steps in completing a Group Project like this one.

Step 1: Form the Group

Mr. Braccio asked for volunteers. Privately, he encouraged his two English-language learners (Sara and Ben) and his two lowest-achieving students (Cliff and Dan) to take part. All four said they would like to work on the mural. Six other children volunteered. It was a diverse group in gender, ethnicity, and ability (the group included high-achieving students, too).

Step 2: Provide an Overview of the Project

The next day, Mr. Braccio met with the group. He showed the children photographs of a mural fifth graders had completed depicting scenes from U.S. history. Mr. Braccio told the group their mural would be similar and suggested eight possible scenes from their city's past:

- Morning at a Gabrielino village—the Gabrielino were the Native tribe that lived where their city now stood
- Mission San Fernando Rey de España—actually a few miles from their city but very important
- A wedding at the rancho that covered most of the land the city now occupied
- The house of the dentist, Dr. David Burbank, who founded the city
- The teacher and her students at the first public school

- Workers entering the Lockheed Aircraft plant, which was the city's largest employer
- Actors, camera operators, and a director making a movie, another of the city's important industries
- Airplanes at the city's regional airport, which opened for commercial passenger service in 1975

The group discussed these scenes. Someone suggested adding a drawing of city hall. The other children agreed; this was not surprising because the old city hall was one of the places the children visited on their field trip of the city. Mr. Braccio suggested they add some buildings damaged in the earthquake of 1994. All agreed this would be a dramatic addition to the mural.

The group decided that, for each of the 10 scenes, they would provide an illustration, title, and a brief caption. The illustrations would be on large sheets of construction paper. When finished, the illustrations would be stapled to a large bulletin board. For example, for the earthquake scene, the title was "1994: Earthquake!" The caption read, "On January 17, 1994, a big earthquake shook our city; 750 buildings were damaged, and 47 people were hurt."

Step 3: Decide What Each Student Will Do

When the group met again, Mr. Braccio made a chart identifying the 10 scenes in their mural. He suggested the group divide into five subgroups of two children each. Each pair would draw and describe two scenes. Mr. Braccio wanted to be sure Sara and Ben did not work together; he also wanted to separate Cliff and Dan. He made a list of the five subgroups and presented it to the group. Then each subgroup selected the scenes it would depict. Mr. Braccio made a chart showing the assignments:

Scene 1: A Gabrielino village—Sara, Debbie

Scene 2: Mission San Fernando—Ben, Denise

Scene 3: The rancho adobe—Sara, Debbie

Scene 4: The dentist's house—Brad, Claudia

Scene 5: The first school—Brad, Claudia

Scene 6: Old city hall—Cliff, Tina

Scene 7: Aircraft plant—Ben, Denise

Scene 8: Making a movie—Cliff, Tina

Scene 9: New airport—Dan, Amber

Scene 10: Earthquake—Dan, Amber

Step 4: Make a List of Materials and Resources

Mr. Braccio and the group decided they would need the following materials:

- Colored marking pens and crayons
- Large white construction paper (18 × 24 inches)

- Websites, including the site for the city of Burbank, California (www.ci.burbank.ca.us); the site for the Bob Hope Airport (www.burbankairport.com); and one for the San Fernando mission (www.californiamissions.com/cahistory/sanfernando.html)
- Study prints (large photo reproductions) of the history of their city
- 10 copies of the softcover social studies textbook on the history of their city, which included other photographs

Mr. Braccio had taken photographs while he and the class were on their field trip. He had good photographs of city hall, the mission, the dentist's house, the first school, the airport, the aircraft plant, and buildings damaged by the earthquake.

Step 5: Establish a Timetable

Mr. Braccio and the group met the next day to begin work. The 10 children agreed on the following timetable:

May 10: Pencil drawings finished for each scene

May 16: Final illustrations

May 17: Rough drafts for titles and captions completed

May 18: Titles and captions completed

May 19: Bulletin board "backed" with powder blue paper, title of mural stapled to board, illustrations and captions stapled to the board

Step 6: Work with Individuals, Subgroups, and the Full Group

This project was completed during the final social studies unit of the year, "Our City Today and Tomorrow." Of the 10 children who worked on the mural, only one set of partners had some problems communicating. Dan and Amber had some trouble working together; Dan wanted to draw both scenes, which gave Amber nothing to do but the captions. Mr. Braccio helped them resolve their differences by leading them to discuss their scenes and agree on the composition of each one. Then they were directed to draw and color both scenes together.

The students did a good job of adhering to the timetable, although one group fell behind because it had trouble getting started. Once Mr. Braccio helped these students "block out" their drawings, they moved along fine. After the mural was finished and displayed for all to see, each student was proud of what he or she had created.

Note: While these 10 students were working on the chronological mural, other students were engaged in different projects in groups or independently. One class group examined what the city might look like in the year 2100 and illustrated a book to share their ideas. Another group conducted a Group Investigation to determine why people might immigrate to their city.

Effective Teaching in Today's Diverse Classroom: Group Projects like this one, and all other forms of cooperative learning, will enrich the educational experiences of all children. Kagan's research shows how consistent use of cooperative learning can

improve intergroup relations. Cooperative learning has great appeal to students who thrive in instructional formats requiring social learning (see Chapter 4).

Cooperative learning is also essential for English learners. Children have the ability to provide comprehensible input to their classmates who are English learners. A student can often explain a difficult idea to a peer more easily, and with more clarity, than an adult can with that same person. Cooperative learning, if done properly, creates an environment free of anxiety because students relax when working with their classmates. Sometimes you will want your English learners to work together under your guidance (so it is easier for you to provide comprehensible input). Usually, though, you should disperse your English learners so they gain the benefits from working with their English-only classmates.

Inquiry and Critical Thinking

In this chapter, you will read about

- Social studies instruction created around inquiry-based activities

- A general teaching sequence for inquiry activities requiring teachers and students to assume roles different from those they traditionally play in social studies lessons

- The Group Investigation and Suchman inquiry models

- Factors enabling all students to participate successfully in fun and challenging inquiry activities

- *Critical thinking,* also referred to as *complex thinking* or *higher-order thinking*

- A taxonomy provided by the National Council for the Social Studies (NCSS) that can be a useful source to order the development of critical thinking skills

- Four instructional approaches to be used to teach critical thinking skills to elementary school children

- How to develop critical thinking through the examination and analysis of auditory media, visual media, or realia (real objects)

Let me begin this chapter with a memory from my own teaching experience. An important part of the fourth-grade curriculum in Burbank, California, was the study of California history. Each year, my fourth graders viewed a filmstrip on the California missions, which were built under the direction of Franciscan missionaries between 1769 and 1823. I remember this filmstrip because it featured excellent photographs of the missions. Today, of course, filmstrips have been replaced by computer-based delivery systems. I preferred showing filmstrips without their accompanying narration so the class and I could linger on interesting images and discuss them.

In the middle of this filmstrip was an old drawing of a group of Natives attacking a mission clergyman (padre). The padre was bound with ropes, and the Natives were beating him with clubs. In previous years, when my classes viewed the same filmstrip, this image did not generate any interest. This time, Susan raised her hand and asked, "Mr. Zarrillo, did that really happen? I don't think anybody would attack a priest." Instead of answering the question, which would have been impossible because I did not know the answer, I decided the question would make an excellent inquiry. It would also be a wonderful opportunity to challenge the students to think critically. I responded by saying I did not know the answer but that a small group of students could work with me to find one. We worked for a month to answer Susan's question. It was an exciting and challenging experience for the students who participated. This inquiry project provided all the students in my class with a better understanding of how California's Natives suffered during the mission era. In this chapter, I describe how to design inquiry activities and how to develop critical thinking . . . and you will learn more about how my students found an answer to Susan's question.

■ ■ ■

Inquiry: An Overview

This chapter describes how to plan inquiry activities and how to help students engage in critical thinking. First, let us look at inquiry. *Inquiry* is a process that begins when a problem is identified either by students or by the teacher. Students then consider the problem, offer possible solutions in the form of hypotheses, gather information, and determine whether a hypothesis is a reasonable solution to the problem. Finally, the initial hypothesis is accepted, revised, or rejected in favor of a different solution (Barell, 2006, 2007; Massialas & Cox, 1966; Wilen & White, 1991). Some social studies educators use the term *problem solving* to describe the inquiry process. The goal of inquiry activities is to help students acquire the ability to resolve problems in a rational and systematic fashion.

Inquiry, or problem solving, has a long history in elementary social studies. John Dewey, as you will recall from Chapter 1, was the greatest thinker of the Progressive era of American education, which began in the late 1800s. Dewey (1933) used the term *reflective thinking* to describe the type of inquiry-based activity he thought should be at the center of Progressive schools. To Dewey, an activity requiring reflective thinking presented children with "a forked-road situation, a situation that is ambiguous, that presents a dilemma that proposes alternatives" (p. 14). Dewey thought the social studies curriculum should give children opportunities to engage in reflective thinking and to become "versed in the methods of experimental inquiry and proof" (p. 217). In Dewey's view, inquiry should be child centered as children define problems and develop plans to gather data and reach solutions. Dewey's ideas continue to serve as the basis for many models of inquiry teaching.

The 1960s saw the introduction of the "New Social Studies" programs. Many of these programs were "inquiry based" because most lessons in a unit of study were based on problem-solving activities. These inquiry-based programs were greatly influenced by Jerome Bruner (1960, 1961). Bruner used the term *discovery learning* to describe inquiry activities. He wanted children to acquire "an attitude toward learning and inquiry, toward guessing and hunches, toward the possibility of solving problems on one's own" (1960, p. 97). Bruner thought children should solve problems the same way as real-life social scientists and become child versions of anthropologists, sociologists, economists, and historians. Many New Social Studies inquiry-based curricula were exciting and challenging for both students and teachers.

Brophy (1990), however, noted several difficulties with these innovative programs. Many problems were too difficult for children. Some activities were based on hypothetical communities or countries, and children did not spend enough time studying real ones. Too often, inquiries were entirely teacher centered. Teachers or the textbook defined the problem and dictated how to solve it. These "problem-solving" activities were really exercises with predetermined answers. Keep these criticisms in mind as we look at how to design inquiry activities.

One factor that should encourage more teachers to plan inquiry activities is the abundance of teaching resources available on the Internet. Thousands of documents, images, and other items that would have been out of reach for teachers are now easily accessed. For example, Rulli (2005) provided a list of sources relating to citizenship education that can be found on the Web. Imagine being able to use many of the resources in the Smithsonian Institution (www.si.edu)! Though developed for secondary school teachers of American history, the Website developed by Historicalthinkingmatters.org is a superb example of how Web-based resources can be used for historical problem solving (Martin, Wineburg, Rosenzweig, & Leon, 2008). An excellent resource for teachers to use when planning inquiries based on Internet resources is the Web Inquiry Projects site developed at San Diego State University (Molebash, 2004).

A Teaching Sequence for an Inquiry

Researchers do not agree on the exact steps an inquiry should follow. For example, Eggen and Kauchak (2005), Massialas and Cox (1966), the Sharans (Sharan & Sharan, 1989–1990; Sharan, 1997), and Suchman (1962, 1966) each developed a unique sequence for an inquiry. A synthesis of their methodologies follows:

1. Define the problem.

2. Speculate on possible answers.

3. Gather information.

4. Analyze the information and test hypotheses.

5. Reach a conclusion.

Let's now take a closer look at each step.

1. *Define the problem.*   The social studies textbook may provide the problem, we may pose the problem, or students may generate the problem. A certain excitement accompanies questions coming from students. Recall the opening vignette to this chapter; Susan's question was a good example of the motivational power of a student-generated question. When she questioned the authenticity of the drawing, several other students

agreed with her, and they were determined to find an answer! Depending on the series, textbooks can be a source of good questions for inquiries. These questions are often at the end of the chapters under subtitles like "On Your Own" or "For Further Research." When teachers plan a unit of study, they should be sure to look at the suggested inquiries in our textbook series.

Inquiry questions can be placed on a continuum. The worst are those having simple answers that can be found in a single source. A question like "What agricultural products are raised in South Africa?" is only an inquiry if the definition of that term is broad. To answer such a question, students do not need to go through the entire sequence of steps to find the answer; such questions are merely exercises in using reference materials. Better, but not perfect, are inquiry questions having complex answers requiring data from more than one source. An example is "Why do people live in our community?" Students can speculate on answers, gather data through a survey, and then reach conclusions. Another example is "How was elementary school in colonial times different from elementary school today?" This question would require students to consult several sources of information and make comparisons with their own classroom and school. The best inquiries have no single correct answers, usually because authorities in the field disagree. Examples are "What happened to the lost colony of Roanoke?" and "Who built the Easter Island monuments and for what purpose?" Questions like these require data from many sources. Because even authorities do not agree on answers to such questions, students will reach solutions solely on the merits of the data rather than by finding verification of their hypothesis in a book. Figure 7.1 illustrates the range of inquiry questions.

Figure 7.1

Range of Inquiry Questions

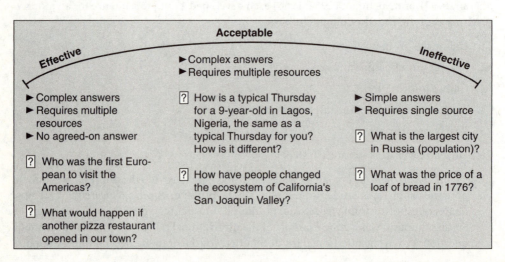

2. *Speculate on possible answers.* After the inquiry question is refined and agreed on, we need to help students make *educated* guesses on possible answers. The discussion will reveal how much students know about the problem. In this sense, the hypothesis-generating discussion will help us assist students in finding information. Some inquiries are done individually, but most involve small groups of students. It is not necessary for students to agree on one possible answer; they may have several hypotheses. Sometimes students may not be able to make a realistic guess, and then we need to broaden their background knowledge before they look for answers. Hypotheses should be recorded, and as the inquiry progresses, they may be revised.

In my class's inquiry into the attack by California Natives against a mission priest, a group of five students agreed to resolve the question. Two competing hypotheses were advanced: One member of the group speculated the picture was accurate, and the Natives had killed a priest; the other students hypothesized that, for some unknown reason, the picture was a fake.

3. *Gather information.* After students have speculated on possible solutions to the problem, it is time for them to gather information. We can break down our question into subtopics and assign students to look for answers in different sources (e.g., Aimee scans the Internet, Fred checks the encyclopedia, and Li looks at information books). It is best if students play a leading role in developing the "research" plan. Our role will vary, depending on the complexity of the question, the abilities of our students, and the difficulty of the sources of data. In some situations, we may only need to point students in the right direction. In others, we may need to locate materials and help students read them.

Many sources of information can become a part of a research plan:

■ *Bibliographic and computer-based information.* Inquiry activities provide perfect opportunities for students to master the use of both computer-based sources, like the Internet and CD encyclopedias, and hard-copy references, like encyclopedias and almanacs.

■ *Primary sources.* The best inquiries ask students to look at original, historic material such as diaries and old newspapers. When an inquiry leads to a primary source, students are doing history like real historians.

■ *Surveys.* Many inquiry-based activities can be based on contemporary issues. For example, one group of third graders was commissioned by the principal to investigate what all the school's students thought about a revised lunch schedule. Should the school move the lunch period up an hour? The third graders surveyed their schoolmates to find out the answer to this question.

■ *Miscellaneous resources.* Just about any teaching resource can be used in an inquiry. For example, an inquiry to determine the links between ancient Egypt and ancient Greece would require an examination of maps, charts, graphs, films, DVDs, CDs, prints, realia, CD and hard-copy encyclopedias, the Internet, and information books. We should not limit our students; rather, we should encourage them to seek information from all appropriate sources.

- *Direct observation.*   Although this data source is essential in the natural and physical sciences, it is more difficult to use in the social sciences, especially in the elementary grades. Many inquiries, however, can be answered through direct observation. A visit to a harbor, for example, helps students answer the inquiry "What different jobs do people perform at the harbor?"

    In my class's inquiry into the attack on the mission priest, students searched through old fourth-grade textbooks, information books in the library, and encyclopedias. In addition, at my suggestion, one student wrote to three professors of California history, each at a different campus of the California State University system. This inquiry activity took place before widespread use of the Internet; today, we could have checked many Websites. One of my favorites is "Spanish Missions of California" (http://library.thinkquest.org/3615/). This site was developed on ThinkQuest by two high school students in southern California, is full of useful information, and is written at a level most fourth graders can understand.

4. *Analyze the data to test the hypothesis.*   Analysis of the information students gather is fairly simple in an inquiry: How do the data support or challenge our hypotheses? As students gather information, they will do one of three things with each of their initial hypotheses: (a) reject it as being too far from the data to be supported, (b) revise it because the information gathered supports some aspect of the hypothesis but not all of it, or (c) accept it because the information indicates the proposed answer was accurate.

    In my class's inquiry, students found that only a few Native uprisings took place in California's Mission era. Interestingly enough, each professor written to wrote back, and *each gave us a different answer.* This was an eye-opener for my students, who at that point seemed stunned that "authorities" would not all give the same answer. Despite the disagreements, all the professors did support the answer the information books had given—that isolated incidents of Native rebellions against mission priests did take place.

5. *Reach a conclusion.*   In the final step of the inquiry, students state an answer and share it with the class. Although most inquiries will result in definitive answers, some will be left "dangling." In some instances, the best that can be done is to state a few possible solutions and admit the data do not warrant a final answer. In other instances, the concluding statements may lead to a new inquiry, and the process can begin again. Whatever the results, students should share what they have learned with their classmates. Following are several possibilities for doing this:

    - *Computer-based multimedia.*   Several computer-based possibilities are suitable for "reports." In many classrooms, students are posting their findings on a class or school Website. Students can also create multimedia reports on a CD through slide shows with images and narrations. Some elementary school students are creating podcasts. Another possibility is a "virtual museum" (Ricchiuti, 1998) that becomes part of a school Website.

    - *Written material.*   Students can write a book or issue a short summary of their inquiry.

- *Illustrations.* Sometimes the answer to an inquiry can be presented visually by using illustrations or photographs displayed on a bulletin board, on an overhead projector, or via computer-based technology.
- *Charts and graphs.* The best way to share numerical data is to communicate the results with charts or graphs.
- *Oral reports.* Oral reports are more successful if students rehearse, if the report is brief, and if the report summarizes the process students followed to find the answer.

My fourth-graders' inquiry concluded when the group made an oral presentation to their classmates. To support their presentation, they compared the three answers the professors offered.

Inquiry as Cooperative Learning: Group Investigation

Group Investigation is an instructional model combining inquiry teaching with the principles of cooperative learning. A group of students chooses a question to investigate and attempts to find possible answers. To answer the question, some group members explore sub-questions. Finally, the group makes a presentation to its classmates summarizing the findings (Gallenstein, 2000). Group Investigation has its roots in the Progressive ideas of John Dewey and has been refined by the Israeli scholars Yael Sharan and Shlomo Sharan (1989–1990; 1997). The Sharans developed their model from earlier work done by Miel (1952) and Thelan (1960). Group Investigation should follow six consecutive stages:

1. *Stage 1: Identify the question to be investigated and organize the group.* Again, the best questions are asked by students. For as many social studies units as possible, the teacher should develop a list of questions that could serve as the focus of a Group Investigation. Once a topic is chosen, it should be phrased as a question. The question should have more than a single simple answer, or else the Group Investigation model will not work. In this first stage, the teacher and students must decide whether the topic in question can be better answered by dividing the investigation into subtopics.

2. *Stage 2: Plan the investigation.* In this stage, students decide what each member of the group will do. For example, two members of the group will read nonfiction books, another will use CD encyclopedias, a fourth will surf the Internet, and a fifth member of the group will write a final report. The group decides what resources it will need. Sharan and Sharan suggest the group writes a plan describing how and when the investigation will be completed.

3. *Stage 3: Carry out the investigation.* Group members gather information, take notes, compare their findings with those other members of the group, and state possible answers to their question.

4. *Stage 4: Prepare the final report.* Quite appropriately, Sharan and Sharan have a liberal definition of *report.* Some groups will report via computer, others will construct

bulletin board displays, and some will perform skits. The key, of course, is that the final presentation answers the question the group has investigated.

5. *Stage 5: Present the final report.*   Teachers should work with students to be sure the prepared presentation is comprehensible. Because it will be presented publicly, written material should be edited, and the final draft should be in an easy-to-read display format. If the final report is oral, students should rehearse.

6. *Stage 6: Evaluate.*   Each member of the group evaluates her or his experience. Simple questions can focus this evaluation: What went well for our group? When did we have difficulty? If we were to do another investigation, what would we do differently?

Suchman's Inquiry Model

The first two models of inquiry teaching I presented in this chapter are quite similar. Richard Suchman, however, developed a unique teaching sequence for an inquiry activity (Eggen & Kauchak, 2005; Suchman, 1962, 1966; Joyce & Weil, 2008). Suchman developed his model of inquiry teaching for the process of investigating and explaining atypical natural phenomena. Although he based his model on the work of physical scientists, Suchman's procedures have been used successfully in social studies. The Suchman teaching sequence is concise, and an activity following the model can be completed in less than an hour because we provide all the information our students require. Another advantage of this model is it encourages students to work together toward resolving the question. This model of inquiry is also called "discrepant event inquiry" (Yell, 2002) and resembles the game of Twenty Questions (Edgington, 2001).

A Suchman inquiry has five phases:

1. *The teacher presents a puzzling situation to students.*   It is essential that the situation confuse the students and lack an obvious explanation. The teacher then might display pictures, diagrams, or maps that visually reveal the problem. Alternatively, the teacher might use eyewitness accounts, newspaper reports, or diary entries. Teachers can also provide students with a fact sheet, a list of information that cannot be presented visually. Whatever the resources, they should present the problem dramatically.

2. *Students ask yes/no questions to verify data.*   This is the unique aspect of the Suchman model. After the teacher presents the problem, students ask questions that can be answered only "yes" or "no." If a student asks a question that cannot be answered yes or no, the question must be restated. At this point, the questions must relate to the presented information and not attempt to answer the inquiry.

3. *Students ask yes/no questions to formulate hypotheses.*   Again, students may ask only questions that can be answered yes or no. This third phase is different from the second in that students should introduce possible solutions in their questions. Their questions should seek to support those solutions.

4. *Students state their explanations and discuss them.*   Each explanation should be fully discussed in the light of the data that have been revealed. Students should

acknowledge the strengths and reveal the weaknesses of each hypothesis. During this phase, the teacher has a decision to make: Should we tell our students "the answer"? This depends. If the students have come up with an answer close to the correct one, the teacher probably should acknowledge and reward them for their success. If students appear frustrated because their answers do not seem adequate, the teacher might want to explain the answer to the problem. If students appear to be interested in gathering more data on the problem, however, the teacher should not give an answer; instead, students should be encouraged to continue to investigate.

5. *Students analyze the inquiry process.* One purpose of the Suchman model is to help students become more proficient at solving problems. After the activity is over, the teacher should lead a discussion about the first four phases: What questions were most effective? How must members of the group work together? What questions might have been asked that would have led to a quicker or more definitive answer?

At the end of the chapter, you will find a description of a lesson using the Suchman inquiry model.

Critical Thinking: An Overview

In social studies, the desire to move students beyond rote memorization to more complex modes of thinking has been a consistent goal for educators since the early 1900s (Parker, 1991). There are many definitions of critical thinking, but for social studies teaching and learning, the focus should be on raising questions about statements of fact and opinion and making judgments about the validity of those statements (Beyer, 1985; Brophy, 1990; Elder & Paul, 2008). Other authorities sometimes use the terms *complex thinking* or *higher-order thinking* to refer to critical thinking.

Educators cannot agree, however, on what critical thinking is or how we can help our students become proficient at it (Wilen & Phillips, 1995). The variety of perspectives on critical thinking is reflected in the number of books written about the topic (e.g., Beyer, 1987; Fisher, 2001; Ruggiero, 2003; Wallace, 2005). Beyond the question of just what types of thinking are "critical thinking" are several viewpoints on the relationship of critical thinking to content. Wright (1995) describes three ways of conceptualizing critical thinking. First, some authorities believe in a set of generic critical thinking skills. Once we learn them, we can use them to think about any topic. Second, critical thinking is different from subject to subject; that is, critical thinking in economics is different from critical thinking in history. Wright prefers a third view, that some critical thinking skills are transferable from subject to subject, and some are not. On a related issue, Olsen (1995) summarizes the arguments in favor of the position that, for our students to develop critical thinking, teachers must cover a topic in depth. This means teachers should cover fewer topics each year because it seems that in-depth coverage presents more opportunities for our students to engage in critical thinking.

Computer-based resources provide teachers with many opportunities to challenge students to think critically.

What Are Critical Thinking Skills?

Beyer's (1987) definition is that critical thinking involves assessing and judging statements. Within this definition are two parts to critical thinking: (a) an analysis of the data or evidence used to support a statement, and (b) an evaluation of whether the data or evidence meets some standard of sufficiency. For example, young children could think critically about the following statement: "Our city has enough parks; we don't need any more." Thus, their teacher would lead the children to gather and analyze data relevant to the statement—data that look for answers to questions such as, How many parks does the city currently have? What are they used for? How many people use them each week? Are any people and groups unable to use the parks because of insufficient time or space? The teacher would then show the children how to analyze the data by using agreed-on criteria. Finally, the children would have to make an evaluation—verbally, in writing, or with charts and graphs—indicating whether the current park system meets the needs of the community.

Other definitions of critical thinking are broader than the one offered by Beyer. Indeed, which thinking skills are "critical" seems to be a somewhat arbitrary decision. Perhaps it would be a good idea to look at one taxonomy, or classification, of social studies thinking skills. Of particular interest is a taxonomy developed by the NCSS Task Force on Scope and Sequence (1989) that mirrors Bloom's cognitive taxonomy (see Chapter 2). The NCSS Task

Force delineated activities identifying lower-level to higher-level critical thinking processes. The six categories where these skills are ordered are listed here:

- *Classify information*
  Identify relevant information
  Group information in categories
  Place information in sequence
- *Interpret information*
  State relationships among sets of information
  Identify cause-and-effect relationships
  Draw inferences
- *Analyze information*
  Divide a topic into subtopics
  Detect bias in information
  Compare and contrast the credibility of different accounts of the same event
- *Summarize information*
  State the significant ideas supported by the information
  State conclusions based on the information
  State hypotheses for future research
- *Synthesize information*
  Propose a plan based on the information
  Speculate on what might happen if the information was different
  Propose a solution to the problem related to the information
- *Evaluate information*
  Judge the source of the information to determine objectivity
  Examine the technical accuracy of the information
  Determine the currency of the information

The sixth category of thinking skills lists criteria students will find useful in examining and evaluating the sources of information. For example, when we admonish our students to "consider the source," we are requesting that they determine whether the information is appropriate for judging data. Several factors are crucial to considering whether sources are appropriate. One of the most obvious factors is if the data used to support a statement comes from an unreliable or, in some cases, unprofessional source. If the answer is yes, then the validity of the data would be in question. *Objectivity* is another essential factor if we are to rely on information. Information provided by sources with a bias should be questioned. Modeling for students statements indicating an author may be biased would alert them to look for a prejudiced opinion or study.

Students should also consider the *technical correctness* of what they read. If, in the critical thinking exercise about the number of parks in the city, information on the level of park use was taken from a survey that improperly defined a sample (e.g., the first week of every month), then the information may provide an inaccurate portrait. Finally, *currency* is essential in social studies. Unless we are examining historical data, the older our information is, the less likely it is to be accurate.

Developing Critical Thinking Skills

Several specific instructional strategies have been promoted as essential for developing critical thinking (see books cited earlier in the chapter). Here, I discuss (a) the application of Fred Newmann's research on critical thinking in high school to elementary social studies, (b) Hilda Taba's instructional strategies for concept formation, (c) the integrative model of teaching reasoning and content developed by Paul Eggen and Donald Kauchak, and (d) a lesson plan model for teaching critical thinking while using visual resources, auditory resources, and real objects.

Barbara Schwartz/Merrill

To solve inquiries, students must use a variety of resources, including maps with very small print.

Newmann's Research on Critical Thinking in Social Studies

Fred Newmann (1990a, 1990b, 1991) has conducted interesting research on the teaching of critical thinking in high school social studies classes. His findings should help elementary teachers become more effective in developing their students' ability to think critically. Newmann (1991) concluded,

> At best, much classroom activity fails to challenge students to use their minds in any valuable way; at worst, much classroom activity is nonsensical or mindless. The more serious problem, therefore, is not the failure to teach some specific aspect of thinking, but the profound absence of thoughtfulness in classrooms. (p. 330)

Newmann (1991) identified six dimensions fundamental for a classroom where critical thinking can be developed:

1. *Sustained examination of a few topics is better than superficial coverage of many.* Newmann noted that "sustained concentration" on a topic is essential for in-depth thinking (p. 330). If teachers are in a position to shape the social studies curriculum for the grade-levels they teach, then they should limit the number of topics that are covered. When it comes to the development of critical thinking, less is more.

2. *Lessons must present content in a coherent, continuous manner.* Newmann reached this conclusion after observing secondary teachers, but this dimension is also crucial to elementary teaching. The content you present to your students should be logically sequenced and well organized. In other words, the concepts you teach should build on one another and be presented in a clear, predictable manner. For example, if a teacher is introducing third-grade students to some principles of economics, then she probably would conduct activities to help students understand the difference between producers and consumers before she explains the law of supply and demand.

3. *Students should be given an appropriate amount of time to think and prepare answers to questions.* As Newmann noted, "thinking takes time" (p. 332). I have found in my observations that teachers are uncomfortable with the silence that should follow a provocative question. It is as if they were engineers of a radio program and had been trained to avoid silent times, which are called "dead air." Critical thinking takes time, and one test of whether a question will stimulate complex thought is that it cannot be answered quickly.

4. *Teachers must ask challenging questions or present challenging tasks.* This dimension, of course, should go without saying. Newmann calls for questions and tasks that "demand analysis, interpretation, or manipulation of information" (p. 332). It takes courage to prepare challenging lessons because some students will find the experience frustrating. The frustration some students feel when confronted with complex tasks is essential for their development as critical thinkers.

5. *Teachers should be models of thoughtfulness.* Teachers should show interest in their students' ideas, explore alternative approaches to problems, show how to think

through a problem, and acknowledge the difficulty in answering some questions. A good way to do this is to work through a problem with students and to "think aloud" so students can see a model of critical thinking.

6. *Students should offer explanations and reasons for their conclusions.* Newmann noted that answers to "higher order challenges are rarely self-evident" (p. 333). Students must be encouraged to explain and support their conclusions. This can be a challenge for elementary teachers, but even the youngest students can be asked to explain why they have adopted a certain perspective.

Newmann's six dimensions are important because they provide a set of fundamental characteristics for creating a classroom environment where children can grow as critical thinkers.

Taba's Strategies for Concept Formation

Hilda Taba, whose ideas on the classification of content in the social studies curriculum were discussed in Chapter 1, developed a set of instructional strategies for teaching critical thinking through social studies. In fact, Taba may have been the first to use the term *instructional strategy*. Taba developed three instructional strategies to help children reason inductively. Each instructional strategy is actually a three-step teaching sequence. The three sets are used for concept formation, interpretation of data, and application of principles (Taba, 1967; Joyce & Weil, 2008).

All three strategies are important. Here I describe the strategy for concept formation because it is simple, applicable to all the elementary grades, and particularly useful for social studies. Taba (1967) thought the strategy for concept formation should be used at the beginning of a unit. I have found, however, that it works better as a concluding activity. The three steps of the Taba strategy for concept formation are as follows:

1. *Enumeration and listing.* In the first step, the teacher begins the activity by asking students to compile a list—for example, "What are some items we can buy at the market?" "Who were some inventors we learned about this week?" "What are some facts we have learned about Mexico?"

2. *Grouping.* In the second step, the teacher asks students, "Do you see some things that belong together?" (Taba, 1967, p. 93). Students may be right or wrong in their groupings; the important thing is that the teacher encourages them to think about what characteristics the items in the list share and what distinguishes the items. The teacher should help students see many possible ways the items can be grouped. For example, students might place the things they learned about Mexico into the following categories: (a) famous Mexican men and women, (b) names of Mexican cities, (c) things Mexico produces, (d) Mexican songs and dances, (e) Mexican folktales, and (f) life in a Mexican city.

3. *Labeling and categorizing.* In the third and final step, the teacher helps students attach labels to the groups they have created. It may be necessary to rearrange lists or to create new categories.

The concept formation teaching sequence has many possible modifications. To make the exercise easier, teachers can provide the list of items. It is a good idea to put each item on a separate card so it can be moved around as students define groups. Teachers can also tell the students how many groups they should form (e.g., "The places we have listed can be placed into five groups"). If students find this type of activity very difficult, the teacher can also provide the titles for each group. Each of the adjustments, however, should serve as "training wheels." They should be discarded as students become more sophisticated in the process.

An Integrative Model for Teaching Reasoning with Content

Eggen and Kauchak (2005) developed an integrative model to teach reasoning while teaching content. This model is a teaching sequence designed for content teaching, especially social studies. The sequence has four phases: (a) describe and compare, (b) explain, (c) hypothesize, and (d) generalize.

1. *Describe and compare.*   The teacher presents students with information presented through charts, graphs, illustrations, or written text. One strength of this model is it lends itself to data presented through charts and graphs, so the integrative model will provide students who are not good readers a chance to practice critical thinking. The teacher asks very specific questions about the information. The students are expected to observe and describe the information. For example, the last unit of the year for a fifth-grade class was "The United States in the 21st Century." Their teacher had prepared a lesson using the integrative model and used Table 7.1 as the basis for the lesson. The students are asked to compare different parts of the data. The logical place to start is with the most obvious similarities and differences between two sets of data. For example, if a group of students is looking at photographs of an ocean liner and a passenger jet, the teacher might direct students' attention to their shape and exterior design. Charts facilitate making comparisons because two sets of data can be placed

Table 7.1   Chart for a Lesson Using the Integrative Model for Teaching Reasoning with Content: Grade 5—Where Will Americans Live in the 21st Century?

State Population by Year in Millions			
State	*1900*	*1950*	*2000*
New York	7.27	14.83	18.98
Pennsylvania	6.30	10.49	12.28
Ohio	4.16	7.95	11.35
Texas	3.05	7.71	20.85
California	1.48	10.57	33.87
Florida	0.53	2.77	15.98

Source: U.S. Census Bureau, www.census.gov.

side by side. Finally, teachers should challenge their students to identify any patterns emerging after comparing and contrasting the data.

2. *Explain.* So far, students have been asked to perform relatively easy thinking skills. Now processing becomes deductive. Teachers ask students why some parts of the data are the same and other parts different. Students must speculate, and teachers must ask "why" questions that students have a reasonable chance of answering. Almost any set of data will suggest questions requiring too much of the students, questions they simply cannot answer. Obviously, teachers should avoid those, and instead develop "why" questions that will generate reasonable speculations based on the data.

3. *Hypothesize.* This phase is closely linked to the one before and the one after. Here the teachers asks students to expand the explanations they offered in phase 2. Teachers do this by presenting a hypothetical situation as the students are forced to apply what they have learned. For example, if a teacher asked the students to think about travel by ship and by airplane, she could present them with a variety of travel scenarios and the task of identifying which mode of transportation they would choose (e.g., "You need to get to Cairo as soon as possible" or "You want to relax while you travel").

4. *Generalize.* The final phase of the integrative model is a chance to summarize. The expectation is that students will state generalizations they have learned during the activity. Many students find this a difficult chore, and primary-grade teachers may have to provide considerable assistance. For example, the teacher could provide the first half of a generalization and ask the students to write the second half (e.g., "If you want to get somewhere in a hurry, then you should _____.").

At the end of the chapter there is a lesson plan a first-grade teacher wrote for an activity based on Eggen and Kauchak's integrative model for teaching reasoning with content.

Critical Thinking and Auditory Media, Visual Media, and Realia

Inquiry and critical thinking activities can use any type of instructional resource. Visual media, auditory media, and realia present excellent opportunities for elementary students to engage in interpretation and analysis. As students are taught to view and listen critically, they will become more proficient in their ability to engage in complex thinking.

Teachers have a wide variety of auditory (or listening) media to use in their classrooms. Technology changes rapidly here; yes, some of us began our careers when students listened to vinyl records. Then, vinyl gave way to audiotapes. Now, of course, teachers have the advantage of auditory recordings stored on Compact Discs (CDs) and iPods. Whatever formats are available, recordings of music, interviews, and other sounds can be a valuable social studies resource (Cooper, 1989; Turner & Hickey, 1991). Visual media have changed, too. Computer technology has provided teachers with a variety of ways to present pictures. Digital Video Discs (DVDs) have become common classroom resources. An endless supply of visual images are available on the Web.

Realia refers to real things (Braun & Cook, 1985; Lankiewicz, 1987; McKoy, 2010; Rule & Sunal, 1994). The use of realia in social studies is essential because it provides three-dimensional objects for students to both see and touch. Realia can be either the real thing or human-made models. The best lessons make use of *artifacts,* real things used by people. Some school districts have collections of items they lend to other schools, like a branding iron, old coins, or a butter churn. Other artifacts can be viewed only at museums, such as Native American baskets or an ancient Egyptian mummy. Below you will find a teaching sequence that can be used when students are asked to examine and analyze a visual image, an auditory source, or realia. Regardless of the resource, the goals of the lesson are the same: We want students to look closely, to notice all the relevant details, and then to engage in critical thinking based on what they have seen (or heard). For this discussion, let's assume students are viewing a visual image projected onto a large screen:

1. First, the teacher *links* the image to what we previously covered in the unit of study. The teacher needs to do this before we show the image (or play the CD or let students examine the artifact). Teachers can establish the connection between the image and what students have been learning in several ways: discussion, a review of information on a chart, or rereading parts of a textbook.

2. Next, the teacher places the image in *context* by establishing time and place. This usually involves using a map and a timeline. For some inquiry and critical thinking activities, however, the teacher may want to eliminate this step because the challenge for students will be to determine the time and place of the slide.

3. The teacher then asks students to take a *first look* (or *listen*): What catches their attention? What would they like to learn more about the image? What questions do they have after a first look? We can do this by having small-group discussions or by having students record their responses in writing. For discussion, the cooperative learning structures of Think–Pair–Share and Three-Step Interview work well. Although this should go without saying, we must be sure the visual image can be seen by all students participating in the activity—and if students are listening to a recording, be sure everyone can hear it. If equipment limits how large an image can be displayed, then we should have students view it in small groups. If we are using an artifact that students can touch, we should arrange a format permitting each student some time with the object.

4. The teacher leads students to a *focused examination* of the image by asking them either to look for specific things or to narrow their focus to a certain part of the image (or recording or artifact). This is more difficult to do with an audio recording or a video.

5. Last, the teacher helps students *interpret and analyze* the image. Here are the types of questions the teacher could ask:
   - Challenge students to find *relationships* between the image and other things. For historic images, recordings, and artifacts, we can help students see the connection between the old and the contemporary. If students were viewing photographs of a fifth-grade classroom of 1900, we could ask them to compare what they see with their own experiences.
   - Help students use the visual image to make broader *inferences* about the people, the place, and the times that produced it. Photographs of the classroom of

1900, for example, would tell us about the relationship between students and their teachers.

■ Work with students to help them detect *bias.* In many paintings, for example, the perspective of the artist leads to distortions of reality. It is important that teachers share with students biographical information about the artist so they can critically analyze a painting or piece of sculpture for evidence of bias.

At the end of the chapter you will find a lesson plan written by a sixth-grade teacher for an activity requiring the critical analysis of photographs of a Roman coin.

Inquiry and Critical Thinking for All Students

Every student can be successful and enjoy inquiry activities and the challenge of being asked to think critically. Students with disabilities and English learners, however, may experience difficulty. For most English learners, inquiry and critical thinking activities can be difficult because the language associated with them is not comprehensible. Problems arise because of the students' level of English proficiency. With students with disabilities, the issue is not second-language acquisition, but rather the complexity of the task. Notice I have tried to use "conditional language" throughout this paragraph because it is a mistake to underestimate the students; they will succeed at times when we may not expect it. Teachers can help their students with inquiry and critical thinking activities:

■ *Use step-by-step guidance.*   Students with disabilities will need help at each step of an inquiry or critical thinking activity. Whereas students with less severe disabilities may breeze through, some students will need considerable help during each step of the process. Explicit instructions, delivered with patience, will be necessary.

■ *Present information through charts, graphs, and pictures.*   Many students with reading difficulties will be unable to participate in an inquiry or critical thinking activity if all the data are written at a level they cannot read. The alternatives are obvious: Use charts, graphs, photographs, illustrations, or films to provide the information needed to resolve the problem. In this regard, the Suchman inquiry model and the integrative model for teaching reasoning with content have particular promise because they work well when the problem and the supporting information are presented visually.

■ *Allow students to work together.*   Almost any child will be able to do more with help. This help can come from the teacher, but it can also be provided by the child's more competent classmates. Thus, inquiry activities that may seem to be beyond some students are "doable" if the students work with their fellow students.

For English learners, we should also consider the following:

■ *Use the primary language.*   Teachers who are bilingual and those with bilingual aides should allow their English learners to complete inquiries and critical thinking activities in their native language. Cummins (1979, 1986a, 1992) made a convincing case that students who learn how to gather data and solve problems in one language will easily transfer those abilities to their second language. Because some important sources of information will be available in languages other than English, the ability to use non-English resources will be an advantage for our English learners. For example, if an inquiry project requires interviews of people living in the community, our bilingual students will be able to gather information from people who speak little or no English.

■ *Remember that comprehensible input is the key.*   Teachers should be sure the English they use when leading an inquiry or critical thinking activity is understandable. They may need to slow down, repeat things, and carefully consider their choice of words. It is important, when working with English learners, to stop from time to time and ask questions to check whether students are following the presentation.

Summary of Key Points

- Inquiry is a process during which a problem is identified. Then students speculate on possible solutions, gather data, analyze the data, and reach a conclusion.

- Two specific models for inquiry activities are the cooperative learning structure called Group Investigation and the Suchman inquiry model.

- Teachers should continue to teach students to use reference books (encyclopedias, almanacs, and atlases).

- *Critical thinking* has many definitions. This type of thinking requires students to go beyond rote memorization to analyze, synthesize, speculate, challenge, verify, and generalize.

- Fred Newmann identified six dimensions fundamental for a classroom where critical thinking can be developed.

- Hilda Taba developed instructional strategies to help children reason inductively.

- An integrative model for teaching reasoning with content provides a format for building content knowledge while students think critically.

- Visual media, auditory media, and realia are excellent resources to use for critical thinking and inquiry activities.

- With a skillful teacher, all students can participate successfully in inquiry and critical thinking activities.

Lesson Plans and Instructional Activities

This chapter concludes with three examples of teaching that fosters critical thinking:

1. A Suchman inquiry lesson for fifth graders that challenges the students to explain why Samoset was able to speak to the Pilgrims in English in March of 1621

2. A lesson plan for first graders, using the integrative model for teaching reasoning with content, on the differences between summer and winter

3. A lesson plan for sixth graders requiring analysis of a Roman coin

Description of a Lesson
Grade Five: A Suchman Inquiry—
Samoset Greets the Pilgrims

Mrs. Kim's fifth graders were working on a 3-week unit on the Pilgrims. The class learned about the suppression of Separatist religious groups in England, how a group of Separatists first emigrated to Holland, the voyage of the Separatists and others to New England aboard the *Mayflower,* and the establishment of the Plimoth colony during January and February 1621. Her students had taken a "virtual field trip" to the wonderful living history museum of Plimoth Plantation, which is an exact replica of the Plimoth colony of 1627. The tour is available on the Plimoth Plantation Website, www.plimoth.org. She used the Suchman inquiry model for a lesson about the appearance of Samoset, a member of the Abenaki tribe, in Plimoth on March 16, 1621.

Step 1. The Teacher Presents a Puzzling Situation to Students

Mrs. Kim started the lesson by reviewing what the students had learned so far. After looking at several sources on the Pilgrims, including Caleb Johnson's superb Website on the *Mayflower* (www.mayflowerhistory.com), she found the best description of Samoset's visit in an old book from the wonderful American Heritage Junior Library, *The Pilgrims of Plymouth Colony* (Ziner, 1961). She wrote and read aloud the following account of an event that occurred on March 16, 1621:

> March 16 was a cool morning in Plimoth. Most of the men had gathered in the Common House for a meeting. The women and children were busy with their chores. A small number of men with guns stood guard. Many of the Pilgrims were ill from the "General Sickness" that had killed over half the people who had sailed on the *Mayflower.* So far, the Pilgrims had only seen a few Natives. Each time, the Natives ran away and hid. But on the morning of March 16, one of the guards looked up and saw a Native man walking toward the village. He was tall, with feathers in his hair. He was smiling and waving at the Pilgrims! The guards shouldered their rifles and were about to demand that he stop. Then the Native shouted at them, "Welcome, English-men! My name is Samoset!" Samoset talked to the Pilgrims in English for quite some time. He told them about the region near the settlement. He talked with them well into the night. The Pilgrims were astonished that Samoset could speak English.

> Mrs. Kim then said, "It was amazing that Samoset could speak English. How did he learn English?"

Step 2. Students Ask Yes/No Questions to Verify Data

Mrs. Kim explained that the class was to figure out how Samoset learned to speak English. She explained the students could ask her any questions they wanted, but there were two rules: (a) She could only answer yes or no, and (b) their questions should try to get more facts. Most questions the students asked were appropriate:

"Had Samoset ever been to England?" (No.)

"Was Samoset really a Native?" (Yes. Students thought Samoset might be an Englishman in disguise.)

Eventually, students asked questions that served as the basis for two possible answers to this historic riddle:

"We learned about Jamestown, in Virginia. Wasn't that before Plimoth?" (Yes. Here, Mrs. Kim went beyond the Suchman format to locate Jamestown and Plimoth on the map. She wrote the year 1607, when Jamestown was founded, on the board.)

"Were the Pilgrims the first English people to visit New England?" (No.)

Step 3. Students Ask Yes/No Questions to Formulate Hypotheses

Mrs. Kim now moved to the third step, where students asked questions that would support possible answers. One group of students thought Samoset had lived for a time in Jamestown. This answer worked until one girl asked, "Had Samoset ever lived at Jamestown?" (No.)

"Had he ever visited the English at Jamestown?" (No.)

Now, three students focused on the English who had visited New England prior to the coming of the Pilgrims. They asked, "Did Samoset ever talk to the English who visited New England before the Pilgrims?" (Yes.)

"Did he work for them?" (The answer to this is not clear because Samoset had sailed with English captains along the Maine and Newfoundland coasts. He may have served as a guide, or he may have just been along for the ride. Again, Mrs. Kim deviated from the Suchman model by replying that Samoset had sailed with English captains who had explored the New England and Canadian coasts.)

Step 4. Students State Their Explanations and Discuss Them

At this point, it was easy for students to state an explanation: Samoset had learned to speak English when he sailed along the coast with the English explorers.

Step 5. Students Analyze the Inquiry Process

Most students said they enjoyed this activity and wanted to do more like it. Some students complained their classmates did not ask good questions. Mrs. Kim was satisfied with the activity, although she was disappointed more students did not participate. Next time, she decided, she would modify the teaching sequence so students could discuss the puzzling event in small groups before they started asking questions.

Mrs. Kim planned the Samoset inquiry for two reasons: (a) She wanted her students to practice the critical thinking that is part of the Suchman model, and (b) she wanted to help her students understand a historical generalization: The English had considerable contact with New England and Canada before the coming of the Pilgrims. After the Samoset inquiry, she used a timeline and a map to show the following events:

1497: John Cabot landed at Cape Breton Island in Canada.

1583: Humphrey Gilbert sailed to St. John's, Newfoundland, and established a temporary English settlement.

1602: Bartholomew Gosnold explored the Maine coast and sailed to Cape Cod—he named it.

1605: Ferdinando Gorges and George Waymouth landed on Monhegan Island off Maine. They supposedly took another Native, Tisqauntum (Squanto), back to England.

1607: Gorges and George Popham established a colony at Sagadahoc (or Popham), Maine. The colony, which was to serve as a base for fishing, failed in 1608.

1614: John Smith, one of the settlers of Jamestown, sailed along the New England coast from Maine to Cape Cod. He made a map and wrote a book, *A Description of New England,* that the Pilgrims took with them on the *Mayflower.*

 Effective Teaching in Today's Diverse Classroom: Let me make this point very clear: All children need to take part in inquiry and critical thinking activities. Children with learning disabilities and English learners may well find these activities challenging, but to assign them to other, simpler activities, is to deny them the opportunity to fully develop as students. In many inquiries and lessons requiring critical thinking, all children can succeed if teachers make minor modifications in how they teach.

One important component of effective instruction for English learners is "primary language support." Primary language support for English learners can be provided by a bilingual teacher, an instructional aide fluent in the student's first language, or bilingual classmates. The support can be oral as the teacher explains an activity in the primary language, or it can be written. In this lesson, the description of Samoset's visit could be translated into the primary language(s) of the English learners in the class. The English learners could read the translation, or the translation could be read to them.

Children with learning disabilities would benefit from a "pre-lesson" coaching session. The teacher would meet with a small group of children who might be overwhelmed by this activity. The teacher would use the model on something not related to the social studies curriculum. Since the Suchman model is essentially the same as playing the game of "20 Questions," the teacher might play that game with objects in the room, like the flag ("I'm thinking of something in the room, you have to guess what it is by asking questions which I can answer with a *no* or a *yes*"). The teacher would help the children learn successful strategies for a Suchman inquiry, which include narrowing the possibilities, rather than guessing the answer ("Is it something in the front of the room?").

Lesson Plan
Grade One: Using an Integrative Model—
Summer and Winter

Overview: To allow for more participation, the lesson was taught three times, each time to a group of seven children. The lesson was part of the thematic unit "The Seasons," which integrated social studies, science, language arts, visual arts, and performing arts.

Resources and Materials: The lesson uses a single resource—a large chart prepared by the teacher. The chart is divided in half, one side labeled "Summer" and the other labeled "Winter." Along the left side of the chart are three categories—"Special Things to Do," "Food," and "Clothing." Each "cell" is illustrated with photographs cut from magazines. For example, under "Summer" in the "Special Things to Do" cell are photographs of people at the beach, children playing baseball, and a family having a picnic in a park. Under "Winter" in the "Special Things to Do" cell are photographs of people making a snowman, children ice skating, and a family gathered indoors around a fireplace. (A large area of the United States does not have snowy, low-temperature winters; if you are located in this area, adjust your discussions of "Winter" cells with the children accordingly.) Under "Summer" in the "Clothing" cell are photographs of people in shorts, sandals, and T-shirts. Under "Winter" in the "Clothing" cell are photographs of people in winter clothing—show heavy jackets, mufflers, knit hats, and gloves. Under "Winter" in the "Food" cell are photographs of a man placing a stuffed turkey into an oven and of a steaming cup of hot chocolate. In contrast, "Summer" "Food" depicts an outdoor barbecue and a pitcher of iced lemonade.

Standard: Standard 15 for grades K–4 of the National Geography Standards is "How physical systems affect human systems." One performance expectation of this standard is that a student be able to "describe how humans adapt to variations in the physical environment, as exemplified by being able to list ways in which people adapt to the physical environment; e.g., choices of clothing" (Geography Education Standards Project, 1994, p. 134).

Content Objectives: Children will learn weather is one factor that determines how people live. Regarding recreational activity, food, and clothing, children will understand the differences caused by winter and summer weather.

Process Objectives: Children will *describe* the recreational activities, food, and clothing typical of winter and summer; *compare and contrast* photographs of summer and winter; *explain* why people participate in different recreational activities, eat different foods, and wear different clothing during summer and winter; *speculate* on which businesses do better in the winter and which do better in the summer; and *state a generalization* summarizing the relationship of weather to the way people live.

Teaching Sequence:

1. Before the lesson, prepare the chart and make a list of the key questions to be asked during each phase.

2. Divide the class into groups of seven children. Have each group sit on the rug, with the chart displayed nearby on an easel. Follow the five-step sequence of the integrative model:

   a. *Describe.*   Introduce the lesson by saying, "Today we are going to look at photographs of things we do, things we eat, and how we dress during the summer and the winter." Direct the children to each of the six "cells" in the chart (Summer/Special Things to Do, Summer/Food, Summer/Clothing, Winter/Things to Do, Winter/Food, Winter/Clothing). For each cell, the key question is, "What do you see in this photograph?" Be sure all significant details are noted. It is best to start with the clothing cells, and you may want to pantomime the differences between summer and winter (for winter, you might have the children shiver, rub their hands together, and say things like, "It's freezing out here!").

   b. *Compare and contrast.*   Help the children make comparisons between each set of photographs. Start with clothing, where the differences are most noticeable. Ask the children to look first at the clothing cell for summer and then to look at the clothing cell for winter. Then ask, "How are the clothes we wear different in summer from the ones we wear in winter?" The children should note winter clothes cover more of our bodies, they are larger, and thicker. Then ask the children to note differences between summer and winter food and between special things to do in the summer and in the winter.

   c. *Explain.*   Ask the first graders why we need to wear different clothes in the summer and the winter, why we eat different foods, and why we do different things. The simple answer, of course, is that it is hot in the summer and cold in the winter. Probe further by asking questions like, "Why wouldn't hot chocolate be good at the beach?" "Why is it possible to barbecue in the summer and not in the winter?"

   d. *Speculate.*   This will be the most difficult part of the lesson for the first graders. On the chalkboard, write the following: "You sell beach umbrellas," "You sell mittens," and other commercial activities that have a busy season. Ask the children to identify which businesses would do better in the summer and which would probably do better in the winter. Help them offer justifications for their answers.

   e. *Generalize.*   Finally, help the children understand the information presented in the lesson supports the statement: The weather is one factor that determines how people live. With first graders, the exact wording is not important. The opening question for this step should be something like,

"What have we learned today?" A more specific prompt is, "Why do people do different activities, eat different foods, and wear different clothes during the summer and the winter?" The lesson on summer and winter should lead children to a simple conclusion: that weather is one factor determining what they do, what they eat, and how they dress.

Effective Teaching in Today's Diverse Classroom: This activity would work well with any group of children experiencing difficulty reading grade-level textbooks. Although most social studies activities require students to read—and, in fact, social studies should be an area of the curriculum helping children become better readers— it is important that not all lessons be based on a text. The goal of this lesson is to promote critical thinking. That goal can be accomplished without the use of written material. The medium used to stimulate thinking was photographs; thus, the lesson would be effective with English learners, especially those whose level of English proficiency allows them to participate in discussions but who lack the ability to read grade-level texts.

Lesson Plan
Grade Six: A Roman Coin

Overview: This lesson would take place during a unit on ancient Rome, planned for a group of approximately 25 students. The images of the Marcus Aurelius coin in the gallery of Roman coins found at www.romancoins.info/ are the key source. Another good source for Websites on ancient Rome is the "Schools of California Online Resources for Teachers" (SCORE) site (www.score.k12.ca.us).

Resources and Materials: (a) A wall map of the Roman Empire; (b) a piece of con- struction paper; (c) the timeline created for the unit on ancient Rome; (d) a sheet of chart paper on which are written three facts about Marcus Aurelius; (e) the photo- graphic images of a Roman coin bearing the likeness of Emperor Marcus Aurelius, one for each side of the coin; (f) a projector capable of displaying the images from the Website; (g) a sheet of chart paper on which focused examination questions are written (see the list in the following section "Focused Examination"); (h) copies of a photograph of Abraham Lincoln from *Lincoln: A Photobiography* (Freedman, 1987) and copies of a photograph of Franklin Roosevelt from *Franklin Delano Roosevelt* (Freedman, 1990); (i) several U.S. pennies and dimes.

Standard: This lesson helps students achieve both history and economic stan- dards. In the *National Standards for History* for grades 5–12, standard 3A is "the student understands the causes and consequences of the unification of the Mediter- ranean basin under Roman rule." One of the performance expectations under this standard is that "the student is able to analyze how Roman unity contributed to the growth of trade among the lands of the Mediterranean basin" (National Center for History in the Schools, 1996, p. 151). Standard VII of the National Social Studies Standards is "production, distribution, and consumption." For the middle grades, performance expectation is that learners can "differentiate among various forms of exchange and money" (NCSS, 1994, p. 96).

Content Objectives: Students will learn introductory biographical information about Marcus Aurelius, the characteristics of Roman coins, the relationship between economic activity and the need for money, and a shared characteristic of Roman and contemporary U.S. coins—the idealized images of leaders on the coins.

Process Objectives: Students will *identify* the reign of Marcus Aurelius (C.E. 161–180) on the timeline, *recall* information they learned about the geography of and economic activity in the Roman Empire, *examine* slides of the coin, *list* three things that caught their eye about the coin, *speculate* on the reasons why economic trade and the amassing of capital requires the use of money, *compare and contrast* the photographs of Lincoln and Roosevelt with their images on coins, and *speculate* on the purposes of idealized portraits placed on coins.

Teaching Sequence:

1. *Link.*   Using a wall map, review the geographic boundaries of the Roman Empire in the second century of the common era. Then, help students recall what they have learned about economic activity during the height of the empire.

2. *Contexts.*   Ask a group of students to help place a piece of construction paper underneath the reign of Marcus Aurelius on the timeline. Share the information about Marcus Aurelius you wrote on a sheet of chart paper (e.g., he lived from C.E. 121 to 180). I would note Marcus Aurelius was both a political leader and a philosopher. I think students would find it interesting to discuss his stoic philosophy that emphasized forgiveness, the absence of selfishness, and the common good. That, though, would require another lesson.

3. *First look.*   For most of the activity, students will work in groups of four. Project the images and ask the students to "look at these photographic images of the front and back of a Roman coin and write down three things that catch your eye." Then use the cooperative learning structure Three-Step Interview to allow each student to share his or her response. Reconvene the group and listen to three or four students present what they wrote.

4. *Focused examination.*   Now ask each group to take another look at the images and, working as a group, to answer the following questions, which were listed beforehand on a sheet of chart paper:
   a. What general shape is the coin?
   b. What do you think the coin is made of?
   c. Do you see any writing on the coin?

    d. Are there any numbers on the coin? Write them down.

    e. What part of Marcus Aurelius can you see?

    Reconvene the whole group and share answers to the questions.

5. *Interpret and analyze.* Working with the whole group, see whether you can help students discern the relationship between economic activity and the need for money. These relationships include complex trade, the division of labor, many workers engaged in "service" jobs, and the amassing of capital requires money; all were present in the Roman Empire. Notice that this lesson helps students acquire Standard 11 of the *National Content Standards in Economics* (National Council on Economic Education, 1997), which reads, "Students will understand that money makes it easier to trade, borrow, save, invest, and compare the value of goods and services." You might ask them to imagine what would happen if we did not have money. Be sure students see the connection between the complex, international system of trade and exchange used by the Romans and the need for money.

    Next, have students once again work in their groups. Distribute the copies of the photographs of Lincoln and Roosevelt, the pennies, and the dimes. Ask each group to look closely and compare and contrast the photographs and the images on the coins. How are the portraits similar, and how are they different? Students should see that the images on the coins make Lincoln and Roosevelt look very good. To make the comparison obvious, choose photographs of Lincoln and Roosevelt near the end of their days as president when, alas, the pressures of the job had aged them. Why? Why might an artist change the way a person looked when designing a coin?

Evaluation: Collect the written responses of each student. These will provide useful information on whether individuals were able to notice details on the Roman coin. You may want to tape-record the whole-group discussions. The tape will help you identify who is talking and whether students have engaged in the type of analytic, speculative thinking the lesson requires. You should certainly take notes while the students work in small groups.

Effective Teaching in Today's Diverse Classroom: The lesson was planned for the entire class (assuming approximately 25 students). For much of the activity, however, students worked in small groups of four. How would you assign your English learners to these groups? You have three choices:

1. If your English learners have an advanced level of oral English proficiency, then it would make sense to spread them out and place them with students who are fully proficient in English (e.g., one English learner with three fully proficient students). Because the data for the lesson are visual and require no reading, this arrangement should work. The English learners will benefit from the comprehensible input provided by their peers who are proficient in English.

2. If you have a group of English learners with limited oral English skills, so limited that they will not be able to converse with students who are fully proficient in English, then the English learners should be grouped together and work with either you or an instructional aide. If you were working with a group of English learners on this lesson, you would need to modify your vocal register. You would speak slowly, repeat things, and limit your vocabulary so the English learners can understand the questions written on the chart paper.

3. Finally, if you have English learners who are in the first stages of acquiring English and who would not understand you even if you used a modified vocal register, then these students can benefit from the lesson only if they are allowed to complete it in their first language. It is, unfortunately, not always possible to find the resources (materials or personnel) to allow students to use their first language. If, for example, you have in your class an Urdu-speaking student who recently emigrated from Pakistan, my guess is you will not have materials written in Urdu or Urdu-speaking teachers or aides to help you. If you cannot provide a setting where the lesson can be completed in languages other than English, you must do your best to help your students who speak little English understand the lesson.

Literacy

Indira Kaur wanted to use computer-based resources with her first graders. Her principal had recommended a book published by the National Council for The Social Studies, *Digital Age: Technology-Based K–12 Lesson Plans for Socials Studies.* Mrs. Kaur decided to modify a unit plan presented in the book to create an electronic "big book" (Gallavan & Juliano, 2007). The children were used to hard-copy books printed on paper 15 × 21 inches, but their electronic big book would be stored in a computer and projected on a large screen. The activity fit perfectly into her social studies unit titled "Children Today and Long Ago." Gallavan and Juliano's project used family photographs accompanied by student-written captions to create a PowerPoint big book. Mrs. Kaur decided instead to create a PowerPoint big book focusing on the uniqueness of each child in her classroom. The project started with the class compiling a wall of words that could be used to describe members of the class. Children then selected five words that fit them individually and wrote them on a sheet of paper. They each took a letter home requesting a family member either to email photographs of the child to the teacher, or provide photographs of the child to be brought to school. The photos could show the child doing something he or she enjoyed, or show the child when she or he was younger, or show the child with family members. The letter stated if the family was not comfortable in sharing photographs, the child could draw pictures using the software Kid Pix. Hard-copy photos would be scanned into a digital format. The letter home also included a written permission form allowing the photos to be posted on the class Website.

Next, the children used the five words they had selected to write two or three-sentence captions to accompany the photographs. Mrs. Kaur then constructed an electronic big book on PowerPoint with all the children's photographs and captions. Each child had two pages in the big book, and they were all excited to see their pages in the class big book! During the PowerPoint presentation of the book, children read their pages aloud individually and had a chance to talk about what the photos represented. Later, Mrs. Kaur posted the PowerPoint version of the big book on the class Website so it would be accessible to the parents, family, and friends of the children in her classroom.

The project was a success. It helped the children meet two of Mrs.Kaur's grade-level social studies standards—understanding each child is unique and special, and learning how the daily lives of children have changed over the years (she would compare the big book photographs with photos of children in the 19th century). At the same time, the project provided opportunities for the children to grow as readers and writers. That is what this chapter is about—the connections between literacy, the ability to read and write, and social studies teaching and learning. The social studies curriculum should provide students with many opportunities to support literacy and become more proficient as readers and writers (Camperell & Knight, 1991; Gilstrap, 1991; Irvin et al., 1995; Roberts, 1996; Selwyn, 1995).

■ ■ ■

Social Studies Textbooks

We will begin our discussion by looking at issues related to use of social studies textbooks. Almost every school district in the United States purchases social studies textbooks as part of a classroom package that usually includes a teacher's edition, student texts, worksheets, and supplemental items like CDs, DVDs, maps, and charts. Please note I distinguish *textbook* from *text*. To me, *text* has a broader meaning and includes anything that is written. For many teachers, the social studies textbook is at the center of social studies instruction. One fairly recent national study revealed 57% of second-grade teachers and 73% of fifth-grade teachers used a social studies textbook in the social studies lesson they taught immediately before responding to the researchers' survey (Leming, Ellington, & Schug, 2006).

Criticisms of Social Studies Textbooks

Despite their widespread use and popularity, social studies textbooks have been criticized (Beck & McKeown, 1991b; Wade, 1993; White, 1988). The criticisms of textbooks can be summarized as follows:

■ *Social studies textbooks tend to avoid controversy and fail to present conflicting points of view.* Textbooks are marketed nationally, with particular attention to California and Texas, where state committees decide which texts will be approved for purchase for the entire state. Publishers try to produce textbooks with wide acceptability; because of the potential for alienating prospective buyers, the presentation of conflicting perspectives is avoided.

■ *Social studies textbooks can be dull.* The writing is bland, and many textbooks ignore interesting historical incidents and people. One research study showed if there were a "voice" to a social studies textbook, students would learn more material (Beck, McKeown, & Worthy, 1995). A passage on British taxation of the American colonists was rewritten so it read more like fiction. The "voiced" version had more action, included quotations, and made connections to the readers' emotions.

■ *Many textbooks do not always present coherent content.* Beck and McKeown (1988, 1991a, 1991b) studied the coherence of elementary social studies textbooks. They concluded that, in many textbooks, the main point is not emphasized; authors stray from their central point with meaningless digressions; examples and comparisons are often inadequate; the reader is given no sense of time; and many passages fail to clearly state the consequences of an event.

■ *Social studies textbooks are written for a generic student.* Even if social studies textbooks were written with more panache and greater clarity, using them would still involve significant problems. Quite simply, many students cannot read their grade-level textbooks. Also, textbook-centered instruction will not be compatible with the learning styles of all students. For example, many of our students learn better from visual images other than text, like charts and photographs, and through hands-on activities.

Fortunately, recent elementary social studies textbooks are an improvement over their predecessors. The illustrations and graphics are excellent and include old paintings, cartoons, and drawings. Timelines, several types of maps, bar graphs, and summary charts present material in a form students readily understand. Recent textbooks have broadened their coverage to include more information about minorities, women, and children. Finally, the most recent textbooks have increased the amount of primary source material they contain. Along with the chapter narrative, readers will find transcripts of oral histories, journal entries, songs, and newspaper articles. Even with these improvements, textbooks should never be the only resource teachers use to teach social studies. Teachers should read the teacher's edition carefully and choose only those portions of a chapter and those instructional activities that will help students achieve grade-level standards.

Instructional Strategies for Reading the Textbook: Activating Background Knowledge

Effective use of instructional strategies can help students read their textbooks (Jones & Lapham, 2004; Tierney & Readance, 2005). Our discussion looks at the following:

- Strategies to help students recall what they know about a topic before they read

- The use of graphic organizers before students start reading

- Strategies to be used to teach new vocabulary

- Strategies that facilitate comprehension and can be used while students read and after they have finished

- A teaching sequence to be used with a textbook-centered lesson

Let's begin our discussion by looking at two strategies that will help students "call to mind" what they already know about a topic: K–W–L charts and PReP.

K–W–L Chart.   The K–W–L chart (Ogle, 1986) has become a popular instructional strategy to help children recall their knowledge of a topic. Let's assume a group of second graders will read a selection in their textbooks about the Pledge of Allegiance. The teacher divides a sheet of chart paper into three parts: one with the heading "What We *K*now About the Pledge of Allegiance," the second column with "What We *W*ant to Learn About the Pledge of Allegiance," and the third with "What We *L*earned About the Pledge of Allegiance." The first two columns are completed during the pre-reading phase of the reading lesson. The third column can be completed either as the material is read or after the reading is completed. If the children do not come up with all the topics the teacher had planned to cover under the "W" portion of the chart, the teacher should add them. If children show a special interest in a topic the teacher had not planned to cover, the plans should be modified so it is covered.

PreReading Plan.   The PreReading Plan (PReP) is another technique to help readers recall what they know about a topic before they start reading (Langer, 1981). For example, a sixth-grade class will read about ancient Egypt. PReP has three phases:

1. In the first phase of PReP, the teacher asks the students to express their initial associations with the topic: "What comes to mind when I say, 'Egypt'?" or "What do you think of when I say, 'Egypt'?"

2. Next, the teacher asks the students to reflect on their initial responses: "What made you think of (whatever the students said)?" This should lead to a discussion during which students explain the sources of their knowledge.

3. Finally, the teacher asks whether the students have any new ideas about the topic or whether they changed their perceptions: "Do any of you have new or different ideas or thoughts about Egypt?"

While using PReP, the teacher will analyze the student responses. Langer (1981) suggests individual responses can be characterized as (a) showing very little knowledge, (b) showing some prior knowledge, or (c) showing much prior knowledge. The teacher should adjust the instructional plan if the students, as a group, reveal a lack of knowledge about the topic. Instead of proceeding with the reading assignment, the teacher should focus on building students' background knowledge.

Instructional Strategies for Reading the Textbook: Graphic Organizers

In addition to activating background knowledge, a teacher may decide to use a graphic organizer to highlight the main points of a textbook (Barron, 1969). A graphic organizer is a diagram showing the structure of something—in this case, a chapter or selection in a social studies textbook. Usually, the teacher's edition of an elementary social studies textbook will have a graphic organizer for each chapter. If a teacher wants to create a graphic organizer, first the teacher identifies the important concepts, the main ideas, of the chapter. Then the teacher selects key words to represent those concepts and prepares a diagram showing the structure of the chapter. The diagram may be placed on a chart or on an overhead transparency and is used in leading a discussion with the students before they read. The discussion may lead students to offer annotations, questions, or comments, which are placed on the graphic organizer. The whole discussion should not take a long time, just 5 to 10 minutes. Figure 8.1 is an example of a graphic organizer prepared for a class of fourth graders who will read a textbook chapter about the physical geography of their state, Connecticut.

To summarize, a graphic organizer is: (1) a chart or diagram showing the main ideas in a textbook chapter, (2) is prepared by the teacher, and (3) is displayed before children read.

Instructional Strategies for Reading the Textbook: Vocabulary

Many educators call the type of writing found in social studies textbooks *academic language*. Academic language is different from the type of writing found in literary (or narrative) texts. There are two types of academic language, both found in social studies textbooks. *Technical*, or specific, academic language includes words related to a specific discipline. In elementary social studies these are words from the social sciences—primarily history and geography, but also words from anthropology, economics, and sociology. For example, for a fourth-grade unit on the geography of California, the technical academic language would include *precipitation, climate, mountain range, delta,* and *desert. Nontechnical* academic language includes words that run across academic disciplines, and would be found in science textbooks as well (e.g., *theory, compare, analyze).* Some authorities also include words and phrases that appear in all texts, but are especially important in textbooks, such as *for instance, on the contrary*, and *to demonstrate* (Schleppegrell, 2004; Zwiers, 2008).

The demands of reading the academic language of social studies textbooks means teachers must be effective teachers of vocabulary. Students will learn little if they are asked to perform the task of looking up the meanings of words in a dictionary or glossary. Other

Figure 8.1

Graphic Organizer

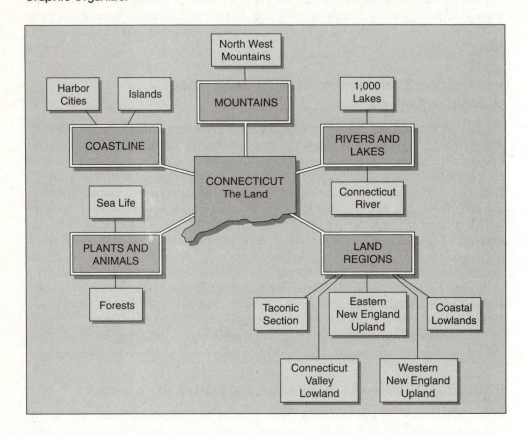

instructional strategies should prove more effective. One guideline to keep in mind is any word selected for a lesson should meet two criteria: It should be a word students do not understand *and* it should be important—a student who does not know what it means will have a difficult time understanding the text. There are dozens of good instructional strategies to teach social studies vocabulary. Here, we will look at (a) contextual redefinition, (b) semantic maps, and (c) a best option approach.

Contextual Redefinition.   For our older students, *contextual redefinition* (Cunningham, Cunningham, & Arthur, 1981) is a strategy to consider. For example, fourth graders will read the portion of a chapter on the California Gold Rush discussing the absence of law in the mining camps. The teacher identifies the following words for contextual redefinition: *bribe* and *vigilante.* Then the teacher finds the first sentence in the chapter where each word appears. Before the lesson, he wrote these sentences, and the ones preceding them, on a sheet of chart paper. For our example, these were the sentences copied from the textbook:

> *Not all elected leaders were honest. Some took* bribes.
>
> *In some mining camps there was so much crime that the citizens did not feel safe. They became* vigilantes *and punished people who had broken the law.*

A contextual redefinition vocabulary lesson has four phases:

1. To begin the lesson, the teacher asks his class to come up with definitions for the words *bribe* and *vigilante* before they see the chart with the sentences. This part of the lesson was done individually, and the teacher made it clear it was okay to write "I don't know."

2. In the next step, the children meet in groups of three or four to compare what they have written. Each child then writes a second definition, based on the discussion, for *bribe* and *vigilante*. Each group attempts to reach consensus on one definition for each word.

3. The teacher shows the sentences on an overhead projector and reads them with the students. The groups reconvene and discuss what they have seen, and each child writes a third definition.

4. Finally, the teacher has the whole group compare the definitions in the glossary of the social studies textbook with the ones the students have written. Contextual redefinition is a powerful teaching tool because it takes advantage of both cooperative learning and the context of the word as it appears in a sentence.

Semantic Maps.   Semantic maps are diagrams allowing students to organize several pieces of information related to a single word (Heimlich & Pittelman, 1986; Johnson & Pearson, 1984; Yopp & Yopp, 1996). Much of the information generated comes from the students themselves, and semantic mapping has the advantage of simultaneously teaching word meanings and activating background knowledge. The teacher starts by writing a word inside a circle in the middle of a piece of chart paper. The students then suggest words and phrases related to the word, which the teacher writes on the chart paper. Finally, the teacher and the students work together to organize the suggested words and phrases in "satellites" linked to the target word. My experience has been that with elementary school children, semantic webbing works better if the teacher provides descriptors for the satellites before beginning the activity. For example, if the target word was *money,* the teacher would begin the activity with the word *money* written in the center of a semantic map including satellites labeled *types of money, what people do with money, how people get money,* and *what money looks like.* The comments of the students would then be recorded around the appropriate satellite. Figure 8.2 shows a semantic map a group of second graders completed for the word *money.*

A Best Option Approach.   Again, there are literally dozens of techniques for teaching word meanings (Reutzel & Cooter, 2008; Tierney & Readance, 2005). A "best option" approach for elementary classrooms allows teachers to make choices and borrows on the

Figure 8.2

Semantic Map: *Money*

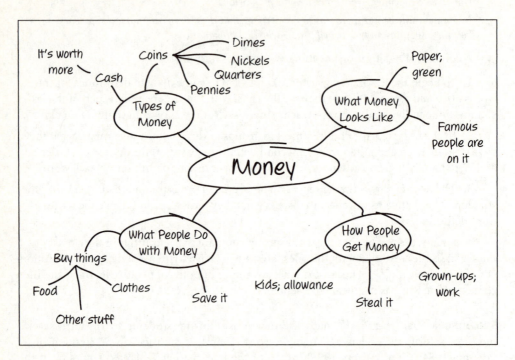

Context-Structure-Sound-Reference approach first proposed by William S. Gray (Ruddell, 1997). This approach works best with small groups of children. It goes as follows:

1. *Display the word in context.* Show the children the word in a sentence, preferably a sentence from the social studies textbook. Underline the target word—for example, *Many farms in our county grow <u>asparagus</u>.*

2. Have the children see if they can *guess a meaning.* If they are close, you may want to add what they need to know, and you can stop right here!

3. For most words, the students will need more help. At this point, you need to make a choice. You have five good options:

   ■ The most effective way to convey the meaning of some words is by presenting *the thing itself or an illustration of it.* For example, if the target word is *asparagus,* your most effective teaching tool is a bunch of fresh asparagus and, not having that, a photograph of asparagus. This will not work for words not having a tangible referent, like *democracy.*

   ■ Another option is to look at the *structure of the word,* focusing on prefixes, root words, and suffixes. For example, a class of third graders was studying their community, and the November election included a local antigrowth initiative.

To teach *antigrowth,* the teacher could focus on the meaning of the prefix *anti-.* With older students this can involve a look at Greek and Latin roots. To teach *democracy,* a group of sixth graders studying ancient Greece would learn the word comes from the Greek words *demos,* which means "the people," and *kratein,* meaning "to govern."

- In some cases, neither *option a* nor *option b* is the best choice because some words are best taught through *synonyms and antonyms.* The target word can be taught by displaying either words with nearly the same meaning or an opposite meaning. This works well with "big" words having a "short" word synonym. For example, to teach *occupation,* it may take no more than displaying and discussing *job.*

- Select *some other method,* such as contextual redefinition or a semantic map. Remember, not all words need to be taught the same way!

- Finally, some words are best taught by referring to a *"kid-friendly" definition.* Sometimes the glossary in a social studies book or a dictionary for children provides a simple definition that will get the job done. For other words, you may have to write one. Display the definition and discuss what it means.

Instructional Strategies for Reading the Textbook: Comprehension

The ultimate goal of all reading, of course, is to understand the text. Many resources are available for teachers who want to learn more about "comprehension building" strategies (Camperell & Knight, 1991; McKeown, Beck, & Blake, 2009; National Institute of Child Health and Development, 2000; Tierney & Readence, 2005). We will focus on (a) developing *strategic reading* through reciprocal teaching, (b) mastering the art of *question classification and answer verification* through the use of question–answer relationships, and (c) using *text structures* to focus students on the most important information in a text.

Teaching Reading Strategies Through Reciprocal Teaching. Reciprocal teaching is a comprehension-building process that has proved effective in several studies (Fisher & Frey, 2008; Lubliner, 2001; Palinscar & Brown, 1984; Pilonieta & Medina, 2010; Rosenshine & Meister, 1994). Reciprocal teaching follows the "gradual release of responsibility" model of teaching. At first, teachers model a reading strategy. Then, students perform the strategy under the teacher's guidance. Finally, students are challenged to perform the strategy independently, while the teacher monitors their output and provides corrective feedback.

The goal is to teach students to use a set of metacognitive strategies independently while they read. *Metacognitive* means thinking about our own thinking. The essential strategies are:

1. *questioning,* as students ask questions reflecting the main idea of the text and probe for inferences;

2. *clarifying* unclear portions of a text, especially words and phrases;

3. *summarizing* the information in the text; and

4. *predicting* what might be learned next.

The text is read in subparts, usually one paragraph in upper-grade texts or one page in primary texts. The teacher may focus on one strategy at a time or work on more than one. Again, at first, the teacher models the strategy, using the technique of "thinking aloud." When the teacher thinks the students can perform the strategy, the students assume that responsibility under the teacher's guidance. Thus, the teacher's role gradually diminishes as students take over more and more responsibility in the group lesson.

Question Classification and Answer Verification Through QARs.   Question–answer relationships (QARs) will help students answer questions more efficiently and accurately (Raphael & Au, 2005). Students need to classify questions by the location of their answers. This will not only make it easier to answer the questions but also help students verify their answers. The fact is many students think every question is *literal,* that is, with a clearly verifiable answer (e.g., The answer is in the second paragraph on page 73). Many questions, however, require *inferential* or *evaluative* comprehension. Inferential questions require the reader to form opinions, often through speculation, while evaluative questions ask readers to make a judgment. In each case, the answer to the question cannot be found in any one place in the text.

In the QAR format, questions and their answers can be placed into four categories according to the relationship between the question and the location of the answer. The four categories are:

1. *Right There.*   The answer to this type of question is explicitly stated in the text and easy to find. These questions reflect the student's ability to perform literal comprehension tasks. For example: *How long did the San Francisco earthquake of April 18, 1906, last?*

2. *Think and Search.*   The answer is stated in the text, but the required information is in more than one place. The reader has to "put together" two or more parts of the text to come up with the answer. These are also literal comprehension tasks, but are more complicated because the verification of the answer requires reference to at least two places in the text. For example: *What three factors led to the "population boom" in southern California in the early 1900s?*

3. *Author and Me.*   The answer is not in the text. The reader synthesizes information in the text with his or her personal knowledge or perspective. Author-and-me questions challenge the student to perform inferential and evaluative comprehension tasks. For example: *We read about the first automobiles driven in California. What changes had to be made once many people began driving automobiles?* (This is an inferential comprehension task because the text did not state the answer.) *Now we have millions of cars in California and thousands of miles of freeways. All in all, has this been good or bad for our state?* (This is an evaluative comprehension task, as students must make a judgment.)

4. *On My Own.*   This type of question is related to information in the text, but the reader could answer it without having the text. For example: *We read about how John Muir and other conservationists worked to create national parks in California. Have you visited a national park in California? Tell us about your visit.*

The purpose of QARs is to teach students to classify questions and verify their answers. This is a different process from the one most teachers follow. The common practice is to simply ask questions and hope some student provides an answer. Using the QARs for question classification and answer verification requires the following steps:

First the teacher asks the question—the teacher should be sure that during the reading lesson all four types of questions will be asked.

Next, *before* the students attempt to answer the question, the students classify the question. Is it a "Right There" question, a "Think and Search" question, an "Author and Me" question, or an "On My Own" question? This takes time—the children will have to be taught the characteristics of each type of question.

Then, students answer the question.

Finally, the teacher asks the student to verify their answers. Why do you think your answer is correct?

For younger children, in grades 1 to 3, a more simple QAR taxonomy has only two categories: Is the answer to the question "In the Book," or "In My Head"? "Right There" and "Think and Search" questions have answers that can be found "In the Book." On the other hand, "On My Own" and "Author and Me" questions have answers that will be found "In My Head." I have seen teachers use this simple categorization effectively with first graders. Before answering a question from their social studies books, the children are challenged to decide if the answer is "In the Book" or "In My Head." If the answer is "In the Book," the teacher asks the students to find the page where the answer is located. If the answer is "In My Head," the children close their books and think about what they have read and what they already know.

Highlighting Important Information Through the Use of Text Structures.   Almost all authorities on reading social studies textbooks promote the use of expository text structures to aid reading comprehension (Reutzel & Cooter, 2008; Tierney & Readence, 2005). *Expository* text is information-based text, as opposed to *narrative* texts, which are stories. Most chapters in social studies textbooks reflect one of the following text structures: (a) cause and effect, (b) problem and solution, (c) comparison/contrast, (d) sequence, and (e) description. Figure 8.3 shows diagrams of these text structures.

For lessons with the social studies textbook, there are two ways to use diagrams based on text structures: as a graphic organizer or a *study guide*. We covered graphic organizers earlier in this chapter. A study guide based on a text structure consists of questions or fill-in-the-blank tasks students complete during and after reading. Both structure-based graphic organizers and study guides focus student attention on the key concepts and supporting details. Figures 8.4 and 8.5 allow you to compare a graphic organizer and a study guide, each based on the cause and effect text structure. Figure 8.4 shows a graphic

Figure 8.3

Diagrams of Expository Text Structures

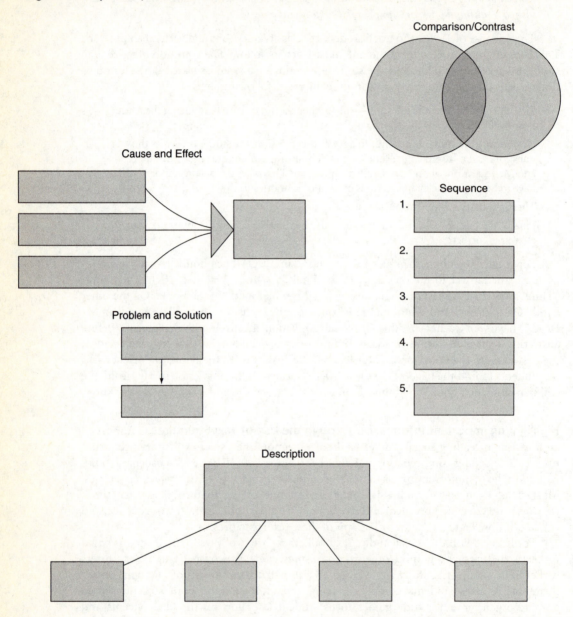

Figure 8.4

Structure-Based Graphic Organizer

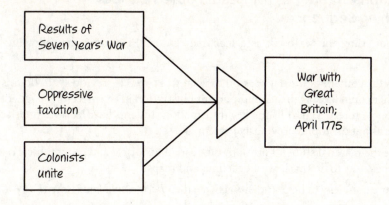

Figure 8.5

Structure-Based Study Guide

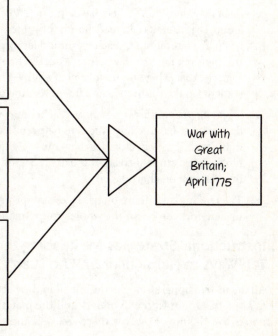

Results of the Seven Years' War
1. Why were the colonists angry with the Proclamation of 1763?
2. Did the colonists need the British army? Why or why not?
3. What new skills did the colonists learn?

Oppressive Taxes
4. Why did Britain need more money?
5. What does "no taxation without representation" mean?
6. How did the colonists protest the Tea Act?

Colonists Unite
7. Why did the first Continental Congress meet in September 1774?
8. How had the colonists' views of themselves and Britain changed in the 20 years from 1754 to 1774?

War with Great Britain; April 1775

organizer for a fifth-grade social studies textbook chapter on the causes of the American Revolution. Figure 8.5 is a structure-based study on the same reading selection.

Instructional Strategies for Reading the Textbook: A Teaching Sequence

For lessons using the textbook as a teaching resource, I suggest the following teaching sequence:

1. *Link* the content of the day's lesson to what was covered previously. To do this, a teacher could look again at an important illustration in the preceding pages of the textbook, reread a chart listing key information students have learned, or ask questions about the topics previously presented.

2. Place the material students are about to read in historical and geographical *context*. The best way to do this is with timelines and maps.

3. Choose a strategy to help students activate their *background knowledge* (K–W–L, PReP).

4. Teach essential *vocabulary*—see strategies covered earlier in the chapter .

5. Set a *purpose* for reading, either orally or in writing. A graphic organizer can be used to do this. Or, I suggest writing the purpose on the chalkboard or on a chart paper. For example, "Today, we are going to read pages 11 to 14 to learn more about firefighters." Another way to do this is to write three or four questions on the chalkboard students should be able to answer after they have done the reading.

6. *Read the material.* Teachers have quite a few options here: (a) The teacher can read aloud, (b) students can read aloud, (c) students can read silently, or (d) students can listen to an audiotape. Teachers should let students who are going to read aloud practice their reading the day before. Also, teachers should never have students read aloud material that is beyond their level of ability. The teacher's goal should be to allow all students in the room to hear a fluent reading of the text.

7. *Focus on essential information.* A teacher may want to use reciprocal teaching, QARs, or structure-based study guides to help students understand important information in the text. To be effective, teachers must highlight the essential information in the block of text students read. It is usually a good idea to summarize the important information on chart paper.

8. The reading experience often serves as a *springboard to other activities.* These follow-up activities can be for the whole group, small groups, or interested individuals.

Instructional Strategies for Reading the Textbook: Ten Ways to Help Children Who "Can't Read" the Textbook

All the instructional strategies described in this section will increase the number of children in your classroom who will understand the material presented in their social studies textbooks. We all know, however, there will be some children who will still find the textbook a mystery that cannot be solved. Some of these children will be English learners who have not acquired English literacy, others will be children with disabilities who find reading a difficult chore. Here is a list of suggestions for helping such children:

1. Tape-record as many chapters in the textbook as possible—this is a great task for a dedicated parent volunteer. Let students listen to the tape before and after the chapter is covered in class.

2. Write a simplified version of a textbook chapter. Yes, I know, this is a very time-consuming task, and it will be impossible to do for all chapters. The goal is to take a chapter and cut it by two-thirds, using smaller words and shorter sentences.

3. Summarize key points in a chapter on a set of study cards. Each card should be large: 8½ × 11 inches, standard paper size, is about right. Prepare a limited number of cards for each chapter, approximately 5 to 10. In simplified language and with large print, restate information presented in the chapter. One card for a fifth-grade chapter on the causes of the American Revolution could read, "The British government made people in the Colonies pay new taxes. The people in the Colonies had no say in the decision to add these taxes."

4. Make good use of graphic organizers and data retrieval charts. Graphic organizers are effective in cueing children to what they will learn. Data retrieval charts summarize what has been learned in a textbook chapter in a highly accessible format (see Figure 8.6).

5. Make your study guides as simple as possible. For example, take a look again at Figure 8.5, the structure-based study guide. A teacher could add page number hints to each question; for example, *4. Why did the British need more money? (see pages 104–105)*.

6. Differentiate your vocabulary instruction. Try to use real objects or illustrations whenever possible. The vocabulary teaching strategies described in this chapter are effective, but they "use words to teach words." It may be necessary to provide additional instruction, typically through discussion, to teach the meanings of some words to children with reading difficulties.

7. Do a selective, second reading of a chapter with children who are struggling. This "skimming" of the chapter would consist of the following: a second look at a graphic organizer; reading and discussing the title of the chapter; reading and discussing all subtitles; reading the first paragraph and a small number of selected paragraphs; looking closely at all illustrations, charts and diagrams; reading the chapter summary.

8. Supplement the textbook with other resources. Many times the material covered in a chapter will be the topic of a children's information book written at a much simpler level. For English learners, resources written in a language other than English will be very valuable.

9. For children with learning disabilities, consider breaking the chapter down into smaller, more manageable units. After the chapter has been covered with the whole class, you may want to meet with children having difficulty and teach three, 15-minute mini-lessons on successive days, each addressing one-third of the chapter.

Figure 8.6

Example of a Data Retrieval Chart

	Native Californians: Comparison of Four Tribes			
Tribe	Region: Where did they live?	Dwellings: What type of homes did they build?	Food: What did they eat?	Other: In what other ways were they different from other tribes?
Yurok				
Yokuts				
Mohave				
Chumash				

10. For English learners, use preview–review whenever it is feasible. Again, in preview–review, the teacher or an aide gives a preview of the contents of the chapter in the students' first language before the chapter-based lesson in English is taught. After the lesson, the teacher reviews the important information presented in English in the students' first language. This is difficult to implement because it requires a teacher who speaks the students' first language and all the English learners in the group must have the same first language.

Children's Literature: Information Books and Biography

Information books are an essential resource for the social studies teacher (Bennett & Groce, 2009; Marinak & Gambrell, 2009; Ogle, Klemp, & McBride, 2007; Sandmann & Ahern, 2002; Zarnowski & Gallagher, 1993). Books about people, places, things, ideas, and events are all information books. The best books are a blend of art and science, a combination of a vivid text, inspired illustration, and uncompromising accuracy (Gill, 2010). Why are information books so valuable for social studies teaching? Books are available on almost any topic. For example, do you know who Esther Morris was? Students who read *I Could Do That! Esther Morris Gets Women the Vote* will learn Esther Morris worked tirelessly to get women the vote in Wyoming and was the first woman in United States history to hold political office (White, 2005). Or, want to know more about candy? Try *How Sweet It Is (and Was): A History of Candy* (Swain, 2003). Another advantage of using information books is they are available at all reading levels, from simple picture books to books for the oldest, ablest students. For example, among the many juvenile biographies on Dr. Martin Luther King, Jr. is the excellent *Martin's Big Words: The Life of Dr. Martin Luther King, Jr.* (Rappaport, 2001), a picture book for young readers. Readers with more advanced abilities could read the more challenging biography by Diane Patrick (1990), *Martin Luther King, Jr.*

Selection of Information Books

Resources.   Hundreds of new information books are published each year and join the thousands already occupying the shelves of public and school libraries. Fortunately, teachers have many good resources to help them find books that fit the social studies standards they are teaching:

■ Each year, a joint committee of the National Council for the Social Studies (NCSS) and the Children's Book Council selects a list of books; the list is titled "Notable Children's Books in the Field of Social Studies." The annotated list of notable books is published annually in the journal *Social Education* (usually in the April/May issue). The NCSS also selects the Carter G. Woodson Book Awards annually. Awards go to outstanding books for young readers that treat topics related to ethnic minorities and race relations sensitively and accurately. Winning books are reviewed in the September issue of *Social Education*.

■ Articles in professional journals discuss books, usually in the context of a specific topic or category of books. See, for example, Stewart's (2006) article on children's books about the life and legacy of Rosa Parks.

■ Reviews of books are an excellent resource and are regularly published in the following journals: *Booklist, Children's Literature Association Quarterly, Hornbook, Interracial Books for Children Bulletin, Language Arts, School Library Journal, Social Studies and the Young Learner, The Reading Teacher, Top of the News,* and *Wilson Library Bulletin.*

■ Books about children's literature can provide a great deal of help. These include large, college-level textbooks on children's literature with good discussions of information books, like Norton, Norton, and McClure's (2003) *Through the Eyes of a Child: An Introduction to Children's Literature.* A book written specifically for elementary teachers is *Transcultural Children's Literature* (Pratt & Beaty, 1999). Two books link children's literature to *Expectations of Excellence,* the NCSS social studies standards (Krey, 1998; Sandmann & Ahern, 2002).

Quality.   Recommendations from the previously listed sources will give us some assurance of quality. This is an important issue because not all information books are worthy of inclusion in our classrooms. We can use two general criteria in evaluating information books:

First, *the content presented in the book should be accurate.* Accuracy, especially in biography, has been a problem in children's information books (Bigelow, 1992; Moore, 1985; Wilton, 1993; Zarnowski, 1990). Authors frequently painted heroic, mythic images of some of their subjects, ignoring or minimizing their faults and failures. Times certainly have changed, however, and more recent biographies for upper-elementary readers reveal things formerly taboo. For example, Freedman's (1993) biography of Eleanor Roosevelt has a full discussion of FDR's adulterous affair with Lucy Mercer (*Eleanor Roosevelt: A Life of Discovery*). Many authors of information books now include a list of sources. For example, Diane Stanley's (1994) picture book biography *Cleopatra* includes a "Note on Ancient Sources." Readers learn there are no existing portraits or statues of Cleopatra and that illustrator Peter Vennema therefore based his pictures on Cleopatra's image on Egyptian coins. Some older information books lack accuracy because people of color often were presented in a biased or racist manner. To provide one example, compare two picture book biographies of Pocahontas (Lechner, 1997). One written in the 1990s, by William Accrosi (1992), is quite good (*My Name Is Pocahontas*). The book has a realistic portrayal of Pocahontas's tribal life, and no "Eurocentric" bias is evident. Compare it with an older biography written and illustrated by Ingri and Edgar Parin d'Aulaire (*Pocahontas,* published in 1946). In this book, Powhatan, Pocahontas's father, is described as a "stern old Indian chief" who "was ugly and cruel." Englishman John Smith, however, "was the handsomest man Pocahontas had ever seen" and was "hardy" and "shrewd." The bottom line was well stated by Tony Sanchez (2001) in an article about how children should learn about "heroes and heroines":

> One crucial aspect of examining the hero is to go underneath the image and myth to reveal the person's strengths and weaknesses. Only a multidimensional portrayal allows students to understand the nature of heroism. (p. 27)

The second general criterion to use in evaluating information books is *the writing and illustration should be very good.* The books we choose should be both good social science and good literature. Again, the previously listed sources usually do an excellent job of screening information books and only recommend those of good quality. Some information books have won the most prestigious awards in children's literature: the Newbery Medal and the Caldecott Medal. Both are awarded by the American Library Association. The Newbery Medal goes to the author of the most distinguished contribution to American literature for children, and the Caldecott Medal is awarded to the artist of the most distinguished American picture book for children. In addition to winners of each medal, the selection committee also recognizes several "honor" books. Recent information book winners include a 2010 Newbery Honor Book, *Claudette Colvin: Twice Toward Justice* (House, 2009); a 2006 Newbery Honor Book, *Hitler Youth: Growing Up in Hitler's Shadow* (Bartoletti, 2005); and a 2005 Newbery Honor Book, *The Voice that Challenged the Nation: Marian Anderson and the Struggle for Equal Rights* (Freedman, 2004). Information book winners include a 2009 Caldecott Honor Book, *A River of Words: The Story of William Carlos Williams* (Bryant, 2008); a 2008 Caldecott Honor Book, *The Wall: Growing Up Behind the Iron Curtain* (Sis, 2007); and, the 2004 Caldecott Medal recipient, *The Man Who Walked Between the Towers* (Gerstein, 2003).

How to Use Information Books to Teach Social Studies

Information books can be used as part of the social studies program in many ways. Usually, an information book is read in one of two ways:

1. *Read independently.* There should be some time every day in our classrooms for our students to read information books. Some children will choose to read information books during time devoted to silent reading—usually called either *sustained silent reading* (SSR) or *drop everything and read* (DEAR). In addition to SSR, on some days our plan for social studies should allow students to read books independently while their classmates work on projects. Students will amass an amazing amount of content knowledge through independent reading. Think of the parallel situation among adults. Most adults realize how much a person can learn from reading fiction and biography; the potential of information books is as great for our students.

2. *Read to find specific information.* Information books are an essential resource for students who are "hunting down" the answer to an inquiry or are looking for facts they need to complete a project. Information books provide more depth than an encyclopedia, which can either be a blessing or a curse, depending on what level of understanding a person requires. Reading to answer an inquiry or complete a project is very different from the more casual, "kick-your-feet-up" reading done during SSR. For one thing, the reader will skip portions of the book because the only parts that matter are those answering the inquiry. This type of reading is called *scanning.* Also, information will have to be recorded, so parts of the text will be read two or three times. As students read, they take notes or write things down on a data retrieval chart.

Children's Literature: Fiction

Many authorities recommend including juvenile fiction when teaching social studies in the elementary school (Field, 1998; Sandmann & Ahern, 2002; Zarnowski & Gallagher, 1993). Three types of fiction can be used in social studies instruction:

1. *Historical novels.*   Many social studies units can be enhanced with *historical novels.* Some of the finest children's books fall into this genre, including Newbery Medal winners like *The Midwife's Apprentice* (Cushman, 1995), *Out of the Dust* (Hesse, 1997), and *A Single Shard* (Park, 2001).

2. *Folktales.*   Folktales can be used when a unit looks at a specific cultural group (Virtue & Vogler, 2009). A *folktale* is a story passed down through generations, typically in oral form. Today, culturally authentic, beautifully illustrated, and well-written versions of tales from cultural groups all over the world are available. One caution is in order when using folktales in social studies. Almost all picture book folktales portray people in preindustrial settings. In folktales, Native Americans and people from Hispanic America, Africa, and Asia all wear traditional costumes and live in villages. It is important to use folktales in combination with information books showing the same group of people as they live today. If, for example, a teacher wanted to develop a mini-unit on the folktales of the Native peoples of Alaska and Northern Canada, then he or she would use the stories in books like *The Girl Who Dreamed Only Geese and Other Tales of the Far North* (Norman, 1997), *Enchanted Caribou* (Cleaver, 1985), *The White Archer* (Houston, 1967), and *Tikta Liktak: An Eskimo Legend* (Houston, 1965). It would be important to have children also become familiar with books showing the Inuit and Inupait in contemporary settings (Corriveau, 2002; Santella, 2001). The best-known Inuit author of books for children is Michael Kusugak. His books, like *Baseball Bats for Christmas* (1990) and *Northern Lights: The Soccer Trails* (1993) show modern Inuit children in their daily lives (Black, 2008). Another important book for this unit is Diane Hoyt-Goldsmith's *Arctic Hunter* (1992). This chronicles the daily life of Reggie, an Inupait boy living in Kotzebue, Alaska. Although much of Reggie's life is that of a traditional Inupait, we also see him riding in a four-wheel-drive truck, living in a modern house with a television and video games, and eating hamburgers and pizza.

3. *Contemporary realistic fiction.*   This is a broad genre of literature incorporating stories taking place during the present or recent past. For many topics in social studies, contemporary stories can be used. For example, Eve Bunting's *A Day's Work* (1994) is a fictional account of a Hispanic day laborer and his grandson. This book not only tells a good story, but also helps children better understand the status of immigrants in the United States. *Too Many Tamales,* by Gary Soto (1993), is a charming Christmas story with Hispanic characters. Both books could be used to illustrate the importance of intergenerational relationships among Hispanic cultural groups (see also Cordier & Perez-Stable, 1996; Cruz, 2007; Main, Wilhelm, & Cox, 1996).

Students will amass an amazing amount of content knowledge when they read, together and alone.

Why Use Fiction?

First, fiction can help children acquire essential social studies content because a story can provide them with a sense of empathy. Books combining thorough research with vivid writing will make children feel transported to another place. Consider Lois Lowry's *Number the Stars* (1989). Readers will share the terror of Ellen Rosen, a Danish Jew, and her best friend, Annemarie Johansen, when the girls are awakened in the night by Nazi soldiers. Also, fiction can help students acquire information about a wide range of topics. This assumes, of course, that a work of fiction is accurate—free of bias, stereotypes, and outright errors. Author-illustrator Paul Goble set a standard more authors should emulate; he cites the sources of his Native American folktales (i.e., *The Girl Who Loved Wild Horses,* 1978; *Buffalo Woman,* 1984; *Lone Bull's Horse Raid,* 1973). His stories are based on oral testimony gathered by anthropologists during the last part of the 19th century and the first decade of the 20th century. Even though authors of historical fiction are not under the same obligation as authors of information books to provide a bibliography, many list the sources of their stories or provide informative essays on the historical context of the books (e.g., Cushman provides a fine note on medieval midwifery at the end of *The Midwife's Apprentice*, 1995).

How to Use Fiction

The same categories of activities presented in the previous section on information books can be used with fiction. The books can be read independently or read to find information to complete an inquiry or a project. Unlike information books, however, fiction is not written to transmit facts and ideas. The goal of the writer of fiction is to tell a story and, in many cases, to shed light on the human condition. Therefore, the best way to use fiction is as an "adjunct" to a unit and to encourage students to read the stories independently. When teachers use fiction as part of social studies, a major caution is in order. Before moving to the social studies content in the book, students should first be allowed to respond to the book as a story. At the end of the chapter is a lesson plan encouraging children to appreciate a good book as literature and then learn social studies content from the story.

Writing in the Social Studies Program

A good elementary school social studies program will require students to write in a variety of formats, many unique to social studies (Beyer & Gilstrap, 1982; Firek, 2006; Gilstrap, 1991; Quigley & Bahmueller, 1991). For many years writing in elementary social studies has, for the most part, been limited to "research" reports, book reports, and filling in the blanks on worksheets (Gilstrap, 1982; Leming, Ellington, & Schug, 2006). This is unfortunate because other forms of writing are relatively easy to use and are more challenging than research and book reports. In the 21st century, it should go without saying that all the forms of writing described in this section should be completed by older elementary students on computers. Our focus here is on (a) forms of writing well suited to the social studies, and (b) writing as a part of civic education.

Forms of Writing Well Suited to the Social Studies

As students gather information, they will do a great deal of information-based writing, primarily in the form of notes written on charts or graphs. Most elementary students need a great deal of help in learning how to take notes. I suggest providing students with *data retrieval charts* to record their data. Data retrieval charts provide an organizational framework for taking notes (see example in Figure 8.6).

Only after students have completed several retrieval charts should they be asked to take notes without any assistance. Taking notes is difficult because it differs from the types of narrative writing students complete during language arts (e.g., journal entries, personal narratives, and stories).

Students enjoy projects in which they write from the perspective of a person living in the past (Firek, 2006; Selwyn, 1995). This is a written form of *role play,* wherein students assume another identity. For example, fifth-grade class students will pretend they are soldiers in the Revolutionary War. Their Valley Forge diaries are to reveal their experiences in the summer of 1777. A good way to begin this assignment is to make a chart of the contextual details students will need when they start writing. They should have a good sense of the setting for their journal entries, including the weather, the clothing people wore, and the design of buildings and other human-made objects. They should read and listen to the words and phrases people in that era used so their written entries "sound" authentic. For another project, students could write the front page of a newspaper the *day after* an important historical event (e.g., July 5, 1776). This type of written project requires students to gather data and incorporate it into the news stories they are writing. Many students enjoy changing their "voice" as they become persons who lived long ago.

Selwyn (1995) suggests two more challenging formats for writing from the perspective of a person who lived in the past. In the first, members of the class assume complementary roles and write to each other (also described by Evans, 1995; see the vignette at the beginning of Chapter 5). For example, during a unit on the Civil War, one student could pretend to be an abolitionist living in Massachusetts, and a classmate could assume the role of a slave owner living in Georgia. Both could write journal entries responding to Lincoln's election in 1860. If students understand the anachronism, it would be fun for them to pretend to be on different sides of a historical issue and send e-mail to each other. Tunnell and Ammon (1996) show how children's literature can provide multiple perspectives on a historical event and help students avoid inaccurate generalizations.

What are the alternatives to the standard "research" report (Dimmitt & Van Cleaf, 1992; Koeller, 1992)? All too often, the assignment to do a report becomes an exercise in "pseudowriting" as students plagiarize material from the Internet and encyclopedias. Rather than assign a topic that appears as an entry in an encyclopedia (e.g., "The Navajo," "Harriet Tubman," or "Russia"), it is better to pose inquiry questions requiring students to find information in more than one place. Topics requiring students to gather data through surveys or interviews will eliminate the possibility of copying from encyclopedias. Finally, not all reports should be written. After gathering information on a topic or question, students can prepare multimedia presentations with software like PowerPoint, create a podcast, or make more traditional oral presentations and bulletin board displays.

Writing as a Part of Civic Education

Civitas, the curriculum framework for citizenship education developed by the Council for the Advancement for Citizenship and the Center for Civic Education, describes several types of "participatory writing" that should be a part of elementary social studies (Quigley & Bahmueller, 1991):

Writing to Gather Social Science Data.   Students can write surveys to be administered to their classmates, families, friends, and neighbors. They can also write to agencies for

Annie Pickert/Pearson

This chapter presents many forms of writing that should be a part of social studies.

information (e.g., League of Women Voters, city council, foreign consulates, and state and federal agencies). A survey project is an excellent experience for students because they do two types of writing: composing questions on the survey and then writing a summary of their findings.

E-Mailing Public Officials.   E-mail has made it much easier for students to send written messages to public officials. They can write to congratulate candidates who win elections, to express support for a policy decision, or to complain. This type of writing will test the ability of students to adjust their writing to fit their target audience. An e-mail or letter to a member of the U.S. Congress, for example, should not sound the same as a message written to a classmate.

Writing Agendas and Minutes.   Students should take part in classroom and school meetings to understand democracy and civil discourse. These meetings should be forums for students to express perspectives and reach decisions. Meetings need agendas and minutes. Writing minutes, especially, is a difficult task. Students will have to master taking notes, pausing to clarify when they are unsure of what was said, and condensing the notes for publication.

Writing for Political Campaigns.   Political campaigns require a great deal of written material—speeches, "mailers," copy for radio and television ads, posters, and position papers. Older students can write campaign materials when they run for classroom and school office positions. Students can also write political texts for state and federal campaigns.

Writing Laws and Rules. The text of a law or classroom or school rule requires a special type of writing; the author must be succinct and convey a precise meaning. Students can write rules for the playground, classroom, and school. Every word of a classroom rule will be important and subject to interpretation.

Summary of Key Points

- Social studies textbooks can be used effectively in elementary classrooms. They should never, however, be the only instructional resource used.

- Teachers should selectively use a variety of instructional strategies with social studies textbooks, including: (a) activating student background knowledge before they read, (b) previewing chapters with graphic organizers, (c) teaching directly essential vocabulary, and (d) building comprehension. .

- As part of social studies, information books should be read independently and used to answer inquiries and complete projects.

- Fiction can provide students with a strong sense of empathy with people living in other places and times.

- Social studies provides students with many opportunities to write, often in formats they seldom use in other areas of the curriculum.

Lesson Plans and Instructional Activities

This chapter concludes with a lesson plan for a third-grade lesson using Allen Say's Caldecott-winning picture book, *Grandfather's Journey*.

Lesson Plan
Grade Three: *Grandfather's Journey*

Overview: Students in a third-grade class have been studying their community, and are working on a unit called "Our City Today." Their city has many residents who are immigrants to the United States. Allen Say's Caldecott-winning picture book *Grandfather's Journey* (1993) will help the children understand that many immigrants to their city are bicultural and have strong emotional attachments to both the United States and their homelands. This lesson is for a third-grade class of 25 students.

Resources and Materials: (a) A hardcover copy of *Grandfather's Journey*, (b) a chart with response options (see the section "Teaching Sequence"), (c) a wall map of the world, (d) various information books, encyclopedias, and atlases.

Standard: In the *National Standards for History,* Standard 3C for the early grades is "the student understands the various other groups from regions throughout the world who came into his or her own state or region over the long-ago and recent past." A performance expectation for this standard is that "the student is able to use a variety of visual data, fiction and nonfiction sources, and speakers to identify the groups that have come into the state or region and to generate ideas about why they came" (National Center for History in the Schools, 1996, p. 30).

Content Objectives: Children will learn that many immigrants retain close feelings for their native lands. One group will identify geographic similarities and differences between Japan and the United States.

Process Objectives: Children will *write* a response to the story and *identify* reasons why Allen Say's grandfather felt attached to both Japan and the United States, and a small group will *compare and contrast* the physical geography of Japan and the United States.

Values Objective: This lesson will help children become sympathetic rather than hostile to the biculturalism of many Americans.

Teaching Sequence:

1. Prepare the chart with the response options and gather information books, encyclopedias, and atlases.

2. Identify for the children Japan and the United States on a wall map of the world. Then read aloud *Grandfather's Journey.*

3. Ask whether any of the children have anything they would like to say about the book. Then call attention to the three journal-writing options you wrote beforehand on chart paper.

   Select one of the following:

   a. Write anything you want about *Grandfather's Journey.*
   b. Grandfather was *astonished* by the ocean, the enormous rocks, the endless fields, and the towering mountains. Write about something you have seen that is *astonishing.*
   c. Why do you think Allen Say's grandfather loved both the United States and Japan?

4. Later that day or the next, bring the class together and reread the story. At the end of the story, ask the class question (c). Discuss possible reasons why Grandfather felt attached to both places. Help children see that Grandfather appreciated the great natural beauty, the different kinds of people, and the wide range of sites and sounds in the United States. At the same time, he could not forget his old friends and the beauty of the places he knew as a boy in Japan.

5. You might also want to go back through the story and point out to the class how Grandfather ages and changes (see illustrations on pp. 4, 5, 16, 18, 25, and 29 of *Grandfather's Journey*).

6. Ask for volunteers for a special project on the geographic similarities and differences between Japan and the United States. This group will use the reference sources to compare the two nations on (a) climate, (b) topography, (c) rivers, (d) population density, (e) cultural groups, (f) industry, and (g) agriculture. The group will decide to report to its classmates with either a bulletin board display or an oral presentation.

Evaluation: To determine whether children have achieved the lesson's content and values objectives, (a) read what they wrote in their journals, (b) listen carefully to what they said during the discussion, and (c) assess the bulletin board display or oral presentation of the children participating in the project.

Effective Teaching in Today's Diverse Classroom: This lesson provides an example of what some educators call an *additive cultural approach* to teaching. This approach calls for a curriculum that takes advantage of the cultural identities of children by using aspects of culture as the focus for lessons. Like Allen Say's grandfather, millions of students are bicultural. Rather than ask a child to abandon his or her native culture, it makes more sense to encourage the child to add the "core" American culture to the one he or she has. For example, if you have Korean American children in your classroom, you should plan a unit that will teach all children about the history and culture of Korea. Such a unit not only would allow your Korean American children to succeed as they read and write about familiar topics but also would provide important information to all your children and help them better understand each other.

Content-Specific Instruction

CHAPTER 9

Democratic Citizenship

In this chapter, you will read about

- Why authorities believe citizenship education is the primary goal of social studies programs

- Competing perspectives on citizenship education: to teach students about how government works and to follow the rules, or to teach students about how to change society for the better

- The content of citizenship education as organized around five concerns stated by the *National Standards for Civics and Government* (Center for Civic Education, 1994): (a) what government is, (b) the basic values of American democracy, (c) the role of the U.S. Constitution, (d) the relationship of the United States to other nations, and (e) the roles and responsibilities of U.S. citizens

- Engle and Ochoa's teaching sequence for value-based decision making

- Forms of civic participation appropriate for elementary school students, including school service, community service, and individual service projects

- How citizenship can be developed as part of a teacher's plan for classroom management

In the primary grades, citizenship can be learned through school service projects. Michiko Murayama, a third-grade teacher, provided her class with an opportunity to welcome new students to their school. Ms. Murayama's school had a significant level of transience among the students, so each year her school service project was "Welcome to Cesar Chavez School." Because each teacher at Cesar Chavez School could expect to lose several students during the year and to gain at least five, the task of welcoming new students was an important one.

The first year Ms. Murayama attempted the "Welcome to Cesar Chavez School" project, she asked her class what could be done to help new students. She had her own ideas, and so did the school principal, but her third graders came up with the following list:

- *Writing and publishing a "Guide to Cesar Chavez School."* Each year, a group of her children worked together to write and illustrate the guide, and she made enough hard copies for all the new students. The guide, written and illustrated by the children, included information on school rules, holidays, as well as the recess and lunch schedule. It contained information on special programs at the school, such as an after-school recreation program run by the city. One year, Ms. Murayama's class included a description of their favorite entrées in the school cafeteria. An electronic version of the guide was posted on the school's Website.

■ *Serving as "First Week Hosts."* Other students took part in this component of the school service project by taking new students on a tour of the school. They ate lunch with the new students and made sure they were not alone at recess.

■ *Serving as translators for non-English-speaking new students at other grade levels.* Several of Ms. Murayama's third graders were bilingual. They spent some days in kindergarten and first-grade classrooms, helping teachers communicate with their new students who spoke little or no English.

School service projects like Ms. Murayama's provide children with opportunities to apply what they have learned about citizenship. Citizenship education is the topic of this chapter.

■ ■ ■

Democratic Citizenship: The First Goal of Social Studies

Good citizenship is widely recognized as the most important goal of social studies. The definition of *social studies* adopted by the National Council for the Social Studies (NCSS) states "the primary purpose of social studies is to help young people develop the ability to make informed and reasoned decisions for the public good as citizens of a culturally diverse, democratic society in an interdependent world" (National Council for the Social Studies, 2010, p. 3). Why a preeminent place for citizenship education? Knowledgeable and active citizens are essential for the survival of our democratic way of life. Consider the following statement: "Ultimately, a free society must rely on the knowledge, skills, and virtue of its citizens and those they elect to public office. Civic education, therefore, is essential to the preservation and improvement of American constitutional democracy" (Center for Civic Education, 1994, p. 1).

Citizenship education is a topic with many facets. A reading of the professional literature on the topic reveals there is no widespread agreement on the core issue, a definition of "effective" or "ideal" citizenship (Bennett, 2006; Carnegie Corporation of New York & The Center for Information and Research on Civic Learning and Engagement, 2003; Parker, 2008; Quigley & Bahmueller, 1991; Westheimer & Kahne, 2004). A major study conducted by Anderson and colleagues (1997) established that teachers have very different perspectives on what citizenship education should accomplish. A good place to start our discussion is with some definitions.

The type of citizenship we are concerned with is broader than legal status as a citizen. *Citizenship* refers to our public life, and is not limited to political activity. The *National Standards for Civics and Government* define this as "civic life," in which individuals are concerned with the "affairs of the community and nation, that is, the public realm" (Center for Civic Education, 1994, p. 7). Within this definition, an active citizen might participate in any of the following: attending a lecture series on world affairs, going to Washington DC to lobby a member of Congress, serving as docent at a museum, hosting a "tea" for a state assembly candidate, or volunteering at a shelter for homeless people. *Democratic citizenship* refers to civic life in a free society wherein decisions are reached in an open and deliberative process. The key is while the "majority rules," the basic rights of any minority are protected.

Civics and government are the two social science disciplines at the heart of citizenship education. *Civics* covers "the rights and responsibilities of citizens and their relationship to one another and to the government," whereas instruction in *government* focuses on "political and legal institutions" (Patrick & Hoge, 1991, p. 428). In elementary school, students should learn about how rules are made, enforced, and interpreted in families, at school, in the classroom, and at the local, state, national, and international levels. Instruction focusing on the functioning of legal systems is called *law-related education* (LRE), and several lessons and units have been produced to accomplish the goals of LRE (Bjorklun, 1995; Hicks & Austin, 1994; Norton, 1992; Smagorinsky, 1994).

Recently, many authorities in the field of social studies have become concerned about the decline in citizenship education in K–12 schools. Two factors seem to be involved: the impact of the federal No Child Left Behind Act, and a narrowing of the focus of public education to producing workers trained for 21st century jobs. As Ted McConnell stated, "Under the cloud of No Child Left Behind, civics has taken a backseat to reading and math, leading to the decline in civic knowledge . . . This trend is especially severe in less advantaged communities, where pressures of school assessment are far more acute" (2008, p. 312). Peggy Atlof (2008) reported about attending a meeting of the Colorado Graduation Guidelines Development Council. Participants were asked to define the primary purposes of education. "Post-secondary readiness" and "Workforce readiness" were the top two vote getters. Only 15% of the participants chose "Responsible citizenry"! Despite these trends, citizenship education should be a primary focus of elementary social studies—and I hope you get the opportunity to participate in a classroom with a strong citizenship curriculum during your professional preparation program.

Citizenship Education and Diversity

Citizenship education must provide for unification and celebrate diversity—at the same time! The values, principles, and beliefs of a democratic way of life are the unifying elements of the United States. The *National Standards for Civics and Government* (Center for Civic Education, 1994) summarize how the democratic ideal binds us as Americans: "Americans are united by the values, principles, and beliefs they share rather than by ethnicity, race, religion, class, language, gender, or national origin" (p. 25). Thus, when students become committed to our democratic system of government, democratic values and beliefs, and democratic civic life, they become Americans.

The NCSS *Curriculum Guidelines for Multicultural Education* makes this same point:

> There is, after all, a set of overarching values that all groups within a society or nation
> endorse to maintain societal cohesion. In our nation, these core values stem from our
> commitment to human dignity, and include justice, equality, freedom, and due process
> of law. (NCSS Task Force on Ethnic Studies Curriculum Guidelines, 1992, p. 284)

In your classroom, among the children there may be a half dozen native languages, national identities encompassing all the continents, and religious affiliations of many kinds. All your students need effective citizenship education that leads to a commitment to the democratic ideals of the United States of America and an understanding of the wonderful freedom we enjoy.

At the same time, citizenship education is education for diversity (Banks and Nguyen, 2008). Our units of study in social studies should help students learn about the many facets of pluralism in the United States. One of the strengths of our democratic system is that it makes diversity in language, culture, religion, nationality, and political philosophy inevitable. Students should see diversity not as a threat to our way of life, but rather a part of America that has always existed and will exist in the future. A key component of citizenship education is students learn our democratic ideal has not always been realized. Even though the United States was founded on values of justice and equality, public policy and private action have sometimes been unjust and unequal. For example, in California, fourth graders who study the history of their state should learn about the internment of Japanese Americans during World War II. Fifth graders who study the creation of the United States should understand that although the Constitution was enacted by "the people," women, Native Americans, enslaved persons, and men without property could not vote in 18th-century elections.

It is important that students who are immigrants to the United States understand our system of government, commit to democratic values and beliefs, and participate in civic life. At the same time, immigrant children should see "links between the reality of immigration today and the historical legacy of immigration to this continent" (Keiper & Garcia, 2009a, p. 1). Teachers should consider:

- Teaching children about the patterns of immigration to the United States—and how at different times, people from different parts of the world have come to this country (Keiper & Garcia, 2009b).

- Weaving citizenship naturalization ceremonies into their curriculum—one curriculum that does this is *The Path to Citizenship* curriculum published by McDougal and Littell (Ullman, 2009).

- Find ways to integrate the personal stories of immigrants both present and past into the grade level curriculum—a study of local, state, or national history will present opportunities to focus on immigration (Colby, 2009). Several excellent Websites can be used (Keiper, Krohn, & Kepner, 2009).

Research on Citizenship Education

With these definitions in mind, let's take a look at the research on citizenship education. Janet Alleman and Jere Brophy (2006) concluded the "studies focusing on elementary students, and especially primary students, have little or nothing to say about children's ideas about democracy or democratic government" (p. 17). In an earlier review, Patrick and Hoge (1991) reached a similar conclusion as they stated "the solid findings are too few and unrelated to help practitioners make a powerful difference in how they teach government, civics, and law, and in what their students learn from them" (p. 434).

Some interesting research has been conducted on what students know and think about government and civics, and how these topics are presented in textbooks. Children do understand rules and laws are a necessary part of life; they tend, however, to see government primarily as a provider of what people need, rather than as an enforcer of the rules (Alleman & Brophy, 2006; Berti, 2005). Alleman and Brophy's (2002a) study of children's understanding of the U.S. presidency revealed that K–3 students know little about the three branches of government and their ideas about the presidency center on material items, such as a big house and a limousine, rather than what the president does. An earlier study by Greenstein (1969) of political understanding among students in grades 4 through 8 still makes interesting reading. Greenstein found that fourth graders idealized political leaders, from their mayor to the president. By eighth grade, this reverence had diminished. Of particular interest is Greenstein's finding that elementary students did not base their feelings on political information; they knew very little about the leaders they held in high regard.

The research on how civics and government are treated in elementary school social studies textbooks is now dated. Wade and Everett (1994) examined how citizenship education was presented in four of the most popular third-grade social studies textbooks of the time. They wanted to find out whether things had changed from the 1960s and 1970s, when textbooks presented an image of a good citizen who was "passive, harmonious, and accepting" (p. 308). All four textbooks devoted several pages to citizenship. Wade and Everett concluded the textbooks they reviewed in the early 1990s were an improvement over earlier ones. A variety of political and social acts were presented as a part of good citizenship. In addition to staying informed, voting, and running for office, good citizens were presented as also taking social action, performing community service, and lobbying public officials. The researchers thought, however, the books did not provide enough information to help students learn the full range of civic options available to citizens of the United States. You could evaluate the social studies textbooks in your school to determine whether or not they promote "passive" citizenship, where good citizens limit their activities to staying informed and voting; or an "active" citizenship, in which good citizens lobby public officials, perform community service, and, when necessary, take part in public protests.

Competing Perspectives on Citizenship Education

Authorities have proffered several perspectives on precisely what citizenship education should try to accomplish. Anderson and colleagues (1997) conducted a study of how elementary and secondary teachers define citizenship education. They found "four coherent, identifiable, and separate viewpoints on citizenship education" (p. 351). A brief description of each should help us understand why this area of social studies is controversial:

■ Some teachers adopt a *critical thinking* perspective. These teachers believe citizenship education should help students question the status quo, develop critical thinking and questioning skills, and encourage open-mindedness and tolerance.

■ Other teachers hold a *legalist* perspective. They believe citizenship education should stress obedience to laws, teach the basic structure of our political system, and inform students of their rights and responsibilities.

■ Teachers who have a *cultural pluralism* perspective define citizenship education as the celebration of diversity and pluralism. These teachers believe that rather than teach the basic structure of our political institutions, citizenship education should expose students to a range of ideologies.

■ Finally, some teachers adhere to an *assimilationist* perspective, which is similar to the views of the legalists. Assimilationist teachers, however, explicitly reject current ideas of "political correctness" and want to transmit to students the dominant values of our society.

This summary categorizes the perspectives of teachers who, at the time, belonged to the NCSS, and reveals the divergent nature of citizenship education. It should also be noted that some teachers hold more than one perspective. To simplify things somewhat, another way to look at the competing views on citizenship education is to examine the "transmission versus transformation" debate (Stanley, 2005). This crystallizes one of the more controversial issues in social studies. Simply put, should teachers limit citizenship education to how government functions, and should their definition of a good citizen be a person who follows the rules and votes (transmission)? Or should teachers teach students how to analyze social conditions *and* then take action to bring about change (transformation)? To paraphrase Parker (2008), should citizenship education be limited to "knowing" democratic things, or should it also include "doing" democratic things (p. 65)?

The *transmission model* is adopted by the legalists and assimilationists described by Anderson and colleagues (1997; see also, Leming, Ellington, & Porter-Magee, 2003). Teachers help students understand the structure and function of local, state, and federal government. Students learn about the rights and responsibilities of citizenship and are encouraged to participate in nonthreatening civic activities, such as working on political campaigns, staying informed, and voting.

The *transformation model* is endorsed by many social studies authorities (Banks & Banks, 2003; Engle & Ochoa, 1988; Jennings, Crowell, & Fernlund, 1994). It is the model used by teachers who have both the critical thinking and the cultural pluralist perspectives described by Anderson and colleagues. Advocates of this model want a curriculum that encourages students to make decisions and *take action* related to the concept, issue, or problem being studied.

Jennings and colleagues (1994) provide specific suggestions for how to implement "transformational social studies." First, we should see our classrooms as places where students can learn about "social relationships, reciprocity, power, and community." This means we should encourage students to analyze how things do or do not work, and make suggestions for improvement. Second, the curriculum should present students with historical problem-solving situations focusing on historical "dilemmas of justice," such as those faced by the abolitionists and advocates for child labor laws. Third, we should encourage students to express their own opinions, not just to restate the positions of others. Fourth, the authors argue, we should teach students the dynamic relationship between pluralism and unity in our constitutional system. Fifth, teachers should plan for students to participate in social action projects to convince them of "the power inherent within cooperative efforts against injustice" (pp. 5–6).

You can see how controversial this could become. I think almost everyone would agree our older students should be taught to understand and analyze a range of perspectives on important current issues. Students should learn about several forms of civic participation. Teachers who encourage students to take action, however, must be sure that they do not steer their students to any one side of a public policy issue or to any one political candidate. In fact, teachers should encourage students to define issues rather than having an agenda presented to them. Finally, teachers should remember they are dealing with elementary school children, and most of these "social action" projects are more appropriate for middle and high school students.

Nonetheless, sometimes all of us can underestimate the potential of elementary school children. One of the most impressive social action projects I am aware of took place in an *elementary* school classroom. Barbara Vogel, a fifth-grade teacher in Aurora, Colorado, had completed a unit with her students on slavery in American history. Shortly thereafter, Associated Press writer Karin Davies completed a story on the slave trade existing in the late 1990s in Sudan. The story ran in a local newspaper, and one of Ms. Vogel's students, Kyle Vincent, decided something should be done to stop slavery in Sudan. The slave trade in Sudan was the result of civil war as local militias, who fought without pay for the Sudanese government, made captives their slaves. International organizations were able to purchase the freedom of some of the enslaved people. Ms. Vogel's class began to raise money, originally collecting coins in jars. This social action project received national media coverage, and eventually large donations began to arrive. By the end of 1998, the project had raised more than $50,000. The money was donated to international organizations and was used to free more than 1,000 enslaved people in Sudan.

National Projects on Citizenship Education

Two attempts to define the scope of citizenship education are worthy of mention. *Civitas* is a curriculum framework developed by the Council for the Advancement of Citizenship and the Center for Civic Education (Quigley & Bahmueller, 1991). *Civitas* is an essential document for school district committees writing instructional units on citizenship education. The *National Standards for Civics and Government* (Center for Civic Education, 1994) could prove to be very influential. I discuss specific sections of the national standards later in this chapter.

Citizenship Education: Content

Citizenship education has three components: content, values, and processes. The *content* is the knowledge students should acquire to be effective citizens, and they need to know a great deal in the fields of civics and government. For most of us, our district curriculum guide and social studies textbooks cover these topics at every grade level. If our district's

Classroom elections provide excellent opportunities for children to practice what they have learned aboutour democratic system of government.

social studies program follows the expanded horizons format, then kindergartners, first graders, and second graders focus on families, classrooms, and schools; third graders look at civic life in their cities; fourth graders study the government of their state; fifth graders learn about the federal government; and sixth graders examine governments of ancient cultures or foreign nations.

The *National Standards for Civics and Government* (Center for Civic Education, 1994) provide a specific description of the civic knowledge our students should acquire. The standards organize content under five questions:

1. *What is government, and what should it do?*   Our students should be able to provide a basic description of government. For example, students should know how rules are made, enforced, and interpreted. Students should have some understanding of the types of legislatures that exist (e.g., school boards, city councils, state assemblies, and U.S. Congress). They should become familiar with courts of law. They should learn about executives, such as their principal, the mayor, and the president. It is important that students see why government is necessary and what life would be like without it. Alleman and Brophy (2006) argue that, unfortunately, "teaching about government in the elementary grades often is not as effective as it could be, either because it is confined to teaching about government leaders and symbols, or because it gets mired in the details of topics like how a bill becomes a law." They argue that the focus should be on "why governments are needed and what they do for their people" (p. 16).

Students should learn about power and authority. Why does a city council have the power to make laws? Where did it get that power? Students should understand the authority of teachers and principals. They should also recognize examples of "power without authority," such as a robber holding up a bank or a playground bully harassing another student. Young students need to explore the purposes of rules and laws. They should recognize that rules describe the way people must behave. Again, critical analysis is necessary for good social studies lessons because the national standards expect students to evaluate laws according to criteria. Are the classroom rules understandable? Is a playground rule equitable? Is a city ordinance possible to follow and not a demand for the impossible? Finally, under this question, students should begin to understand the concept of limited government. They should see that everyone, including our most powerful elected and appointed officials, must obey the law.

At the end of the chapter is a lesson plan for a "walking field trip." A second-grade teacher takes her students on a walk to the city library. On the way, students examine several signs stating rules of public behavior—a good way to introduce children to the purpose of laws created by government, in this case a municipal government.

2. *What are the basic values and principles of American democracy?*   As a knowledge goal, we want students to describe the important values and principles of our system of government and civic life.

3. *How does the government established by the Constitution embody the purposes, values, and principles of American democracy?*   Elementary students should know what the U.S. Constitution is and the important ideas in it. Most social studies programs save most of this material until fifth grade. An important topic that should be explored before fifth grade is how the Constitution and the federal government protect individual rights. Students should begin to understand their First Amendment freedoms. Most fourth graders will learn about their state government and the specifics of their legislature, judiciary, and executive. Third grade has usually been the place where students study municipal government. In any case, by the end of fourth grade, the national standards state students should know what services their local government provides, how the services are funded, and how people can participate in local government.

4. *What is the relationship of the United States to other nations and to world affairs?*   Remember, a valid criticism of the expanded horizons curricular framework is the lack of global education in grades K–5. The national standards call for students in grades K–4 to develop knowledge in several international areas. Students should understand the concept of *nation*. I have found this to be difficult for young students, who frequently cannot understand the difference between a state in the United States, such as Vermont, and a sovereign nation, such as Germany. One concept students can begin to understand is the interdependence of nations. They should be able to identify cultural exchanges (e.g., music from another nation), trade (products grown or manufactured in other nations), and military linkages (multinational military operations). Students should learn about examples of how nations solve problems peacefully.

5. *What are the roles of the citizen in American democracy?*   Students are expected to know the definition of *citizenship*, how people become citizens of the United States, their rights and responsibilities, how their leaders are selected, and how U.S. citizens can participate in their government.

At the end of this chapter, you will find a mini-unit developed by a fifth-grade teacher with the goal of teaching her students about a basic right afforded us in the U.S. Constitution—a fair trial.

Teaching the Electoral Process

Children in elementary schools should learn about the electoral process in democratic societies (Gandy, 2004; Haas, 2004; Ledford & Lyon, 2004). One way for children to learn about elections is for them to participate in a mock election. Haas (2004) believes these elections should refrain from asking children to vote on actual candidates for local, state, or federal office. Rather, she recommends that teachers should "focus instead on key concepts about . . . the voting process" (p. 340). From her perspective, to teach the full electoral process, it is best to have an election about a class- or school-related issue (e.g., How should we spend $100 donated by the PTA?).

After a problem has been identified, the next step is to define a small number of possible solutions. Some children then choose or are assigned to be advocates for each solution. It is probably a good idea to have at least half the class be "nonpartisan," so the campaigners have someone to sway. A campaign manager is selected for each rival solution. The mock campaign can include campaign posters, speeches, and, in the upper grades, the development of video ads and campaign Websites. Though real political campaigns these days are poor examples, the emphasis should be on positive and accurate advocacy. Children should learn the vocabulary of free elections as they prepare for the election (e.g., poll, secret ballot, etc.). The actual election should include all the elements of real elections. The children could be asked to fill out a simple voter registration form. There should be a private polling place and, since many elementary schools serve as polling places for real elections, you might be able to use the actual polling booths used by adult voters. To ensure fairness, students from another class might be "hired" to monitor the voting and to count the ballots, with observers from each campaign on hand. Finally, the entire process should be analyzed. An important lesson would be to ask students to consider the key elements of a free election. Teachers should also ask the students to evaluate the effectiveness of the campaigns. If they had it to do all over again, what would they do differently?

There is much to say for Haas's approach—focusing on a classroom or school issue for a mock election. It should be noted, however, that many elementary schools do conduct mock elections on local and statewide issues, and for statewide and national candidates. The popular Kids Voting USA program allows children to learn about democracy through a combination of classroom activities, an actual voting experience, and family discussions. The program is run through state and local affiliates. In the 2008 presidential election, over 1.8 million K–12 students voted through an online balloting process—President Obama and Senator Biden received 1,173,217 votes, Senator McCain and Governor Palin received 604,754, and the remainder of the votes went to other candidates.

Citizenship Education: Values

Values are standards we use to judge human behavior. *Civic values* are values relevant to our public life. The *National Standards for Civics and Government* (Center for Civic Education, 1994) are a realistic statement of civic values. The standards call for students to become knowledgeable about the basic values of American democracy. This knowledge "is an essential first step in fostering a reasoned commitment to them" (p. 22). The standards offer this list of fundamental values of American democracy: (a) individual rights to life, liberty, and pursuit of happiness; (b) the public or common good; (c) justice; (d) equality of opportunity; (e) diversity; (f) truth; and (g) patriotism.

The national standards (Center for Civic Education, 1994) address the relationship of unity and diversity. They state that, by the end of fourth grade, "students should be able to explain the importance of Americans sharing and supporting certain values, principles, and beliefs" (p. 25). The United States is a place of many cultural groups, languages, and religions, and the standards correctly state that "the identity of an American is defined by shared political values, principles, and beliefs" (p. 25). At the same time, "students should be able to describe diversity in the United States and identify its benefits" (p. 26). A diverse country provides for new ideas, a range of perspectives on any issue, and choices in all aspects of life (e.g., the arts and politics). The standards call for students to understand how diversity can lead to conflict through discrimination and alienation. Social studies programs should help students see how such conflicts can be avoided and resolved.

Teaching Democratic Values: A Model and an Example

Engle and Ochoa (1988) comment that, for teachers, "the temptation is to indoctrinate children with the 'right' democratic values" (p. 66). Instead, they call for an analytic study of values. The national standards call for knowledge of values that will lead to a "commitment" to them. Thus, for teachers it seems the first goal should be to help students understand a value and then to analyze the issues which can arise when the value guides behavior. Finally, teachers should want students to study controversial issues and make decisions on the basis of those values.

Engle and Ochoa (1988) define a seven-step process for value-based decision making on public issues. As an example, we will consider this process as it was used in a sixth-grade classroom. The principal of the school asked students to suggest how there could be fewer disputes over use of various areas of the playground. Younger children complained that older children monopolized the more desirable areas. Engle and Ochoa's seven steps are similar to those for the processes of inquiry and critical thinking described in Chapter 7.

Step 1: Identify and Define the Problem

In this case, the principal, acting in response to student complaints, defined the problem: How can the various areas of the playground be used so there are fewer arguments about who should be playing where? Some sixth graders did not think this was a problem. They cited two reasons. First, when they were younger, the older students "hogged" the good areas. Second, the younger children did not know how to play some of the games that could be played only in certain areas. At this point, the teacher turned the discussion toward definitions. Engle and Ochoa note this is an important prerequisite to value-based decision making. The teacher wanted agreement on what constituted an "area." After some discussion, the sixth graders generated a list of six playground areas (e.g., jungle gym, dodgeball circles).

Step 2: Identify Value Assumptions

Returning to the issue his sixth graders had raised, that there was no problem regarding the playground areas, the teacher decided to focus on two values: (a) justice, and (b) respect for the rights of others. Engle and Ochoa (1988) wrote "identifying value assumptions is not limited to any one phase of the decision-making process" (p. 74). It is a good idea, though, to clarify and consider values at this stage.

The sixth graders had an extended discussion about justice, equity, and sharing. The teacher asked for definitions of *justice*. Students responded by saying it meant people "were fair" and "things happened according to fair rules." The value of justice would seem to require sharing the playground areas. Although all the students believed in fairness, some had difficulty with the application of this value in this case. This small group said justice meant that because they were treated unfairly by older students when they were small, it was perfectly fair for them to treat current fourth graders the same way (fourth, fifth, and sixth graders had recess at the same time). Other students pointed out "two wrongs don't make a right" and "fourth graders have rights, too." The vast majority of the students agreed that, to respect the rights of all students, the playground areas would have to be shared.

Step 3: Identify Alternatives

Engle and Ochoa (1988) state "values, previous knowledge, and experience are all involved in identifying alternatives" (p. 74). At this point, the teacher could have had his class work in small groups to maximize the number of students who could participate vigorously. He thought, though, the whole-group discussion was progressing well. So far, this was a civil discussion. Students had not personalized comments, exchanged threatening looks, or made rude interruptions. The teacher had two students transcribe ideas as they were offered. Two "solution alternatives" survived the discussion:

- Because nine classes were at recess together (three classes each in grades 4, 5, and 6), nine areas should be designated and the classes rotate through them—this became known as the "rotation" plan.
- Students could play in any area they wanted, and two sixth-grade monitors would be assigned to each area. The monitors would ensure all students would have a chance to play the area's game—this became known as the "monitor" plan.

Step 4: Predict Consequences

Engle and Ochoa suggest two questions be considered: (1) What effects will follow from each alternative? and (2) What effect will each alternative have on all parties? Some students noted the consequence of the rotation plan would be they would be giving up their prerogative of what to play. Others noted that they would not be able to "play handball everyday, like we want to." Other students interjected the value of justice idea again at this point as they considered the second question. The strength of the rotation plan was its equity; all classes would have the same opportunity to use each area of the playground.

The monitor plan was criticized widely when the sixth graders considered its consequences. First, several sixth graders would not be playing anything; they would be acting as organizers and referees. Although many of the sixth graders would do a good job at these tasks, they would be "giving up" their chance to play. A few noted the problem might not be solved in the monitor plan. Each area would contain fourth, fifth, and sixth graders. The younger students might continue to be pushed aside. Finally, one student commented that the younger students could not compete with them and "some of the fourth graders" might get hurt.

Step 5: Reach Decisions

Engle and Ochoa note that reaching decisions can be filled with tension because, in most cases, no solution satisfies everyone. After considering the consequences, however, this group of sixth graders almost unanimously recommended the rotation plan.

Step 6: Justify Decisions

Once again, the discussion turned to values. When the teacher asked for reasons why the rotation plan was best, several students noted it was "fair" and would give all classes "the same chance." This was a reliance on justice as a rationale. Other students commented it seemed to be better than any other plan they could think of. Three students were chosen to present the class's recommendation to the principal.

Step 7: Tentativeness of Decision Making

The teacher wanted his students to understand that their suggested rotation plan seemed like a good one but might not work. He prompted his students to remain open-minded and to accept that they may need to revise their perspectives. In this case, it was not necessary. The principal adopted the rotation plan. It worked well and has been in place for 9 years now.

Citizenship Education: Processes

The processes of effective citizenship should be practiced at home, in the classroom, on the playground, in the community, and at the state, national, and international levels. A good place to discuss the "doing" of citizenship education is with a set of attitudes, called *dispositions,* that students should adopt. The *National Standards for Civics and Government* (Center for Civic Education, 1994) argues these dispositions will enhance "citizen effectiveness and promote the healthy functioning of American democracy" (p. 37). These dispositions are beliefs that guide behavior. They include individual responsibility, self-discipline, civility, respect for the rights of other individuals, honesty, respect for the law, open-mindedness, critical-mindedness, negotiation and compromise, persistence, civic-mindedness, compassion, and patriotism. Each of these dispositions involves a process. For example, the process of open-mindedness has many components that can be practiced and developed in the classroom. First, students can learn to listen, without interruption and without preconceived notions, to the opinions of other students. Next, students should learn to question

Anthony Magnacca/Merrill

Social studies should teach our students to be good citizens. A key component of good citizenship is participation in community service projects.

the perspectives of others without personalizing their comments. Finally, students should learn to accept the valid points that another person makes rather than reject the whole message because some parts make little sense.

This open-mindedness is part of civil discourse, the polite way citizens in a democracy discuss public issues. Civil discourse is an essential process for students to learn (Parker, 1995, 2001, 2006). In *Civitas,* the curriculum framework developed through the Center for Civic Education, two essential components of civil discourse are defined (Quigley & Bahmueller, 1991, p. 13):

- *Addressing the issue.* Participants in a discussion focus on their contributions to the issues at hand and do not engage in personal attack.

- *Respecting the right of others to be heard.* Civil discourse requires good listening participants in a discussion should not disrupt other speakers.

The guidelines presented in Chapter 5 in the section "Speaking and Listening in the Social Studies Program" will encourage the development of appropriate civic discourse.

The national standards go on to define "the means by which citizens can influence the decisions and actions of their government" (Center for Civic Education, 1994, p. 38). These are (a) read about public issues; (b) discuss public issues; (c) communicate with public offi-cials; (d) vote; (e) take an active role in interest groups, political parties, and organizations; and (f) attend meetings of governing agencies, work in campaigns, circulate petitions, take part in peaceful demonstrations, and contribute money to parties, candidates, and causes. Each of these can be implemented in some form in the elementary classroom:

Read About Public Issues. News magazines written for children, like *Weekly Reader,* do an excellent job of presenting national and global issues to children. Online com-puter resources are beginning to provide accessible information to elementary stu-dents (e.g., the online resource KidsNet). Our oldest and most able elementary students can read articles in newspapers, magazines, and on appropriate Websites on the Internet.

Discuss Public Issues. Children at all elementary levels should discuss issues relating to their classroom, school, and community. Older elementary children who have read a variety of perspectives should be encouraged to discuss state, national, and global issues.

Communicate with Public Officials. One of the first public officials students should communicate with is their teacher. Students, at the proper time and in a respectful manner, should have the opportunity to talk with their teachers about topics of concern. Students at all levels should learn how to speak and write to their princi-pal on school issues. Teachers should encourage older students to write to their school board, city council and mayor, state legislature and governor, representatives in Congress, and the president. The teacher's goal is to present information, to allow a range of perspectives to be heard, and to model written and oral formats of communicating.

Vote. Elementary students should take part in classroom and school elections. These elections should be as close to the real thing as possible. All elections should pro-vide for a secret ballot, even those in the classroom. Many schools are voting places in "real" elections, and it is a good idea to let students experience a voting booth as they vote in mock state and federal elections.

Take an Active Role in Interest Groups, Political Parties, and Organizations. A variety of youth organizations encourage civic life, such as Girl Scouts, Boy Scouts, and youth groups in religious institutions. All elementary schools, however, should have stu-dent governments. Heath and Vik (1994) report how elementary school student councils allow children to exercise leadership, share ideas, resolve problems, and manage projects.

Attend Meetings of Governing Agencies, Work in Campaigns, Circulate Petitions, Take Part in Peaceful Demonstrations, and Contribute Money to Parties, Candidates, and Causes. Students should learn the petitioning process in elementary school. They can petition for changes in classroom and school policies. I know teachers who have encouraged students to consider community issues, define a position, and make presentations to the city council. Students can participate in fund-raising drives, but this must be done cautiously. The cause should be noncontroversial and school related, and the process should protect those students who are unable to make a financial contribution. Students should see they can make contributions in other ways, such as collecting things (e.g., newspapers or cans) or giving one's time.

The real test of the effect of citizenship education is whether our students become active citizens when they are older—whether they, in fact, participate when they are not directed to do so by a school assignment. The activities planned as part of the social studies curriculum should show students the range of options available to active citizens in a democratic society.

Service Learning

The NCSS position statement on service learning provides a definition, rationale, and guidelines for successful practice (NCSS Select Subcommittee, 2001). First, service learning "connects meaningful service in the school or community with academic learning and civic responsibility" (p. 240). Service learning is different from community service or voluntarism in two ways. First, the service activity is part of the curriculum and helps students acquire social studies content and civic values. Second, service learning requires reflection and, in some cases, related assignments for the students (Wade, 2008). Two of the positive features of service learning are (1) it provides opportunities for "intergenerational learning," as children interact with adults in their schools and communities; and (2) it allows students to be good citizens and make their schools and communities better places since almost all service learning projects attempt to solve problems (Levin-Goldberg, 2009; Morris, 2003). Quality service-learning activities meet these four criteria:

1. The activity provides opportunities for both the students and representatives from other agencies to design the experience (i.e., if students participate at a senior living facility, residents of the facility help plan the scope of the students' involvement).

2. The activity includes both meaningful service and the opportunity to learn social studies content.

3. The activity requires students to reflect on their service experience and the connection between the experience and democratic values.

4. The activity should focus on how to create a better society rather than simply providing charity that perpetuates the status quo.

Wade (2008) reviewed the research on service learning and social studies. Unfortunately, the research in this area is subject to significant challenges. Many "studies" on service learning are actually progress reports required by a funding agency, while others lack control groups and tracking of participants over time. Further, the results are mixed, regardless of the outcome being measured. Having noted that, Wade concluded that research shows service learning can have positive effects on items related to academic success, like student conduct at school, student motivation, and student attendance. Research shows student participants in service learning can show increases in self-esteem, social responsibility, identity development, and concern for others. Does participation in service learning increase academic achievement? Wade concluded that the "research results in this area are mixed and inconclusive" (p. 112). Future research should focus on the variables essential to the relationship of service learning and academic achievement, such as matching the experience to relevant standards, the quality of reflection after the service learning activity is finished, and the number of hours necessary for service learning to result in academic gains.

Proctor and Haas (1993) and Wade (1994) discuss service learning as a part of citizenship education for elementary students. Proctor and Haas argue that participation in service projects should "be a part of formal education beginning in the primary grades and continuing through graduation. The responsibilities and opportunities for community and social behaviors are present and need to begin at an early age" (p. 381). They describe a hierarchy of service projects:

■ *Service projects in schools and classrooms.*   These include cross-age tutoring, planting trees, raising money to buy computers for the school, and the venerable clean-campus crusade. Many of these projects can be run by the school Parent-Teacher Association. At the end of this chapter is a description of how a second-grade teacher designed school service projects for her students.

■ *Service projects in the community.*   These serve the neighborhood and the community. Proctor and Haas suggest they that begin in third grade. Community service projects typically involve cooperation with out-of-school agencies; examples are collecting food for victims of a disaster and converting a vacant lot into a park.

■ *Individual service projects.*   Proctor and Haas (1993) suggest these are appropriate for middle school and high school students. These projects involve a commitment of many hours over an extended period of time, such as volunteer work at a preschool or a senior citizen center.

Service learning can involve students of every grade level. For example, Willison and Ruane (1995) describe how students in each elementary grade provided service to local senior citizens. Kindergartners made holiday cards for residents of a nursing home. First and second graders sang and performed in theatrical programs at the nursing home. Third and fourth graders had senior pen pals and visited seniors who lived on their own. Fifth and sixth graders visited their "adoptive grandparents" at the nursing home, read to them, and played games with them. All the students studied their own grandparents and the elderly to break down stereotypical images of old people.

Service learning is an excellent way to integrate the curriculum. Continuing with the specific example of providing service to seniors, Wade (1994) shows how students could prepare a survey asking seniors what services they need (language arts). A school project could require fund-raising, which entails bookkeeping (mathematics). Environmental projects, like a community garden, demand knowledge in botany and ecology (science). Finally, service learning can incorporate the use of technology. Harwood and Chang (1999) describe strategies for using the Internet to enhance service learning. Students can find information to help them focus their project. A group concerned about a local environmental issue, for example, will find information, cataloged by ZIP code, on waste sites and other local topics in a database maintained by the Environmental Protection Agency (www.epa.gov). To provide another example of how technology can be used in service learning, e-mail can be used to communicate with people working in agencies and to share reflections on the service experience.

Citizenship and Classroom Management

A discussion of classroom management, the process of promoting and maintaining a productive environment for students, is beyond the scope of a social studies methods textbook. We should realize, however, that citizenship and classroom management are related topics (Brophy, 1985; Goodman, 1992; Hoover & Kindsvatter, 1997; Ross & Bondy, 1993; Schimmel, 1997; Wolfgang & Kelsay, 1995). Although some aspects of classroom management must be exercised by adults, classrooms should have some level of democracy. Ross and Bondy note that although teachers and students will never be equals, more teachers should "shift the emphasis away from controlling students' behavior to teaching them how to be responsible members of a community" (p. 328). Students at all grade levels should be allowed to do each of the following:

- *Play some role in the development of classroom and playground rules.* Teachers should establish some nonnegotiable rules (e.g., keep your hands and feet to yourself). Many aspects of classroom life, however, lend themselves to a variety of possible rules. Students need the experience of considering possible rules and the consequences of their implementation. Schimmel (1997) makes a persuasive argument that the development of school and classroom rules should involve everyone in the school community—students, parents, and staff.

- *Resolve problems through collaborative effort.* Students should approach their teachers with problems they think should be addressed. Likewise, teachers should bring some problems to their classroom community for consideration. Some problems have to be resolved only by the teacher and the student(s) directly involved (e.g., problems revealing private information about students). On the other hand, some issues should be brought before the whole class for an open and democratic discussion. Conflict resolution activities will give students a chance to practice civil discourse and value-based decision making. One possibility teachers should explore is helping students see the relationship between interpersonal conflicts in their classroom and international conflicts between nations (Bickmore, 2002).

- *Make decisions about how they allocate their time and about what activities they pursue.* Of course, teachers plan activities for each school day. However, students should have some blocks of class time to make choices about what they will do. Likewise, teachers select most topics covered in class. Students, though, should be able to choose areas of personal interest to study, especially in literature, social studies, and science. Democracy requires choices, and the elementary school day should present opportunities for students to learn how to make reasoned and informed decisions.

Schimmel (1997) makes two other important points about classroom rules and citizenship education. First, any list of classroom or school rules should include a list of student rights. Any just legal system is a balance of responsibilities and rights. Too many classroom rule systems are lists of things students may *not do;* there is no corresponding list of what students *may do.* For example, students should have the right to free expression as long as it does not interfere with teaching and learning, the right to a safe classroom environment, the right to participate in classroom activities, and the right to make their grievances known to school authorities.

Second, classroom rules should be taught like any other part of the curriculum. Schimmel (1997) correctly points out that, all too often, classroom rules are presented on the first day of class with little or no explanation. After parents and students have their chance to help create the classroom rules, the rules should be taught through small-group discussion and simulation. Lessons on classroom rules should be part of a unit on laws in broader jurisdictions, like the school, the city, the state, and the nation. At the very least, students should understand the rationale for each classroom rule. The bottom line is we cannot expect our students to become effective citizens in a democracy if their classroom experiences are completely undemocratic. Hoover and Kindsvatter (1997) sum it up: "What students learn from our disciplinary activities can significantly shape their future behavior as citizens in our democratic society" (p. 71).

Summary of Key Points

- The development of good citizens is the most important goal of social studies.

- Controversy surrounds whether citizenship education should be limited to information on how government works with a definition of a good citizen as a person who follows the rules and votes (transmission), or whether citizenship education should teach students to analyze current issues and take action for social change (transformation).

- The content of citizenship education is government and civics. Students should learn what government is, what government should do, the basic principles and values of American democracy, the U.S. Constitution, the relationship of the United States to other nations, and the nature of good citizenship.

- Social studies programs should make students knowledgeable about basic American civic values. This knowledge should serve as the basis for a commitment to those values.

- A process of value-based decision making includes identifying social problems, relevant values, alternative courses of action, and predicting consequences of actions, reaching a decision, and justifying a decision.

- Good citizens in a democracy are active. Active citizenship requires participation: reading about public issues and discussing them, communicating with public officials, voting, taking an active role in political organizations, and attending meetings.

- Elementary school children can participate in a variety of school and community service projects.

- We cannot expect our students to become effective citizens in a democracy if their classroom experiences are completely undemocratic; students should play some role in developing rules, resolve problems through collaborative effort, and make decisions about how they spend their time.

Lesson Plans and Instructional Activities

Here you will find two examples of innovative social studies teaching, one focusing on the nature and purpose of laws, the other on the American concept of a fair trial: (a) A lesson plan for a "walking field trip" for a second-grade class, challenging students to understand the rules they see displayed on signs around their school; and (b) A fifth-grade mini-unit on fair trials, featuring a mock trial and an analysis of a trial depicted in the Newbery-winning novel, *The Witch of Blackbird Pond*.

Lesson Plan
Grade Two: Walking Field Trip—Rules on Signs

A second-grade teacher took her class on a "walking field trip" to the local branch of the city library every month (for another example of a walking field trip, see Morris, 2006). They looked forward to this event because the children's librarian read aloud a picture book to them, and the children could use their library cards to check out books. The distance from the school to the library was about three-quarters of a mile. Two parent volunteers and two sixth graders accompanied the class. The teacher was in the middle of a unit called "Rules and Laws." She decided to use the walk to the library as an opportunity to show her class the many rules posted as signs. Her lesson plan follows:

Overview: This lesson is for second graders. It is part of a unit on rules and laws.

Resources and Materials: (a) A digital camera, (b) a projector capable of displaying digitized photographs, (c) chart paper.

Standard: One of the *National Standards for Civics and Government* for grades K–4 is "students should be able to explain the purposes of rules and laws and why they are important in their classroom, school, community, state, and nation" (Center for Civic Education, 1994, p. 18, Standard IE [1]).

Content Objectives: Children will understand that many rules are posted as signs, that rules describe what people may and may not do, that some rules provide for order and safety, and others protect the rights of people.

Process Objectives: Children will *read* four signs during their walk to the library, *describe* how each rule displayed on a sign limits behavior, and *define* a purpose (safety or protect rights) for each sign.

Values Objectives: This lesson, along with many others, will help children understand and become committed to the democratic value of "the public good," that individual behavior must be limited to achieve an orderly and equitable society.

Teaching Sequence:

1. Explain to the children that on this walking trip to the library they will stop to look at rules written on signs. Also review the rules for a walking field trip. Permission slips from parents would have been collected earlier.

2. Stop at the gate of the fence surrounding the playground and grass field. The sign reads:

   > **Public welcome to use school grounds when school is not in session. Gates are locked each night at dusk. Use of the following is strictly prohibited:**
   >
   > **Golf clubs**
   >
   > **Alcoholic beverages**
   >
   > **Tobacco products**
   >
   > **Motor vehicles**
   >
   > **Bicycles, skateboards, roller skates, and in-line skates (roller blades)**

   Read the sign aloud to the children. Make sure they understand the specific items that may not be used on the playground or grass field. Photograph the sign.

3. Stop along the sidewalk to read to the children the next sign: **No Parking Monday 8–10 A.M.** Photograph the sign.

4. Stop at the speed limit sign and read it aloud: **35 mph.** Photograph the sign.

5. At the library, stop at the sign that reserves parking spaces for people with disabilities. The sign is blue and has a white logo for handicapped parking (a person in a wheelchair). Read it aloud to the children: **Reserved for Handicapped.** Photograph the sign. Tell the children you will use the photographs later for a classroom discussion about the signs.

6. Make a chart with three columns: "Rule," "How It Limits Us," and "Why." Show the photograph of the first sign prohibiting the use of certain things on the playground and on the grass field. Read it aloud and discuss it. On the chart, summarize it as "Public use of playground." Help the children understand this rule limits the items people can use on the playground. Under the second heading, "How It Limits Us," write down the statement the children generate; it will probably go something like "Things that can't be used on the playground." The children should understand that many people would like to use the prohibited items on the weekends and early evenings at the school. Do not be surprised if some children have seen this rule being violated. Help the children understand this is a safety rule because the use of golf clubs, alcohol, and skateboards creates many dangers. So, under "Why," write "Makes the playground and grass field safe for everyone."

7. Follow the same procedure for the no parking sign, the speed limit sign, and the handicapped parking sign. The no parking and speed limit signs also are safety signs. The handicapped parking sign is different because it protects the rights of people with disabilities. It is a good example of a rule reflecting a commitment to the common good and respect for minority rights—the majority of the population, who do not have disabilities, give up the chance to park in the reserved spots so people with disabilities can more easily use the library.

Effective Teaching in Today's Diverse Classroom: This activity could be difficult for your English learners. In Cummins's terms, "cognitive demand" is high. Therefore, you need to "embed" the lesson "contextually" to support your English learners as they tackle a challenging lesson. What could you do? First, your English learners could have difficulty reading the sign on the playground. You might want to take them aside the day before the lesson and paraphrase the message of the sign in simplified English they can understand. Fortunately, the other signs are easy to understand (no parking, 35 mph, and handicapped logo). Unless your English learners have a high level of oral English proficiency, they will not be able to participate in completing the chart. After your English learners listen to the class discussion that leads to completion of the chart, you should work with them in a group and discuss the chart in its final form.

Mini-Unit

Grade Five: Fair Trials

This mini-unit is appropriate for a fifth-grade class engaged in a larger unit on the U.S. Constitution. This mini-unit looks at sections of the Fifth and Sixth Amendments, which guarantee the rights constituting the basis for a fair trial. This mini-unit is one of many examples of using children's literature for law-related education (Landman, 2008). Students will participate in a mock trial, *The State v. The Big Bad Wolf,* based on a journal article by Judith Norton (1992). This simulation is an excellent way for students to learn about the U.S. system of criminal trials. Students will analyze a fictional judicial procedure presented in the award-winning historical novel *The Witch of Blackbird Pond* (Speare, 1958).

Part I: Organizing Framework

Standard: The *National Standards for Civics and Government* (Center for Civic Education, 1994) provides the organizing framework for the mini-unit. The performance expectation is part of the national standards for grades 5 through 8 (see p. 75 of the standards):

(1) *Personal Rights.* Students should be able to evaluate, take, and defend positions on issues involving personal rights. To achieve this standard, students should be able to identify personal rights and identify the major documentary sources of personal rights (e.g., U.S. Constitution).

This mini-unit will teach students about the specific rights listed in the Fifth and Sixth Amendments, collectively referred to as the right to a fair trial. This mini-unit answers three questions:

Unit Question 1: What rights in the Fifth and Sixth Amendments to the U.S. Constitution guarantee a fair trial for people accused of crimes?

Unit Question 2: What happens during a trial of someone accused of a crime?

Unit Question 3: Can we identify the rights that were not respected in criminal trials conducted in the United States before the Constitution was written?

Part II: Instructional Activities

Unit Question 1: What rights in the Fifth and Sixth Amendments to the U.S. Constitution guarantee a fair trial for people accused of crimes?

Teacher-Directed Lesson on the Fifth and Sixth Amendments

Content Objectives: Students will learn the specific rights guaranteed by the Fifth and Sixth Amendments.

Process Objectives: Students will *identify* the Fifth and Sixth Amendment rights of people accused of crimes; *define* capital crime, indictment, double jeopardy, self-incrimination, jury, and witness; and *speculate* on what would happen if the rights did not exist.

1. Provide copies of the Fifth and Sixth Amendments to each student. Show the class transparencies of the amendments on the overhead projector.

2. With the class, create a chart listing the following rights:

    Rights of People Accused of Crimes from the Fifth Amendment:

    1. Cannot be tried for capital crime without a grand jury indictment
    2. Cannot be tried for the same crime twice (no double jeopardy)
    3. Cannot be made to testify (no self-incrimination)

    From the Sixth Amendment:

    4. Right to a speedy trial
    5. Right to a public trial
    6. Right to be judged by a jury
    7. Right to be informed of the nature of the crime
    8. Right to confront witnesses
    9. Right to summon witnesses
    10. Right to be represented by a lawyer

Discuss each of these rights with the class. Be sure students understand terms such as *capital crime, indictment, double jeopardy, self-incrimination, jury,* and *witness.* Then, for each right, help students understand what would happen if that right did not exist. For example, ask, "What would happen if we did not have a right to a public trial?" (Help students understand that trials conducted in private could ignore all the rights protected by the amendments—public trials guarantee the procedure can be evaluated for fairness.)

Unit Question 2: What happens during a trial of someone accused of a crime?

Mock Trial

Content Objectives: Students will learn the definitions of several crimes; the roles of the judge, the clerk, the defendant, attorneys, the jury, and witnesses in a criminal trial; and how the rights in the Fifth and Sixth Amendments are applied in a criminal trial.

Process Objectives: Students will *understand* the definitions of seven crimes, *identify* which crimes the wolf should be charged with, *play the role* of one of the participants in the trial, *gather and analyze* physical evidence, *participate* in the mock trial, and *distinguish* which rights were essential parts of the trial.

Note: This activity will take from 4 to 7 days.

1. Read aloud a version of the fairy tale "Little Red Riding Hood." Then present the revised set of facts on page 5 of Judith Norton's article (the wolf beats, not eats, Grandma; the wolf strikes a police officer prior to arrest; the wolf has marijuana in his pocket).

2. Distribute a copy of the "criminal code" from page 5 of Norton's article. The code defines seven crimes: battery, assault, theft, possession of marijuana, resisting arrest, disorderly conduct, and felonious restraint. Help students understand the definition of each. Then ask the class to decide the crimes with which the wolf should be charged.

3. Begin work on the mock trial. Norton's simulation has the following roles: judge, court clerk, defendant (the wolf), defense attorneys, prosecuting attorneys, the jury, and witnesses (Little Red Riding Hood, Grandma, and arresting officers). Norton suggests you create some defense witnesses who try to provide the wolf with an alibi or vouch for his character. You can even add "expert witnesses."

4. Gather the physical evidence for the case. This can include a medical report on Grandma's beating, a blood-stained carpet, paw prints, and the police report.

5. Be sure the witnesses know what they are supposed to say. Then work with the defense attorneys on their case. What questions will they ask? Work with the prosecuting attorneys. How will they present their evidence? What should they ask each witness?

6. Meet with the judge and the clerk and discuss the conduct of the courtroom.

7. Discuss with the entire class the rules of court procedure and proper courtroom conduct (see page 6 of Norton's article).

8. Today is the trial! Norton provides excellent descriptions of how the case should proceed. The key to a good simulation is working with each student before the trial begins so everyone is comfortable and confident.

9. After the mock trial is over, take another look at the list of rights you compiled in the first lesson (the teacher-directed lesson on the Fifth and Sixth Amendments). Which rights were evident in the mock trial? (Almost all were—public trial, jury, accused informed of nature of crime, accused able to summon and confront witnesses, and accused represented by a lawyer.)

Unit Question 3: Can we identify the rights that were not respected in criminal trials conducted before the Constitution was written?

Readers' Theater: The Trial in The Witch of Blackbird Pond

Content Objectives: Students will learn some trials conducted in colonial America failed to protect the rights of the accused.

Process Objectives: Students will *dramatize* the trial in Chapter 19 of the book *The Witch of Blackbird Pond* and analyze the proceedings to identify which rights were denied the accused during the trial.

1. Before the other activities start and while they are progressing, read aloud to the class *The Witch of Blackbird Pond* (Speare, 1958). This is an excellent piece of historical fiction with an appealing story line. The book fits perfectly with the fifth-grade social studies curriculum in most schools—which usually includes colonial America. This is the story of 16-year-old Katherine (Kit) Tyler, who is the orphaned daughter of English royalists. She comes to live with her Puritan relatives in Connecticut in 1687 and is accused of being a witch.

2. About a week prior to the performance, select actors for a readers' theater presentation of Chapter 19. Suggest students rehearse their parts so this exciting chapter can be presented with appropriate characterization. Present Chapter 19 to the class through readers' theater. In Chapter 19, Kit is tried as a witch in a judicial proceeding similar to a current-day preliminary hearing. The hearing is conducted by the town magistrate, who serves as judge along with two local clergymen. After the presentation, have the class analyze the proceeding. One hundred years after this fictional event, the U.S. Constitution granted all Americans fundamental judicial rights. What rights was Kit granted? Students should see she was informed of the charges against her; witchcraft in colonial Connecticut was a capital offense. Her hearing meets the requirement of a preliminary proceeding in capital cases (the Fifth Amendment mentions a grand jury indictment). As Chapter 19 explains, Kit was not entitled to a jury at this phase because the hearing would determine whether she would be sent to the capital of the colony for a jury trial. Kit was denied certain rights that present-day defendants have in their preliminary hearings. Students should recognize she did not have an attorney. Also, Kit was forced to testify. Finally, Kit was not allowed to question witnesses, nor was she allowed to call her own witnesses.

3. Although this might be too complicated for fifth graders, you could point out another difference between the proceeding in *The Witch of Blackbird Pond* and present-day trials: Today, a judge decides at the preliminary hearing whether the accused must stand trial. In *The Witch,* the local judge was joined by two Puritan ministers. The 19th-century New England witch trials were one of the few times in the history of the United States that criminal proceedings were mixed with "ecclesiastical" courts. Ecclesiastical, or religious, courts were common in Europe during the Middle Ages, with full power to convict and punish people. They exist in some nations today, though no person in the United States today can be tried by a religious group unless she or he agrees to participate in the proceeding.

Effective Teaching in Today's Diverse Classroom: The mock trial is a real challenge for fifth graders. There are parts for everybody to play, but try to avoid assigning the most prominent roles only to your most able students. Although students should not be asked to perform publicly at a level beyond their ability, you will be surprised how most students can rise to the occasion and exceed your expectations, especially with a little extra help from you! For your gifted children, this mini-unit could be an excellent stimulus for a *depth* activity, one that allows students to learn more about a topic previously covered. Gifted students could be challenged to find out more about the qualifications for judges at the municipal, state, and federal level. Do these minimal qualifications seem adequate? Other students could look at another example of the systematic denial of fair trials in our history, the vigilante justice practiced in California's gold fields in the late 1840s and 1850s.

History

Scott Cunningham Merrill

Nancy Grant's third graders were working on a unit entitled "All About Us." The children were to complete a project on a history of their families. The choices were (a) complete a family tree, (b) write a biography of one of their grandparents, and (c) make a family timeline. Lourdes Delgado wanted to make a family timeline. Mrs. Grant explained Lourdes would have to be selective because it would be impossible to include every important event. The first step, then, was to compile a list of dates to be charted. After talking with her mother and father, Lourdes decided on the following:

1994: The Delgado family takes a vacation to Yellowstone National Park.

1992: Maria Chacon, Lourdes's great-great-grandmother, dies at the age of 101.

251

1987: Lourdes Delgado is born.

1978: The first of Lourdes's three brothers is born.

1977: Lourdes's father and mother buy a house in Burbank, where the family has lived ever since.

1974: Hector Delgado and Teresa Chacon marry at Mission San Fernando.

1973: Hector Delgado (her father) and Teresa Chacon (her mother) graduate from California State University, Northridge.

1949: Lourdes's grandfather and grandmother Delgado move from Mexico City to California.

1937: Lourdes's grandfather and grandmother Chacon move from Guadalajara to California.

Next, Mrs. Grant helped Lourdes figure the time span to be covered by the timeline. It would have to cover 58 years (1937 to 1995). Lourdes wanted to make her timeline on a sheet of poster board 2 feet by 3 feet. If she left room for margins, she would have to place 58 years on a line 30 inches long (so each side would have a 3-inch margin). To make it easier, Mrs. Grant suggested Lourdes have the timeline cover 60 years so each half inch would represent a year. After Mrs. Grant helped Lourdes figure the proper scale for the timeline, the rest was easy. She left space at the top of the poster for her title—"The History of My Family: Lourdes Delgado." Lourdes then drew her line and marked the 2-inch intervals. Mrs. Grant suggested she place larger marks for the years 1940, 1950, 1960, 1970, 1980, and 1990. This confused Lourdes for a moment, before she realized she needed to measure halfway between the mark for 1939 and the mark for 1941 to find the correct location for 1940. She then wrote "1940" in bold numbers below the mark. Then Lourdes wrote the years below the marks for the designated years: 1937, 1949, 1973, 1977, 1978, 1987, 1992, 1994. She found she had to write small and stagger the placement of the years. Finally, she wrote brief captions under each year, explaining what happened. With great pride, Lourdes displayed her timeline on a side bulletin board with projects the other children completed.

This project was valuable because Lourdes learned a great deal about her family and the history of her community in southern California. At the same time, she experienced firsthand the "doing" of history— gathering data, organizing it chronologically, and presenting it in a format easily understood by other people. One thing to note here—Lourdes completed this project in 1995. Today, she could work with an adult and use a computer software system like Timeliner, TimelineMaker, or Timeglider. It is interesting to compare the challenges faced by a child, like Lourdes, making a timeline without software with the challenges faced by a child making a computer-based timeline.

■ ■ ■

History in the Elementary School: Overview and Research

History has been a part of the elementary school curriculum ever since the United States became a nation (Brophy & Van Sledright, 1997; Downey, 1985; Downey & Levstik, 1991; Levstik, 1991). As noted in Chapter 1, controversy, however, has surrounded two issues: (a) The role history should play in the social studies curriculum, and (b) the historical content that should be taught. Regarding the first issue, the argument is: Should elementary social studies focus primarily on history? Or, should history assume a less central role as time is devoted to the other social sciences, such as anthropology, economics, and political science; and topics of special interest, like environmental education and global education? Currently, almost all the state standards for social studies place history in the primary position. If you teach elementary school anywhere in the United States, you will teach a great deal of history. The second issue, about historical content, will always generate controversy as advocates of a "traditional" curriculum clash with people wishing to include multiple perspectives on events in the past and provide more information on women, people of color, and leaders of dissenting organizations. Almost any time someone attempts to define the history content children should learn, sparks fly as they did in Texas in 2010 or in Minnesota in 2003 (Spies et al., 2004).

Many elementary school children, especially if their social studies curriculum follows the "expanding environments" model, receive virtually no historical content until fourth grade, when they study their state. A rationale for delaying the study of the past has been the now disproven perspective that small children are unable to understand historical concepts (Barton, 1997, 2008; Barton & Levstik, 1996; Brophy, 1996; Levstik, 1991; Thornton & Vukelich, 1988). One reason why educators misunderstood the capacity of children to learn history is that a previous model of the child's cognitive development and historical thinking, called the "Piaget-Peel-Hallam" model, underestimated what children can learn (Brophy, 1996; Downey & Levstik, 1991). British scholars E. A. Peel and Roy Hallam applied Jean Piaget's stage theory of cognitive development to historical thinking. They concluded that children need to be at the "formal level" of cognitive operations to understand the past. History would have to wait until junior high school! This model is flawed because it was based on faulty experimental tasks and does not represent an accurate portrait of the abilities of children.

Jere Brophy's (1996) excellent review of the research on the ability of children to learn history explains that children gradually develop the ability to understand the past rather than developing this capacity in Piagetian-like stages. For example, children initially fail to perceive the causal relationships of historical events. Then children take a "mechanistic view of causal determination," believing linked events were inevitable (p. 6). Only later do young learners see there can be multiple causes of an event and if the causal events had not all occurred, the result would have been different. Similar developmental patterns exist for a child's ability to empathize with people from other eras and to cope with conflicting accounts of the same historical event.

One important study of children's understanding of history was completed by Keith Barton and Linda Levstik (1996). The authors were critical of previous studies, noting almost all earlier research on this topic suffered from one of the following flaws: (a) The researchers drew conclusions without evidence, (b) the researchers failed to consider the possibility that children younger than age 8 could understand historical concepts, and (c) the studies reflected a limited view of history, focusing solely on the sequence of dates. Barton and Levstik asked children from kindergarten to grade 6 (a) to place nine pictures in sequence, and (b) to explain their rationale for doing so. The pictures, both photographs and drawings, depicted scenes from 1772 to 1993. The results revealed the youngest students *can* make distinctions in historical time. Kindergartners and first graders were able to go beyond a simple split between pictures belonging either in "long ago" or "close to now" categories. Most kindergartners and first graders and *all* the second graders identified other categories as they recognized some pictures were older than the ones they had seen previously. Other pictures were identified as being newer, and some were placed between the previous pictures.

Interestingly enough, kindergartners, first, and second graders have no sense of what dates signify. Not until third grade do children try to assign dates to the pictures. Beginning in fourth grade, dates are useful to children, although not until fifth or sixth grade did children in the study use dates to identify the pictures accurately. Finally, almost all children, regardless of age, seem to think "a particular time is characterized by only one image" (Barton & Levstik, 1996, p. 440). For example, children in the study did not seem to understand that illustrations continued to be drawn after the invention of photography; thus, they thought any drawing was automatically older than any photograph. Nor did they understand that while pioneers were building cabins in the 1880s, large cities were being built in other geographic areas. Their rationale was "first there were pioneers, then there were cities" (p. 440). As with any study, the results of this one may later be challenged, but it seems safe to say children at all elementary grades should have a social studies curriculum that includes historical content.

Another important body of research has examined the effects of culture, national identity, ethnicity, and gender on student's historical knowledge and beliefs. In their review, Epstein and Shiller (2005) reached this conclusion: At every grade level, including kindergarten, what children know about history, and how they view the history they are taught, will be influenced by their culture, national identity, ethnicity, and gender. The authors noted "there are limits to what and how much children or adolescents will adopt from teachers or texts, especially when school-based historical content conflicts with history accounts learned in the home" (p. 203). For example, when shown a photograph of a 1960s antiwar protest, African American fifth graders thought it was a picture of a rally against racism or a dangerous place for African Americans to be (there were armed, white soldiers in the photo). On the other hand, the European American fifth graders thought the photo showed an event in the American Civil War (Levstik & Barton, 1996).

History in the Elementary School: Content

The expanding environments approach to social studies defined a curriculum with little historical content until students reached the fourth grade. Kindergarten and first- and second-grade social studies curricula have focused on social development, the school, the family, and the neighborhood. Third graders studied their community, with a small amount of local history. Not until fourth grade, when students learn about their state, was any significant historical content presented. Fifth-grade social studies, following the expanded environments framework, has always been historical, as students learned about the history of the United States. Sixth grade covered foreign regions or nations—typically Canada, Mexico, Central America, and South America. So, in the traditional scheme, global content has been covered in grade 6 but virtually not before that grade level.

Although they have generated considerable controversy, the national history standards represent the combined effort of many dedicated historians and educators. Let's take a look at the proposed topics for grades K–4 included in the *National Standards for History* (National Center for History in the Schools, 1996). The eight content standards listed will help us understand what students in K–4 classrooms should know:

1. *Students should understand family life now and in the recent past and family life in various places long ago.*   Most state social studies standards include a focus on family life in one or more of the primary grades, consistent with this national standard. Rather than learn only political and economic history, students should learn about their personal histories and the everyday lives of people in the past.

2. *Students should understand the history of their own local community and how communities in North America varied long ago.*   Community history has traditionally been a part of elementary social studies. Students should use a variety of resources to learn about their community, including field trips, old photographs, newspapers, and interviews with senior citizens.

3. *Students should understand the people, events, problems, and ideas that were significant in creating the history of their state.*   State history, long the focus of fourth-grade social studies, should cover the Natives who first lived in the state, the early non-Native explorers of their state, and the people who have moved to their state throughout its history.

4. *Students should understand how democratic values came to be and how they have been exemplified by people, events, and symbols.*   Many state social studies standards reflect this national standard—rather than delaying discussion of citizenship education until the fifth grade. This national standard bridges history and citizenship and calls for students to understand how the United States was formed through a revolution with England and to identify the basic principles in the Declaration of Independence and the U.S. Constitution. Other parts of this standard are familiar topics for the early grades: national holidays, American symbols, the Pledge of Allegiance, and the national anthem.

5. *Students should understand the causes and nature of various movements of large groups of people into the United States now and long ago.*   This standard combines history and geography. Included here would be the forced relocation of Native Americans; the stories of immigrant groups who have come to the United States throughout our history; the internal migrations of African Americans, Mexican and Puerto Rican workers, and Dust Bowl families; and the 20th-century migration of Americans from farms to cities.

6. *Students should understand folklore and other cultural contributions from various regions of the United States and how they help form a national heritage.*   Students should be able to describe regional folk heroes, stories, and songs; use folk literature to describe the way people lived in various sections of the United States; and describe the national influence of regional art, crafts, music, and language. Most state social standards include some coverage of American folklore in the primary grades.

7. *Students should understand selected attributes and historical developments of societies in such places as Africa, the Americas, Asia, and Europe.* This standard represents an attempt to internationalize the social studies curriculum and is an important addition to the typical K–3 fare of family, classroom, neighborhood, and city. Students would compare and contrast different structures of family life, retell folktales and legends, describe significant historical achievements of many cultural groups, and analyze the art produced by various cultural groups. Almost all of the state social studies standards have ignored this focus—other than to include international folktales in the primary grades, usually as a part of language arts.

8. *Students should understand discoveries in science and technology, some of their social and economic effects, and the major scientists and inventors responsible for them.* The content in this standard seems like a worthwhile addition to the elementary curriculum, especially as students face technological change at an unprecedented pace. Students would examine changes in transportation and communication and learn about the technological achievements of many cultural groups, such as Chinese paper, Mayan calendars, Egyptian mummies, and English steam engines. Few state social studies standards reflect this national standard at the elementary level—this focus on the relationship of technological innovation and social studies is left to the middle and high schools.

The *National Standards for History* for fifth and sixth graders call for a detailed study of United States history and world history. There are 31 standards for fifth and sixth graders in United States history and 39 standards for fifth and sixth graders in world history. Almost all state social studies standards call for a fifth-grade curriculum on United States history and a sixth-grade curriculum that either focuses on some period of world history or a study of some international region.

History in the Elementary School: Processes

In addition to their acquiring historical information, we want students to become proficient at several historical processes. This is the "doing" of history, as students begin to think and act like historians. The *National Standards for History* (National Center for History in the Schools, 1996) provides a useful categorization of the thinking and doing skills of history. These include the following:

1. *Chronological thinking.* This includes the ability to distinguish past, present, and future time; establish temporal order in constructing their own historical narratives; measure and calculate calendar time; make and interpret timelines; and explain continuity and change over time.

2. *Historical comprehension.* Students should be able to reconstruct the literal meaning of a historical passage, identify important questions and historical perspectives, use historical maps, find information in illustrations, and understand data in charts and graphs.

Shutterstock

One important skill all students should acquire is the ability to read accounts of historical events and develop questions for further study.

3. *Historical analysis and interpretation.* This is an essential set of skills for the historically literate. It includes the ability to formulate questions for inquiry, compare and contrast different ideas, distinguish fact from fiction, compare different versions of the same event, explain causes in historical events, and hypothesize how the past has influenced the present.

4. *Historical research capabilities.* Students should be able to state historical questions, locate historical data, interpret data, and use their knowledge to write a story, explanation, or narrative.

5. *Historical issues:* Analysis and decision making. These important critical thinking skills include the ability to identify issues in the past, compare the interests and values of various people, suggest alternative choices for solving a historical problem, prepare a position on an issue, and evaluate the consequences of a decision.

These historical processes usually are taught through participation in lessons presenting historical content. It is possible, however, to design lessons that focus solely on historical processes. At the end of this chapter, you will find a mini-unit that teaches students the methodology of "real" historians.

Teaching History in the Elementary School

Perhaps it would be a good idea for us to review here the elements of effective social studies teaching in a classroom with a diverse student population. Because teaching history is so much a part of teaching social studies, the elements are worth repeating:

■ For our English learners, learning history will require a great deal of contextual support—cooperative learning, visual aids, hands-on activities, modification of how the teacher talks, and primary-language support.

■ For children with mild learning disabilities, teachers will need to modify curricular content, perhaps by dividing material into smaller units; modify instructional processes, which could include the use of instructional prompts and cues; and modify student work products, such as providing more time to finish a task.

■ A variety of lesson plans and teaching sequences should be used to teach history. For some lessons, a model of direct instruction, like a direct instruction seven-step plan, will work; for others, we may want to use a teaching sequence designed for inquiry, the use of artifacts, or critical thinking.

■ Cooperative learning can be used effectively to teach historical content; it is essential for students to practice historical analysis and interpretation.

■ Because the events of the past are subject to many interpretations, activities requiring critical thinking, like the integrative model for teaching reasoning and content, are important in teaching history. Inquiry activities should be a part of every unit with historical content (Levstik & Barton, 2005).

■ History must be taught through a variety of resources: textbooks, children's literature, reference material, charts and graphs, films, realia, and computer-based resources. Illustrations should be used frequently as a teaching tool, and students should be encouraged to show what they know by drawing.

■ The history curriculum should be transformed so our students learn about women, children, immigrants, African Americans, Native Americans, religious minorities, and those who have dissented from the majority. Also, history should be personalized and localized; an effective means is through oral history. Barton and Levstik (1996) argue that "the most accessible knowledge for younger children [is] related to material culture and the patterns of everyday life" (p. 442). The best way to introduce students to another time is through food, clothing, household tools, schools, play, and other things and experiences children know firsthand.

As with other aspects of social studies, historical teaching in the elementary school has been too dependent on the textbook. Isabel Beck, Margaret McKeown, and their colleagues have published some revealing research about how history is presented in elementary social studies textbooks (Beck, McKeown, & Worthy, 1995; McKeown, Beck, Sinatra, & Loxterman, 1991). Generally, they found textbooks do a poor job of presenting historical material and textbook passages can be rewritten so they are easier to understand. Children do not

History comes alive! Field trips to living history sites, like this one-room schoolhouse, will significantly increase students' understanding of how people lived in the past.

understand historical cause and effect and will need clarification and explanation. Also, when historical passages had a "voice" and sounded more like historical fiction, children learned more history. Textbooks should never be the sole resource for teaching historical content; rather, they should be used in concert with other resources.

Let's now look at four resources essential for good history teaching in an elementary classroom: (a) primary sources, (b) children's fiction, (c) timelines, and (d) field trips, virtual field trips and online expeditions.

Primary Sources

The essential resource for the professional historian is the *primary source* (Potter, 2003). A primary source is a document, work of art, or artifact produced during the period being studied. To teach history well, we must have our students work with primary sources. Teaching with primary sources has two problems: (a) We must locate sources relevant to the time period we are covering, and (b) the sources must be comprehensible to our young students. Actually, primary sources can be found in many places—the Internet has become an excellent resource. Many Websites provide primary source material suitable for elementary students; for example try "Poetry and Music of the War Between the States" (www.civilwarpoetry.org). This site has poetry written by women on the home front, from both the North and South.

Primary source documents can be found in each issue of the journal *Social Education* in the "Teaching with Documents" feature. It should be noted, however, that some of the documents are too difficult for elementary school children to read. Nonetheless, many of the featured documents will work with students in grades 4 and up, and each article includes both a copy of the historical document and several teaching ideas.

Fortunately, the newest elementary school social studies textbooks incorporate more primary source material than textbooks published in the past. Many now include excerpts from diaries and newspapers and reproductions of old maps and paintings. When it comes to artifacts, a good museum is essential, and many cities have excellent museums of local history. Field trips to museums give students a chance to examine historical artifacts. The Internet has made it possible to take virtual tours of museums (please see the discussion below). Also, we should not forget many of our students have old items at home that, with parental cooperation, can become a learning resource.

Although some historical documents can be read by elementary students, most are too difficult. Some of these primary sources can be adapted for young readers, and many fine children's books have done exactly that. For example, the well-known children's author Margaret Wise Brown edited a version of *Mourt's Relation* for children. *Mourt's Relation* is a journal written by several *Mayflower* pilgrims, most notably William Bradford and Edward Winslow. It was first published in 1622 and is the basis for much of what is known about the early days in Plimoth, but it is far too difficult for elementary students to read. Brown's adaptation, called *Homes in the Wilderness* (1988), is delightful and well within the reading ability of most third and fourth graders. Also noteworthy are the books written by Brett Harvey, who has used the diaries of women who lived in the past as the basis of easy-to-read but historically accurate picture books. His books include *My Prairie Year: Based on the Diary of Elinore Plaisted* (1986), *Cassie's Journey: Going West in the 1860s* (1988), and *Immigrant Girl: Becky of Eldridge Street* (1987).

Though it is a great deal of work, teachers can adapt primary source documents so their students can read them. While students may initially view a copy of what the primary source really looks like, the teacher should provide students with an edited version to read. Wineburg and Martin (2009) provided excellent suggestions on how teachers can make a primary source accessible to their students:

1. *Focusing.*   For most documents, the teacher should consider only the most relevant part(s) of the document. This means much of it may be eliminated. For upper elementary school students, the document should be 200–300 words at the most.

2. *Simplification.*   Teachers should convert complex sentences into simple ones; they should make spelling and capitalization standard and contemporary; and they should simplify the vocabulary of the document.

3. *Presentation.*   The document should be formatted so the text is clear and easy to read. The typeface should be at least 16 point with ample margins.

Finally, please remember that songs are primary sources, too. Many old ones reveal a great deal about a time or place. Noteworthy is *The Laura Ingalls Wilder Songbook* (Garson, 1999), which includes the words and lyrics to all the songs mentioned in the *Little House* books. Most elementary music texts contain several historical songs. My favorite anthology of American folk songs is *Gonna Sing My Head Off: American Folk Songs for Children* (Krull, 1992).

Teaching Sequence for a Primary Source.   Both historical comprehension and historical analysis can be developed through work with primary sources. For lessons using primary sources, I suggest the following teaching sequence, which is similar to the one presented for realia, visual media, and auditory media in Chapter 7.

1. *First, establish time and place.*   Before sharing a primary source with students, it should be placed in context. This usually requires using a timeline to establish time and a map to establish location. A good idea is to bring out a summary chart, a data retrieval chart, or a Web made earlier in the unit. It is important that students should not have the primary source "thrown at them," without a meaningful context.

2. *Present the primary source.*   If a primary source is written, it should be neatly reproduced or displayed on a large screen through an LCD (liquid crystal display), an overhead projector, or a photographic slide. Even when presented in a reader-friendly fashion, many written primary sources will have to be read aloud to students. Artifacts must be presented so every student can see them easily. Sometimes this means letting students look at the artifact in small groups. Students should then examine the primary source to "identify" it: Is it a photograph, a diary entry, a newspaper article, or something else?

3. *Start with open-ended questions.*   "Does anyone wish to make a comment?" "Who has a question about the diary entry (or letter, newspaper advertisement, coin, and so on)?"

4. *Ask very specific questions.*   These questions should require students to take a closer look at the primary source. With some written primary sources, it helps to number the lines of the text like a legal document and then ask students about specific words, phrases, and sentences. If the primary source mentions names, places, or things, students should take notice of them. With artifacts, questions should narrow students' focus, such as, "What do you see in the upper-right corner of the painting?" or "What places are mentioned in the diary entry?" The purpose of these questions is to call attention to the specifics so the students will remember.

5. *Analyze the primary source.*   The analysis is the most important part of a lesson with a primary source because it engages students in the same type of critical thinking real historians practice, often called "source work." Van Sledright (2002a, 2002b, 2004), based on his own experience with fifth graders, provides excellent ideas on how to proceed. Students need to ask and answer questions about the person(s) who created the primary source. Once they are clear about that person, they need to ask questions about possible bias. For example, "Did the person have an agenda?" Then students assess the source against what else they know to determine the source's reliability.

Does the source match what they know or does it present a different perspective? Finally, teachers should sum up what has been learned. "What new things does it show us?" "How does it change what we know [about the topic being studied]?"

Several lessons and activities presented in this book use primary sources. You can find them at the end of the relevant chapter:

Chapter 2: The opening vignette and the lesson plans based on the painting *Buffalo Chase, Upper Missouri*

Chapter 4: Lesson plan based on *To Be a Slave*

Chapter 5: The oral history project "The History of Our School"

Chapter 7: Lesson plan examining a Roman coin

Children's Fiction: History as a Story Well Told

Fiction written for children has excellent potential as a resource for teaching history. Beck and colleagues (1995) and Levstik (1986, 1989, 1990) have written about the power of presenting history through narrative. Simply put, children learn more through stories than they do with other forms of presentation, most notably, textbook selections. A great deal has been written about how teachers can use fiction to teach history (Field, 1998; McGowan, Erickson, & Neufeld, 1996; Stewart & Marshall, 2009; Zarnowski & Gallagher, 1993).

Historical fiction written for children is of two forms: (a) novels for older children and (b) picture books aimed at the youngest students. Some of the finest children's books ever written are historical fiction, including Newbery Medal winners like *Island of the Blue Dolphins* (O'Dell, 1960), *Johnny Tremain* (Forbes, 1943), *Sarah, Plain and Tall* (MacLaughlin, 1985), *The Witch of Blackbird Pond* (Speare, 1958), and *The Bronze Bow* (Speare, 1961). More recent Newbery winners include *Good Masters! Sweet Ladies! Voices from a Medieval Village* (Schlitz, 2007), *Kira Kira* (Kadohata, 2004), *Crispin: The Cross of Lead* (Avi, 2002), and *A Single Shard* (Park, 2001). Many excellent picture books tell stories that take place in other times, like *Thy Friend, Obadiah* (Turkle, 1969), *Ox-Cart Man* (Hall, 1979), *How My Parents Learned to Eat* (Friedman, 1987), and *Follow the Drinking Gourd* (Winter, 1988).

Harms and Lettow (1994) provide a useful set of criteria for selecting picture books with historical settings. This includes

1. *Developmental appropriateness.* The book should be written and illustrated at a level children in your classroom can understand.

2. *Quality.* The book should be a good book, one children will find appealing and at least some authorities consider to be well illustrated and written.

3. *Authenticity.* Historical accuracy extends to both text and illustration. In more and more historical picture books, authors and illustrators include a list of their sources or bibliographic notes that reveal and/or comment on the sources the author and illustrator used.

4. *Complementary text and illustration.* This is a characteristic that all good picture books share. Text and illustrations should work together rather than appear disjointed. Harms and Lettow note this is essential in picture books with historical settings because the illustrations can enhance the level of historical understanding the reader acquires.

5. *Three-dimensional central characters.* As noted previously, children can understand historical concepts when the past is presented as a well-told story. Good stories require well-developed characters with whom children can develop a sense of empathy. This is a real challenge for authors and illustrators of picture books because of the limited space in picture books; most have fewer than 40 pages.

6. *Freedom from bias.* Teachers should avoid books presenting stereotypes or biased views, although older children should read such books for the purpose of detecting bias. We should seek books showing events from the perspectives of all the participants in an event. Harms and Lettow, for example, note that in Jean Fritz's *The Great Adventure of Christopher Columbus* (1992), the Natives who greet Columbus are portrayed as "uncultured and witless," unable to understand Columbus and too willing to accept trinkets in exchange for valuable information (Harms & Lettow, 1994, p. 153). It would be interesting for older children to compare this book with Jane Yolen's *Encounter* (1992) or Michael Dorris's *Morning Girl* (1992), books presenting the perspectives of the Taino Natives. A well-told story can provide children with a sense of empathy because fiction that is well researched and well written will make children feel transported to another place. After listening to their teacher read *Thy Friend, Obadiah* (Turkle, 1969), for example, children will have a sense of the clothing, buildings, and means of transportation in 19th-century Nantucket.

Children's fiction can be used in several ways. Children can read books independently. Historical novels and picture books can be read a second time to provide the specific information needed to answer inquiries and to complete projects. Fiction should be used as part of teacher-directed lessons in social studies. A word of caution is in order, however. Fiction is not written with the same purpose as a textbook; rather, the goal of the author is to tell a story. It seems reasonable that we should allow children to respond to the book as a story before they move on to a history lesson. We can do this by asking open-ended questions encouraging children to express their personal feelings, interpretations, and opinions about the story (Zarrillo, 1994).

At the end of the chapter is a lesson plan providing an example of teaching history with a picture book.

Timelines

Timelines are charts showing the chronological intervals between events. Timelines can be used as an instructional tool to present information to students. Students could also construct them as part of instructional units with a historical focus (Hoone, 1989). Students can make many types of timelines, encompassing the following characteristics:

- Timelines can be either vertical, with the earliest date at the top of the line and the most recent date at the bottom, or horizontal, with the earliest date on the reader's left and the most recent on the reader's right.

- The standard form of a timeline has a long line with intervals of time designated by short perpendicular marks (the intervals may be 1 month, 1 year, 10 years, or 100 years). Marks are added to the line at the appropriate time place to designate significant events, and each event is given a brief description in words (e.g., 1993: my little sister is born).

- Picture timelines use illustrations for historical people, places, and events. For example, a timeline of the history of flight could include a drawing of Lindbergh's plane, *The Spirit of St. Louis.*

- Object timelines use real things. For example, students could construct a timeline using objects that have changed over time, like men's dress shoes, writing pens, or football helmets.

- Other timelines do not use paper. It is possible to make a "clothesline" timeline. A string is stretched across a space, clothespins are placed on the line at appropriate points to designate historical events, and written descriptions or illustrations can be attached to the line with the clothespins.

- . . . and computer software has made it much easier to produce accurate, neat timelines. Perhaps the most popular software package is Timeliner, produced by Tom Snyder Productions. The software includes 400 historical photographs and clip art images and allows students to import images from the Internet and place them on their timelines. Other timeline software systems include TimelineMaker and Timeglider.

Field Trips, Virtual Field Trips, and Online Expeditions

There is nothing like a field trip—an educational excursion to a place that can help children better understand social studies content. I have many wonderful memories of the field trips my classes took when I taught elementary school in Burbank, California—trips to places like Mission San Fernando, the L. A. Harbor, the *Los Angeles Times* headquarters, and Los Angeles International Airport. To help children better understand the past, teachers should plan field trips to living history sites like Pleasant Valley School, a restored one-room schoolhouse in Stillwater, Oklahoma (Buckner, Brown, & Curry, 2010). At living history sites, docents dress in period costumes, speak in period dialect, and perform tasks with period tools. Not all historic sites provide living history through docents. Trips to historic sites, however, are an important part of social studies because they are, in fact, primary sources (White, 2010). Here are some keys to a successful field trip to a historic site:

- Though this can take time and effort, I think any trip is enhanced if the teacher visits the site before the day of the field trip and takes photographs. The photographs can show the children what they will see and what they should closely examine.

- Take advantage of historic site staff. If there are docents available to provide an insight on certain displays, be sure they know you are coming and have worked your class into their schedule.

- I always liked to have some sort of study guide, 2 or 3 pages, the students would complete while on the field trip. The guide would include questions and fill-in-the-blank exercises the children would compete while examining certain parts of the historic site. The study guide shouldn't be an overwhelming experience—we don't want to spoil the day for our students—but the trip is an educational experience, after all.

- Before you go on the field trip have clear rules for student behavior, including for the trip to and back from the site, and rules of conduct while at the historic site. I recall, for example, having to set real limits on how many students could enter gift shops at historic sites, how much they could spend, and how much time they could devote to buying souvenirs!

- Be sure parent volunteers understand their role during the field trip.

The Internet provides wonderful opportunities for students to experience other people and places through virtual reality. Students living in any state can visit the White House, and students anywhere in the world can join a group of explorers for an expedition to the Andes. A *virtual field trip* takes students to a museum or historical site through the Web (Risinger, 2005; Wilson, Rice, Bagley, & Rice, 2001). Many locations have well-planned virtual tours easily accessible by even our youngest students. Two good resources for virtual field trips are the "Schools of California Online Resources for Educators" site (www.score.k12.ca.us) and the articles written by C. Frederick Risinger appearing in almost every edition of the journal *Social Education* (Risinger, 2010). An *online expedition,* on the other hand, allows students to share the experiences of current explorers on expeditions (Delaney & Oyler, 2001).

Like a real field trip, a virtual field trip can be either a meaningful learning experience helping students acquire social studies content and master important processes, or an excursion with little educational value. The key is teacher preparation. One issue that has emerged with virtual field trips is the tendency for students to visit a Website solely for the purpose of "cutting and pasting" either text or images from the site onto a student report of some sort. Wilson et al. (2001) correctly state the teacher needs to structure the virtual field trip so students "explore a site thoroughly, analyze the information critically, and present their findings in their own words" (p. 152). Here are some things teachers should do. First, either bookmark the URL of the site or begin the trip with the site's home page on the screen. There is no reason to have students struggle to find the Website since the goal of a virtual field trip is to experience a remote location, not to teach students how to find relevant Websites. Then provide the students with a study guide focusing their attention on the most significant information in the site. Next, and this is important, write instructions on how to navigate the site. A virtual field trip does not accomplish very much if the students do not get beyond the site's home page. Once all students have completed the trip, teachers should lead a "debriefing" discussion, clarifying the information they wanted students to learn, analyzing it critically, and synthesizing it with what has been learned previously. Students can then use what they have learned to create any of a number of projects in either hard-copy or computer-based formats.

Perhaps the best way to take part in an online expedition is through the GlobaLearn Website (Delaney & Oyler, 2001). The GlobaLearn site (www.eduserveinc.com) allows students to take part in live expeditions via the Web. For each adventure, students meet a host—a young person from 11 to 15 years old who lives in the nation or region where the expedition will take place. During an online expedition, the explorers document their experiences with digital cameras, audio and video recorders, and journal entries. All this information is transmitted to the classrooms, where students are following along. The GlobaLearn server is in Connecticut, and the information is edited and posted on their Website. Students use e-mail to communicate both with the explorers and with students in other classrooms who are participating in the expedition. Students usually keep their own journals and complete a variety of assignments related to the expedition. This could include creating an expedition page on a school Website, complete with maps, charts of geographic data, like temperature and rainfall, images pasted from the expedition Website, and written reports on any of a number of topics.

At the end of the chapter is a lesson plan for fifth graders taking a virtual field trip to Monticello, Thomas Jefferson's private residence outside Charlottesville, Virginia.

Summary of Key Points

- History has always been an important part of the elementary school curriculum. Publication of the national history standards generated considerable debate about what historical content students should learn.

- Children have the cognitive capacity to learn historical concepts if they receive appropriate instruction.

- Elementary students should learn about the history of their families, schools, communities, and state; the history of the United States; the history of people living in other nations; and the historical contributions of women, people of color, and common people.

- Students should develop the ability to think and act like historians; the "doing" of history is an important part of teaching history.

- Throughout the book, I have presented teaching ideas essential to teach history in a diverse classroom; these include contextual support, multiple lesson formats, cooperative learning, critical thinking, and a variety of resources.

- Four types of lessons are essential to teach history to children: (a) those using primary sources, (b) those incorporating children's fiction, (c) those using timelines, and (d) those that are part of field trips, virtual field trips, and online excursions.

Lesson Plans and Instructional Activities

This chapter concludes with three examples of teaching history and geography to elementary school children:

1. For sixth graders, a mini-unit titled "The Historian as Detective," that teaches historical processes.

2. A kindergarten lesson that shows how children's literature, in this case the picture book *Ox-Cart Man,* can be used to teach historical content.

3. For fifth graders, a lesson plan for a virtual field trip to Jefferson's home, Monticello.

Description of a Mini-Unit

Grade Six: The Historian as Detective

Gavrish (1995) describes a unit titled "The Historian as Detective." Although designed for secondary students, it could be adapted to teach historical methodology in elementary classrooms.

Part I: Organizing Framework

From the national history standards (National Center for History in the Schools, 1996) Standard 3: Historical Analysis and Interpretation: (D) distinguish fact and fiction, and (G) consider multiple perspectives.

In this mini-unit, students will be asked to think like historians as they deal with the unreliability of eyewitness accounts, work with primary sources, and challenge the accuracy of a document. This mini-unit answers three questions:

Unit Question 1: To the historian, how reliable are eyewitness accounts?

Unit Question 2: What are primary sources, and why are they more valuable than secondary sources?

Unit Question 3: How do historians challenge the accuracy of documents they read?

Part II: Instructional Activities

Unit Question 1: To the historian, how reliable are eyewitness accounts?

Activity 1

Content Objectives: Students will learn eyewitness accounts are not always trustworthy and this causes a problem for the historian.

Process Objectives: Students will *examine* the geographic figures on the board, *draw* what they recall, and *assess* the accuracy of their recollections.

1. Tape three diagrams to the chalkboard. Each should have an outer figure (e.g., circle or square) of one color and an inner figure of another color. Tell the students, "Look at these diagrams." Leave the diagrams on the board for a short time and then remove them. Then ask the students to draw each diagram from memory: What shape is the outer figure? What color? What shape is the inner figure? What color? This task puts students in the same place as the historian, who cannot replay events. Have the students work in small groups to determine the accuracy of their drawings.

2. Help students draw the comparison between this exercise and eyewitness accounts of historical events. Why might historical events be faulty? (With the diagrams, bias is not the issue.) Like eyewitnesses to real events, the students (a) may have faulty memory, and (b) probably did not look as carefully as they would have had they known they would be asked to recall specific details.

Unit Question 2: What are primary sources, and what is their value to the historian?

Activity 2

Content Objectives: Students will learn the definition of primary sources and understand their value to the historian.

Process Objectives: Students will *list* and evaluate the value of the sources they could use to write an accurate autobiography. They will *define* primary source and *state* the value of primary sources to historians.

1. In the second activity, students consider what sources of information they would use to answer questions such as the following: Where were you born? How much did you weigh at birth? What age were you when you took your first step? What age were you when you said your first word? Read aloud the questions. Then ask the class what sources of information they would use to answer those questions. Students will probably say they would just ask their parents (or other family members). Ask the students to recall what they learned in the previous lesson about the unreliability of eyewitness accounts. Then ask them what other sources they could use besides parents or other family members. Help students see that several sources would be useful: birth certificates, baby books, and photographs. Have documents for one student (or even yourself) available to use as examples (these should be copies, and the parents and the student must approve their use). Point out these are all *primary sources*.

2. Tell the class if a classmate were to write a biography of you, that biography would be a *secondary source.* Make sure the class understands the distinction between primary and secondary sources. Finally, ask the students why primary sources are so valuable to the historian.

Unit Question 3: How do historians challenge the accuracy of documents they read?

Activity 3

Content Objectives: Students will see not all written documents are accurate.

Process Objectives: Students will *read* the historical letter prepared by the teacher and *identify* examples of historical inaccuracy.

1. In this third activity, students are told about a recently "discovered" letter. Actually, you will have to create such a letter or use the one created by Gavrish (1995) in his article. His fake letter was supposedly written by George Washington. You could write your own as long as the letter is full of historical errors (anachronisms) making it an obvious fake. The sample letter provided by Gavrish has many errors. It is written to Queen Victoria, it is written in Chicago, and it mentions the use of tanks in battle. Show the students the letter and challenge them to find each error.

2. I would have students work in small groups and share the errors they find. This lesson helps students learn to analyze a document. It shows historians must view primary sources with a critical eye.

Effective Teaching in Today's Diverse Classroom: The first two activities in this mini-unit have features making them appropriate for a diverse student population. In the first, when students are drawing the geometric figures from memory, they do not need to be able to read grade-level texts to be successful. The second activity is based on shared, personal experience of the students—their births! One caution is in order here, though. Some students will have access to more primary source data about their births than their classmates. Whereas some students will have baby books, photographs, and birth certificates, others will not (for any number of reasons). Try to obtain birth-related primary source material for four or five students and use it for the lesson. The third activity is a challenging one. To find the errors in the historically inaccurate letter, students will need to know enough historical information to spot the mistakes. Because you will write the fake letter (or use the one from Gavrish, 1995), I suggest you write it so your students will find it easy to read. Your goal is to help them see that written documents can be inaccurate, and this can be accomplished with an easy-to-read document.

Lesson Plan
Kindergarten: *Ox-Cart Man*

In a journal article, I describe history lessons that can be taught with children's literature (Zarrillo, 1989). An exciting, cross-curricular lesson can be developed with *Ox-Cart
Man,* a Caldecott-winning picture book written by Donald Hall (1979) and illustrated
by Barbara Cooney. This book tells the story of a New England farmer and his family,
apparently in the early 19th century.

Overview: This lesson is for a kindergarten class of 25 children.

Resources and Materials: (a) A copy of the book *Ox-Cart Man* (Hall, 1979), and
(b) chart paper and an easel.

Content Objectives: Children will understand life in times past was different from
life today. Specifically, they will see differences in clothing, tools, transportation, and
food preparation. They will also learn about the work done on a farm many years ago.

Standard: From ***The National Standards for History,*** grades K–4, Standard 1, the
student is able to "Compare and contrast family life now with family life over time"
(National Center for History in the Schools, 1996, p. 26).

Process Objectives: Children will *listen* and *watch* as their teacher reads aloud the
book and demonstrates the productive activities of the farmer, his wife, son, and
daughter; *pantomime* those activities under the teacher's direction; and *distinguish*
differences between how the farmer and his family lived and how we live today (clothing, transportation, and food preparation).

Teaching Sequence:

1. Before the lesson, write the following on a sheet of chart paper: carve a new
   yoke, saw planks for a new cart, split shingles, embroider clothing, make can-
   dles, tap syrup, shear sheep, spin yarn, plant crops.

2. Display the chart on an easel.

3. Ask the children to come to the read-aloud area and to sit cross-legged on
   the floor.

4. Read aloud *Ox-Cart Man.*

5. Ask the children whether they have any questions or comments about the story.

6. Read aloud each farming activity on the chart and demonstrate, through pantomime, how each would be done.

7. Ask the children to stand and, under your guidance, pantomime each activity.

8. Point to the illustrations in the book showing how the farmer and his family dressed, how they prepared food, the tools they used, and how they transported goods. Allow the children to look at each illustration closely and to talk about what they find interesting. Then ask, "What is different about how the farmer lived and how we live today?"

Evaluation: You may want to tape-record the children's responses to the question "What is different about how the farmer lived and how we live today?" The comments will reveal to what extent the children understand the lesson's content objective.

Effective Teaching in Today's Diverse Classroom: Howard Gardner has written about *multiple intelligences* (1991, 2006). This concept defies the older idea that intelligence is a single entity that can be measured and quantified (with an intelligence quotient [IQ]). It seems to make sense some people are gifted (or challenged) in one area, like the arts, but challenged (or gifted) in another, like mathematical thinking. In any case, some children are frustrated with school because they typically have so few opportunities for learning and expression through the arts. This activity will make their day by providing an opportunity to assume the roles of the ox-cart man and his family.

Lesson Plan
Grade Five: A Virtual Field Trip to Monticello

Overview: This lesson would take place during a unit on the American Revolution and the founding of the United States. The field trip is completed by visiting the Monticello Website, www.Monticello.org, maintained by the Thomas Jefferson Foundation. Monticello, of course, was Thomas Jefferson's private residence and is located outside Charlottesville, Virginia. Students would work in pairs to complete the lesson, following the directions and answering the questions on the study guide. The study guide is designed to allow the students to complete the virtual field trip with little teacher intervention. The lesson assumes students have visited several Websites and have a reasonable level of Web literacy. Students should already know about Jefferson's role in writing the Declaration of Independence. It would be a good idea to teach the meanings of a few words before the students take the tour (e.g., *ploughing* and *nailery*).

Resources and Materials: (a) Access to the Website, www.Monticello.org, and (b) the study guide created by the teacher, "A Virtual Field Trip to Monticello."

Standard: From the *National Standards for History,* Grades 5–12, Era 3, "Revolution and the New Nation," Standard 1B, "The student understands the principles articulated in the Declaration of Independence," and Standard 2C, "The student understands the Revolution's effects on different social groups" (National Center for History in the Schools, 1996, pp. 86–87).

Content Objectives: Students will learn that Monticello provides evidence Jefferson was a product of the Enlightenment. This is reflected in his interests in learning, architecture, art, and science. Students will also learn that Jefferson owned enslaved persons who worked at both manufacturing and agriculture.

Process Objectives: Students will follow the directions provided in the study guide to *navigate* the Website; *examine* photographs, illustrations, and diagrams; *read* sections of the Website; and *answer* the questions listed on the study guide.

Teaching Sequence: The students follow the directions of the study guide provided here:

Study Guide: A Virtual Tour of Monticello

1. We are going on a trip to Thomas Jefferson's home. The house and the land around it are called Monticello. Follow all the directions in this guide. Let's go!

2. Monticello's home page should be on the screen. To get a good look at the house, scroll down to "The House" and click. Then scroll down to "Frequently Asked Questions about Monticello." Click on it.

3. We are not going to answer the questions. We just want to look at two good photographs of the house from a distance. Click on the first question, "What is the architectural style of the house?" Look at the photograph. Click on the "Back" button on the toolbar at the top of the screen. Let's look at one more photograph. Click on "Which is the front side of the house?"

4. Let's go inside the house. Scroll to the bottom of the page and click on "The House." We see a diagram of all the rooms of the house. Click on "Entrance Hall (3)." Read the section titled "Purpose of the Room" and answer questions a and b.

   a. What were the two purposes of the Entrance Hall?

   b. What types of things did the museum have in the Entrance Hall?

5. Now here comes a fun part. Scroll up and click on "Virtual Reality Panorama." Look at the photo of the room. Now click on the (+) to zoom in and get a closer look. Click on the (−) to pull back. Wow, that was like walking through the room!

6. Click on the "Back" button to get back to the Entrance Room page. Let's go visit another room. Scroll down and click on "Parlor (9)." Read the "Purpose of the Room" section. Put an (×) by every activity that took place in the room.

   a. Which of the following activities took place in Monticello's parlor?

   ____music   ____cooking   ____games

   ____reading   ____weddings   ____basketball

   ____gardening   ____dances

7. Let's take a look at Jefferson's favorite chair. Scroll down to "Furnishings of Note." Then look for the link "A Delightful Recreation." Click. Look at the illustration of the campeachy or siesta chair.

   a. Does Jefferson's siesta chair look comfortable to you? Why or why not?

8. Click on "Back" to return to the Parlor page. We only have time for one more room. Scroll down to "Library or Book Room (5)." Click. Read the section on the "Purpose of the Room." Answer two questions:

   a. How many books did Jefferson own?

   b. What happened to his books?

9. We can do a virtual reality tour of this room, too. Scroll up and click on "Virtual Reality Panorama." Again, click on the (+) to zoom in and the (−) to zoom out.

10. It is time to leave the house. Let's learn more about farming and the enslaved people at Monticello. Click on "Back" to return to the Library and Book Room main page. Scroll down to the bottom of the page and click on "The Plantation." Read the text and answer the following questions:

    a. How big was the plantation at Monticello?

    b. How many farms were there?

    c. How many enslaved people worked on the farms?

11. Scroll down and click on "Work: The Industries and Activities Pursued at Monticello." Find and click on "Ploughing. "Let's learn more about how the fields were ploughed at Monticello. Read the second and third paragraphs and answer these questions:

    a. How much did Jefferson pay for the plough he bought from George Logan?

    b. How old was the slave Robin when Jefferson wrote Robin "works well at the plough already"?

    c. What evidence is there that women did much of the ploughing?

12. Click "Back" to return to the Work page. Scroll down and click on "Nailmaking." That's right! To make money when the farm was not producing many crops, Jefferson relied on the making of nails. Read the second paragraph and answer these questions:

    a. How many young male enslaved persons worked at the nailery?

    b. Read carefully! How old were the enslaved people who worked there?

    c. What happened to most of the enslaved people who worked at the nailery?

13. It's time to come home! Click "Back" to return to the Plantation page. Scroll down and click on the home page. The computer is now ready for someone else. Thank you.

Once all students have completed this virtual field trip, the teacher will lead a discussion. The first goal will be to review the answers to the questions on the study

guide. Then the students will break into small groups to answer these questions:
(a) We have learned Jefferson, like other leaders of his time, was interested in many different topics. What evidence did we see of this in our tour? (b) We saw Monticello was home to many enslaved people who worked in the nailery and on the plantation. From Jefferson's standpoint, what were the financial advantages of using slave labor? If slavery had been abolished, what would have happened at Monticello? From the perspective of the enslaved persons, what hardships did they experience? (c) Did the Declaration of Independence and the American Revolution change the lives of the enslaved people at Monticello?

Students may return to the Website to complete some of the projects which are part of the unit. For example, if some students are developing a "Who's Who of the American Revolution" page to be posted on the school Website, they may want to cut and paste images of Monticello to accompany their text on Jefferson. Students completing a bulletin board display on "Life in the United States, October 11, 1803" can use what they learned to create a section called "Homer Watson, Age 14, Enslaved Person at Monticello."

 Effective Teaching in Today's Diverse Classroom: This activity could prove very difficult for a child with a learning disability. Sometimes it is necessary to select more than one instructional modification to help children succeed with an activity. Here, a teacher might use *instructional prompts and cues* and breaking the task into *smaller, manageable units.* For example, consider Step 11 in the activity: *Scroll down and click on "Work: The Industries and Activities Pursued at Monticello." Find and click on "Ploughing." Let's learn more about how the fields were ploughed at Monticello.* It might be necessary to print a copy of the computer screen the children would view and highlight, with a yellow marker, *Ploughing.* This visual clue will make the task less abstract and increase the chances that all children will click on the correct link. This activity has 13 steps, which may be too many for some students with disabilities. Teachers could consider an abbreviated form of the lesson, with only six or seven steps.

CHAPTER 11

Geography

In this chapter, you will read about

- A definition of geography that is broad, and not limited to the memorization of the names and locations of a few geographic features, like oceans, rivers, mountain ranges, and capital cities

- The research on children's understanding of geography, which reveals that there are significant challenges to teaching geographic concepts to young children

- The appropriate geographic content children should learn, including physical characteristics of a place, geopolitical information, demographics, and economic information

- The essential geographic processes children should master

- How to teach children to read map symbols, understand scale on a map, use grids on maps, and develop a sense of directionality

- How to teach children to make mental, relief, and thematic maps

- How to use computer-based Geographic Information Systems to teach geographic concepts

Rather than begin this chapter with a single vignette, I will share some of the activities described in a special edition of *Social Studies and the Young Learner* devoted to geographic education (Bennett, 2007):

- Second graders used aerial maps available through GoogleMaps or MapQuest to learn more about their school and neighborhood. They examined aerial maps over a ten-year time span and then drew illustrations with colored pencils to predict what their neighborhood would look like in the future.

- Primary level students considered the many features of a single place. After taking a walking field trip visiting four places in their neighborhood (e.g., bus stop, market), each student selected one place. On a sheet of paper divided into four quadrants, each student drew a picture of the place in one of the quadrants, wrote words describing the place in the second quadrant, listed things "created by nature" and things "made by people" in the third quadrant, and people who use the place in the fourth quadrant.

■ Fourth and fifth graders took part in several activities related to yard sales, each teaching geographic concepts. Students found four yard sales listed in the classified section of the local newspaper on a hard-copy map; created directions for going from their school to the location of each of the yard sales—a "yard sale circuit," used maps to calculate the distance of their yard sale circuit, and planned an itinerary so they would arrive at each yard sale as close as possible to the time it opened.

■ Three third-grade teachers had their students participate in "The Great Mail Race." Each class wrote and mailed 50 letters to elementary schools, one in each of the United States. The letters asked students in the 50 schools to complete a survey about their classroom and their school. Students used maps to select the schools receiving the letters and surveys. The students used the Website www.50states.com to locate specific school addresses. When the responses arrived, students analyzed the data to draw conclusions about their national sample of third-grade classrooms and schools.

■ Fourth graders took a field trip to New Orleans that challenged them to visit 20 landmarks in the French Quarter. Students used a Global Positioning System (GPS), digital cameras, MP3 players, and hand-held I-Paqs during the field trip. Organized in groups of four, one student was the navigator, another the cartographer, the third the journalist, and the fourth the photographer. Accompanied by an adult chaperone, each group used the GPS to find the landmark, then took photographs and interviewed either a local business owner or a tourist. As a final project, students created both a PowerPoint presentation with graphs, text, and photographs and a movie about their adventure using Photo Story software.

■ ■ ■

Geography in the Elementary School: Overview and Research on Children's Understanding of Geography

Although there is near-universal agreement that geography is an essential component of the school curriculum, geography has struggled to find a significant place in the schools (Douglass, 1998; Geography Education Standards Project, 1994; Gersmehl, 2005; Gregg & Leinhardt, 1994; Stoltman, 1991). There are really two issues here: (1) Will geography in any form be taught as part of social studies? and (2) If it is taught, will geographic education go beyond memorizing the names and locations of a few items, such as oceans, rivers, lakes, and capital cities? Important information about the first issue can be found in the review of the research on K–12 geographic education provided by Segal and Helfenbein (2008). They reported that by 2004 all states except Rhode Island and Iowa had some form of standards for geography—certainly good news. However, they also reported that only about half the states included geography on their mandated state examinations. Interestingly enough, these authors report that even among social studies professionals, geography gets little attention. Segal and Helfenbein concluded "research articles in/on geography education area a rare occurrence" in social studies journals.

As to the second issue, meaningful geographic curricula require a broad view of geography. A simple definition is that geography is the study of place just as history is the study of the past. The important thing is to make geography more than bits of information; it should be seen by teachers as "a way of knowing," a process that evolves as students learn "to think in terms of spatial interactions" (Douglass, 1998, p. xvi). Gregg and Leinhardt (1994) provide a definition we should consider:

> Geography uses the language of maps to communicate ideas about the context and distribution of phenomena and processes important for human decision making, issues of scale, the dynamic nature of phenomena, and cultural perspective. (p. 328)

This definition, though complex, provides a basis for understanding the geographic component of the social studies. Geography requires that students know how to read and make several types of *maps*. Thus, geographic understanding is a form of literacy, though in this case it is the ability to read and write maps, not words. Through geographic lessons, students should understand how people, resources, and products are *distributed* over the earth. Geographic study should provide a *context* for understanding events as students see how the *decisions* people make are influenced by their physical surroundings. Finally, students should learn how people interact with the environment and, as a result, how both people and places *change* (Gersmehl, 2005).

Apparently, we must do a great deal to increase the level of geographic knowledge our students have. Two national assessments of geographic understanding have been completed as part of the National Assessment of Educational Progress, one in 1994, the other in 2001. The results of each study were consistent, with slight improvement occurring in 2001. The number of students at the "advanced" level is small (1994: 3%; 2001: 2%); the number at the "proficient" level in both studies was 19%. Fortunately, the percentage of students who scored at or above the basic level increased from 48% in 1994 to 53% in 2001 (the complete results are at the U.S. Department of Education Website, under "The Nation's Report Card," www.nces.ed/gov/nationsreportcard). In the winter of 2010, the NAEP geography examinations will be administered again; the results will be available sometime in 2011.

Research on Geographic Learning and Teaching

Several comprehensive reviews of the research on geographic learning and teaching have been published (Douglass, 1998; Forsythe, 1995; Gersmehl, 2005; Gregg and Leinhardt, 1994; Segal & Helfenbein, 2008; Stoltman, 1991). Fortunately, there is a body of research that can help elementary school teachers be effective teachers of geography. While some professional journals in social studies rarely publish research articles on geographic topics, *The Journal of Geography* has increased the number of studies it publishes and the journal *Research in Geography* is solely devoted to research reports. Our discussion will focus on research:

- Completed by the great child psychologist Jean Piaget
- Measuring the ability of children to read symbols and understand scale

- Examining the cognitive processes involved in map reading
- Evaluating classroom practice

Jean Piaget investigated the map-reading abilities of children (Piaget & Inhelder, 1969). He thought that children go through three stages in their ability to see things from a different perspective, an ability which is prerequisite to reading maps. At first, children are in a "topographical" stage, unable to use directional labels (e.g., north and south). Then children pass through a "projective" stage, when they can determine location in relation to their own position—they know what is to the right and left of them. The final stage, usually reached between ages 10 and 12, Piaget labeled as "Euclidean," as children have an accurate perception of spatial relationships. As is so often the case in developmental studies, other researchers have challenged Piaget's conclusions. Using different methods (e.g., familiar cartoon characters), researchers have shown that children are able to do more with maps at an earlier age than Piaget thought they could.

A body of research is available on the child's ability to read symbols. Some amusing studies have shown that children tend to interpret symbols literally, stating the urban centers colored yellow on a map were eggs or firecrackers (Liben & Downs, 1989). Children, however, can understand symbols on maps represent things. The more difficult task for children is to see the relationships among the represented items. Generally, the ability of children to understand symbols on a map is influenced by the "degree of abstractness of the symbol and the amount of detail on the map" (Gregg & Leinhardt, 1994, p. 333).

Likewise, several studies have been conducted on the ability of children to understand scale. Gregg and Leinhardt (1994) concluded three things are necessary for children to read and use scale. First, they must have developed proportional reasoning; they must have a sense that the relationships among items remain constant even if the unit of comparison has shrunk. Second, they must be able to measure in the units used on the map; on the simplest maps, this involves inches and miles or centimeters and kilometers. Finally, they must have a sense of the frame of reference of the map. Maps are selective in what they reveal. No map can show everything about a place, and to understand scale children must understand the level of detail in the map.

Research on the cognitive processes involved in map reading is complex. Researchers have investigated how the information on a map is recognized, how their images are stored in memory, and how that information is recalled. Gregg and Leinhardt (1994) concluded, "From a cognitive perspective, it is not easy to make sense of the symbols and letters superimposed on the complex visual fields referred to as maps" (p. 343). Maps, through the use of symbol and scale, can convey large amounts of important information. Map reading is not easy; it places unique demands on the developing thinking abilities of children. Muir and Frazee (1986) noted a significant cognitive challenge for young map readers is understanding that maps require a "bird's-eye" rather than a "ground-level" perspective. Some children, when asked to read maps, have great difficulty because they are not able to make this shift in perspective.

Unfortunately, few studies shed much light on how to teach geography. J. W. Miller (1974, 1982) did show that the design of maps makes a difference. Children find it easier to read maps with a limited number of different typefaces, clearly differentiated symbols, a compass rose, a grid system of latitude and longitude, boldly marked boundaries, and all labels in a horizontal format. Atkins (1981) found young children can be taught to read simple maps if the instruction is presented in a clear and structured manner. In conclusion, it is important to note at least one authority reached the same conclusion about the child's capacity to learn geography that others have reached about history. Karen Trifonoff (1997) stated "many early geographic educators believed children to have a poorly developed sense of space. Most modern studies suggest the opposite. Students do have well-developed spatial understanding, and they continue to astound researchers with their advanced mapping behaviors" (p. 17). Although it is essential that our teaching be developmentally appropriate and not ask children to perform tasks beyond their abilities, it also appears that, regarding history and geography, educators have underestimated the capacity of children to learn essential concepts.

Geography in the Elementary School: Content

Geography should include each of the following:

- Physical characteristics, such as elevation of land and types of vegetation;

- Geopolitical information, like boundaries and capital cities;

- Demographics, including the size, density, and identity of population; and

- Economic information, such as the type and volume of agricultural and manufactured products produced in places.

Students should learn the relationships between this information, especially how places change over time. The most important scheme for organizing geographic content was created for the national standards for geography. The geographic content students should learn is organized under six elements: (a) the world in spatial terms, (b) places and regions, (c) physical systems, (d) human systems, (e) environment and society, and (f) the uses of geography (Freese, 1997; Geography Education Standards Project, 1994). Let's take a closer look at the elements. Eighteen standards are organized across these six elements:

1. *The world in spatial terms.*   The national standards seek to develop the "geographically informed person." Such a student is expected to have basic map-reading skills and the ability to produce maps summarizing geographic information. Students should be able to read and make maps showing the spatial relationships of people, places, and environments.

2. *Places and regions.*   The world's resources, both human and natural, are not evenly distributed over the earth. Each place is unique, and the earth's landmasses can be divided into regions with clearly defined characteristics. Students should learn the physical and human characteristics of places. They should know, for example, what makes Hawaii and Alaska different from each other.

3. *Physical systems.*   This is a part of social studies that overlaps science. Students should understand the physical processes that shape the earth's surface (e.g., floods, volcanoes, and earthquakes) and the concept of an ecosystem.

4. *Human systems.*   This element looks at the three ways human beings relate to the surface of the earth: (a) People shape the surface of the earth by consuming resources and altering natural patterns; (b) people build structures that become a part of the surface of the earth; and (c) people compete for control of the surface of the earth.

5. *Environment and society.*   People modify the physical environment of the earth. An easy example for students to understand is how the construction of a dam creates a lake. Sometimes the relationship between nature and people is reverse as nature "strikes back" and physical systems alter those things people have constructed. For example, a hurricane destroys buildings; over a longer period of time, persistent drought leads to mass migration.

6. *The uses of geography.*   The sixth and final element states students should know how to apply geographic knowledge to interpret the past, understand the present, and plan for the future.

Almost all state social standards include each of these six geographic themes. The level of emphasis, however, varies widely from state to state. Some state standards focus mainly on the second element—the physical characteristics of the place being studied (e.g., for third graders, the geographic focus in the physical geography of the local region; for fourth graders, the focus is the physical geography of the state). You would need to check your relevant state standards to assess the status of geographic education where you will teach. Virtually none of the state social studies standards is as ambitious as the national standards.

Geography in the Elementary School: Processes

The five sets of geographic skills proposed in *Guidelines for Geographic Education: Elementary and Secondary Schools* (Joint Committee on Geographic Education, 1984), listed next, are widely accepted as an outline of what students should be able to do in geography. The national standards in geography incorporate them.

■ *Asking geographic questions.* Students must learn how to ask questions in geographic terms. "Where is something located?" "How did it get there?" "Why is it located where it is?" "How is one place different from another?" Specifically, students should be able to

Ask geographic questions about current events

Distinguish between questions that can be answered with geographic data and those that cannot

■ *Acquiring geographic information.* As with history, geographic data can be found in both primary and secondary sources. Primary data are gathered through fieldwork as students distribute surveys, take photographs, and record their observations on field trips. Secondary data are maps, databases, and books. Specifically, students should be able to

> Make records of geographic data on field trips
>
> Use their mathematical skills to count and measure
>
> Read maps, charts, graphs, and tables with geographic data

■ *Organizing information.* Geographic data can be organized in several ways. Maps, of course, are the primary tool for organizing what students learn about a place. Students should also learn how to construct charts, graphs, and tables. Specifically, students should be able to

> Prepare maps, charts, graphs, and tables with geographic data
>
> Write concise summaries of geographic data

■ *Analyzing geographic information.* It is often difficult to distinguish the processes of gathering and analyzing geographic data. They tend to occur simultaneously. Specifically, students should be able to

> Interpret data in maps, graphs, charts, and tables
>
> Discover trends, relationships, and patterns in geographic data

■ *Answering geographic questions.* Finally, students should see the relationships among the data they have gathered and analyzed. They should reach generalizations that are true across time and place. Specifically, students should be able to

> Present oral and written reports accompanied by maps, charts, graphs, and tables
>
> Apply geographic knowledge to interpret the past, understand the present, and predict the future

Teaching Geography: Challenges and Principles of Instruction, Map Reading, and Map Making

Our discussion of how to teach geography in the elementary school will be divided into two parts. In this first section, the discussion will first examine fundamental issues of geographic instruction, including the challenges teachers face. The discussion will then turn to the key components of teaching children to read maps: understanding how symbols, scale, grids, and direction are used by map makers. Finally, the first section will address the types of maps children should create. The second section will look at how elementary school teachers can use computer-based resources to teach geography.

Challenges and Principles of Instruction

Geography presents a unique challenge to teachers, primarily because geographic information is presented in an unfamiliar format. Maps and globes require a different type of reading from the expository text students read in textbooks and encyclopedias. Further,

Shutterstock

Reading maps is not easy for children—they must understand the symbols and scale of each map they examine.

elementary students will work with a variety of maps, each with its own category of information. For example, one type of climate map shows precipitation for South America, whereas another, historical map shows European colonies in South America during the early 19th century. Another complicating factor with world maps is the difference between conformal maps and equal area maps. The *Mercator projection* produces a *conformal map;* all the landmasses retain their appropriate shapes. Unfortunately, this type of map is distorted; Greenland appears larger than Africa. *Equal-area maps,* in contrast, show land areas with proper relative sizes. Unfortunately, this requires a distortion of the earth's landmasses. The good news is most social studies textbooks present maps that are developmentally appropriate for the children who read them. Further, schools should have globes and maps specially designed for young learners. For example, globes at many levels of sophistication are available. The simplest ones avoid detail, include only the names of nations and their capital cities, and use bright colors to distinguish boundaries.

As with many social studies processes, map-reading skills should be developed through both repeated practice and direct instruction. Students will become geographically literate if they are *repeatedly* asked to use maps; there is no substitute for practice. At the same time, teachers should plan *developmental* lessons to help their students understand the special language of maps. All geography teaching with children should move from the concrete to the abstract, from the simple to the complex. If possible, developmental map-reading activities should use the following progression:

1. First, children should participate in activities using their bodies as points of reference.

2. Next, children should use three-dimensional maps.

3. Then children should use simplified maps for use in the elementary classroom.

4. Finally, children should be asked to complete activities with maps that are real and have been produced for use outside the classroom. The mini-unit presented at the end of this chapter on using a grid system follows this progression.

To both gather and report geographic information, elementary students must become sophisticated with four aspects of maps: symbols, scale, grid, and direction.

Reading Maps: Symbols

Maps use symbols to report information. Some symbols represent things with a fixed, physical presence, such as highways and rivers; others reveal patterns of data, such as levels of unemployment. Consider the challenge children face. Written material, such as a textbook, uses a single, unvarying set of symbols—the 26 letters of the English alphabet. Most maps, in contrast, have their own set of symbols. A red circle on one map may represent a city with a population of 100,000, whereas on another map a red circle may represent the location of a water treatment plant. The key concept for children to understand is that once a certain symbol stands for something on a map, it will always have the same meaning for that particular map. The *legend* on a map tells what the symbols mean.

Our youngest learners should be exposed to maps with three-dimensional symbols that look a great deal like what they represent. A three-dimensional map of the neighborhood, for example, might have milk cartons represent houses and a large shoe box, with doors and windows painted on it, represents the school. Next, students work with maps with symbols that are pictographs, or "pictorial" symbols, the symbols are drawings for what they represent. The next level of abstraction is "semi-pictorial" symbols, which look something like, or retain a single feature of, what they represent (e.g., a church is represented by a cross). When symbols no longer "look" like what they represent (e.g., the symbol for the state capital is a star), then the maps should be simplified and include very few symbols. Following are some activities that teach children to understand map symbols:

■ *Group symbols.* If students are seated in groups, have each group choose a symbol to represent themselves. The symbols cannot have any writing; they may be pictorial, but eventually they should be abstract—for example, blue circles or red triangles. Use the symbols in class schedules and on charts.

■ *Symbols in the community.* Develop a lesson with symbols used in the community and in the media. Students will recognize some commercial symbols—like the golden arches for McDonald's or the Nike swoosh, and others used in public places—like symbols for men and women on bathroom doors or symbols for railroad tracks.

■ *Matching symbols with what they represent.* Prepare simple pictorial symbols for a set of photographs. For a picture of a school, the symbol could be a simple drawing of a building with a flag; for a picture of a forest, the symbol could be a triangular treetop with a narrow, rectangular trunk, like a stylized Christmas tree. Shuffle the symbols and the photographs and then have students match each symbol to its photograph.

■ *Simplified maps.* If the textbook does not have them, make some maps that (a) have few places represented (few details), and (b) use pictorial symbols. Students will need repeated practice with these simplified maps (see Figure 11.1 for an example).

Reading Maps: Scale

Our youngest students should work with some life-size maps. For example, it is possible to create a life-size map of the top of a teacher's desk. Eventually, the possibilities for life-size maps are exhausted, and students will have to understand scale to use maps. My experience is that this is a very difficult concept for young children. Most maps that I have seen primary-level children produce, prior to a good unit on maps, are more illustrations than maps. The problem is that the scale on these maps produced by primary-age children is inconsistent. I recall that, when I asked them to draw a map of the neighborhood, for example, most children drew houses that were grossly out of scale and covered an area that should represent an entire block. Our older students, in contrast, should be able to calculate the exact distance between two places on a map. Following are some activities to help children understand scale:

■ Compare the furniture in a first-grade classroom with the furniture in a fifth-grade classroom. The chairs the children use will make the point dramatically. Then have the children think about the relative sizes of first graders and fifth graders. Help the children see the furniture has been "built to scale"—smaller chairs for smaller children, larger chairs for larger children.

■ Have the children draw maps of the classroom. Focus on scale. The children must represent their desks in a way that makes them smaller than the teacher's desk—assuming the teacher's desk is larger than the students'. Then have the children try making maps of the school. First, you may want to measure the size of some of the buildings in the school complex. Help the children see that the smaller buildings at the school must look that way on their maps.

■ When you think the children are ready, teach a series of lessons on using the scale of miles. The goal should be to have the children calculate actual distances between places by using the scale.

At the end of the chapter, you will find an example of this type of lesson, an activity in which students determine the distance between two places.

Figure 11.1

Simplified Map to Teach Children How to Use a Grid System

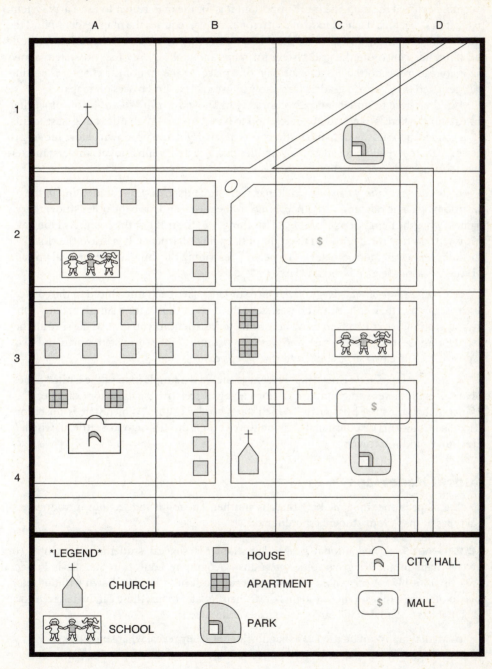

Reading Maps: Grids and Direction

The more detailed the map, the more important it is for the map reader to use a grid system. To locate a street on a detailed map of a city, for example, requires the map reader to find the street name in an index and then use the *coordinates* (e.g., E5) to narrow the search. Latitude and longitude constitute the grid system for maps and globes. Use of a grid system allows the map reader to find the *absolute location* of a place. At the end of the chapter is a mini-unit designed to help third graders learn how to use grids to find places on maps.

Children need to understand directionality to know the *relative location* of something. For example, where is San Antonio in relation to New Orleans? With our youngest students, it is a good idea to start with familiar directions of left-right and up-down before moving to the compass rose. Following are some activities that will help your students understand relative location and directionality:

■ *Directions in the classroom.* Challenge your students to describe something in the classroom by using references to other things in the room, and have the other students try to guess what the item is. For example, "This thing is in the front of the room. As I look at it, it is to the left of the flag and to the right of the pencil sharpener. It is below the clock" (the item was a wall thermometer). The person describing the thing may *not* reveal physical characteristics (e.g., it is red and large).

■ *Compass rose on the playground.* Once students have been introduced to the compass rose and north, south, east, and west, take the class outdoors for a simple activity. On the playground, ask students to move according to instructions you give. Make sure all the instructions use north, south, east, and west, for example, "Take three steps north and two steps south," "Take two steps south and three steps east."

■ *Relative location on a real map.* Present to the class a simple map of the United States. Have students answer some simple questions involving relative location, for example, "Which state is north of Missouri?" "Which states border Utah?" "Which state is closer to Arizona—California or Louisiana?" "If you were going from Chicago to Seattle, in which direction would you travel?"

Student-Made Maps

Reading maps is one thing; making them is another. The following sections introduce several types of maps your students should make.

Mental Maps. The national geography standards suggest students use mental (or sketch) maps to answer geographic questions (Geography Education Standards Project, 1994, pp. 146–147). A *mental map* is a map "inside your head" and is drawn without reference to other resources. When students draw their mental maps, these can be referred to as "sketch maps." Mental maps can be used in several ways:

■ Mental maps can be used as a diagnostic tool. They reveal what students know about the region being mapped. More important, they reveal the mapmaker's attitude toward the places represented. The familiar and the important tend to be drawn larger than the less familiar and less important.

■ For some geographic tasks, a sketch map serves us well. *Sketch maps* can help us recall the relative locations and sizes of places. A sketch map could help us remember what nations a person must travel through to go from Paris to Moscow or to show someone how to get from school to the airport.

Relief Maps.   For more than 100 years, elementary school children have made three-dimensional relief maps. *Relief maps* reveal the topography of a region because mountain ranges and valleys can be shown. To help your students be successful, consider conducting the following activity:

1. Build an outline map on an inflexible surface, such as plywood (cardboard tends to buckle, so do not use it).

2. Start with a good "outline" map. An *outline map* shows some geographic features but omits others. Commercially produced outline maps of the world, the continents, the United States, and each of the 50 states are available. The outline map used for a relief map must be either drawn or projected on the surface. Do not make the outline map too small; a relief map must be large enough to show the important physical features of the region.

3. Sketch the outline of the features in the model (e.g., mountains, rivers, and valleys) on the surface. Students will need an easy-to-read map to show the physical geography of the region they are mapping. It is essential they have a good idea of the scale of things (e.g., how tall one mountain is in relation to another).

4. There are many recipes for making relief maps. The old tried-and-true recipe is salt and flour. Mix equal parts of salt and flour and add a minimal amount of water—just enough to keep the glob together. I prefer to use clay, but it is more expensive.

5. Have patience! It is not easy to make a mountain. Work with students to consider scale and expect some initial efforts will need to be reshaped.

6. Relief maps look better if they are painted (e.g., mountains, brown; valleys, green; and rivers, blue). Tempera paints work fine.

Thematic Maps.   In her excellent article, Trifonoff (1997) challenges primary-level teachers to allow their students to make thematic maps. Almost all the maps elementary students read or make are location maps, which show where things are. Thematic maps, in contrast, "illustrate a single idea, distribution, or relationship" (p. 17). An example of a thematic map is a map of the United States showing the rate of coronary-related deaths among 100 people. States are divided into four categories based on the data on coronary-related deaths. Each category is assigned a color, and on the thematic map of coronary-related deaths in the United States, each state is colored according to the data. Anyone looking at the map can easily compare the data on any two states, and, more important, regional trends (if any) are easy to spot.

To make a thematic map, start with a blank map of a region (e.g., your school, neighborhood, city, or state). The map must have clearly defined subregions (e.g., the map of the state must show counties, the map of the school must show each classroom). Next, students need to gather data and compile it in a table. For example, students could do a survey to determine how frequently students in each classroom eat in the cafeteria. Then students would have to organize the data so they fall into four or five categories. Each classroom must fit into one of the categories based on the average number of students who eat in the cafeteria each day. For example, on the average, (a) more than 75% of students in the classroom eat in the cafeteria, (b) 50% to 74% of students in the classroom eat in the cafeteria, (c) 25% to 49% of students in the classroom eat in the cafeteria, and (d) less than 24% of students in the classroom eat in the cafeteria. A color must be assigned to each category (e.g., over 75%, red; 50%–74%, blue; 25%–49%, green; and 24% and under, yellow). A legend must be added explaining what the colors mean, and students would have to color each classroom on the map accordingly.

Teaching Geography: Computer-Based Resources

The introduction of computer-based resources has had a profound impact on the teaching of geography. Our discussion will (1) discuss the variety of Geographic Information Systems (GIS) available to teachers, and (2) present guidelines for using GIS in the elementary school classroom.

Geographic Information Systems

Geographic Information Systems (GIS) have revolutionized the field of geography. GIS provide layers of geographic information in computers and allow previously unheard of opportunities to retrieve, store, and manipulate geographic data. GIS come in all levels of sophistication—the most advanced GIS allow a user to pan across maps, access data sets, view 3-D images, and zoom into specific locations. In addition, some of the maps in GIS are interactive in that the user can add information to the maps. GIS are used widely in both the private and public sectors for such purposes as military intelligence, market analysis, and assessing real estate. And, GIS are increasingly an important part of K–12 geographic instruction. Some GIS are available as software, such as the popular MyWorld GIS, which was developed by the Geographic Data Education Initiative at Northwestern University (www.myworldgis.org). Other GIS are Web-based, and are available through the Internet—they are called "Internet-based Geographic Systems (IGIS)." The general public uses simple IGIS featuring satellite imagery—like GoogleMaps (www.maps.google.com) and MapQuest (www.mapquest.com). Popular GIS appropriate for elementary students include Google Earth (www.earth.google.com). Google Earth is a virtual globe available via the Internet. Google Earth features three-dimensional images of buildings, aerial images of places, and several types of maps. More advanced IGIS include the National Atlas (www.national-atlas.gov) and Globalis (www.globalis.gvu.unu.edu). The professional literature includes several articles about using GIS in K–12 settings (Britt & LaFontaine, 2009;

Shutterstock

Today, more and more geography lessons for elementary school children will require the use of computer-based Geographic Information Systems (GIS).

Hammond & Bodzin, 2009; Milson & Curtis, 2009; Milson, Gilbert, & Earle, 2007; Shin & Alibrandi, 2007; Todd & Delahunty, 2007).

What does the research say about this use of GIS in the classroom? So far, though, "relatively little is known about how such systems influence younger learners" (Segal & Helfenbein, 2008). The research does reveal that relatively few teachers use GIS, for a variety of reasons including inadequate teacher training and limited access to relevant hardware and software. One study did show in a fifth-grade class, the use of GIS lead to students *practicing* geographic skills rather than merely *memorizing* facts (Keiper, 1999). Other studies show the use of computer-based resources helps students develop spatial understanding and enhance their problem-solving skills (Segal & Helfenbein, 2008).

The advantages of planning and implementing classroom projects and units of study include:

- Projects and units with GIS will push students to go beyond simply reading maps and engage them in data gathering, data analysis, and data reporting;

- GIS projects and units are easy to design as inquiries that foster critical thinking; and

- Projects and units with GIS, while difficult for children, are highly motivating—they are fun (Hammond & Bodzin, 2009).

Guidelines for GIS Projects or Units

A teacher planning a GIS project or unit with elementary school students should follow the guidelines you see below, which I adapted from articles written by Britt and La Fontaine (2009), Hammond and Bodzin (2009), Milson and Curtis (2009), Shin and Alibrandi (2007), and Todd and Delahunty (2007). Projects usually are problem-solving inquiries taking several days. Units of study using GIS, especially for elementary students may not be focused on solving a problem; rather they look forward to develop geographic understanding in young learners by introducing them to computer-based maps, images, and data sets.

(1) Pre-Implementation Planning.   The teacher must address each of the following issues:

1. The teacher will decide what GIS will be used. Most GIS are complex and should be used with upper elementary school students. Younger children, however, can use the simpler GIS with plenty of help from their teacher. Britt and LaFontaine described a unit that used GoogleEarth with first graders! The GIS selected must be (a) accessible to the children and (b) fit the topic of the project or unit.

2. Decide what resources you will use in addition to the GIS. For example, in Britt and LaFontaine's description of a first-grade unit featuring Google Earth, Gus LaFontaine, the classroom teacher, began his unit with a tour of the school, using a hand-drawn map. For a GIS project or unit, teachers may also use hard-copy maps, the social studies textbook, realia, or children's literature. Hard-copy maps can be compared with computer versions of the same place. Children's books frequently are a good supplementary resource. For their second-grade unit using aerial maps through MapQuest, Todd and Delahunty (2007) shared with their students three picture books with aerial perspectives: *Madlenka* (Sis, 2000), *Mirette on the High Wire* (McCully, 1992), and *As the Crow Flies* (Hartman, 1993).

3. The teacher must define the tasks the students will complete. The goal of GIS projects should be to solve a problem. Milson and Curtis designed a high school project in which students would use the MyWorld GIS (a) to find the best location for a new business of their choice, and (b) justify their choice through a PowerPoint presentation. GIS units are planned to introduce students to the variety of geographic data available. Teachers will usually include two parts to their projects or units. The first challenges students to gather and analyze data and reach some conclusion. The second requires the students to report their findings.

4. Teachers then need to decide what "scaffolds" they will need to help students accomplish their tasks. For elementary school students, teachers should consider developing hard-copy step-by-step directions.

5. Finally, in the pre-implementation phase, the teachers must decide if the students are going to work in groups or individually.

(2) Data Gathering. GIS data will be presented in a variety of formats: maps, data sets, or images, usually some combination of each. As Hammond and Bodzin (2009) noted, "Before students can begin to work with the GIS, they must understand what they are looking at—what is on-screen and where is it located?" (p. 120). Elementary school students will need help accessing the data in the GIS—the teacher may have to provide considerable guidance in bringing up the appropriate screens. Students will then need help understanding what they are looking at. Most class sessions will need to start with tutorials on how to read the data the students are going to see. Usually, there will be much to consider—it is important to narrow the students' focus to locate the relevant information. I suggest students have either a study guide or a data retrieval chart (see Chapter 8) to focus their examination of the data. Our youngest students may simply be asked to look carefully at the images they see and take part in a focused discussion.

(3) Data Analysis. Once the students have gathered their data, they must make sense of what they have learned. This requires critical thinking and the teacher will need to serve as a guide. The purpose, of course, is to solve the problem. The challenge here is the students probably will have to synthesize several bits of data, often from different sources in the GIS. The teacher might well have to develop a set of questions the students must answer. The analysis need not always be complex—as part of Britt and LaFontaine's first-grade unit, the students used what they had learned to write directions to a local restaurant. In the second-grade unit using aerial maps described by Todd and Delahunty, a problem for analysis emerged from the examination of chronological aerial images of their school. Students noticed their school had a new building that did not exist ten years earlier. Why was the new wing built? Students used aerial images to learn the expansion of their school was the result of a change in their neighborhood—many new houses and apartments had been built over the ten-year period.

(4) Data Sharing. The student presentations to their classmates could use digital resources and include text, images, and maps. Milson and Curtis (2009) had their high school students report their conclusions using PowerPoint. With help from the teacher, PowerPoint can be used with elementary school students. With our youngest learners, sharing what has been learned may rely on more traditional resources. In Britt and LaFontaine's first-grade project, students created models of landforms they had seen on Google Earth with good, old-fashioned Play-Doh.

Summary of Key Points

- Teachers should adopt a broad definition of geography so their students do more than just memorizing geographic data.
- Maps are difficult to read because information is presented in an unfamiliar format.

- Research on the cognitive development of children and geography shows children can learn geographic concepts, although there are developmental limits.

- Geography is the study of place, including physical characteristics, geopolitical information, demographics, and economic information.

- The processes of geography include the ability to ask and answer geographic questions by acquiring, organizing, and analyzing geographic information.

- To read maps, children must understand symbols, scale, grid, and direction.

- Computer-based Geographic Information Systems have become a powerful resource for teaching geography.

Lesson Plans and Instructional Activities

This chapter concludes with three examples of teaching history and geography to elementary school children:

1. A lesson plan for fourth graders that challenges the students to use a scale of miles to calculate the distance between two places

2. A third-grade mini-unit on "Using Grid Systems to Find Places on Maps"

3. A WebQuest project for sixth graders on ancient Egypt

Lesson Plan
Grade Four: Using a Scale of Miles to Calculate Distance: A First Lesson

The first time students use a scale of miles to calculate the distance between two points on a map, it helps if they are not confronted with distances in fractions of inches. If 1 inch equals 100 miles, it is easy to figure out how far apart two places are if they appear 3 inches apart on the map (3 inches × 100 miles/inch = 300 miles). It is quite another task if they are 1-3/4 inches apart.

Overview: This lesson is for a small group of fourth graders, six students.

Resources and Materials: Beforehand, make a map of either your state or the United States; cities should be placed on the map so each city is exactly 1, 2, 3, or 4 inches from the other cities (no fractional distances). This will involve minor adjustments in placing some cities. Base the scale of miles on 1 inch (1 inch equals 50 miles or 100 miles, whichever is appropriate). Have available (a) a plastic transparency of the map, (b) six copies of the map, (c) six sets of colored pencils, and (d) six rulers.

Standard: From the *National Curriculum Standards for Socials Studies*, the National Council for the Social Studies (NCSS) curriculum standards, thematic strand III, "People, Places & Environments," Process Learning Expectation (d) for the middle grades: "The learner will be able to calculate distance, scale, and area, to inform study of historic or current national and global environments" (NCSS, 2010, p. 101).

Content Objectives: Students will calculate the actual distance between two points on a map by using scale.

Process Objectives: Students will *calculate* the actual distance between cities on the map.

Teaching Sequence

1. Display the plastic transparency of the simplified map. Explain that each student will receive a copy of this map. Point out the scale of miles.

2. Using the distance between any two cities as an example, (a) draw a straight line between two cities (e.g., from Kansas City to Detroit), (b) measure the line, and (c) multiply the distance by 100 (or whatever distance is equivalent to 1 inch on this map).

3. Ask students to use their red pencils to draw a line between two other cities on their own copies of the map. Next, have students measure the line. Help them set up the multiplication problem and do the calculation.

4. Present other combinations of cities for students to calculate. For each pair of cities, have the class use a different-colored pencil. Help students with the standard process: draw the line, measure the line, and multiply to find the real distance.

Evaluation: Your observation of the students will tell you who is having difficulty using a scale of miles. Collect each student's map for further analysis.

Effective Teaching in Today's Diverse Classroom: This lesson is planned for a small group of students. I have planned this as a first lesson on using a scale of miles. Although some of your more able students will find this an easy task, most elementary students find it challenging. For children with mild learning disabilities, you may need to provide extra support through one-to-one tutoring or small-group coaching. One more thing: Although you probably realize this, students cannot use a scale of miles to calculate distance on a map if they cannot perform the required multiplication (in this lesson, multiplying two-digit numbers by one-digit numbers).

Mini-Unit

Grade Three: Using Grid Systems to Find Places on Maps

Part I: Organizing Framework

Standard: The organizing framework for this mini-unit comes from the national geography standards (Geography Education Standards Project, 1994): Standard 1 for grades K–4, The World in Spatial Terms, performance expectation (c), "The student is able to use a map grid to answer the question—What is this location?—as applied to places chosen by the teacher and the student" (p. 107).

This mini-unit answers one question:

Unit Question: How can we use the grid system to help us locate things on maps?

Part II: Instructional Activities

Activity 1: The Grid Game

Content Objectives: Using the classroom as an example, children will understand how a grid system works.

Process Objectives: Children will *identify* coordinates for several locations in the room and *use* coordinates to find the absolute location of several classmates.

Arrange the classroom so the children are seated in rows. Label each row: If you have six rows, they should be labeled A, B, C, D, E, and F. Then label the position of each chair in each row. If each row has five chairs, the first chair would be 1, the second chair would be 2, and so on. Now each child has an absolute location with a set of coordinates (e.g., the child sitting in the fourth chair in the first row would be A4). Attach large signs in front of each row with the correct label (A, B, C, and so on) and do the same for the position of the chairs (you might have to use easels so the children can see the labels). To begin, stand next to a child and ask the class what the coordinates are ("I am standing next to José. What are his coordinates?" If José is in the last seat of the fifth row, the answer is E5). On a set of index cards, print all the possible coordinates (A1–A5, B1–B5, and so on). Shuffle the cards and pull out one at a time. Then ask, "Who is seated in D3?" (B2? A5? and so on).

Activity 2: Locating a Place on a Map of a Model City

Content Objectives: Children will understand how a grid system can be "placed" on a three-dimensional map.

Process Objectives: Children will *construct* a three-dimensional map of a hypothetical city, use yarn to *create* a grid system for the city, and *locate* places on the three-dimensional map by using the grid system.

Have the class make a three-dimensional map of a model city. This will require milk cartons, shoe boxes, and other paper containers that can be modified to resemble structures. The model should include businesses, parks, hospitals, houses, apartment buildings, and schools. After the children have finished this three-dimensional map, place a grid system "over" it with yarn. This is somewhat tricky, but be sure the spaces between the vertical and horizontal pieces of yarn are equivalent. Then label the grid. Again, the vertical rows can be labeled A, B, C, and so on and the horizontal rows 1, 2, 3, and so on. First, help children see every place on the model city map can be identified by a set of coordinates (e.g., the hospital is in C4). Ask the children what they see in a variety of places (e.g., "What is in B3?"). Then give the class a list of places and have them identify the proper coordinates.

Activity 3: A Simplified Map

Content Objectives: Children will move from a three-dimensional map to a two-dimensional map and understand how a grid system can be used on a flat map.

Process Objectives: Children will *locate* places on a simplified map of a city by using a grid system.

Have children work with simplified grid systems. Many social studies textbooks include these. If yours does not, it is easy to develop your own. Figure 11.1 shows a simplified grid system one teacher created for his third-grade class.

First, the simplified map should have a limited number of coordinates (no more than four vertical and four horizontal). Thus, the "squares" defined by the grid system are large. Second, the map should have a limited number of places represented on the map. The simplified map in Figure 11.1 includes only seven symbols. Challenge the class to find places by using the grid system. Ask them, "Where are the two parks?" (C1 and C4). You can also ask more difficult questions, like, "Do the people who live in B4 have a church nearby?" (Yes, one is in B4). A final important activity with the simplified map: Prepare an index of locations. This should list the coordinates for the places on the map (e.g., City Hall—A4; Churches—A1 and B4; and Schools—A2, C3). Have children verify the information of the index.

Activity 4: A Real Map of Your City

Content Objectives: Children will now see how a grid system on a real map of their city can be used to locate places.

Process Objectives: Children will *locate* places on a real map of their city by using a grid system.

Third graders will appreciate the challenge of using a real city map as their parents do. Obtain several copies of a map of your city, but be sure the map has a good grid system. Have the children work in groups. Because this activity is difficult, you may want to have cross-age helpers from the sixth grade come to your room to help each group. Give children a list of 10 places to find on the map. These should include a school, a park, and a library. First, have the children use the index to find the coordinates for each place. Then ask the children to find the place by using the coordinates on the map. Finally, for a real challenge, give each group a set of cross streets to locate (e.g., Adams and Elm). They will need to find both streets on the index and then locate their intersection.

Effective Teaching in Today's Diverse Classroom: James Cummins has described how skills learned in one language transfer to another (1979, 1986a, 1986b, 1989, 1992). Because reading maps is dependent on symbols unrelated to English, the geographic processes described in this section of the textbook can be learned in any language. If a student learns to use symbols, a scale of miles (or kilometers), and a grid system in any language, then those skills can be used to read maps written in other languages. Admittedly, most English-language learners attend schools where too few, if any, teachers and aides can provide primary-language instruction. When the possibility exists, however, it makes sense to use the primary language to teach map-reading skills to English-language learners who speak little English. For children with learning disabilities, you may need to *adapt the lesson materials* by providing *instructional cues* on the city maps they use. Rather than have the children find the appropriate page in the map book on their own, provide students with a photocopy of the correct page in the map book with the appropriate columns highlighted (e.g., if a park is located in *4G,* highlight in yellow the *4* at the top of the page and *G* on the side of the page). This will make the task much easier, while still teaching the concept of a map grid system.

Description of a WEB-BASED PROJECT
Grade Six: A WebQuest on Ancient Egypt

One promising format teachers can use to help students make good use of the Internet is WebQuest (Milson & Downey, 2001). The structure of WebQuest was developed by Bernie Dodge at San Diego State University. Resources for teachers who want to build a WebQuest are available at the WebQuest site, www.WebQuest.org. For a given topic or area of study, the teacher selects relevant Websites and creates a Web page. The page leads the students through a cooperative inquiry in five stages: introduction, task, process, evaluation, and conclusion.

The WebQuest reported by Milson and Downey (2001) took place in Downey's sixth-grade classroom in Illinois. The WebQuest allowed students to use several sites to learn more about ancient Egypt. Downey selected many sites, including those developed by the Library of Congress, the National Archives, the Smithsonian Institution, the Egyptian Ministry of Tourism, and the PBS television program *Nova.* Each student created a "Time Traveler's Guidebook," consisting of information they considered most relevant for a traveler to ancient Egypt. The guidebooks were pocket pages allowing students to insert hypertext cards with text and images. One point to note here is teachers planning a computer-based project, like the "Time Traveler's Guidebook," can direct their students to a variety of software. The simplest option is entering text with a word processing program.

Downey's WebQuest consisted of six learning stations: (a) Land and Time, (b) Daily Life, (c) People and Culture, (d) Arts, (e) Science and Technology, and (f) Mummies and Pyramids. Each station presented information in a variety of formats: books, bulletin board displays, and instruction cards. The students worked in four teams, with three teams at stations and the fourth at the six classroom computers. While at the computers, students gathered information from the Websites listed on the WebQuest page Downey had created. One interesting feature of this inquiry was the Websites were used to support the hard-copy resources at the stations. When students had difficulty finding information at the stations, they wrote questions on index cards and brought them to the students working on the computers. Students at the computers used the links on the WebQuest page to gather information to answer these questions.

Milson and Downey (2001), in their evaluation of this activity, found advantages to the WebQuest format. Because the teacher had built the WebQuest page with links to good Websites, students did not struggle with finding relevant sites. This activity provided an opportunity for students to sharpen their Web-based data-gathering skills. Also, Downey did not have to worry about her students ending up on inappropriate sites. Another strength was the project worked in a classroom with a limited number of computers because the data-gathering process involved both traditional, hard-copy resources and the Web.

Effective Teaching in Today's Diverse Classroom: For our English learners, experiences with computers need to be "sheltered" so every child can be successful. Figure 2.2 (see Chapter 2) summarized those instructional strategies that help English learners acquire social studies content. With this WebQuest project, two interventions would be important if it were tried with a classroom with English learners. First, instruction on how to move through the Websites must be carefully designed. If possible, it would be ideal to offer that instruction in the students' first language. Teachers should frequently check on the progress of English learners as they work with a Website and provide immediate corrective feedback. Second, effective vocabulary teaching would be very important. English learners would need to know key words in two categories: those relating to Web literacy (e.g., *click* and *scroll*) and those relating to ancient Egypt (e.g., *pyramid* and *agriculture*).

CHAPTER **12**

The Other Social Sciences and Topics of Special Interest

In this chapter, you will read about

- How anthropology can be an important part of elementary social studies
- How our students can participate in an archaeological dig
- Integrating economic concepts into the social studies curriculum
- A six-step process students can use when they analyze economic problems
- How concepts from psychology and sociology will help students better understand themselves and other people
- How to make global education, environmental education, and current events part of your social studies curriculum

Two years ago, a curriculum committee in Darlene Hoyer's school district decided key concepts from psychology should be a part of the social studies curriculum. For each grade level, projects or units were designed to help students learn how to develop positive interpersonal relationships. Mrs. Hoyer engaged her fifth-grade students in an anger management project. Students in Mrs. Hoyer's classroom were expected to learn about how they could limit and control their anger. During this project, some students conducted a survey of their classmates to find out what made them angry, others interviewed the school psychologist to find out what coping mechanisms could be used to exercise control over anger, and a third group read information books to learn about the causes and control of anger.

The goal of the project was to produce a video that could be used with other classes. Once informed about anger management, members of Mrs. Hoyer's class would write the video script, shoot the necessary footage, and edit the footage. Students determined that they should make two versions of the video: one for children in the primary grades, and one for students in the upper elementary grades. Much of the video would be simulated scenarios, with Mrs. Hoyer's students playing the roles. The simulations would illustrate how to decrease the chances of someone would get angry and, if anger did come to the surface, how to cope with the hostile feelings. This project on anger management is an example of how the social science disciplines can be used to enrich the elementary social studies curriculum.

■ ■ ■

Completing the Social Studies Curriculum

Citizenship education, history, and geography traditionally have been the main focus in the elementary social studies curriculum. Content from the other social sciences, however, must also be included in the elementary curriculum. The "other" social sciences normally included are anthropology, economics, sociology, psychology, and political science. Content from these areas is essential because, without it, students will have only a partial understanding of the world they live in. In this chapter, we look at anthropology, economics, psychology, and sociology (political science was covered in Chapter 9).

It is important to note that each social science includes both a body of knowledge (content) and a way of learning about people (process). For example, the content of anthropology includes information about ancient cultural groups of the Americas, like the Aztec. Students should learn this information. At the same time, the social studies curriculum should help students understand how practitioners in each discipline gather information. For example, anthropologists who study ancient cultures learn about the Aztec through several processes, primarily by analyzing artifacts obtained through excavation. If students understand how social scientists gather and analyze data, they will have a better sense of how these experts reached their conclusions. In this chapter, we also examine two emerging fields of study in social studies: global education and environmental education. The chapter concludes with a discussion of how to teach current events.

Anthropology

Several authorities have written about how teachers can make anthropology a part of elementary social studies: Barnes (1991), Jantz and Klawitter (1991), Laney and Moseley (1990), Little Soldier (1990), Nelson and Stahl (1991), and White (1989). *Anthropology* is the study of the physical and cultural characteristics of people. Jane White (1989) stated the goal of this discipline:

> The central goal of anthropologists is to explain why groups of people are different
> from each other; to explain why they have different physical characteristics, speak
> different languages, use different technologies, and why they think, believe, and act so
> differently. (p. 31)

Anthropology comprises two broad fields: physical anthropology and cultural anthropology. *Physical anthropology,* which explores the evolution and physical differences of people, is rarely a part of the elementary curriculum. Some sixth-grade social studies curricula, however, do cover the origins of humankind, introducing students to the work of Mary and Richard Leakey in East Africa (human paleontology is part of physical anthropology). *Cultural anthropology,* which is the study of the culture, should be an integral part of social studies in the elementary curriculum. When teachers plan and present units on the Navajo or ancient Rome, they are teaching cultural anthropology. Many aspects, or "manifestations," of culture can serve as the focus of elementary social studies lessons:

■ *Getting food.* How is food gathered or produced? How is food distributed? Most elementary school students assume that all other people—both those living today and those who lived in the past—live the same way the students do. It may never occur to a third grader, for example, that some people do not get their food in a grocery store. Social studies should teach students about groups who depend on hunting and/or agriculture for food.

■ *Economic systems.* What resources does the cultural group use? How are resources converted to useful things? What must they trade for? How are resources allocated? What system of money is used for exchange?

■ *Social stratification.* What social groups exist within the cultural group? What advantages are reserved for members of some groups (economic, power, or prestige)? What is denied to other groups?

■ *Patterns of residence.* Who lives with whom? What determines where a person lives? Although it is worthwhile to learn about different human dwellings, it is more important to consider the cultural rules determining who resides in a home.

■ *Political organization.* Who makes the laws? Who enforces the laws? How are conflicts resolved?

■ *Religion.* What religions are practiced by members of the cultural group? What are the fundamental beliefs? What rituals are religious in nature?

■ *Arts.* What forms of visual arts are produced and valued by members of the cultural group? What media are preferred? What types of performing arts are practiced by members of the cultural group?

Social studies units that introduce children to a cultural group do have a "bottom line," however. What is most important? *Curriculum Guidelines for Multicultural Education* (National Council for the Social Studies [NCSS] Task Force on Ethnic Studies Curriculum Guidelines, 1992) states we want students to learn a cultural group's "ideas, ways of thinking, values, symbols" (p. 276). White (1989) summarizes this point:

> All too often, well-intentioned teachers will teach about "our neighbors across the border" by having their class, for example, break a piñata or eat tamales. They may not realize these events are the tips of a cultural iceberg . . . these isolated experiences do not really capture the more central values of how the Mexicans make meaning out of their own culture. (p. 35)

Single-Group Studies

A *single-group study* is a unit on one cultural group, for example the Kikuyu, the Nez Percé, or modern Germany. In another book, I stated some important points to consider when teaching about cultural groups (Zarrillo, 1994):

■ *Don't lump groups of people together.* For example, if a teacher presents a unit on the "American Indian," students will be left with the impression that all Native groups shared a common culture. This, of course, is far from the truth. The Huron and the Hopi are as different as the Swedes and the Greeks. At the very least, a unit should cover a small group of tribes who inhabited a common physical region (e.g., "Natives of the Pacific Northwest"). A unit on a single tribe will provide depth of understanding and diminish the chances students will learn inaccurate information about a cultural group.

■ *Be specific about the historical period.* All cultural groups change over time, so our units of study must have chronological boundaries. For example, the Chinese of the Han dynasty (206 B.C. to A.D. 220) share many cultural traits with the Chinese of the present day, yet there are some striking differences. Thus, well-defined units should state a time span—for example, "Mexico in the 20th Century," "Medieval Japan," or "Ancient Egypt."

■ *Avoid stereotyping.* This can be difficult because anthropologists describe a norm, and it is easy for children to assume that all members of a cultural group conform to the norm. Every cultural group, however, contains variation.

■ *Use as many resources as possible.* These should include DVDs, CDs, the Internet, software, information books, biographies, and reference books. The more resources teachers use, the better the chances students will acquire more than a superficial understanding of the cultural group. What if a resource is guilty of bias? Biased materials should be either excluded or presented as biased. Materials created by members of the cultural group being studied are a significant addition to any unit.

■ *Include lessons on many facets of the cultural group.* For example, it should be clear to students what roles men and women fill. As noted earlier, it is essential that students become aware of the values and beliefs of the cultural group, so lessons on religion are important. The students I taught, for example, were fascinated with the marriage and courtship rituals of other cultural groups.

■ *Do some background work on the group of people to be studied.* No one should expect the teacher to become an expert. Instruction will be more successful, however, if the teacher takes time to read about the cultural group students will study.

One final point: Students should make comparisons among cultural groups, contrasting the way we live with the ways of other groups. The purpose of a cultural comparison is to learn about ourselves and others, not to judge whether one group of people is better or worse than another. The NCSS Task Force on Ethnic Studies (1992) states study of different cultural groups should help students see that:

> Each individual and each ethnic group has worth and dignity. Students should be taught that persons from all ethnic groups have common characteristics and needs, although they are affected differently by certain social situations and may use different means to respond to their needs. (p. 286)

Doing Anthropology: A Dig

One activity that will give students some sense of how anthropologists work is a "dig." This is one way that *archaeologists,* those anthropologists investigating cultural groups from the past, gather data. During a dig, archaeologists excavate a site in search of artifacts. Several articles can help us in planning a dig with our students: Carrol (1987), Hightshoe (1997), LaRue (2010), Ovoian and Gregory (1991), Owen (1982), and Passe and Passe (1985). I also recommend two children's books: *Going on a Dig,* by Velma Morrison (1981), and *Digging to the Past: Excavations in Ancient Lands,* by W. John Hackwell (1986).

Students who participate in a dig will learn how knowledge of a past culture is pieced together from the available evidence. Teachers can plan two types of digs for students. The first type is a *simulation* (Chisholm, Leone, & Bentley, 2007). The teacher gathers old coins, pieces of inexpensive jewelry, old tools, and perhaps animal bones (e.g., from last night's roasted chicken). Then, the teacher buries these items, either in a sandbox on the playground or in a specially constructed dig box. A dig box can be a plastic container, about 3 feet long, 2 feet wide, and at least 8 inches deep. If the items are buried in a dig box, they should be buried in sand, mulch, peat moss, or kitty litter. Hightshoe (1997) recommends constructing excavation boxes, which are 1 meter square and 15 centimeters deep. The members of the class then conduct the excavation. They collect the items and analyze them for information on the hypothetical civilization that created them.

The other type of dig is an *excavation* of some part of the school grounds or an area in the community. It is best to conduct this type of dig with the assistance of an anthropologist. Anthropologists are not difficult to find; almost every college has some! The simplest example is an excavation of an area where children have played for a long time.

One teacher I worked with conducted a successful dig of the bench area where children sat when their team was at bat during softball games. Other school and community digs are a more serious matter, must be conducted with an anthropologist, and commence only after receiving permission from the owners of the site. Susan Hightshoe (1997) describes a good combination of the two types of digs: Students study a local area that may have artifacts. The actual dig is a simulation, and the planted artifacts are representative of what might have been found at the actual site. This requires cooperation from a local history center or museum.

Here are some steps to consider when planning a dig for a class:

1. *Make sure students understand why archaeologists conduct excavations.* Young children do not understand why things get buried over time. Earthquakes, volcanic eruptions, and the gradual accumulation of mud, sand, and gravel bury the remains of a civilization.

2. *Provide students with an outline of the process before they start digging.* Students must understand why certain sites are selected for excavation. Explain the actual physical act of digging must be performed with utmost care. Students should realize that once artifacts are unearthed, their work is just beginning. The exact location of each artifact must be recorded. Once removed from their burial places, the artifacts must be cleaned, measured, and weighed. Each artifact must be analyzed to determine what it is and how it was used. Finally, artifacts should be displayed with an accompanying explanation.

3. *Prepare the excavation site.* Obviously, excavations on school grounds must be approved by the school principal before any digging begins. Excavations at off-school sites must be approved by the principal and the owner of the property. For a simulation, bury the fake artifacts ahead of time. Bury one set of artifacts at one level (e.g., 12 inches deep) and another set, belonging to an earlier culture, even deeper (e.g., 30 inches). This would approximate the layers of artifacts archaeologists often find at a single site. Then "square" the excavation by using wooden stakes and lengths of strings to create a grid. Make each square in the grid large enough for two or three students to work within it— at least 5 feet square. Label each square by using a grid system (make horizontal spaces A, B, C, D, and so on and vertical spaces 1, 2, 3, and so on). Thus, students will be able to determine and record the precise location of each artifact they discover.

4. *Train students in excavation techniques.* Students must be careful. They should wear gloves for safety and use garden tools, kitchen utensils, and even whisk brooms to excavate the artifacts. Students must be cautious so that they do not break an item. When students discover something, its exact location should be recorded before the item is moved. Then it should be removed and placed into a plastic bag and labeled with the following information: date, time, coordinates of the square where it was found, approximate depth where it was found, and name of the person who found it. Students can also sift for artifacts. A simple sifter can be made by nailing an 18-inch screen to a wooden frame. Students pour dirt through the sifter so small items are caught on the screen.

5. *Analyze each artifact in a laboratory setting.* First, artifacts should be cleaned, usually with an old toothbrush. Then each item should be measured and weighed. Items recovered intact are easy to identify (e.g., most coins). Other items are pieces of something else (e.g., a *shard* is a broken piece of pottery). Students should identify the item, speculate on what it reveals about the people who made or used it, and try to figure out the age of the item. The whole group needs to share findings because the discovery of any item sheds light on all others.

6. *Consider creating a classroom museum.* An exciting way to share the results is on a "virtual" tour of a classroom museum (Ricchiuti, 1998). Students could create the tour on a school or classroom Website or on a CD. A "real" museum is fun to create and would require only a corner of a classroom. Students write descriptions of each item, listing its measurements, where it was found, its age, what it is, and how it was used.

Economics

Economics is the study of the production, distribution, and consumption of goods and services. Although economics has been called the "dismal science" by those who find it dull, economics can be an exciting part of an elementary social studies program (Armento, 1991; Kourilsky, 1977, 1987; Schug, 1985; Schug & Lopus, 2008; Schug & Walstad, 1991; Schug & Western, 2003, 2007; Schug & Wood, 2009; VanFossen & Nagel, 2010). Traditional primary-level units with an economic focus have included some elementary school classics, like "The Farm" or "The Market." In the upper grades, economics usually has been presented as a part of historical units or area studies. For example, during a unit on the American colonies,

Hands-on activities, like the one pictured here, are an essential part of teaching children the role money plays in a complex economic system.

students learn about triangular trade routes; during a unit on Saudi Arabia, students learn about oil production. Recently, there has been considerable interest in linking school and 21st-century careers so students learn about the world of work and acquire skills they will need after they leave school. Forty-five states have economics-related standards in their social studies standards (Miller & VanFossen, 2008). Several organizations promote economic education, including the National Council on Economic Education, the Foundation for Teaching Economics, and the National Association of Economic Educators. These three groups formed a partnership to develop national standards for economics—the voluntary *National Content Standards in Economics* (National Council on Economic Education, 1997). Our discussion of economic education examines research on the development of economic thinking, the content and processes of economics that should be included in the elementary curriculum, and some teaching ideas.

Several researchers have examined how children acquire economic concepts: Armento (1991), Berti and Bombi (1988), Brophy and Alleman (2002), Danziger (1958), Jahoda (1979), Miller and VanFossen (2008), Schug (1983, 1994), and Schug and Walstad (1991). Most researchers posed economic problems to children and then interviewed them about their proposed solutions. This body of research leads to the following two conclusions:

1. *Children's economic thinking becomes more abstract and flexible with age.*   Younger children are very concrete and literal in the way they view economic activity. For example, when asked to explain the exchange of money in a market, young children state that this is a form of ritual without economic meaning, the exchange is required by law, or the store is the place where money was produced (Armento, 1991). Young children have expressed the misconception that the price of a good is determined by the size of the price tag and the value of money is determined by the size and color of the currency or coin (Schug, 1994).

2. *Children's mature reasoning does not emerge at the same rate for all economic concepts.*   Abstract thinking comes sooner for some aspects of economics than for others. For example, although young children usually are aware of their relative poverty or affluence, they often fail to grasp the relationship between work and income. Interestingly enough, at the same time a child understands she will receive 50¢ if she performs a household chore, she may fail to comprehend that her parents' jobs are linked to the household's financial status. As children mature, the economic relationship of labor and compensation becomes clearer and is generalized to all jobs. Our oldest students can understand the relationships among the parties in an economic system. For example, that jewelry salespersons depend on goldsmiths, who depend on gold miners. Upper-grade students can provide explanations for economic phenomena; for example, why an airline slashes fares. Finally 10–12 year olds usually can state the implications of economic policies, such as how a temporary embargo on Japanese-manufactured cars could lead to fewer jobs in U.S. automobile dealerships.

Brophy and Alleman's (2002) study examined children's understanding of the economic aspects of shelter. Their findings are consistent with the two previously stated conclusions. This study of students in grades K–3 provides us with a better understanding of what children know about "cultural universals." Cultural universals are experiences common to all people, like the need for shelter, food, clothing, transportation, and some sort of government. This study showed children have "limited, disconnected, and frequently distorted ideas" about these universals, in this case, shelter (p. 464). For example, most children confused apartments and hotels and did not understand the concept of rent. This study makes a strong argument that we should not assume our students are well-informed about these cultural universals. Indeed, there is much we will need to teach.

Economics: The Curriculum

Almost all social studies textbooks have economic content. As I noted earlier, primary texts have focused on the production and distribution of common goods, such as food available in supermarkets and clothing in department stores. Upper-grade texts have included economics as part of historical units or area studies. Two curriculum developers, however, have played a significant role in bringing economics to the elementary classroom. Lawrence Senesh (1963) and Marilyn Kourilsky (1977, 1987) have shown basic economic concepts can be taught to young children. Senesh was the author of a popular series of texts titled *Our Working World*. Kourilsky wrote curricula based on classroom mini-societies and simulated economies in which students developed their own laws, money, and government. Eventually, each class created a unique economic system, including entrepreneurial enterprises and taxes.

One of the most influential national documents in K–12 economics education was *A Framework for Teaching Economics: Basic Concepts,* published in 1977 under the sponsorship of the Joint Council on Economic Education (Hansen, Bach, Calderwood, & Saunders, 1977). The framework defined a K–12 economic curriculum with basic concepts from *microeconomics* (the working of specific markets), *macroeconomics* (the working of the national economy), and international economics. The framework was revised in 1984 and, despite its significant contribution to the social studies curriculum, was criticized by several leading economists (Saunders, Bach, Calderwood, & Hansen, 1984).

In 1997, the voluntary *National Content Standards in Economics* were published under the leadership of the National Council on Economic Education. These standards were authorized and funded by the Goals 2000 legislation of 1994. The 20 standards are written in plain English and provide "benchmarks" at grades 4, 8, and 12. The benchmarks are objectives stating what students are expected to know and be able to do (Meszaros, 1997; Meszaros & Engstrom, 1998). Earlier, in 1994, *Expectations of Excellence: Curriculum Standards for the Social Studies,* produced by the NCSS, also attempted to define the scope of economic content children should learn. Of the 10 strands in the NCSS standards, one, Strand 7: Production, Distribution, & Consumption, is devoted entirely to economics.

Both sets of standards expect elementary children to acquire a great deal of basic economic knowledge and to perform economic analysis. For example, Content Standard 11 in the national economic standards is "Students will understand that money makes it easier to trade, borrow, save, invest, and compare the value of goods and services." One knowledge objective in the benchmarks for this standard is that, by the completion of fourth grade, "students will know that money makes trading easier by replacing barter with transactions involving currency, coin, or checks." One performance objective for this standard is that fourth graders will be able to "decide whether they would rather have a suitcase full of money or one full of food when stranded on a deserted island" (National Council on Economic Education, 1997, pp. 20–21).

Both sets of standards expect children to know:

- Resources are limited and people must choose to have some things and not have others,

- Economic decisions require an analysis of costs and benefits,

- Economic systems are complex and involve several institutions, such as households, corporations, banks, and labor unions,

- The nature of various economic systems,

- How supply and demand, prices, incentives, and profits function in a market system,

- The difference between private and public sectors of the economy,

- How jobs become specialized,

- Various forms of exchange and money,

- How income is determined by market conditions,

- The nature of investment and entrepreneurship, and

- The impact of government policy on a market system.

Both sets of standards also expect children to think critically about the economic content they learn. For example, children should be able to (a) compare economic systems according to who determines what is produced and distributed; (b) explain historical events from an economic perspective; and (c) use economic reasoning to evaluate policy proposals for contemporary issues like unemployment and pollution. Lessons with economic content should present opportunities for children to both gather and produce data in tables, charts, and graphs.

Teaching Ideas for Economics

Schug (1996) provides a framework for elementary students to use as they analyze economic problems or conditions. Use of the framework helps students grasp a fundamental concept: Economic decisions are the result of choices people make on the basis of expected costs and expected benefits. The teacher presents a question ("Why do people save money?") or makes a statement ("We have cars in the United States made in many different nations"). Working in small groups or as a whole group, students then apply the six statements of Schug's framework.

1. *People choose to do things they think are best for them.*　　Children need to understand economic events are not accidental or random. A third-grade class studying their local airport must see the decision to build the airport was a difficult choice for citizens of the community. After a long debate, the airport was approved by voters because the majority thought the airport would help them. At this point, it is important for us to help children see the rationale behind economic choices.

2. *People's choices have costs.*   The decision to build the new airport had costs. Children should realize the full range of costs beyond the money needed to acquire the land and pay for the terminal, runways, and supporting structures. Other costs included the relocation of people living on the land purchased for the airport, the "quality of life" costs to the airport's new neighbors, and the cost of not using for other purposes the resources allocated for the airport.

3. *People choose to do things for which they are rewarded.*   Incentives encourage people to act. Wentworth and Schug (1994) note "incentives may involve an increase in expected benefits, a decrease in expected costs, or some combination of the two" (p. 11). Teachers might help children understand the nature of an incentive by noting some incentives used at school, like rewards for positive behavior. To encourage people to vote for the airport, supporters offered the incentive of easier access to airline flights because the other nearest airport was 83 miles away.

4. *People create rules that affect their choices and actions.*   Economic choices can be made only within the context of the existing laws governing economic activity. Construction of the airport was possible because federal laws allow for the private ownership of air-lines and state laws permit local governments to purchase private land for a public purpose. For each economic condition children study, they should see the choices people make are restricted or enabled by laws.

5. *People gain when they decide to trade freely with others.*   The key here is for children to understand that voluntary trade helps both traders. In the case of the airport, airline tra-vel is a trade. Passengers exchange money for a ride on the airplane. Both sides benefit: The passengers reach their destinations, and the airline makes money. Children should understand not all trade is voluntary. When children study the European colonization of North America and examine the economic relationships among the Native tribes and the Europeans, they will see an example of involuntary or exploitative trade in which only one side benefited.

6. *People's immediate choices today have future results.*   The construction of the new air-port changed the community. New people arrived because of the jobs created by the airport. Some members of the community living near the airport, however, continued legal action because of increased noise and traffic. Speculation is an important part of economic analysis, and we should encourage children to predict what they think the future will be like if an economic decision is made. Another, simpler way to help chil-dren analyze an economic decision is to prepare a two-column chart. On one side, list the benefits coming from the decision, and on the other side, list the costs. Challenge children to consider both short-term and long-term benefits and costs. Sometimes it is worthwhile to have children make a choice before doing the analysis and then to see how many have changed their minds after the cost–benefit analysis.

School to Career.   A key part of economic education is to prepare students for the world of work in the emerging information age (Hembacher, Okada, & Richardson, 2004). This is sometimes called *school-to-career or workforce education.* Much of the focus at the secondary level has been on reforming the high school curriculum to fit the expectations of the contemporary workplace. At the elementary level, initiatives have expanded coverage of the requirements and responsibilities of contemporary jobs. Students are curious about "grown-up jobs," and teachers should plan some of the following activities for elementary students:

- *Job shadowing.* Students spend time with someone while at work, for example, a student spends a day with a dental hygienist.

- *Career inquiries.* Students find out all they can about a job: required schooling, scope of the tasks the job entails, special challenges of the job, tools used by people holding the job, and so on. Students should interview adults who currently are employed in the type of job being studied.

- *Career days.* Members of the community come to school to share information about their jobs.

- *Career opportunities.* Students use the classified section of the newspaper to learn about the jobs available in their community.

- *Entrepreneur fair.* Teresa Moore (2010) described an "entrepreneur fair" at Stonewall Elementary School in Lexington, Kentucky. Each year, hundreds of fifth graders create one-day businesses. Some are solo efforts (sole proprietorships), while other businesses are developed by groups of students (partnerships). The children set up booths in the school gym and sell to other students, teachers, parents and community members during a four-hour period. One girl named her business, "One Sassy Chick," and made a net profit of $124 selling embellished picture frames.

- *Simulations.* Students pretend to have a certain type of job, and then make the decisions that person would have to make. Van't Hooft and Anstadt (2007) described a unit of study for third to fifth graders based on the popular software game Lemonade Tycoon, a business simulation challenging students to turn a lemonade stand into a big business. Or, upper-grade elementary school students can pretend to be stockbrokers managing a mutual fund (Hembacher et al., 2004).

- *Children's books.* Literature written for children includes many books that can be used to teach about different careers. In addition to information books written about a specific job, other books can be used as well. For example, Hembacher (2004) and her coauthors proposed a lesson plan challenging third graders to be community planners. The lesson used *The Little House* (Burton, 1942), *The House on Maple Street* (Pryor, 1992), and *In My Own Backyard* (Kurjian, 1993).

At the end of the chapter is an example of this type of lesson as sixth graders analyze a classified ad for the position of controller at a furniture-manufacturing company.

Focus on the Consumer. A variety of interesting social studies activities can be built on the economic concept of consumption. Following are examples:

- *Best buys.* Challenge older children to gather comparative price data on similar products. Most markets now include unit prices beneath items (e.g., 16¢ per oz). Students should look at several brands of a product, such as orange juice, paper plates, or ice cream.

For each, they should conclude which is the "best buy." Remind students, of course, that price is only one feature a consumer considers.

■ *Analysis of television advertisements.* The economic concept of distribution includes advertising and marketing. For this activity, record commercials appearing on television. Then challenge students to explain, for each commercial, how the advertiser has tried to make the product more appealing. Some television ads mention price or specific features of the product, but most use other factors, too.

■ *Budgets.* Preparation of a budget requires choices and economic analysis. Ask students to prepare proposed budgets for real situations. For example, if a fund-raiser has provided each classroom with $100 to spend on instructional materials, what should be purchased? Young children can prepare a sample budget for a set of economic conditions. For example, you have $300 to spend on new clothes. You must purchase shoes, pants, a shirt, and a jacket. How will you spend your money? Older students can work with more complicated hypothetical budgets. For example, prepare a yearly budget for a family of five with an annual income of $50,000. This is a difficult project, requiring students to investigate the actual costs of daily living.

■ *Economize.* The recession of 2008–2010 has led to a period of corporate and governmental "downsizing" as families, schools, businesses, and all levels of government have made cuts in their expenditures. *Economizing* is economic analysis with the goal of saving money. Challenge students to think of ways money could be saved in the classroom, the school, their community, and state and federal governments.

Psychology and Sociology

Psychology and sociology have played relatively minor roles in the elementary social studies curriculum (Nelson & Stahl, 1991). Six major areas of psychology could be included in a social studies curriculum: (a) psychological research methods, (b) growth and development, (c) cognition and learning, (d) personality, (e) mental health, and (f) social psychology (Baum & Cohen, 1989). Most of the areas related to psychology focus on the personal identity of each child and how children can deal with emotions like anger, fear, and jealousy. *Sociology,* the study of human society, and how individuals relate to each other, examines group behavior. Attempts to infuse sociological content into the social studies curriculum have focused on the high school (Angell, 1981; Gray, 1989; Jantz & Klawitter, 1991; Switzer, 1986). Elementary school students should examine several aspects of group behavior and understand the roles people play in primary groups, like their families, and secondary groups, like a church choir or softball team. Attitudes toward other groups, especially stereotyping and prejudice, should be addressed in the social studies curriculum (Walsh, 1992).

Expectations of Excellence (NCSS, 1994), the national social studies standards, have incorporated important concepts from psychology and sociology in Strand IV, "Individual Development and Identity" and Strand V, "Individuals, Groups, and Institutions." Strand IV states "social studies programs should include experiences that provide for the study of individual

Anthony Magnacca/Merrill

Social studies incorporates content from all the social science disciplines, including psychology and sociology. Social studies activities should help students abandon prejudicial attitudes and form lasting friendships with their classmates.

development and identity" (p. 57). Strand V proposes "social studies programs should include experiences that provide for the study of interactions among individuals, groups, and institutions" (p. 57). The content of these two strands asks students to learn about the following:

- Personal changes, in terms of both physical growth and personal interests; personal connections to places, like home and school
- Unique features of families; how learning and physical development affect behavior; how families, groups, and community influence a person's daily life
- Factors contributing to one's personal identity; how to work independently and cooperatively
- Roles people fill as members of groups
- Group and institutional influences on people and events
- Tensions between individuals and groups
- Tension between an individual's beliefs and government policies and laws
- How groups and institutions work to meet individual needs and the common good

Following are some activities that incorporate psychology and sociology:

■ Suggest students write autobiographies, using photographs of themselves as illustrations. The photographs will show how the students have changed physically. Have students complete "then and now" surveys to identify changing interests and attitudes. If your school has a Website, the autobiographies could become part of it. Upper elementary school students who have a "tech-savvy" teacher could make a digital documentary movie with Photo Story 3 or Apple iMovie (Fein, Johnson, & Smith, 2010).

■ A very interesting activity is to have students continue their autobiographies as speculative works of fiction. Ask them to write about themselves at each of the following ages: 18, 25, 35, 50, and 70. Where will they live? What jobs will they have?

■ Have students make a mini-mural showing the significant places in their lives. Each student can make one by dividing a piece of 12 × 18-inch drawing paper into four or eight sections. Then students can add to each section an illustration of the significant places in their lives (e.g., home, classroom, baseball field, and grandma's house).

■ Have students make a list of things they can do now that they could not do when they were younger (e.g., compare age 3 and age 8). This list should include physical tasks (e.g., shoot a basket), academic performance (e.g., add large numbers), home chores (e.g., dry the dishes), and other daily activities (e.g., answer the telephone).

■ Suggest a group of students interview their classmates and make a chart with three columns of activities: those best done individually, those best done in a small group, and those best done as a whole class.

■ Help students see they belong to many groups and help them understand their role within each group. Request that students complete a chart listing the groups to which they belong, identifying their roles therein, and describing their responsibilities in those roles. The chart should have three columns: "Group," "Role," and "Responsibilities." For example, a student would write "Group: Chavez School Student Council," "Role: representative and treasurer," and "Responsibilities: represent class, keep track of council budget." Students would make other entries for other groups, such as "Mr. Kim's class," "my family," "the East Park Rangers" (soccer team), and "Temple Beth Torah."

■ Help students consider the consequences of yielding to peer pressure. Tell small groups to report on how peer pressure affects the way their classmates dress, the slang they use, and the out-of-school activities they consider worthwhile. Students should discuss the importance of maintaining a strong sense of self.

■ Allow interested students to prepare a movie on "America's Dissenters." Students can make movies, incorporating images, sounds, music, and special effects using Photo Story 3, which does not allow students to use video clips, or Applie iMovie, which does allow video clips. Elementary students, of course, would need considerable help from their teacher (Fein, Johnson, & Smith, 2010). The national standards state students should be able to "identify and describe examples of tension between an individual's beliefs and government policies and laws" (NCSS, 1994, p. 60). The display could be become a PowerPoint presentation with text and images. It could include political leaders who opposed adoption of the Constitution (e.g., Patrick Henry), early practitioners of civil disobedience (e.g., Henry David Thoreau), Native Americans who fought the expansion of the United States (e.g., Geronimo), abolitionists (e.g., Frederick Douglass), advocates of women's suffrage (e.g., Susan B. Anthony), prohibitionists (e.g., Carrie Nation), civil rights leaders (e.g., Medgar Evers), and consumer advocates (e.g., Ralph Nader).

■ Invite students to go into the community to find out more about organizations that promote the common good, such as the Red Cross, service clubs, and groups raising money to battle diseases. Students could write a book for their classmates on these groups. Or, invite the community to come to your classroom as representatives of these organizations, and visit your room to make presentations to your students.

Reducing Stereotyping and Prejudice

Aspects of psychology and sociology come into play when we try to reduce stereotypical and prejudicial attitudes in our classrooms. Gloria Ladson-Billings (1992) provides excellent suggestions:

1. *Assess our teaching.*   Ladson-Billings asks teachers to consider what conclusions an observer would reach after spending time in their classrooms. We would hope people with overt biases never enter our profession, and I think teachers as a group are among the most sensitive and least prejudiced people in our society. Nonetheless, many teachers do things that are biased. For example, what is the seating pattern in the room? Are members of minority groups clustered together? Are boys and girls intermixed? Does the teacher, in fact, have different discipline procedures for some students, and if so, are those students disproportionately members of a minority group? What does the room environment reveal? Are images of successful people from all groups displayed?

2. *Check our teaching materials.*   Although textbooks, films, children's books, and other resources have come a long way in the past 20 years to remove stereotyped and biased portrayals, it is a good idea to assess the materials used in the classroom.

3. *Transform the curriculum.*   Teachers should incorporate diverse content and perspectives.

4. *Strive for integration.*   Students of both genders, of challenging conditions, of all ethnic groups, and of each social class should work together during the year. If teachers allow students to select the projects they will complete, we must be sure a pattern does not develop of some groups having only girls, only African Americans, and so on. Consistent, positive interactions through cooperative learning can improve intergroup relations (Kagan, 1989–1990).

5. *Do not ignore incidents of student prejudicial behavior.*   When students express stereotypical or biased feelings toward other students, whether through words or actions, teachers should intervene. Teachers should work with students to find the source of these attitudes and then provide information to show a better picture of the disparaged group. Students who use racial slurs need to know the full impact of those words.

A student who says all members of a group behave in one way should be taught about intragroup diversity. Finally, teachers should make it clear to their students that prejudiced behavior on campus will not be tolerated.

Families and Friendship

The traditional social studies curriculum in the early grades has devoted attention to families and friendship, two topics that can help children learn key concepts in sociology and psychology. With some political and religious groups advocating only one type of family be promoted in the schools, discussion of the diversity of family composition has become a hot issue. My suggestion is to take an anthropological view: The definition of family varies widely from cultural group to cultural group, and any cultural group will always contain variations from the norm. Children know the other members of their nuclear family, and in the contemporary United States, families will include a variety of people other than mom and dad, brother and sister. I think the goals of family-related lessons should be to (a) show how families contribute to each child's identity, and (b) help children see how the cooperative efforts among family members can serve as a model for classrooms, schools, communities, states, and nations. Remember, lessons on the family should be preceded by a letter to parents describing the activities that will take place in the classroom. Not all information should be revealed in the classroom, and parents should be aware of what the unit of study is going to cover. The focus on friendship should help children understand the challenges and rewards of being a good friend. Friendship comes easily to many children, but others will benefit from an exploration of the characteristics and responsibilities of friends. The opening vignette in Chapter 4 described how one teacher implemented the unit "Families and Friends." Following are some other activities that could be a part of a unit on families and friends:

■ *Compile family trees.* This project requires students to interview parents, grandparents, and other family members. You will need to help students develop the survey questions and provide a model for the actual family tree to be completed.

■ *Make a class quilt.* The beautiful children's book *The Patchwork Quilt* (Flournoy, 1985) provides a perfect introduction to making a family quilt. In another excellent children's book, *The Secret of Freedom,* a young African American girl learns about slavery from her great aunt's quilt (Vaughn, 2001). Some elementary teachers have the expertise to help their students make real, sewn quilts. Most of us, though, will have to settle for helping students make quilts with sections of paper pasted together. Like any quilt, each section of each student's quilt should be special and, in this case, represent something about the student's family. McCall (1994) discusses the use of quilts in elementary social studies. Her article focuses on the significance of quilting in people's lives and portrayals of history through quilts.

■ *Make semantic maps.* Create a semantic map with the word *Friend* in the middle. Ask students what makes a good friend. Record what they say, linking common characteristics.

■ *Sing songs about families and friends.* One of my favorites is "Five People in My Family" from *The Sesame Street Song* (Moss, Raposo, & Cert, 1994). Another of my favorites is the song "I Live in the City," by Malvina Reynolds. This song expresses multicultural cooperation as people of many colors build a city. "I Live in the City" can be found in many kindergarten, first-grade, or second-grade music textbooks.

■ *Read books about families and friends.* Some of the best children's picture books address themes related to families and friends (Zarrillo, 1994). I provide a list of multicultural children's picture books focusing on families and friendship in Figure 12.4 at the end of the chapter.

■ *Tell family stories.* Give students the opportunity to tell the stories of their families, through timelines, chronologies, murals, and biographies.

At the end of the chapter, you will find a writing project challenging children to discover some of the special aspects of their families.

Global Education, Environmental Education, and Current Events

Global Education

Revolutionary advances in technology and transportation have brought the people of the world closer together. "Global education" should be more than a slogan; the elementary social studies curriculum must be international in scope (Case, 1993; Hicks, 2003; Kniep, 1985, 1986; Lamy, 1987; Massialas, 1991; Merryfield, 2004, 2008; NCSS Ad Hoc Committee on Global Education, 1987; Tye, 1990; Zong, Wilson, & Quayshiga, 2008). Global education has meant different things to different people. Robert Hanvey (1976) and Willard Kniep (1985) were early and influential advocates of global education, and each provided a definition frequently cited by other writers. Case (1993) synthesized Hanvey's and Kniep's work and argued for two dimensions to global education: a *substantive* dimension, "knowledge of various features of the world and how it works," and a *perceptual* dimension, which is "an outlook or orientation" (p. 318).

The substantive dimension includes five categories of content:

1. *Universal and cultural values and practices.*   Students should learn about the many cultural groups inhabiting the earth and discover the similarities and differences among groups.

2. *Global connections.*   Our curriculum should include units and lessons showing how people are linked by global economic, political, ecological, and technological systems.

3. *Contemporary worldwide concerns and conditions.*   Our students should learn about issues and problems that are global in scope and require international solutions.

4. *Origins and past patterns of worldwide affairs.*   This category requires a curriculum to help students understand the history of international current events.

5. *Alternative future directions in worldwide affairs.*   Among the essential activities in global education are those requiring speculation and that challenge students to predict the global consequences of political and economic decisions.

Case's (1993) perceptual dimension is more difficult to define. This dimension is part of the affective domain; the goal is a social studies program leading students to adopt a perspective that includes "open-mindedness, anticipation of complexity, resistance to stereotyping, inclination to empathize, and non-chauvinism" (p. 320). To Case, open-mindedness is crucial to global education. After all, it makes little sense to develop units of study presenting global content if students will ignore the information because of previous biases or prejudices.

Social studies can help students learn about other people and places, but only if they are willing to accept their preconceptions may be inaccurate. Global systems in economics, ecology, politics, communication, and transportation are complex. It should go without saying that social studies programs should help students resist stereotyping. Teachers inadvertently lead to stereotyping by using descriptors that fail to distinguish the differences between nations, groups, and people (e.g., "The Third World"). Repeated references to "Eastern Europe," for example, can lead students to conclude there are no differences between life in the Czech Republic and Bulgaria; in fact, the status of those two nations in the post-Soviet era is not at all alike. Likewise, lessons and units covering a topic superficially can result in stereotyping. For example, a short unit on Egypt could lead students to think this nation is "a museum or curiosity piece as the land of pyramids and sphinxes" (Case, 1993, p. 322).

The national social studies standards (NCSS, 1994) emphasize the importance of "internationalizing" the social studies curriculum. One of the 11 strands is "Global Connections" (Strand 10). The standards are ambitious and call for students in the upper-elementary grades to learn about a wide range of global topics and issues, such as the following:

■ How aspects of culture, such as language, the arts, and belief systems, can both facilitate and impede global understanding

■ Examples of conflict and cooperation among nations and cultural groups

■ Effects of technology on the global community

■ Causes and possible solutions of global issues, such as health, security, and environmental quality

■ The relationship between national sovereignty and global interests

■ Standards and concerns related to universal human rights

■ The purpose and status of international organizations

Teaching Global Education

The traditional expanded environments framework leads to a social studies curriculum lacking global content (Akenson, 1989; Larkins & Hawkins, 1990). The primary grades focus on awareness of self, primary social groups like the school and family, the neighborhood, and the community. Fourth grade focuses on the geography and history of the state. Fifth grade is a survey of U.S. history. Not until sixth grade does the curriculum become international. Alternatives, however, place greater emphasis on global education. Social studies at every grade level should include lessons and units that take a global perspective (Diaz, Massialas, & Xanthopoulos, 1999).

With global education, environmental education, and current events, we can adopt three approaches:

1. Address it as a "stand-alone" component of the social studies curriculum, with separate units of study,

2. Integrate topics into the units we teach, or

3. A combination of the stand-alone and the integration approaches. Global education units include those on other places, in both historical and contemporary context (e.g., "South Africa Today" or "The Aztec"), cross-cultural units (e.g., "Going to School in Colombia, Kenya, and Indonesia"), thematic units (e.g., "Cooperation and Conflict Among Nations"), units on events with global implications (e.g., "The Volcanic Eruption In Iceland"), and units on global problems (e.g., "Famines: Causes and Solutions"). Whether or not the curriculum includes separate units of study, every social studies unit should explore global connections. For example, a unit on families can introduce children to families in other nations. If the fourth-grade curriculum is the geography and history of our state, we can incorporate considerable global content. For example, a unit on the early history of North Carolina should include information on a slave economy closely linked to Africa and the Caribbean. A unit on contemporary North Carolina should help students understand how many jobs in the state are either with foreign-owned companies or with firms dependent on foreign trade.

The following are some specific teaching ideas for global education:

■ Use many topics lending themselves to cross-cultural comparison (e.g., clothing, shelter, school, government, sports, and food). For example, if students in a third-grade class take part in a unit on transportation in Los Angeles, they should also learn about transportation systems in other places. Students in Los Angeles would learn about freeways, the metropolitan bus system, and southern California's light rail system. They would also become acquainted with historical means of transportation in southern California, such as horse-powered wagons, early automobiles, and the efficient system of light-rail "red cars" discontinued in the 1950s. To internationalize this unit, the teacher could select another large city for investigation, such as Beijing, where urban transit is not based on the automobile.

■ Conduct this common global activity with your class: Have them gather data on the source of products in their homes or at school. For example, you could ask your students to select three shirts or blouses. On a data retrieval chart, the students would note where each item was produced (found on the clothing labels). Tally class totals and have students use maps to locate the places where the clothes were made. In most situations, students will see almost everyone has clothes made overseas, especially in Asia and the Spanish-speaking Americas. Students should explore the economic factors that have led U.S. corporations to build factories in other nations and consider the consequences for workers here and abroad.

■ Plan a unit on international organizations for your upper-grade students. This is a good Jigsaw project, as small groups gather information on different organizations and then share what they have learned with their classmates. Students could learn about the United Nations (UN), the Organization of American States (OAS), the International Red

Cross, Amnesty International, the North Atlantic Treaty Organization (NATO), the World Health Organization (WHO), or the International Olympic Committee (IOC).

■ Use people in your community as resources for global education. Some of your students, their parents, or grandparents, are immigrants and can share information about their native lands. An increasing number of "local" businesses actually are international in scope and include employees who can talk about their work with colleagues overseas. Almost every university in the United States has faculty and students who are citizens of other countries. In addition to encyclopedias, books, films, the Internet, and other computer-based resources, people in your city with global experience can help your students with global projects.

■ Teach more elementary units looking at foreign nations in a contemporary context. So often, students study places like China or Mexico only as history. Learning about life today in another nation can be important learning experiences for your students. Ensure that the resources you use are accurate. Fortunately, several excellent nonfiction children's books on other nations are available with updated information presented through well-researched text and attractive photographs. When planning these units, take time to avoid superficial coverage and misunderstandings. Topics should include economics, the arts, recreation, education, and religion. There are many excellent sources on the Web. For example, the site Kids World Japan (web-jpn.org/kidsweb/index./html), could be used for a study of contemporary Japan as children "visit" a Japanese elementary school, take a bike ride around Kyoto, and meet the Imperial Family (Merryfield, 2008).

■ Challenge your students to create an atlas for a region. This is challenging because students will have to make several maps. These student-made books make an excellent group project. For example, an atlas on Southeast Asia would include a world map highlighting the region, a map of the region itself, a map of each nation in Southeast Asia, maps of large cities in the region, topographical maps, economic maps, and historical maps showing the political boundaries of the past.

■ Suggest your students create a "virtual tour" of a nation or region. Virtual tours can be a part of a Website or can be recorded on a CD. Photographs and maps can be "clipped" from Internet sites as long as they have no copyright restriction. Students would write the text and organize the sequence of the tour.

■ Assign your class a similar project, the "travel brochure." This is an old social studies favorite. Students design a document promoting a nation or a region as a travel destination. To avoid superficial coverage, I suggest each brochure promotes a tour lasting at least 15 days. Then students will have to include information about several locations in the nation. Stress to students that these brochures should highlight the places tourists would want to visit.

Environmental Education

Environmental education is highly interdisciplinary. Much of what students learn about their environment is a part of science, as they study the plants and animals and other organisms that share the planet. Many traditional elementary school learning activities, like nature study and outdoor education, are a part of environmental education. As a part of social studies, the focus is how the actions of people affect the air, water, and other living things (Charles, 1985; Simmons, 1994, 1995; Wilkie, 1993). Simmons (1995) provides a summary of the content of environmental education:

- An affective component—sensitivity and appreciation of environmental issues and topics
- Ecological knowledge—a part of the science curriculum, including the biology of plants and animals and the relationships within an ecosystem
- Sociopolitical knowledge—how human activities influence the environment
- Knowledge of current environmental issues
- Environmental skills, including the ability to use primary and secondary sources to learn about environmental topics and issues
- Environmental responsibility and citizenship—an understanding of what individuals and groups can do to preserve and protect the environment

As with the other topics covered in this chapter, environmental topics can either be integrated with existing units of study or serve as the basis for separate units. Following are some teaching ideas for the social studies part of environmental education:

- Ask students to examine the contents of school wastebaskets. This is sometimes recommended as an exercise in anthropology, as students examine the contents as artifacts revealing aspects of their culture. With an environmental focus, students classify the items according to whether they could be reused or recycled. This task helps students see they can play a role in conserving our natural resources.

- Plant a tree. This is an activity full of educational potential. Students will become botanists as they learn about the structure of the tree and how it lives. They will also see how people determine whether the tree survives. Initially, the tree will need to be nurtured and protected. As the tree grows stronger, both single incidents of irresponsibility and the long-term effects of human-made pollution will threaten the tree. In addition to the science-related activities surrounding the tree planting, ask students to provide complete answers to the questions "What can we do to help the tree grow?" and "What might people do that will harm the tree?"

- Suggest reading. Many excellent children's books address environmental issues. For example, Lynn Cherry's *The Great Kapok Tree* (1990) helps students realize the full impact of cutting down a tree in the Amazon rain forest.

- Urge older students to analyze the consumption of energy at home and school. What appliances use the most energy? What use is essential? What use can be reduced? Challenge students to develop precise energy conservation plans for home, school, and classroom.

- Suggest students share information on several endangered species. This is not only a good Jigsaw project but also a good mix of science and social studies. Assign each group of students a different species; each group is responsible for gathering information on that species and what actions by people have placed it at risk of extinction.

■ See whether students can create pictorial flowcharts showing the process of converting crude oil to consumable energy. The chart should show drilling for oil, the work of an oil refinery, and the many products (e.g., gasoline and asphalt) ultimately produced from oil.

■ Help students prepare a PowerPoint display on some of the leading ecologists who have helped bring about changes in environmental policy (e.g., John Muir, Gifford Pinchot, and Rachel Carson).

■ Challenge older students to analyze contemporary environmental issues and consider policy alternatives. These can be local issues, such as the construction of a highway, or national and global issues, such as toxic waste, global warming, or ozone depletion.

■ Help your youngest students learn about the plants and animals sharing their immediate environment at school. This can begin with a simple inventory of all the living things that either live at the school (e.g., trees, grass, and insects) or regularly visit (e.g., birds). This requires a nature walk around your school.

■ A great source for teaching resources is the Website of the Environmental Education Network (www.envirolink.org).

Current Events

Many of us can remember the dreadful chore of searching for a "current event" in the newspaper. Our time came, and we would find ourselves in front of our classmates, struggling to explain the content of our clipping. Fortunately, now, there are many alternatives for incorporating current events into the school day (Passe, 1988). As a separate part of social studies, one option is to schedule current events activities for a special time each week (e.g., every Friday morning). Another option is to integrate current events into our units of study; some important current events, however, will not fit into our units. A third option is a combination approach. We would be ready to modify our unit plans to include current events and, at the same time, reserve a time each week for the current events activities. Current events provide an opportunity for students to apply what they have learned about citizenship, history, geography, and the other social sciences.

The exploration of current events, if done properly, can be controversial. Our goal is to increase students' understanding of the event, and this requires an effort to be sure we present multiple perspectives. The presentation and exploration of diverse views, however, is not as easy because attached to some topics is intense pressure to present only a popular view (Soley, 1996). Teachers need to screen the news stories our students want to share. There are some stories, such as many crimes, children are too young to discuss. For the most part, however, our students already have been exposed to major news events through television. The extra knowledge we help them acquire will often make them less anxious about troubling events. For example, Pang and her colleagues (2008) and Passe (2008) described a number of instructional strategies and activities to help students impacted by the 2007 wildfires in southern California reduce their anxiety.

In addition to television, radio, the Internet, and print media available to adults, several news resources are designed for children. Print media include *Weekly Reader, NewsCurrents,* and *Scholastic Newstime.* These print newsmagazines now all have Web-

These children are practicing active citizenship, the ultimate goal of social studies, as they help define their classroom rules of behavior.

based versions teachers and students can access online. The following are teaching ideas for current events:

■ Plan a unit or mini-unit on the news media. Writing about teaching media literacy, Passe (1994) stressed the importance of helping children understand the news they see presented in the media. Children need geographic and historical information to make sense of some events. Help students identify the major issues surrounding an event, which is often a challenge, given the amount of coverage major events receive. Also be sure students learn to look for balance in coverage, detecting bias in the perspectives of advocates of certain positions. Involve students in news production as they make classroom or school newspapers. Work with students to produce video news broadcasts, complete with news anchors, on-the-spot reporters, and commentators.

■ Teach students how to use the newspaper as a data source (Oldendorf & Calloway, 2008; Rhoades, 1994). Like an encyclopedia or a Website, the newspaper is a tremendous source of information. Have older students identify the sections of a major newspaper, use the index to find a desired section, and distinguish commentary from news reporting. The Internet provides access to all the nation's major newspapers [e.g., the *Los Angeles Times* at www.latimes.com, the *New York Times* at www.nytimes.com, and the *Washington Post* at www.washingtonpost.com].)

■ As for the stand-alone approach, reserve a time for activities relating to current events. The use of student newspapers, like *Weekly Reader,* will help. Encourage, but do not require, students to bring in clippings of news stories they find interesting. Teachers can record portions of televised newscasts for use later in the week. Assign a small group of students to keep an "In the News" bulletin board up to date.

■ Encourage small groups of interested students to "follow" a story and keep their class-mates up to date. Members of the group will need to watch television newscasts and read newspapers to obtain information for their daily or weekly reports to the class. One interesting activity is to have a group of students follow each candidate during a political campaign. Each group could trace their candidate's travels on a map, follow the candidate's changing fortune as reflected in the polls, and make a display of the candidate's position on the major issues.

■ Use current events as the catalyst for further study by students. Some events will stimulate students to complete written, audio, artistic, or dramatic projects. One digital option is for students to create a podcast (Berson, 2009).

Summary of Key Points

■ Anthropology should have a prominent place in the elementary social studies curricu-lum, as students learn about other cultural groups and participate in anthropological data-gathering activities, like a dig.

■ National standards in economics emphasize the importance of economic content and analysis in elementary social studies.

■ Instructional activities drawing content from psychology and sociology will help stu-dents learn more about themselves and the people around them.

■ Global education, environmental education, and current events are essential compo-nents of social studies; content from these areas should be integrated into all units of study and should serve as the focus for separate units.

Lesson Plans and Instructional Activities

In this chapter, you will find (a) A lesson plan for sixth graders, "Jobs Offered—The Classified Ads" which challenge the students to analyze the components of a standard employment advertisement in a newspaper; and (b) A description of a group project for second graders, "A Mini-Book on My Family," in which each student writes a small book about his or her family.

Lesson Plan
Grade Six: Jobs Offered—The Classified Ads
This lesson was part of a sixth-grade unit on careers. The lesson examined an adver-tisement in the classified section of the local newspaper that read as follows:

Controller
High-energy, top-notch accounting person needed for a manufacturer of office furniture. Handle management reporting, financial analysis, and internal control. Supervise employees in payroll, payables, and receiving. Should have

BA/BS degree with emphasis in accounting; CPA is a plus; heavy computer exposure, experience in managing people. FAX resume and salary history to 925-290-xxxx, or email to Fsuzuki@Kottingerfurniture.com.

Overview: This lesson is for a sixth-grade class of 30 students.

Resources and Materials: (a) 30 copies of the same issue of the local newspaper, and (b) a chart with six focus questions you prepare ahead of time.

Standard: From the *National Curriculum Standards for Social Studies*, Strand VII, "Production, Distribution, & Consumption," Knowledge Learning Expectation (g) for the middle grades: "The learner will understand how markets bring buyers and sellers together to exchange goods and services" (NCSS, 2010, p. 112).

Content Objectives: Students will understand the specialized nature of jobs and how each job has unique requirements and responsibilities.

Process Objectives: Students will *identify* the responsibilities and requirements for the position of controller, *identify* the responsibilities and requirements for any other position advertised in the want ads, and *compose* an ad for one of the jobs at their school.

Teaching Sequence:

1. Acquire 30 copies of the same issue of the local newspaper. Most newspapers will provide teachers with copies, especially day-old papers. Circle the same want ad in each of the 30 newspapers. If you cannot obtain 30 copies of the newspaper, make photocopies.

2. Prepare the chart with the focus questions (see step 5).

3. Review with the class the previous week's activities, all on careers, and distribute the newspapers. Tell students to open the paper to the page where the circled ad is located.

4. Explain businesses with open jobs often advertise them in the newspaper. The classified ads have many sections, and the section with available jobs is often called "Jobs Offered." Explain the newspaper charges the employer to run the ad, usually by the number of words, so the text of the ads will appear "choppy" and have lots of abbreviations to keep them short.

5. Direct students to the ad for the controller. Help them answer the six questions you wrote on the chart paper:

    What is the name of the job?

    What type of business has placed the ad in the paper?

    What are the responsibilities of the person who will fill the job? What will the successful applicant do?

What requirements must applicants fulfill?

How much will the job pay?

How do applicants contact the employer?

You will need to explain some of the vocabulary in the ad (e.g., *internal control* and *CPA*). Also, point out that all ads do not include an answer to each question on the chart.

6. Tell students they may work individually, with a partner, or in small groups. Tell them to select a different ad and to answer the questions on the chart. If this appears too challenging, select simple ads for each group to examine. Circulate among the students and ask, "How are the requirements for the job you selected different from the requirements for the job of controller?"

7. Extend the lesson by presenting a project. A group of students could write an ad for one of the jobs at school (e.g., teacher, principal, custodian, or secretary). This would require students to do some research on the requirements and responsibilities of the job. Be sure to give students a word limit; for example, each ad must not exceed 50 words.

Evaluation: Collect and review students' answers to the six questions when they selected an ad in the paper. As you circulate among the students, note how many understand the different requirements for jobs.

Effective Teaching in Today's Diverse Classroom: *Scaffolding* is a word used by many educators to describe the help teachers provide to students. The use of *scaffold* is a metaphor. Just as a scaffold helps workers reach heights they could not reach on their own, an instructional scaffold helps students accomplish things they could not do on their own. The word was first used in the area of language development as a descriptor for the ways adults helped children expand their oral language (Cazden, 1983). Now the concept has taken on a broader meaning and is often used to describe what teachers do to help English learners and children with difficulty learning, to succeed in mathematics, science, and social studies. To use Cummins's ideas, scaffolds provide more contextual support for the learner. The words are not important, but the concept is. The "scaffolding" you provide your English learners could be each of the following:

■ In the second part of the lesson, when students select an ad and respond to the questions, be sure your English learners are in a group with someone who can help them understand the text of the ad (the help can be provided by you, an aide, or a classmate who is a good reader).

■ Help English-language learners select a relatively easy ad to read.

■ Be prepared to work with each group that has an English learner. You may have to paraphrase the content of the ad in words your English learners can understand.

Description of a Group Project
Grade Two: A Mini-Book on My Family

As part of a unit on the family, children wrote and illustrated four-page books, including the covers, on their families.

Standard: From the *National Curriculum Standards for Social Studies,* Strand IV, "Individual Development & Identity," Knowledge Learning Expectation (b) for the early grades, "Learners will understand concepts such as: growth, change, learning, self, family, and groups" (NCSS, 2010, p. 76).

Phase 1

In the first phase of the project, the children surveyed their families by using the data retrieval chart reproduced as Figure 12.1. The chart was titled "3 Fascinating, Funny,

Figure 12.1

Data Retrieval Chart: Mini-Book on My Family

3 Fascinating, funny, incredible, wonderful, heroic, commendable, or ordinary things someone in *my family did*.

1. Who, what, when?

2. Who, what, when?

3. Who, what, when?

Incredible, Wonderful, Heroic, Commendable, or Ordinary Things Someone in My Family Did." The three cells are labeled 1, 2, and 3, and each cell contains the questions "Who, What, When?" The teachers stressed everything recorded on the charts had to be true and it was okay to include things that were less than extraordinary. Funny events were definitely to be included! Children took their charts home and talked with members of their families. More able children wrote the information down; other children had their parents do the writing.

In one second-grade classroom, the completed charts made great reading. One child recorded, "My grandfather met George Clooney in a restaurant." Another student noted, "My sister, Elva, scored three goals last Saturday." A third wrote, "Uncle Luis can make it sound like a frog is singing 'Happy Birthday'."

Phase 2

In the second phase of the project, teachers handed out a template for the book. Each page would be half of an 8-1/2 x 11-inch sheet of paper. Each book would be four pages, including a cover. (Templates are included as Figures 12.2 and 12.3.) The children colored the numeral 3 at the top of their covers and then added, in their own writing the title "Fascinating, Funny, Incredible, Wonderful, Heroic, Commendable, or Ordinary Things Someone in My Family Did." On each page, children provided an illustration and a description of the noteworthy event.

Effective Teaching in Today's Diverse Classroom: This would be a good opportunity to use a variation of the *language experience approach* (LEA) for children with learning disabilities. The LEA is a method of teaching children to read. The child tells the story of a personal experience to an adult, who writes down what the child says. Then the child and the adult read the dictation aloud. Children who are not yet ready to do the writing required in this project could dictate their descriptions to an adult. The child would first draw the illustrations and then dictate a description. The adult would transcribe what the child said. Finally, the child and the adult would read aloud the dictated description.

Figure 12.2

Mini-Book on My Family: Cover and Page 1

Figure 12.3

Mini-Book on My Family: Pages 2 and 3

3 THREE 3

2 TWO 2

Figure 12.4

Families and Friends: A List of Multicultural Picture Books

Baylor, Byrd. *Hawk, I Am Your Brother*. This is a story of the friendship of a boy and an animal.

Bunting, Eve. *The Wall*. A Mexican American boy and his father visit the Vietnam Veterans' War Memorial.

Choi, Yangsook. *The Name Jar*. A Korean American child is embarrassed by her name. A friend helps.

Clifton, Lucille. *My Friend Jacob*. This is the story of a friendship between an African American boy and another who is mentally challenged.

Crews, Donald. *Bigmama's*. African American author-illustrator Crews reminisces about trips to his grandparents' farm.

Dorros, Arthur. *Abuela*. A Latina girl and her grandmother fly above New York; some text is in Spanish.

Flournoy, Valerie. *The Patchwork Quilt*. An African American girl helps her mother make a quilt.

Friedman, Ina. *How My Parents Learned to Eat*. The book tells how a boy's father, a U.S. sailor, and his Japanese mother met.

Garza, Carmen Lomas. *Family Pictures*. This book, with text in English and Spanish, tells about growing up in a small Texas town.

Grifalconi, Ann. *Osa's Pride*. An African girl alienates friends with stories about her dead father.

Havill, Juanita. *Jamaica Tag-Along*. An African American brother thinks his little sister is a nuisance.

Keats, Ezra Jack. *Peter's Chair*. An African American boy decides to run away because of the arrival of his new sister.

Kerley, Barbara. *You and Me Together: Moms, Dads, and Kids Around the World*. Illustrated with photographs, this book shows a wide range of cultural groups.

Miller, Montazalee. *My Grandmother's Cookie Jar*. A Navajo girl and her grandmother eat cookies and share stories.

Monk, Isabel. *Family*. Mom is Black, Dad is White.

Morris, Ann. *Loving*. This is an information book that shows parents, friends, siblings, and pets from all over the world.

Polacco, Patricia. *Chicken Sunday*. A European American girl and her African American friends figure out a way to get a hat for Grandma Eula.

San Souci, Robert. *The Faithful Friend*. A retelling of a folktale from the island of Martinique, two friends break the spell of a wizard.

Say, Allen. *The Lost Lake*. A Japanese American boy and his father go backpacking.

Scanlon, Liz. *All the World*. Delightful picture book follows a multicultural family during one summer day.

Soto, Gary. *Too Many Tamales*. A Mexican American girl loses her mother's diamond ring on Christmas Eve.

Steptoe, John. *Stevie*. An African American boy deals with his foster brother.

Turkle, Brinton. *Thy Friend, Obadiah*. This book is a good introduction to religious minorities. A Quaker boy befriends a duck.

Uchida, Yoshiko. *Sumi's Special Happening*. A Japanese girl must find a gift for a 99-year-old relative.

Updike, John. *A Child's Calendar*. Trina Schart Hyman's illustrations accompany Updike's poems, describing a biracial family's experiences.

Vander Zee, Ruth. *Always With You*. The true story of a Vietnamese girl who loses her mother when her village is bombed. An American soldier rescues her and takes her to an orphanage.

Williams, Sherley Anne. *Working Cotton*. The author recalls her African American family's life as migrant workers in California's central valley.

Williams, Vera. *A Chair for My Mother*. (See the lesson plan in Chapter 1.)

Woodson, Jacqueline. *The Other Side*. Two girls from different ethnic groups fight barriers to become friends.

Children's Literature to Support Social Studies Instruction

Accrosi, W. (1992). *My name is Pocahontas.* New York: Holiday House.

Adler, D. (2004). *George Washington: An illustrated biography.* New York: Holiday House.

Amster, M. (2000). *Sybil Ludington's midnight ride.* Minneapolis: Carolrhoda.

Ancona, G. (1985). *Freighters: Cargo ships and the people who work them.* New York: Crowell.

Anderson, L. H. (2008). *Independent dames: What you never knew about women and girls of the American Revolution.* New York: Simon & Schuster.

Anderson, W. (2008). *Prairie girl: The life of Laura Ingalls Wilder.* New York: Collins.

Atkin, S. B. (Ed.). (1993). *Voices from the fields: Children of migrant farmworkers tell their stories.* Boston: Little, Brown.

Avi. (2002). *Crispin: The cross of lead.* New York: Hyperion.

Baker, O. (1981). *Where the buffaloes begin.* New York: Frederick Warne.

Bartoletti, S. C. (2005). *Hitler Youth: Growing up in Hitler's shadow.* New York: Scholastic.

Barton, B. (1968). *Boats.* New York: Crowell.

Baylor, B. (1976). *Hawk, I am your brother.* New York: Scribner.

Bernard, C. (1974). *The book of fantastic boats.* New York: Golden Press.

Bourne, M. A. (1983). *Uncle George Washington and Harriet's guitar.* New York: Coward.

Brenner, B. (1994). *If you were there in 1776.* New York: Bradbury.

Brown, D. P. (1985). *Sybil rides for independence.* Niles, IL: Albert Whitman.

Brown, M. W. (1988). *Homes in the wilderness.* New York: William Scott. (Original work published 1939.)

Bryant, J. (2008). *A river of words: The story of William Carlos Williams.* Grand Rapids, MI: Eerdmans.

Bunting, E. (1990). *The wall.* New York: Clarion.

Bunting, E. (1994). *A day's work.* New York: Crown.

Burton, V. (1942). *The little house.* Boston: Houghton Mifflin.

Carter, K. (1963). *Ships and seaports.* Chicago: Childrens Press.

Chandra, D., & Comora, M. (2003). *George Washington's teeth.* New York: Farrar, Straus & Giroux.

Cherry, L. (1990). *The great Kapok tree.* San Diego: Harcourt Brace Jovanovich.

Choi, S. N. (1991). *The year of impossible goodbyes.* Boston: Houghton Mifflin.

Choi, Y. (2001). *The name jar.* New York: Knopf.

Clapp, P. (1977). *I'm Deborah Sampson: A soldier in the War of Revolution.* New York: Lothrop, Lee & Shepard.

Cleaver, E. (1985). *Enchanted caribou.* New York: Atheneum.

Clifton, L. (1980). *My friend Jacob.* New York: Dutton.

Collier, J. L., & Collier, C. (1974). *My brother Sam is dead.* New York: Four Winds.

Collier, J. L., & Collier, C. (1981). *Jump ship to freedom.* New York: Delacorte.

Collier, J. L., & Collier, C. (1983). *War comes to Willy Freeman.* New York: Delacorte.

Collier, J. L., & Collier, C. (1984). *Who is Carrie?* New York: Delacorte.

Colman, P. (2008). *Thanksgiving: The true story.* New York: Henry Holt.

Cook, N. (2001). *The world's fastest boats.* Mankato, MN: Capstone.

Corriveau, D. (2002). *The Inuit of Canada.* Minneapolis: Lerner.

Cox, C. (1999). *Come all you brave soldiers: Blacks in the Revolutionary War.* New York: Scholastic.

Creech, S. (1994). *Walk two moons.* New York: HarperCollins.

Crews, D. (1991). *Bigmama's.* New York: Greenwillow.

Cushman, K. (1995). *The midwife's apprentice.* New York: Clarion.

D'Aulaire, I., & D'Aulaire, E. P. (1946). *Pocahontas.* New York: Doubleday.

DePaola, T. (1999). *26 Fairmount Avenue.* New York: Putnam.

Dorris, M. (1992). *Morning girl.* Boston: Hyperion.

Dorros, A. (1991). *Abuela.* New York: Dutton.

Flack, M. (1946). *Boats on the river.* New York: Viking.

Flournoy, V. (1985). *The patchwork quilt.* New York: Dial.

Forbes, E. (1943). *Johnny Tremain.* Boston: Houghton Mifflin.

Frank, A. (1967). *The diary of a young girl* (Rev. Ed., B. M. Mooyart, Trans.). New York: Doubleday.

Freeman, M. S. (1999). *Fire boats.* Mankato, MN: Capstone.

Freedman, R. (1987). *Lincoln: A photobiography.* New York: Clarion.

Freedman, R. (1988). *Buffalo hunt.* New York: Holiday House.

Freedman, R. (1990). *Franklin Delano Roosevelt.* Boston: Houghton Mifflin.

Freedman, R. (1993). *Eleanor Roosevelt: A life of discovery.* New York: Clarion.

Freedman, R. (2004). *The voice that challenged a nation: Marian Anderson and the struggle for equal rights.* New York: Clarion.

Friedman, I. R. (1987). *How my parents learned to eat.* Boston: Houghton Mifflin.

Fritz, J. (1967). *Early thunder.* New York: Coward McCann.

Fritz, J. (1992). *The great adventure of Christopher Columbus.* New York: Putnam & Grosset.

Garson, E. (1999). *The Laura Ingalls Wilder songbook: Favorite songs from the Little House books.* New York: Scholastic.

Garza, C. L. (1990). *Family pictures* (as told to Harriet Rohmer, Spanish text by R. Zubizarreta). San Francisco: Children's Book Press.

Gerstein, M. (2003). *The man who walked between the towers.* New York: Roaring Brook.

Gibbons, G. (1991). *Surrounded by sea: Life on a New England fishing island.* Boston: Little, Brown.

Goble, P. (1978). *The girl who loved wild horses.* Scarsdale, NY: Bradbury.

Goble, P. (1984). *Buffalo woman.* Scarsdale, NY: Bradbury.

Goble, P., & Goble, D. (1973). *Lone Bull's horse raid.* Scarsdale, NY: Bradbury.

Goldstein, P. (1991). *Lóng is a dragon: Chinese writing for children.* San Francisco: China Books.

Grifalconi, A. (1990). *Osa's pride.* Boston: Little, Brown.

Hackwell, W. J. (1986). *Digging to the past: Excavations in ancient lands.* New York: Scribner.

Hall, D. (1979). *Ox-cart man.* New York: Viking.

Hartman, G. (1993). *As the crow flies.* New York: Simon & Schuster.

Harvey, B. (1986). *My prairie year: Based on the diary of Elinore Plaisted.* New York: Holiday House.

Harvey, B. (1987). *Immigrant girl: Becky of Eldridge Street.* New York: Holiday House.

Harvey, B. (1988). *Cassie's journey: Going West in the 1860s.* New York: Holiday House.

Hautzig, E. (1968). *The endless steppe.* New York: Crowell.

Havill, J. (1989). *Jamaica tag-along.* Boston: Houghton Mifflin.

Hesse, K. (1997). *Out of the dust.* New York: Scholastic.

Hillstrom, L. C. (2007). *The Thanksgiving Book.* Detroit: Omnigraphics.

Hodges, M. (1989). *The arrow and the lamp.* Boston: Little, Brown.

House, P. (2009). *Claudette Colvin: Twice toward justice.* New York: Farrar, Straus, & Giroux.

Houston, J. (1965). *Tikta Liktak: An Eskimo legend.* New York: Harcourt.

Houston, J. (1967). *The white archer.* New York: Harcourt.

Hoyt-Goldsmith, D. (1992). *Arctic hunter.* New York: Holiday House.

Hubbell, P. (2009). *Boats: Speeding! Sailing! Cruising!* Tarrytown, NY: Martin Cavendish.

Humble, R. (1991). *Ships, sailors, and the sea.* New York: Franklin Watts.

Huynh, Quang Nhuong. (1982). *The land I lost: Adventures of a boy in Vietnam.* New York: Harper.

Ichord, L. F. (2003). *Skillet bread, sourdough, and vinegar pie. Cooking in pioneer days.* Minneapolis: Millbrook.

Kadohata, C. (2004*). Kira kira.* New York: Atheneum.

Keats, E. J. (1967). *Peter's chair.* New York: Harper & Row.

Kentley, E. (1992). *Boat.* New York: Knopf.

Kerley, B. (2005). *You and me together: Moms, dads, and kids around the world.* Washington, DC: National Geographic Children's Books.

Krull, K. (Ed.). (1992). *Gonna sing my head off: American folk songs for children.* New York: Knopf.

Kurjian, J. (1993). *In my own backyard.* Watertown, MA: Charlesbridge.

Kusugak, M. (1990). *Baseball bats for Christmas.* Toronto: Annick.

Kusugak, M. (1993). *Northern lights: The soccer trails.* Toronto: Annick

Lester, J. (1968). *To be a slave.* New York: Dial.

Levine, E. (Ed.). (1993). *Freedom's children: Young civil rights activists tell their own stories.* New York: Putnam.

Loeb, R. H. (1979). *Meet the real Pilgrims: Everyday life on Plimoth Plantation in 1627.* Garden City, NY: Doubleday.

Loeper, J. J. (1973). *Going to school in 1776.* New York: Atheneum.

Lord, B. B. (1984). *In the year of the boar and Jackie Robinson.* New York: Harper & Row.

Lowry, L. (1989). *Number the stars.* Boston: Houghton Mifflin.

Macauley, D. (1993). *Ship.* Boston: Houghton Mifflin.

MacLaughlin, P. (1985). *Sarah, plain and tall.* New York: Harper & Row.

McCully, E. (1992). *Mirette on the high wire.* New York: G. P. Putnam.

McGovern, A. (1975). *The secret soldier: The story of Deborah Sampson.* New York: Four Winds.

McKissack, P. (2001). *Goin' someplace special.* New York: Antheneum.

Meltzer, M. (Ed.). (1984). *The Black Americans: A history in their own words.* New York: Harper & Row.

Meltzer, M. (1986). *George Washington and the birth of our nation.* New York: Franklin Watts.

Meltzer, M. (1987). *The American revolutionaries: A history in the their own words, 1750–1800.* New York: Crowell.

Miller, B. M. (2005). *Declaring independence: Life during the American Revolution.* Minneapolis: Lerner.

Miller, M. (1987). *My grandmother's cookie jar.* Los Angeles: Sloan.

Monk, I. (2001). *Family.* Minneapolis: Carolrhoda.

Moore, K. (1998). *If you lived at the time of the American Revolution.* New York: Scholastic.

Morris, A. (1990). *Loving.* New York: Lothrop, Lee & Shepard.

Morrison, V. F. (1981). *Going on a dig.* New York: Dodd, Mead.

Moss, J., Raposo, J., & Cerf, C. (1994). *The Sesame Street Songbook: 64 favorite songs.* Los Angeles: Alfred.

Myers, W. D. (2001). *Bad boy: A memoir.* New York: HarperCollins.

Nabakov, P. (Ed.). (1978). *Native American testimony: An anthology of Indian and White relations.* New York: Crowell.

Norman, H. A. (1997). *The girl who dreamed only geese and other tales of the Far North.* New York: Harcourt Brace.

O'Dell, S. (1960). *Island of the blue dolphins.* Boston: Houghton Mifflin.

Ofinoski, S. (1997). *Into the wind: Sailboats then and now.* Tarryton, NY: Benchmark.

Park, L. S. (2001). *A single shard.* New York: Clarion.

Patrick, D. (1990). *Martin Luther King, Jr.* New York: Franklin Watts.

Penner, L. R. (1991). *Eating the plates: A Pilgrim book of food and manners.* New York: Macmillan.

Polacco, P. (1992). *Chicken Sunday.* New York: Philomel.

Pryor, B. (1992). *The house on Maple Street.* New York: Mulberry/William Morrow.

Rachlis, E. (1960). *Indians of the Plains.* New York: American Heritage.

Rappaport, D. (2001). *Martin's big words: The life of Dr. Martin Luther King, Jr.* New York: Jump at the Sun/Hyperion.

Reiss, J. (1976). *The upstairs room.* New York: Crowell.

Rockwell, A. F. (2002). *They call her Molly Pitcher.* New York: Alfred Knopf.

St. George, J. (2001). *John and Abigail Adams: An American love story.* New York: Holiday House.

San Souci, R. D. (1995). *The faithful friend.* New York: Simon & Schuster.

Santella, A. (2001). *The Inuit.* New York: Children's Press.

Say, A. (1982). *The bicycle man.* Boston: Houghton Mifflin.

Say, A. (1989). *The lost lake.* Boston: Houghton Mifflin.

Say, A. (1993). *Grandfather's journey.* Boston: Houghton Mifflin.

Scanlon, L. G. (2009). *All the world.* San Diego: Beach Lane Books.

Schanzer, R. (2004). *George vs. George: The Revolutionary War as seen by both sides.* Washington, DC: National Geographic Children's Books.

Shea, P. D. (2007). *Patience Wright: America's first sculptor and revolutionary spy.* New York: Henry Holt.

Schlitz, L. A. (2007). *Good masters! Sweet ladies! Voices from a medieval village.* Cambridge, MA: Candlewick.

Shulevitz, U. (2008). *How I learned geography.* New York: Farrar, Straus & Giroux.

Sis, P. (2000). *Madlenka.* New York: Frances Foster.

Sis, P. (2007). *The wall: Growing up behind the iron curtain.* New York: Farrar, Straus & Giroux.

Soto, G. (1993). *Too many tamales.* New York: G. P. Putnam.

Speare, E. G. (1958). *The witch of Blackbird Pond.* Boston: Houghton Mifflin.

Speare, E. G. (1961). *The bronze bow.* Boston: Houghton Mifflin.

Spier, P. (1970). *The Erie Canal.* New York: Doubleday.

Stanley, D. (1994). *Cleopatra.* New York: Morrow Junior.

Stephens, B. (1984). *Deborah Sampson goes to war.* Minneapolis: Carolrhoda.

Steptoe, J. (1969). *Stevie.* New York: Harper & Row.

Stokes, J. (1978). *Let's make a toy sailboat.* New York: David McKay.

Swain, R. F. (2003). *How sweet it is (and was): A history of candy.* New York: Holiday House.

Tunis, E. (1952). *Oars, sails, and steam: A picture book of ships.* Cleveland: World.

Tunis, E. (1957). *Colonial living.* Cleveland: World.

Tunis, E. (1961). *Frontier living.* Cleveland: World.

Tunis, E. (1979). *Indians* (Rev. ed.). New York: Crowell.

Turkle, B. (1969). *Thy friend, Obadiah.* New York: Viking.

Uchida, Y. (1966). *Sumi's special happening.* New York: Scribner.

Uchida, Y. (1971). *Journey to Topaz.* New York: Scribner.

Vander Zee, R. (2008). *Always with you.* Grand Rapids, MI: Eerdmans.

Vaughn, M. (2001). *The secret of freedom.* New York: Lee & Low.

Wallner, A. (2001). *Abigail Adams.* New York: Holiday House.

Waters, K. (1989). *Sarah Morton's day: A day in the life of a Pilgrim girl.* New York: Scholastic.

Waters, K. (2001). *Giving thanks: The 1621 harvest feast.* New York: Scholastic.

Weitzman, D. (2003). *Old Ironsides: Americans build a fighting ship.* San Anselmo, CA: Sandpiper.

Weitzman, D. (2009). *Pharaoh's boat.* Boston: Houghton Mifflin.

White, L. A. (2005). *I could do that! Esther Morris gets women the vote.* New York: Farrar, Strauss & Giroux.

Wibberly, L. (1959). *Johnny Treegat's musket.* New York: Farrar, Straus.

Wilder, L. I. (1935). *Little house on the prairie.* New York: Harper & Row.

Williams, S. A. (1992). *Working cotton.* San Diego: Harcourt Brace Jovanovich.

Williams, V. B. (1982). *A chair for my mother.* New York: Greenwillow.

Winnick, K. (2000). *Sybil's night ride.* Honesdale, PA: Boyd's Mills.

Winter, J. (1988). *Follow the drinking gourd.* New York: Knopf.

Wolf, D. (1975). *Chinese writing: An introduction.* New York: Holt, Rinehart & Winston.

Wong, J., & Miran, K. (2002). *Chinese calligraphy: Learn the beautiful art of Chinese writing.* New York: Troll.

Woodson, J. (2001). *The other side.* New York: Putnam.

Yolen, J. (1992). *Encounter.* New York: HarperCollins.

Ziner, F. (1961). *The Pilgrims of Plymouth Colony.* New York: American Heritage.

References

Adams, D. M., & Hamm, M. E. (1992). Portfolio assessment and social studies: Collecting, selecting, and reflecting on what is significant. *Social Education, 56,* 103–105.

Akenson, J. E. (1989). The expanding environments and elementary education: A critical perspective. *Theory and Research in Social Education, 27,* 33–52.

Alibrandi, M., Beal, C., Thompson, A., & Wilson, A. (2000). Reconstructing a school's past using oral histories and GIS mapping. *Social Education, 64,* 134–140.

Alleman, J., & Brophy, J. (1994). Taking advantage of out-of-school opportunities for meaningful social studies learning. *The Social Studies, 85,* 262–267.

Alleman, J., & Brophy, J. (1998). Assessment in a social constructivist classroom. *Social Education, 62,* 32–34.

Alleman, J., & Brophy, J. (2000). On the menu: The growth of self-efficacy. *Social Studies and the Young Learner, 12*(3), 15–19.

Alleman, J., & Brophy, J. (2001a). Assessment in the elementary grades. *Social Studies and the Young Learner, 14*(1), 13–19.

Alleman, J., & Brophy, J. (2001b). *Social studies excursions, K–3. Book one: Powerful units on food, clothing, and shelter.* Portsmouth, NH: Heinemann.

Alleman, J., & Brophy, J. (2002a). Growing up to be President: Interviews with K–3 students. *Social Studies and the Young Learner, 15*(1), 17–20.

Alleman, J., & Brophy, J. (2002b). *Social studies excursions, K–3. Book three: Powerful units on childhood, money, and government.* Portsmouth, NH: Heinemann.

Alleman, J., & Brophy, J. (2002c). *Social studies excursions, K–3. Book two: Powerful units on communication, transportation, and family living.* Portsmouth, NH: Heinemann.

Alleman, J., & Brophy, J. (2004). Building a learning community and studying childhood. *Social Studies and the Young Learner, 17*(2), 16–18.

Alleman, J., & Brophy, J. (2006). Introducing children to democratic government. *Social Studies and the Young Learner, 19*(1), 17–19.

Alleman, J., Brophy, J., & Knighton, B. (2008). How a primary teacher protects the coherence of her social studies lessons. *Social Studies and the Young Learner, 21*(2), 28–31.

Alter, G. (Ed.). (1995). Variations on "ten themes": Applying the social studies standards to the elementary classroom [Special issue]. *Social Studies and the Young Learner, 8*(1).

Alvi, K. (2001). At risk of prejudice: Teaching tolerance about Muslim Americans. *Social Education, 65,* 344–348.

Anand, B., Fine, M., Perkins, T., & Surrey, D. S. (2002). *Keeping the struggle alive: A guide to doing oral history.* New York: Teachers College Press.

Anderson, C., Avery, P. G., Pederson, P. V., Smith, E. S., & Sullivan, J. L. (1997). Divergent perspectives on citizenship education: A Q-method study and survey of social studies teachers. *American Educational Research Journal, 34,* 333–364.

Angell, R. C. (1981). Reflections on the project Sociological Resources for the Social Studies. *American Sociologist, 16,* 41–43.

Armento, B. J. (1991). Learning about the economic world. In V. A. Atwood (Ed.), *Elementary school social studies: Research as a guide to practice* (pp. 85–101). Washington, DC: National Council for the Social Studies.

Aronson, E., Blaney, N., Stephen, C., Sikes, J., & Knapp, M. (1978). *The Jigsaw classroom.* Beverly Hills, CA: Sage.

Atkins, C. L. (1981). Introducing basic map and globe concepts to young children. *Journal of Geography, 80,* 228–233.

Atlof, P. (2008). Citizenship must not be the last of the three "C's". *Social Education, 72,* 379.

Au, K. H. (1980). Participation structures in a reading lesson with Hawaiian children: Analysis of a culturally appropriate instructional event. *Anthropology and Education Quarterly, 11,* 91–115.

Au, K. H. (1993). *Literacy instruction in multicultural settings.* Fort Worth, TX: Harcourt Brace.

Au, K. H. (2009). Isn't culturally responsive instruction just good teaching? *Social Education, 73,* 179–183.

Banks, J. A., & Banks, C. A. M. (Eds.). (2003). *Multicultural education: Issues and perspectives* (5th ed.). New York: Wiley.

Banks, J. A., Cookson, P., Gay, G., Hawley, W. D., Irvine, J. J., Nieto, S., Schofield, J. W., & Stephan, W. G. (2005). Education and diversity. *Social Education, 69,* 36–40.

Banks, J. A., & Nguyen, D. (2008). Diversity and citizenship education: Historical, theoretical, and philosophical issues. In L. S. Levstik & C. A. Tyson (Eds.), *Handbook of research in social studies education* (pp. 137–151). New York: Routledge.

Barell, J. (2006). *Problem-based learning: An inquiry approach.* Los Angeles: Corwin.

Barell, J. (Ed.). (2007). *Why are school buses yellow? Teaching inquiry.* Los Angeles: Corwin.

Barnes, B. R. (1991). Using children's literature in the early anthropology curriculum. *Social Education, 55,* 17–18.

Barnes, M. K., Johnson, E. C., & Neff, L. (2010). Learning through process drama in the first grade. *Social Studies and the Young Learner, 22*(4), 19–24.

Barron, R. F. (1969). The use of vocabulary as an advance organizer. In H. L. Herber & P. L. Sanders (Eds.), *Research in the content areas: First-year report* (pp. 29–39). Syracuse, NY: Reading and Language Arts Center.

Barton, K. C. (1997). History—it can be elementary: An overview of elementary students' understanding of history. *Social Education, 61,* 13–16.

Barton, K. C. (2008). Research on students' ideas about history. In L. S. Levstik & C. A. Tyson (Eds.), *Handbook of research in social studies education* (pp. 239–258). New York: Routledge.

Barton, K. C., & Levstik, L. S. (1996). "Back when God was around and everything": Elementary children's understanding of historical time. *American Educational Research Journal, 33,* 419–454.

Baum, C. G., & Cohen, I. S. (1989). Psychology and the social science curriculum. In *Charting a course: Social studies for the 21st century* (pp. 65–69). Washington, DC: National Commission on Social Studies in the Schools.

Beck, I. L., & McKeown, M. G. (1988). Toward meaningful accounts in history texts for young learners. *Educational Researcher, 17*(6), 31–39.

Beck, I. L., & McKeown, M. G. (1991a). Research directions: Social studies texts are hard to understand: Mediating some of the difficulties. *Language Arts, 68,* 482–489.

Beck, I. L., & McKeown, M. G. (1991b). Substantive and methodological considerations for productive textbook analysis. In J. P. Shaver (Ed.), *Handbook of research on social studies teaching and learning* (pp. 496–512). New York: Macmillan.

Beck, I. L., McKeown, M. G., & Worthy, J. (1995). Giving a text voice can improve students' understanding. *Reading Research Quarterly, 30,* 220–239.

Bennett, L. (Ed.). (2006). Children's voices for democracy [special issue]. *Social Studies and the Young Learner, 19*(1).

Bennett, L. (Ed.). (2007). Geography in a small world [special issue]. *Social Studies and the Young Learner, 20*(2).

Bennett, L., & Groce, E. (Eds.). (2009). Nonfiction and comprehension [Special issue]. *Social Studies and the Young Learner, 21*(3).

Bernard-Powers, J. (2002). Hilda Taba. In M. S. Crocco & O. L. Davis (Eds.), *Building a legacy: Women in social education, 1784–1984* (pp. 57–58). Silver Spring, MD: National Council for the Social Studies.

Berson, I. R. (2009). Here's what we have to say! Podcasting in the early childhood classroom. *Social Studies and the Young Learner, 21*(4), 8–11.

Berson, I. R., & Berson, M. J. (2001). Growing up in the aftermath of terrorism. *Social Studies and the Young Learner, 14*(2), 6–9.

Berson, M. J., & Berson, I. R. (2001). Developing thoughtful "cybercitizens." *Social Studies and the Young Learner, 16*(4), 5–8.

Berti, A. (2005). Children's understanding of politics. In M. Barrett & E. Buchanan-Barrow (Eds.), *Children's understanding of society* (pp. 69–103). New York: Psychology Press.

Berti, A. E., & Bombi, A. S. (1988). *The child's construction of economics.* Cambridge, UK: Cambridge University Press.

Beyer, B. K. (1985). Critical thinking: What is it? *Social Education, 49,* 270–276.

Beyer, B. K. (1987). *Practical strategies for the teaching of thinking.* Boston: Allyn & Bacon.

Beyer, B. K., & Gilstrap, R. L. (Eds.). (1982). *Writing in elementary school social studies.* Boulder, CO: Social Science Education Consortium.

Bickmore, K. (2002). Conflicts global and local: An elementary approach. *Social Education, 66,* 235–238.

Bigelow, W. (1992). Once upon a genocide: Christopher Columbus in children's literature. *Language Arts, 69,* 112–120.

Bjorklun, E. C. (1995). Teaching about personal injury law: Activities for the classroom. *The Social Studies, 86,* 78–84.

Black, M. V. (2008). Teaching about aboriginal Canada through picture books. *Social Education, 72,* 314–318.

Bloom, B. S. (Ed.). (1956). *Taxonomy of educational objectives: The classification of educational goals. Handbook 1: The cognitive domain.* New York: David McKay.

Boggs, S. T., Watson-Gegeo, K., & McMillen, G. (1985). *Speaking, relating, and learning: A study of Hawaiian children at home and at school.* Norwood, NJ: Ablex.

Boykin, A. W. (1982). Task variability and the performance of Black and White schoolchildren: Vervistic explorations. *Journal of Black Studies, 12,* 469–485.

Brandt, R. (Ed.). (1992). Using performance assessment [Special issue]. *Educational Leadership, 49*(8).

Braun, J. A., & Cook, M. L. (1985). Making heritage experiences come alive for elementary school social studies students. *The Social Studies, 76,* 216–219.

Britt, J. & LaFontaine, G. (2009). Google Earth: A virtual globe for elementary geography. *Social Studies and the Young Learner, 21*(94), 20–23.

Brophy, J. (1985). Classroom management as instruction: Socializing self-guidance in students. *Theory Into Practice, 24,* 233–240.

Brophy, J. (1990). Teaching social studies for understanding and higher order application. *Elementary School Journal, 90,* 351–417.

Brophy, J. (1996). Introduction. In J. Brophy (Ed.), *Advances in research on teaching, volume 6: Teaching and learning history* (pp. 1–18). Greenwich CT: JAI.

Brophy, J. (1999). Elementary students learn about Native Americans: The development of knowledge and empathy. *Social Education, 63,* 39–45.

Brophy, J., & Alleman, J. (2002). Primary-grade students' knowledge and thinking about the economics of meeting families' shelter needs. *American Educational Research Journal, 39,* 423–468.

Brophy, J., & Alleman, J. (2008). Early elementary social studies. In L. S. Levstik & C. A. Tyson (Eds.), *Handbook of research in social studies education* (pp. 33–49). New York: Routledge.

Brophy, J., & Van Sledright, B. (1997). *Teaching and learning history in elementary schools.* New York: Teachers College Press.

Bruner, J. (1960). *The process of education.* Cambridge, MA: Harvard University Press.

Bruner, J. (1961). The act of discovery. *Harvard Educational Review, 31,* 21–32.

Bruner, J., Goodnow, J., & Austin, G. (1956). *A study of thinking.* New York: Wiley.

Buckner, D. L., Brown, P. U., & Curry, J. (2010). The Pleasant Valley School: A living history project. *Social Education, 74,* 65–66.

Burstein, J. H., & Hutton, L. (2005). Planning and teaching with multiple perspectives. *Social Studies and the Young Learner, 18*(1), 15–17.

California Department of Education. (1992). *Handbook for teaching Korean American students.* Sacramento: Author.

California Department of Education. (1998). *History-social science content standards for California public schools: Kindergarten through grade twelve.* Sacramento: Author.

Camperell, K., & Knight, R. S. (1991). Reading research and social studies. In J. P. Shaver (Ed.), *Handbook of research on social studies teaching and learning* (pp. 567–577). New York: Macmillan.

Carnegie Corporation of New York and the Center for Information and Research on Civic Learning and Engagement (2003). *The civic mission of schools.* New York: Author.

Carrol, R. F. (1987). Schoolyard archaeology. *The Social Studies, 78,* 69–75.

Case, R. (1993). Key elements of a global perspective. *Social Education, 57,* 318–325.

Cazden, C. (1983). Adult assistance to language development: Scaffolds, models, and direct instruction. In R. P. Parker & F. A. Davis (Eds.), *Developing literacy: Young children's use of language* (pp. 3–18). Newark, DE: International Reading Association.

Center for Civic Education. (1994). *National standards for civics and government.* Calabasas, CA: Author.

Charles, C. (1985). Using the natural world to teach and learn globally. *Social Education, 49,* 213–215.

Chisolm, A. G., Leone, M. P., & Bentley, B. T. (2007). Archaeology in the classroom: Using the "dig box" to understand the past. *Social Education, 71,* 272–277.

Colby, S. (2009). Finding place in state history: Connecting to students through diverse narratives. *Social Studies and Young Learner, 22*(2), 16–18.

Cooper, B. L. (1989). Popular records as oral evidence: Creating an audio time line to examine American history, 1955–1987. *Social Education, 53,* 34–40.

Cordier, M. H., & Perez-Stable, M. A. (1996). Latino connections: Family, neighbors, and community. *Social Studies and the Young Learner, 9*(1), 20–22.

Crawford, J., & Krashen, S. (2007). *English Language Learners in American classrooms: 101 questions, 101 answers.* New York: Scholastic.

Cremin, L. (1961). *The transformation of the school: Progressivism in American education.* New York: Knopf.

Cruz, B. C. (2007). Stories from afar: Using children's and young adult literature to teach about Latin America. *Social Education, 71,* 170–176.

Cruz, B. C., & Thornton, S. J. (2009). Social studies for English Language Learners: Teaching social studies that matters. *Social Education, 73,* 271–274.

Cruz, B. C., Nutta, J. W., O'Brien, J., Feyton, C. M., & Govoni, J. M. (2003). *Passport to learning: Teaching social studies to ESL students.* Silver Spring MD: National Council for the Social Studies.

Cummins, J. (1979). Linguistic interdependence and the educational development of bilingual children. *Review of Educational Research, 49,* 222–251.

Cummins, J. (1986a). Empowering minority students: A framework for intervention. *Harvard Educational Review, 56,* 18–36.

Cummins, J. (1986b). The role of primary language development in promoting educational success for language minority students. In *Schooling and language minority students: A theoretical framework* (pp. 3–49). Los Angeles: CSULA Evaluation, Dissemination, and Assessment Center.

Cummins, J. (1989). *Empowering minority students.* Sacramento: California Association for Bilingual Education.

Cummins, J. (1992). Language proficiency, bilingualism, and academic achievement. In P. A. Richard-Amato & M. A. Snow (Eds.), *The multicultural classroom: Readings for content-area teachers* (pp. 16–26). White Plains, NY: Longman.

Cunningham, J. W., Cunningham, P. M., & Arthur, S. V. (1981). *Middle and secondary school reading.* New York: Longman.

Czartoski, S., & Hickey, G. (1999). All about me: A personal heritage project. *Social Studies and the Young Learner, 11*(4), 11–14.

Danziger, K. (1958). Children's earliest conceptions of economic relationships. *Journal of Social Psychology, 47,* 231–240.

Darling-Hammond, L., Ancess, J., & Falk, B. (Eds.). (1995). *Authentic assessment in action: Studies of schools and students at work.* New York: Teachers College Press.

Delaney, M., & Oyler, C. (2001). Online expeditions: Strengths and limitations. *Social Studies and the Young Learner, 13*(3), 6–9.

Dewey, J. (1900). *The school and society.* Chicago: University of Chicago Press.

Dewey, J. (1902). *The child and the curriculum.* Chicago: University of Chicago Press.

Dewey, J. (1933). *How we think.* Boston: Heath. (Original work published 1910)

Diaz, C. F., Massialas, B. G., & Xanthopoulos, J. A. (1999). *Global perspectives for educators.* Boston: Allyn & Bacon.

Diaz-Rico, L. T., & Weed, K. Z. (2005). *The cross-cultural, language, and academic development handbook: A complete K–12 reference guide* (3rd ed.). Boston: Allyn & Bacon.

Dimmitt, J. P., & Van Cleaf, D. W. (1992). Integrating writing and social studies: Alternatives to the formal research paper. *Social Education, 56,* 382–384.

Douglass, M. P. (1967). *Social studies from theory to practice in elementary education.* Philadelphia: JB Lippincott.

Douglass, M. P. (1998). *The history, psychology and pedagogy of geographic literacy.* Westport, CT: Praeger.

Downey, M. T. (Ed.). (1985). *History in the schools.* Washington, DC: National Council for the Social Studies.

Downey, M. T., & Levstik, L. S. (1991). Teaching and learning history. In J. P. Shaver (Ed.), *Handbook of research on social studies teaching and learning* (pp. 400–410). New York: Macmillan.

Duplass, J. A. (2007). Elementary social studies: Trite, disjointed, and in need of reform? *The Social Studies, 98*(4), 137–144.

Echevarria, J., & Graves, A. (2010). *Sheltered content instruction: Teaching English Language Learners with diverse abilities* (4th ed.). Boston: Allyn & Bacon.

Echevarria, J., Vogt, M., & Short, D. (2003). *Making content comprehensible to English language learners: The SIOP model* (2nd ed.). Boston: Allyn & Bacon.

Edgington, W. D. (2001). Solving problems with twenty questions. *Social Education, 65,* 379–382.

Edwards, S. A., & Maloy, R. W. (2007). Walking back in time: Local history explorations. In L. Bennett & M. Berson (Eds.), *Digital age: Technology-based K-12 lesson plans for social studies,* pp. 14–17. Silver Spring, MD: National Council for the Social Studies.

Eggen, P. & Kauchak, D. P. (2005). *Strategies and models for teachers: Teaching content and thinking skills* (5th ed.). Boston: Allyn and Bacon.

Eisner, E. (1991). Art, music, and literature within social studies. In J. P. Shaver (Ed.), *Handbook of research on social studies teaching and learning* (pp. 551–558). New York: Macmillan.

Elder, L., & Paul, R. (2008). Critical thinking in a world of accelerating change and complexity. *Social Education, 72,* 388–391.

Elnour, A., & Bashir-Ali, K. (2003). Teaching Muslim girls in American schools. *Social Education, 67,* 62–64.

Ember, C. R., & Ember, M. R. (2010). *Cultural anthropology* (13th ed.). Upper Saddle River, NJ: Pearson.

Engle, S. H. (1986). Late night thoughts about the New Social Studies. *Social Education, 50,* 20–22.

Engle, S. H., & Ochoa, A. S. (1988). *Education for democratic citizenship: Decision making in the social studies.* New York: Teachers College Press.

Epstein, J., & Shiller, T. (2005). Perspective matters: Social identity and the teaching and learning of national history. *Social Education, 69,* 201–204.

Evans, M. D. (1995). Exchanging opinions through letters and editorials: A social studies activity. *Social Education, 59,* 158.

Evans, R. W. (1989). A dream unrealized: A brief look at the history of issue-centered approaches. *The Social Studies, 80,* 178–184.

Evans, R. W. (2004). *The social studies wars: What should we teach the children?* New York: Teachers College Press.

Evans, R. W. (2006). The social studies wars, now and then. *Social Education, 70,* 317–321.

Evans, R. W., & Passe, J. (2007). Dare we make peace: A dialogue on the social studies wars. *The Social Studies, 98*(6), 251–256.

Fein, B., Johnson, M, & Smith, T. (2010). Far beyond show and tell: Strategies for integration of desktop documentary making into history classrooms. *Social Education, 74,* 101–104.

Fenton, E. (1991). Reflections on the new social studies. *The Social Studies, 82,* 84–90.

Field, S. L. (1998). (Ed.). Social studies: Gateway to literacy [Special issue]. *Social Studies and the Young Learner, 10*(4).

Field, S. L., & Finchum, M. (Eds.). American Indian culture and history [Special issue]. *Social Studies and the Young Learner, 18*(4).

Field, S. L., Wilhelm, R., Nickell, P., Culligan, J., & Sparks, J. (2001). Teaching middle school social studies: Who is at risk? *Social Education, 65,* 225–230.

Finchum, M. (2006). "I" is for Indian? Dealing with stereotypes in the classroom. *Social Studies and the Young Learner, 18*(4), 4–6.

Firek, H. (2006). Creative writing in the social studies classroom: Promoting literacy and content literacy. *Social Education, 70,* 183–186.

Fisher, A. (2001). *Critical thinking.* London: Cambridge University Press.

Fisher, D., & Frey, N. (2008). *Better learning through structured teaching: A framework for the gradual release of responsibility.* Alexandria, VA: Association for Supervision and Curriculum Development.

Fitzpatrick, C. (2000). Navigating a new information landscape. *Social Education, 64,* 33–35.

Forsythe, A. S. (1995). *Learning geography: An annotated bibliography of research paths.* Indiana, PA: National Council for Geographic Education.

Fraenkel, J. R. (1992). Hilda Taba's contributions to social studies education. *Social Education, 56,* 172–178.

Freese, J. R. (1997). Using the National Geographic standards to integrate children's social studies. *Social Studies and the Young Learner, 10*(2), 22–24.

Gallavan, N. P. (2008). *Developing performance-based assessments, grades K–5.* Los Angeles: Corwin Press.

Gallavan, N. P., & Juilano, C. (2007). What does family mean to you? Constructing an electronic big book. In L. Bennett & M. Berson (Eds.), *Digital age: Technology-based K–12 lesson plans for social studies,* pp. 6–10. Silver Spring, MD: National Council for the Social Studies.

Gallenstein, N. L. (2000). Group investigation: An introduction to cooperative research. *Social Studies and the Young Learner, 13*(1), 17–18.

Gandy, S. K. (2004). Teaching the electoral process in ten days. *Social Education, 68,* 332–338.

Garcia, E. (1994) *Understanding and meeting the challenge of student cultural diversity.* Boston: Houghton Mifflin.

Gardner, H. (1991). *The unschooled mind: How children think and how school should teach.* New York: Basic Books.

Gardner, H. (2006). *Multiple intelligences: New horizons in theory and practice.* New York: Basic Books.

Gavrish, M. J. A. (1995). The historian as detective: An introduction to historical methodology. *Social Education, 59,* 151–153.

Gay, G. (1991). Culturally diverse students and social studies. In J. P. Shaver (Ed.), *Handbook of research on social studies teaching and learning* (pp. 144–156). New York: Macmillan.

Gay, G. (2000). *Culturally responsive teaching: Theory, research and practice.* New York: Teachers College Press.

Geography Education Standards Project. (1994). *Geography for life: National geography standards.* Washington, DC: Author.

Gersmehl, P. (2005). *Teaching geography.* New York: Guilford Press.

Gill, S. R. (2010). What teachers need to know about the "new" nonfiction. *The Reading Teacher, 63,* 260–269.

Gilles, R. M. (2007). *Cooperative learning: Integrating theory and practice.* Los Angeles: Sage.

Gilliland, H. (Ed.). (1992). *Teaching the Native American.* Dubuque, IA: Kendall/Hunt.

Gilstrap, R. L. (1982). Writing in elementary social studies: Report of a personal search. In B. K. Beyer & R. L. Gilstrap (Eds.), *Writing in elementary school social studies* (pp. 19–29). Boulder, CO: Social Science Education Consortium.

Gilstrap, R. L. (1991). Writing for the social studies. In J. P. Shaver (Ed.), *Handbook of research on social studies teaching and learning* (pp. 578–587). New York: Macmillan.

Goldston, S. (2010). The civic mission of schools. *Social Education, 74,* 4–6.

Goodman, J. (1992). *Elementary schooling for critical democracy.* Albany: State University of New York Press.

Grant, S. G. (1997). Appeasing the Right, missing the point? Reading the New York state social studies framework. *Social Education, 61,* 102–107.

Grant, S. G. (2007). High-stakes testing: How are social studies teachers responding? *Social Education, 71,* 250–254.

Grant, S. G., & Salinas, C. (2008). Assessment and accountability in the social studies. In L. S. Levstik & C. A. Tyson (Eds.), *Handbook of research in social studies education* (pp. 219–238). New York: Routledge.

Gray, P. S. (1989). Sociology. In *Charting a course: Social studies for the 21st century* (pp. 71–75). Washington, DC: National Commission on Social Studies in the Schools.

Greenbaum, P. E. (1985). Nonverbal differences in communication style between American Indian and Anglo elementary classrooms. *American Educational Research Journal, 22,* 101–115.

Greenstein, F. I. (1969). *Children and politics.* New Haven, CT: Yale University Press.

Gregg, M., & Leinhardt, G. (1994). Mapping out geography: An example of epistemology and education. *Review of Educational Research, 64,* 311–361.

Gronlund, N. E., & Brookhart, S. M. (2008). *Gronlund's writing instructional objectives* (8th ed.). Upper Saddle River, NJ: Pearson.

Grossman, H. (1984). *Educating Hispanic students: Cultural implications for instruction, classroom management, counseling, and assessment.* Springfield, IL: Charles C. Thomas.

Haas, M. E. (2004). The presidency and presidential elections in the elementary classroom. *Social Education, 68,* 340–346.

Haas, M. E. (2008). Conducting interviews to learn about World War II. *Social Education, 72,* 264–267.

Hammond, T. C., & Bodzin, A. M. (2009). Teaching with rather than about Geographic Information Systems. *Social Education, 73,* 119–123.

Handley, L. M., & Adler, S. (1994). Standards in social studies: Curriculum concerns. *Social Studies and the Young Learner, 6*(3), 17–19.

Hanna, P. R. (1963). Revising the social studies: What is needed. *Social Education, 27,* 190–196.

Hanna, P. R. (Ed.). (1987a). *Assuring quality for the social studies in our schools.* Stanford, CA: Hoover Institution Press.

Hanna, P. R. (1987b). Society-child-curriculum. In P. R. Hanna (Ed.), *Assuring quality for the social studies in our schools* (pp. 11–19). Stanford, CA: Hoover Institution Press. (Original work published 1956).

Hansen, W. L., Bach, G. L., Calderwood, J. D., & Saunders, P. (1977). *A framework for teaching economics: Basic concepts.* New York: Joint Council for Economic Education.

Hanvey, R. G. (1976). *An attainable global perspective.* New York: Global Perspectives in Education.

Harms, J. M., & Lettow, L. J. (1994). Criteria for selecting picture books with historical settings. *Social Education, 58,* 152–155.

Harwood, A. M., & Chang, J. (1999). Inquiry-based service-learning and the Internet. *Social Studies and the Young Learner, 12*(1), 15–18.

Heath, J. A., & Vik, P. (1994). Elementary school student councils: A statewide study. *Principal, 74*(1), 31–32.

Heath, S. B. (1986). Sociocultural contexts of language development. In *Beyond language: Social and cultural factors in schooling language-minority students* (pp. 143–186). Los Angeles: California State University Evaluation, Dissemination, and Assessment Center.

Heimlich, J. E., & Pittelman, S. D. (1986). *Semantic mapping: Classroom applications.* Newark, DE: International Reading Association.

Hembacher, D., Okada, D., & Richardson, T. (2004). "School to career" and social studies: Making the connection. *Social Studies and the Young Learner, 16*(4), 20–23.

Hertzberg, H. W. (1981). *Social studies reform 1880–1980.* Boulder, CO: Social Science Education Consortium.

Hess, D. E. (2004). Discussion in social studies: Is it worth the trouble? *Social Education, 68,* 151–155.

Hess, D. E. (2008). Controversial issues and democratic discourse. In L. S. Levstik & C. A. Tyson (Eds.), *Handbook of research in social studies education* (pp. 124–136). New York: Routledge.

Hickey, G. M. (1991). "And then what happened, Grandpa?": Oral history projects in the elementary classroom. *Social Education, 55,* 216–217.

Hickey, G. M. (1999). *Bringing history home: Local and family history projects for grades K–16.* Boston: Allyn & Bacon.

Hickey, G. M., & Kolterman, D. L. (2006). Special women in my life: Strategies for writing women into the social studies curriculum. *Social Education, 70,* 190–196.

Hicks, D. (2003). Thirty years of global education: A reminder of key principles and precedents. *Educational Review, 55,* 265–275.

Hicks, K., & Austin, J. (1994). Experiencing the legal system: Fairy-tale trials for fifth graders. *The Social Studies, 85,* 39–44.

Hightshoe, S. (1997). Sifting through the sands of time: A simulated archaeological dig. *Social Studies and the Young Learner, 9*(3), 28–30.

Hinde, E. R. (2005). Revisiting curriculum integration: A fresh look at an old idea. *The Social Studies, 96,* 105–111.

Hinde, E. R., & Ekiss, G. O. (2005). No child left behind . . . except in geography? GeoMath in Arizona answers a need. *Social Studies and the Young Learner, 18*(2), 27–29.

Hines, A. (2008). Reflecting on the Great Black Migration by creating a newspaper. *Social Studies and the Young Learner, 21*(2), 4–7.

Hirshfield, C. (1991). New worlds from old: An experience in oral history at the elementary school level. *Social Studies, 82*(3), 110–114.

Hollingsworth, J. R., & Ybarra, S. E. (2008). *Explicit direct instruction (EDI): The power of well-crafted, well-taught lessons.* Los Angeles: Corwin Press.

Hollins, E. R., & Oliver, E. I. (Eds.). (1999). *Pathways to success in school: Culturally responsive teaching.* Mahwah, NJ: Erlbaum.

Hollins, E. R., Smiler, H., & Spencer, K. (1994). Benchmarks in meeting the challenges of effective schooling for African American youngsters. In E. R. Hollins, J. E. King, & W. C. Hayman (Eds.), *Teaching diverse populations: Formulating a knowledge base* (pp. 163–174). Albany: State University of New York Press.

Hoone, C. (1989). Teaching timelines. *Social Studies and the Young Learner, 2*(2), 13–17.

Hoover, R. L., & Kindsvatter, R. (1997). *Democratic discipline: Foundation and practice.* Upper Saddle River, NJ: Merrill/Prentice Hall.

Huerta, G. C., & Flemmer, L. A. (2001). Latina women speak: Using oral histories in the social studies curriculum. *Social Education, 65,* 270–277.

Hunter, M. (1984). Knowing, teaching, and supervising. In P. L. Hosford (Ed.), *Using what we know about teaching* (pp. 169–192). Alexandria, VA: Association for Supervision and Curriculum Development.

Irvin, J. L., Lunstrum, J. P., Lynch-Brown, C., & Shepard, M. F. (1995). *Enhancing social studies through literacy strategies.* Washington, DC: National Council for the Social Studies.

Jaffee, C. (2004). Teaching about the Middle East: Challenges and resources. *Social Education, 68,* 46–50.

Jahoda, G. (1979). The construction of economic reality by some Glaswegian children. *European Journal of Social Psychology, 19,* 115–127.

Jantz, R. K., & Klawitter, K. (1991). Anthropology and sociology. In V. A. Atwood (Ed.), *Elementary school social studies: Research as a guide to practice* (pp. 102–118). Washington, DC: National Council for the Social Studies.

Jennings, T. E., Crowell, S. M., & Fernlund, P. F. (1994). Social justice in the elementary classroom. *Social Studies and the Young Learner, 7*(1), 4–6.

Johnson, D. D., & Pearson, P. D. (1984). *Teaching reading vocabulary.* New York: Holt, Rinehart & Winston.

Johnson, D. W., & Johnson, F. P. (2005). *Joining together: Group theory and group skills* (9th ed.). Boston: Allyn & Bacon.

Johnson, D. W., & Johnson, R. T. (1989–1990). Social skills for successful group work. *Educational Leadership, 47*(4), 29–33.

Johnson, D. W., & Johnson, R. T. (1992). Approaches to implementing cooperative learning in the social studies classroom. In R. J. Stahl & R. L. Van Sickle (Eds.), *Cooperative learning in the social studies classroom: An introduction to social study* (pp. 44–51). Washington, DC: National Council for the Social Studies.

Johnson, D. W., & Johnson, R. T. (1998). *Learning together and alone: Cooperative, competitive, and individualistic learning* (5th ed.). Boston: Allyn & Bacon.

Johnson, D. W., Johnson, R. T., & Holubec, E. J. (1994). *The new circles of learning: Cooperation in the classroom and school.* Alexandria, VA: Association for Supervision and Curriculum Development.

Johnson, D. W., Maruyama, G., Johnson, R. T., Nelson, D., & Skon, L. (1981). Effects of cooperative, competitive, and individualistic goal structures on achievement: A meta-analysis. *Psychological Bulletin, 89,* 47–62.

Joint Committee on Geographic Education. (1984). *Guidelines for geographic education: Elementary and secondary schools.* Washington, DC: Association of American Geographers and National Council for Geographic Education.

Jones, R. C., & Lapham, S. S. (2004). Teaching reading skills in the elementary social studies classroom. *Social Studies and the Young Learner, 17*(2), pullout section.

Joyce, B. R., & Weil, M. (2008). *Models of teaching* (8th ed.). Boston: Allyn & Bacon.

Kagan, S. (1989–1990). The structural approach to cooperative learning. *Educational Leadership, 47*(4), 12–15.

Kagan, S. (1997). *Cooperative learning.* San Juan Capistrano, CA: Author.

Keiper, T. A. (1999). GIS for elementary students: An inquiry into a new approach to learning geography. *Journal of Geography, 98*(2), 17–59.

Keiper, T., & Garcia, J. (2009a). Editor's notes. *Social Studies and the Young Learner, 22*(2), p. 1.

Keiper, T., & Garcia, J. (Eds.). (2009b). Immigration and citizenship [Special issue]. *Social Studies and the Young Learner, 22*(2).

Keiper, T., Krohn, C., & Kepner, G. (2009). Immigration: Resources for teachers. *Social Studies and the Young Learner, 22*(2), 27–28.

Kellough, R. D. (Ed.). (1995). *Integrating language arts and social studies for intermediate and middle school students.* Upper Saddle River, NJ: Merrill/Prentice Hall.

Kerckhoff, A. C. (1986). Effects of ability grouping in British secondary schools. *American Sociological Review, 51,* 842–858.

Kilpatrick, W. H. (1918). The project method. *Teachers College Record, 19,* 319–333.

Kilpatrick, W. H. (1925). *Foundations of method.* New York: Macmillan.

Kleg, M. (1993). On the NCSS curriculum guidelines for multicultural education. *Social Education, 57,* 58–59.

Kniep, W. M. (1985). *A critical review of the short history of global education: Preparing for new opportunities.* New York: Global Perspectives in Education.

Kniep, W. M. (1986). Defining a global education by its content. *Social Education, 50,* 437–446.

Koeller, S. (1992). Social studies research writing: Raising voices. *Social Education, 56,* 379–382.

Kourilsky, M. (1977). The kinder-economy: A case study of kindergarten pupils of economic concepts. *Elementary School Journal, 77,* 182–191.

Kourilsky, M. (1987). Children's learning of economics: The imperative and the hurdles. *Theory Into Practice, 26,* 198–205.

Krashen, S. (2003). *Explorations in language acquisition and use.* Portsmouth, NH: Heinemann.

Krashen, S. D., & Terrell, T. D. (1995). *The natural approach: Language acquisition in the classroom.* New York: Phoenix ELT.

Krey, D. M. (1998). *Children's literature in social studies: Teaching to the standards.* Washington, DC: National Council for the Social Studies.

Kurtz-Costes, B., & Pungello, E. P. (2000). Acculturation and immigrant children: Implications for educators. *Social Education, 64,* 121–125.

Ladson-Billings, G. (1992). I don't see color, I just see children: Dealing with stereotyping and prejudice in young children. *Social Studies and the Young Learner, 5*(2), 9–12.

Ladson-Billings, G. (1995). Toward a theory of culturally relevant pedagogy. *American Educational Research Journal, 32,* 465–492.

Lamy, S. L. (1987). *The definition of a discipline: The objects and methods of analysis in global education.* New York: Global Perspectives in Education.

Landman, J. (2008). Using literature to teach the rule of law. *Social Education, 72,* 165–170.

Landorf, H., & Lowenstein, E. (2004). The Rosa Parks "myth": A third grade historical investigation. *Social Studies and the Young Learner, 16*(3), 5–9.

Laney, J. D., & Moseley, L. (1990). Who packed the suitcase? Playing the role of an archaeologist/anthropologist. *Social Studies and the Young Learner, 2*(3), 17–19.

Langer, J. A. (1981). From theory to practice: A prereading plan. *Journal of Reading, 25,* 106–110.

Lankiewicz, D. (1987). Our museum of American life. *Clearing House, 60,* 256–257.

Larkins, A. G., & Hawkins, M. L. (1990). Trivial and noninformative content in primary grade social studies texts: A second look. *Journal of Social Studies Research, 14,* 25–32.

La Rue, P. (2010). Students preserve an emancipation site with archaeological technology, *Social Education, 74,* 58–60.

Laughlin, M., Black, P., & Loberg, M. (1991). *Social studies readers' theater for children: Scripts and script development.* Englewood, CO: Teacher Idea Press.

Lechner, J. V. (1997). Accuracy in biographies for children. *New Advocate, 10,* 229–242.

Ledford, C. C., & Lyon, A. (2004). Election resources and activities for grades K–5. *Social Studies and the Young Learner, 17*(1), 19–21.

Leming, J., Ellington, L., & Porter-Magee, K. (Eds.). (2003). *Where did social studies go wrong?* Washington, DC: Fordham Institute.

Leming, J. S., Ellington, L., & Schug, M. (2006). The state of social studies: A national random survey of elementary and middle school social studies teachers. *Social Education, 70,* 322–327.

LeRiche, L. W. (1987). The expanding environments sequence in elementary social studies: The origins. *Theory and Research in Social Education, 5,* 137–154.

Levstik, L. (1986). The relationship between historical response and narrative in a sixth-grade classroom. *Theory and Research in Social Education, 21*(1), 1–15.

Levstik, L. (1989). Historical narrative and the young reader. *Theory Into Practice, 28,* 114–119.

Levstik, L. (1990). Mediating content through literary texts. *Language Arts, 67,* 848–853.

Levstik, L. (1991). Teaching history: A definitional and developmental dilemma. In V. A. Atwood (Ed.), *Elementary school social studies: Research as a guide to practice* (pp. 68–84). Washington, DC: National Council for the Social Studies.

Levstik, L. (2008). What happens in social studies classrooms. In L. S. Levstik & C. A. Tyson (Eds.), *Handbook of research in social studies education* (pp. 50–62). New York: Routledge.

Levstik, L. S., & Barton, K. C. (1996). They still use some of their past: Historical salience in elementary children's chronological thinking. *Journal of Curriculum Studies, 28,* 531–576.

Levstik, L. S., & Barton, K. C. (2005). *Doing history: Investigating with children in elementary and middle schools* (3rd ed.). New York: Erlbaum.

Levstik, L., & Tyson, C. A. (Eds.). (2008). *Handbook of research in social studies education.* New York: Routledge.

Lewis, R. B., & Doorlag, D. H. (2010). *Teaching students with special needs in general education classrooms* (8th ed.). Upper Saddle River, NJ: Pearson.

Liben, L., & Downs, R. (1989). Educating with maps: Part I. The place of maps. *Teaching Thinking and Problem Solving, 11*(1), 6–9.

Little Soldier, L. (1990). Making anthropology a part of the elementary social studies curriculum. *Social Education, 54,* 18–19.

Losey, K. M. (1995). Mexican American students and classroom interaction: An overview and critique. *Review of Educational Research, 65,* 283–318.

Lou, Y., Abrami, P. C., Spence, J. C., Poulson, C., Chambers, B., & D'Apollonia, S. (1996). Within-class grouping: A meta-analysis. *Review of Educational Research, 66,* 423–458.

Lubliner, S. (2001). *A practical guide to reciprocal teaching.* Bothel, WA: Wright.

Lybarger, M. (1991). The historiography of social studies: Retrospect, circumspect, and prospect. In J. P. Shaver (Ed.), *Handbook of research on social studies teaching and learning* (pp. 3–15). New York: Macmillan.

Lyman, F. T. (1992). Think-Pair-Share, Thinktrix, Thinklinks, and weird facts: An interactive system for cooperative thinking. In N. Davidson & T. Worsham (Eds.), *Enhancing thinking through cooperative learning* (pp. 169–181). New York: Teachers College Press.

Lyman, L., Foyle, H. C., & Azwell, T. S. (1993). *Cooperative learning in the elementary classroom.* Washington, DC: National Educational Association.

Mager, R. F. (1997). *Preparing instructional objectives: A critical tool in the development of effective instruction* (3rd ed.). Atlanta, GA: The Center for Effective Performance.

Mahood, W. (1980). The land of milk and honey: Simulating the immigrant experience. *Social Education, 44,* 22–27.

Main, M., Wilhelm, R. W., & Cox, A. R. (1996). Mi communidad: Young children's bicultural explorations of the meaning of family. *Social Studies and the Young Learner, 9*(1), 7–9, 14.

Marchand-Martella, N. E., Slocum, T. A., & Martella, R. C. (2003). *Introduction to direct instruction.* Boston: Allyn & Bacon.

Marinak, B. A., & Gambrell, L. B. (2009). Ways to teach about informational text. *Social Studies and the Young Learner, 22*(1), 19–22.

Martin, D., Wineburg, S., Rosenzweig, R., & Leon, S. (2008). Historicalthinkingmatters.org: Using the web to teach historical thinking. *Social Education, 72,* 143–158.

Massialas, B. G. (1991). Education for international understanding. In J. P. Shaver (Ed.), *Handbook of research on social studies teaching and learning* (pp. 448–458). New York: Macmillan.

Massialas, B. G., & Cox, C. B. (1966). *Inquiry in social studies.* San Francisco: McGraw-Hill.

Mayhew, K. C., & Edwards, A. C. (1936). *The Dewey School: The Laboratory School of the University of Chicago 1896–1903.* New York: Appleton-Century.

McCall, A. L. (1994). Including quilters' voices in the social studies curriculum. *Social Studies and the Young Learner, 7*(1), 10–14.

McConnell, T. (2008). Not by votes alone . . . the vital imperative of restoring the civic mission of the schools. *Social Education, 72,* 312–313.

McCormick, T. M. (2004). Letters from Trenton, 1776: Teaching with primary sources. *Social Studies and the Young Learner, 17*(2), 5–12.

McCracken, H. (1959). *George Catlin and the old frontier.* New York: Dial.

McGowan, T. M., Erickson, L., & Neufeld, J. A. (1996). With reason and rhetoric: Building the case for the literature–social studies connection. *Social Education, 60,* 203–207.

McKeown, M. G., Beck, I. L., & Blake, R. G. K. (2009). Rethinking reading comprehension instruction: A comparison of instruction for strategies and content approaches. *Reading Research Quarterly, 44,* 218–255.

McKeown, M. G., Beck, I. L., Sinatra, G. M., & Loxterman, J. A. (1991). The contribution of prior knowledge and coherent text to comprehension. *Reading Research Quarterly, 27,* 79–93.

McKoy, K. (2010). Realia: It's just not about field trips anymore. *Social Education, 74,* 73.

McLaughlin, B. (1987). *Theories of second-language learning.* London: Edward Arnold.

Mehaffy, G., Sitton, G., & Davis, O. L. (1979). *Oral history in the classroom.* Washington, DC: National Council for the Social Studies.

Mehlinger, H. D. (2002). Teaching about September 11 and its aftermath. *Social Education, 66,* 303–306.

Merryfield, M. M. (2004). Elementary students in substantial culture learning. *Social Education, 68,* 270–273.

Merryfield, M. M. (2008). Scaffolding social studies for global education. *Social Education, 72,* 363–366.

Meszaros, B. (1997). Economic standards: A guide for curriculum planners. *Social Education, 61,* 324–328.

Meszaros, B., & Engstrom, L. (1998). The voluntary national content standards in economics: From standards to classroom implementation. *Social Studies and the Young Learner, 11*(2), 7–12.

Miel, A. (1952). *Cooperative procedures in learning.* New York: Teachers College Press.

Miller, F. (2000). Biography buddy: Interviewing each other. *Social Studies and the Young Learner, 12*(3), 13–14.

Miller, J. W. (1974). Comparisons of conventional "subdued" to vivid "highly contrasting" color schemes for elementary school maps: Report of an experiment. *Journal of Geography, 73*(3), 41–45.

Miller, J. W. (1982). Improving the design of classroom maps: Experimental comparison of alternative formats. *Journal of Geography, 81*(2), 51–55.

Miller, S. L., & VanFossen, P. J. (2008). Recent research on the teaching and learning of pre-collegiate economics. In L. S. Levstik & C. A. Tyson (Eds.), *Handbook of research in social studies education* (pp. 284–306). New York: Routledge.

Milson, A. J., & Curtis, M. D. (2009). Where and why there? Spatial thinking with Geographic Information Systems. *Social Education, 73,* 113–188.

Milson, A. J., & Downey, P. (2001). WebQuest: Using Internet resources for cooperative inquiry. *Social Education, 65,* 144–146.

Milson, A. J., Gilbert, K. M., Earle, B. D. (2007). Discovering Africa through internet-based Geographic Information Systems: A Pan-African summit simulation. *Social Education, 71,* 140–145.

Molebash, P. (2004). Web historical inquiry projects. *Social Education, 68,* 226–229.

Moore, A. W. (1985). A question of accuracy: Errors in children's biographies. *School Library Journal, 31*(6), 34–35.

Moore, T. (2010). The entrepreneur fair: Creating fifth grade student businesses. *Social Studies and the Young Learner, 22*(3), 8–13.

Morris, R. V. (2003). Colonial America and service learning in the fifth grade. *Social Studies and the Young Learner, 15*(4), 11–14.

Morris, R. V. (2006). The land of Hope: Third-grade students use a walking tour to explore their community. *The Social Studies, 97*, 129–132.

Muir, S. P., & Frazee, B. (1986). Teaching map-reading skills: A developmental perspective. *Social Education, 50*, 199–203.

Nash, G. B., & Dunn, R. E. (1995). History standards and culture wars. *Social Education, 59*, 5–7.

National Center for History in the Schools. (1996). *National standards for history: Basic edition.* Los Angeles: Author.

National Council for the Social Studies. (2008a). *Curriculum guidelines for social studies teaching and learning.* Silver Spring, MD: Author.

National Council for the Social Studies. (2008b). A vision of powerful teaching and learning in the social studies: Building effective citizens. *Social Education, 72*, 277–280.

National Council for the Social Studies. (2009). Powerful and purposeful teaching and learning in elementary social studies. *Social Studies and the Young Learner, 22*(1), 31–38.

National Council for the Social Studies. (2010). *National curriculum standards for social studies: A framework for teaching, learning, and assessment.* Silver Spring, MD: Author.

National Council for the Social Studies Ad Hoc Committee on Ability Grouping. (1992). Ability grouping in social studies. *Social Education, 56*, 268–270.

National Council for the Social Studies Ad Hoc Committee on Global Education. (1987). Global education: In bounds or out? *Social Education, 51*, 242–249.

National Council for the Social Studies Select Subcommittee. (2001). Service-learning: An essential component of citizenship education. *Social Education, 65*, 240–241.

National Council for the Social Studies Task Force on Early Childhood/Elementary Social Studies. (1989). Social studies for early childhood and elementary school children preparing for the 21st century. *Social Education, 53*, 14–23.

National Council for the Social Studies Task Force on Ethnic Studies. (1992). Curriculum guidelines for multicultural education. *Social Education, 56*, 274–294.

National Council for the Social Studies Task Force on Revitalizing Citizenship Education. (2001). Creating effective citizens. *Social Education, 65*, 319.

National Council for the Social Studies Task Force on Scope and Sequence. (1989). In search of a scope and sequence for social studies: Report of the National Council for the Social Studies Task Force on Scope and Sequence. *Social Education, 53*, 375–387.

National Council on Economic Education. (1997). *National content standards in economics.* New York: Author.

National Institute of Child Health and Development. (2000). *Report of the National Panel. Teaching children to read: An evidence-based assessment of the scientific research literature on reading and its implication for reading instruction. Reports of the subgroups.* Washington, DC: National Institute for Child Health and Human Development/U.S. Department of Education/National Institute for Literacy. www.nationalreadingpanel.org.

Nebel, M., Jamison, B., & Bennett, L. (2009). Students as digital citizens on Web 2.0. *Social Studies and the Young Learner, 21*(4), 5–7.

Neill, M., & Guisbond, L. (2005). Excluding children, lost learning: The costs of doing business with NCLB. *Social Studies and the Young Learner, 17*(4), 31–32.

Nelson, M. R., & Stahl, R. J. (1991). Teaching anthropology, sociology, and psychology. In J. P. Shaver (Ed.), *Handbook of research on social studies teaching and learning* (pp. 420–426). New York: Macmillan.

Newmann, F. M. (1990a). Higher order thinking in social studies: A rationale for the assessment of classroom thoughtfulness. *Journal of Curriculum Studies, 22,* 41–56.

Newmann, F. M. (1990b). Qualities of thoughtful social studies classes: An empirical profile. *Journal of Curriculum Studies, 22,* 253–275.

Newmann, F. M. (1991). Promoting higher order thinking in social studies: Overview of a study of 16 high school departments. *Theory and Research in Social Education, 19,* 324–340.

Nickell, P. (Ed.). (1999). Authentic assessment in social studies. [Special issue]. *Social Education, 63*(6).

Nitko, A. J., & Brookhart, S. M. (2006). *Educational assessment of students* (5th ed.). Upper Saddle River, NJ: Prentice Hall.

Norton, D. E., Norton, S. E., & McClure, A. (2003). *Through the eyes of a child: An introduction to children's literature* (7th ed.). Upper Saddle River, NJ: Merrill/Prentice Hall.

Norton, J. (1992). The State v. the Big Bad Wolf: A study of the justice system in the elementary school. *Social Studies and the Young Learner, 5*(1), 5–9.

Oakes, J. (1985). *Keeping track: How schools structure inequality.* New Haven, CT: Yale University Press.

O'Connor, K. A., Heafner, T., & Groce, E. (2007). Advocating for social studies: Documenting the decline and doing something about it. *Social Education, 71,* 255–260.

Ogle, D. (1986). K-W-L: A teaching model that develops active reading of expository text. *The Reading Teacher, 39,* 564–570.

Ogle, D., Klemp, R. M., & McBride, W. (2007). *Building literacy in social studies: Strategies for improving comprehension and literacy.* Alexandria, VA: Association for Supervision and Curriculum Development.

Oldendorf, S. B., & Callaway, A. (2008). Connecting children to a bigger world: Reading newspapers in second grade. *Social Studies and the Young Learner, 21*(92), 17–19.

Olmedo, I. M. (1996). Creating contexts for studying history with students learning English. *The Social Studies, 87,* 39–43.

Olsen, D. G. (1995). "Less" can be "more" in the promotion of thinking. *Social Education, 59,* 130–134.

Ovoian, G., & Gregory, D. (1991). Can you dig it? *Social Studies Review, 30*(3), 83–88.

Owen, R. C. (1982). Anthropology and a social science/social studies: One more plea. *Social Studies, 73,* 207–211.

Palinscar, A. S., & Brown, A. L. (1984). Reciprocal teaching of comprehension-fostering and comprehension-monitoring activities. *Cognition and Instruction, 2,* 117–175.

Pang, V. O., Madueno, M., Atlas, M., Stratton, T., Oliger, J., & Page, C. (2008). Addressing the trauma of the California wildfires. *Social Education, 72,* 18–23.

Parker, F. W. (1883). *Talks on teaching.* New York: Kellogg.

Parker, F. W. (1894). *Talks on pedagogics.* New York: Kellogg.

Parker, W. C. (1991). Achieving thinking and decision-making objectives in social studies. In J. P. Shaver (Ed.), *Handbook of research on social studies teaching and learning* (pp. 345–356). New York: Macmillan.

Parker, W. C. (1995). Assessing civic discourse. *Educational Leadership, 52*(5), 84–85.

Parker, W. C. (2001). Classroom discussion: Models for leading seminars and discussions. *Social Education, 75,* 111–115.

Parker, W. C. (2006). Talk isn't cheap: Practicing deliberation n school. *Social Studies and the Young Learner, 19*(1), 12–15.

Parker, W. C. (2008). Knowing and doing in democratic citizenship education. In L. S. Levstik & C. A. Tyson (Eds.), *Handbook of research in social studies education* (pp. 65–80). New York: Routledge.

Partnership for 21st Century Skills and the National Council for the Social Studies. (2008). *21st Century skills map.* (www.21stcenturyskills.org/documents/ss_map_11_12_08.pdf).

Pascopella, A. (2005). Staying alive: Social studies in elementary schools. *Social Studies and the Young Learner, 17*(3), 30–32.

Passe, J. (1988). Developing current events awareness in children. *Social Education, 52,* 531–533.

Passe, J. (1994). Media literacy in a global age. *Social Studies and the Young Learner, 6*(4), 7–9.

Passe, J. (2008). A counter-intuitive strategy: Reduce student stress by teaching current events. *Social Studies and the Young Learner, 20*(3), 27–31.

Passe, J., & Passe, M. (1985). Archaeology: A unit to promote thinking skills. *Social studies, 76,* 238–239.

Patrick, J. J., & Hoge, J. D. (1991). Teaching government, civics, and law. In J. P. Shaver (Ed.), *Handbook of research on social studies teaching and learning* (pp. 427–436).New York: Macmillan.

Paul, R. (Ed.). (2007). Teaching social studies to English-language learners [Special issue]. *The Social Studies, 98*(5).

Phillips, S. U. (1972). Participant structures and communicative competence: Warm Springs children in community and classroom. In C. B. Cazden, V. P. John, & D. Hymes (Eds.), *Functions of language in the classroom* (pp. 370–394). New York: Teachers College Press.

Phipps, S., & Adler, S. (2003). Where's the history? *Social Education, 67,* 296–298.

Piaget, J., & Inhelder, B. (1969). *The psychology of the child* (H. Weaver, Trans.). New York: Basic Books.

Pilonieta, P., & Medina, A. (2010). Reciprocal teaching for the primary grades: "We can do it too!" *The Reading Teacher, 63,* 120–129.

Potter, L. A. (2003). Teaching U.S. history with primary sources [Special issue]. *Social Education, 67*(7).

Powe, F. (1998). Perspectives on the American landscape. *Social Education, 62,* 126–133.

Pratt, L., & Beaty, J. J. (1999). *Transcultural children's literature.* Upper Saddle River, NJ: Merrill/Prentice Hall.

Proctor, D. R., & Haas, M. E. (1993). Social studies and school-based community service programs: Teaching the role of cooperation and legitimate power. *Social Education, 57,* 381–384.

Qin, Z., Johnson, D. W., & Johnson, R. T. (1995). Cooperative versus competitive efforts and problem solving. *Review of Educational Research, 65,* 129–143.

Quigley, C. N., & Bahmueller, C. F. (Eds.). (1991). *Civitas: A framework for civic education.* Calabasas, CA: Center for Civic Education.

Ramirez, M., & Castaneda, A. (1974). *Cultural democracy, bicognitive development, and education.* New York: Academic Press.

Raphael, T. E., & Au, K. H. (2005). QAR: Enhancing comprehension and test taking across grades and content areas. *The Reading Teacher, 59,* 206–221.

Reutzel, D. R., & Cooter, R. B. (2008). *Teaching children to read: The teacher makes the difference* (5th ed.). Upper Saddle River, NJ: Pearson.

Rhoades, L. (1994). Quick-start ideas for teaching current events with newspapers. *Social Education, 58,* 173–174.

Ricchiuti, L. (1998). Hanging in the Louvre: Virtual museum. *California Council for the Social Studies, 38*(1), 57–63.

Risinger, C. F. (2005). Take your students on virtual field trips. *Social Education, 69,* 193–294.

Risinger, C. F. (2010). Learning and writing about local history using the Internet. *Social Education, 74,* 76–77.

Ritchie, D. A. (1995). *Doing oral history.* New York: Twayne.

Roberts, P. L. (1996). *Integrating language arts and social studies for kindergarten and primary children.* Upper Saddle River, NJ: Merrill/Prentice Hall.

Rodriguez, H. M., Salinas, C., & Guberman, S. (2005). Creating opportunities for historical thinking with bilingual students. *Social Studies and the Young Learner, 18*(2), 9–13.

Rosenbaum, D., Potter, L. A., & Eder, E. (2008). Letter to, and paintings by, George Catlin. *Social Education, 72,* 171–176.

Rosenshine, B., & Meister, C. (1994). Reciprocal teaching: A review of the research. *Review of Educational Research, 64,* 479–530.

Ross, D. D., & Bondy, E. (1993). Classroom management for responsible citizenship: Practical strategies for teachers. *Social Education, 57,* 326–328.

Rossi, J. A. (1996). Creating strategies and conditions for civil discourse about controversial issues. *Social Education, 60,* 15–21.

Ruddell, M. R. (1997). *Teaching content reading and writing* (2nd ed.). Boston: Allyn & Bacon.

Ruggiero, V. R. (2003). *Beyond feelings: A guide to critical thinking* (7th ed.). New York: McGraw-Hill.

Rule, A. C., & Sunal, C. S. (1994). Buttoning up a hands-on history lesson: Using everyday objects to teach about historical change. *Social Studies and the Young Learner, 7*(2), 8–11.

Rulli, D. (2005). Websites for primary sources and civics education. *Social Education, 69,* 412–413.

Sanchez, T. (2001). Heroes and heroines: Biographies to live by. *Social Studies and the Young Learner, 13*(1), 27–29.

Sandmann, A. L., & Ahern, J. F. (2002). *Linking literature with life: The NCSS standards and children's literature for the middle grades.* Silver Spring, MD: National Council for the Social Studies.

Saunders, P., Bach, G. L., Calderwood, J. D., & Hansen, W. L. (1984). *A framework for teaching economics: Basic concepts* (2nd ed.). New York: Joint Council on Economic Education.

Saxe, D. (1991). *Social studies in schools: A history of the early years.* Albany: State University of New York Press.

Saxe, D. W. (1992). Framing a theory for social studies foundations. *Review of Educational Research, 62,* 259–278.

Saxe, D. W. (1996). The national history standards: Time for common sense. *Social Education, 60,* 44–48.

Schimmel, D. (1997). Traditional rule making and the subversion of citizenship education. *Social Education, 61,* 70–74.

Schleppegrell, M. J. (2004). The language of schooling: A functional linguistic approach. Mahwah, NJ: Erlbaum.

Schug, M. C. (1983). The development of economic thinking in children and adolescents. *Social Education, 47,* 141–145.

Schug, M. C. (Ed.). (1985). *Economics in the school curriculum, K–12.* Washington, DC: Joint Council on Economic Education and the National Education Association.

Schug, M. C. (1994). How children learn economics. *International Journal of Social Education, 8,* 25–34.

Schug, M. C. (1996). Introducing children to economic reasoning: Some beginning lessons. *The Social Studies, 87,* 114–118.

Schug, M. C., & Lopus, J. (2008). Economic and financial education for the 21st century. *Social Education, 72,* 359–362.

Schug, M. C., & Walstad, W. B. (1991). Teaching and learning economics. In J. P. Shaver (Ed.), *Handbook of research on social studies teaching and learning* (pp. 411–419). New York: Macmillan.

Schug, M. C., & Western, R. D. (Eds.). (2003). Raising interest in economics [Special issue]. *Social Education, 67*(2).

Schug, M. C., & Western, R. D. (Eds.). (2007). Teaching economics in U. S. history [Special issue]. *Social Education, 71*(2).

Schug, M. C., & Wood, W. C. (Eds.). (2009). Teaching economics in a time of unprecedented change [Special issue]. *Social Education, 73*(2).

Schwartz, S. (2000). My family's story: Discovering history at home. *Social Studies and the Young Learner, 12*(3), 6–9.

Segal, A. (2003). Maps as stories about the world. *Social Studies and the Young Learner, 16*(1), 21–25.

Segal, A., & Helfenbein, R. J. (2008). Research on K–12 geography education. In L. S. Levstik & C. A. Tyson (Eds.), *Handbook of research in social studies education* (pp. 259–283). New York: Routledge.

Seikaly, Z. A. (2001). At risk of prejudice: The Arab American community. *Social Education, 65,* 349–351.

Selwyn, D. (1995). *Arts and humanities in the social studies.* Washington, DC: National Council for the Social Studies.

Senesh, L. (1963). *Our working world: Families at work.* Chicago: Science Research Associates.

Shade, B. J. (1986). Is there an Afro-American cognitive style? An explanatory study. *Journal of Black Psychology, 13,* 13–16.

Shade, B. J., & New, C. A. (1993). Cultural influences on learning: Teaching implications. In J. A. Banks & C. A. M. Banks (Eds.), *Multicultural education: Issues and perspectives,* (pp. 317–331). Boston: Allyn & Bacon.

Shaftel, F., & Shaftel, G. (1967). *Role playing for social values: Decision making in the social studies.* Upper Saddle River, NJ: Merrill/Prentice Hall.

Sharan, S. (Ed.). (1997). *Handbook of cooperative learning methods.* New York: Praeger.

Sharan, Y., & Sharan, S. (1989–1990). Group investigation expands cooperative learning. *Educational Leadership, 47*(4), 17–21.

Sheehan, J. J., & Sibit, S. A. (2005). Adapting lessons for the special needs student. *Social Studies and the Young Learner, 18*(1), 4–6.

Shin, E. K., & Alibrandi, M. (2007). Online interactive mapping: Using Google Earth. *Social Studies and the Young Learner, 19*(3), p1–p4.

Short, D. J., Mahrer, C. A., Elfin, A. M., Liten-Tejada, R. A., & Montone, C. L. (1994). *Protest and the American Revolution: An integrated language, social studies, and culture unit for middle school American history.* Washington, DC: National Center for Research on Cultural Diversity and Second Language Learning and Center for Applied Linguistics.

Simmons, D. (1994). "Think globally, acting locally": Using the local environment to explore global issues. *Social Studies and the Young Learner, 6*(4), 10–13.

Simmons, D. (1995). Environmental education, social studies, and education reform: Why is environmental education essential education? *Social Studies and the Young Learner, 8*(1), 9–11.

Simpson, M. (Ed.). (2001). Teaching about tragedy [Special issue]. *Social Education, 65*(6).

Simpson, M. (Ed.). (2009a). Social studies 2.0: Thinking, connecting, and creating technology [Special issue]. *Social Education, 73*(3).

Simpson, M. (Ed.). (2009b). Understanding history through the arts [Special issue]. *Social Education, 73*(4).

Singleton, L. R. (2001). Following a tragic event: A necessary challenge for civic educators. *Social Education, 65,* 413–418.

Slavin, R. E. (1978). Student teams and achievement divisions. *Journal of Research and Development in Education, 12,* 39–49.

Slavin, R. E. (1980). Cooperative learning. *Review of Educational Research, 50,* 315–342.

Slavin, R. E. (1987). Ability grouping and achievement in elementary school: A best evidence synthesis. *Review of Educational Research, 60,* 471–499.

Slavin, R. E. (1989–1990). Research on cooperative learning: Consensus and controversy. *Educational Leadership, 47*(4), 52–55.

Slavin, R. E. (1990). On making a difference. *Educational Researcher, 19*(3), 30–34.

Slavin, R. E. (1992). Cooperative learning in the social studies: Balancing the social and the studies. In R. J. Stahl & R. L. Van Sickle (Eds.), *Cooperative learning in the social studies classroom: An introduction to social study* (pp. 21–25). Washington, DC: National Council for the Social Studies.

Slavin, R. E. (1994a). *Cooperative learning: Theory, research, and practice on line* (2nd ed.). Boston: Allyn & Bacon.

Slavin, R. E. (1994b). *Using student team learning* (2nd ed.) Baltimore: Johns Hopkins University Center for Research on Elementary and Middle Schools.

Sloyer, S. (1982). *Readers' theatre: Story dramatization in the classroom.* Urbana, IL: National Council of Teachers of English.

Smagorinsky, P. (1994). Bring the courtroom to the classroom: Develop civic awareness with simulation activities. *The Social Studies, 85,* 174–180.

Soley, M. (1996). If it's controversial, why teach it? *Social Education, 60,* 9–14.

Spies, P., Bloom, J., Boucher, J., Lucking, C., Norling, L., & Theisen, R. (2004). From crisis to civic engagement: The struggle over social studies standards in Minnesota. *Social Education, 68,* 457–463.

Stahl, R. J., & Van Sickle, R. L. (1992). *Cooperative learning in the social studies classroom: An introduction to social study.* Washington, DC: National Council for the Social Studies.

Stahl, R. J., Van Sickle, R. L., & Stahl, N. N. (Eds.). (2009). *Cooperative learning in the social studies classroom.* Silver Spring, MD: National Council for the Social Studies.

Stanley, W. B. (2005). Social studies and the social order: Transmission or transformation? *Social Education, 69,* 282–286.

Steele, M. M. (2005). Teaching social studies to students with mild disabilities. *Social Studies and the Young Learner, 17*(3), 8–10.

Stevens, R. (2002). A thoughtful patriotism. *Social Education, 66,* 18–24.

Stevens, R. L., & Starkey, M. (2007). Teaching an interdisciplinary unit on shelter. *Social Studies and the Young Learner, 20*(1), 6–10.

Stewart, L. (2006). Celebrating the life and legacy of Rosa Parks. *Social Studies and the Young Learner, 19*(1), 23–26.

Stewart, L. M., & Marshall, J. (2009). Denied access: Using African American children's literature to examine the anatomy of social justice. *Social Studies and the Young Learner, 22*(1), 27–30.

Stokes, S. M. (1997). Curriculum for Native American students: Using Native American values. *The Reading Teacher, 50,* 576–584.

Stoltman, J. P. (1991). Research on geography teaching. In J. P. Shaver (Ed.), *Handbook of research on social studies teaching and learning* (pp. 437–447). New York: Macmillan.

Stone, L. (1991). Intercultural and multicultural education: In V. A. Atwood (Ed.), *Elementary school social studies: Research as a guide to practice* (pp. 34–54). Washington, DC: National Council for the Social Studies.

Suchman, R. (1962). *The elementary school training program in scientific inquiry: Report to the U.S. Office of Education Project Title VII, Project 216.* Urbana: University of Illinois.

Suchman, R. (1966). *Inquiry development program: Developing inquiry.* Chicago: Science Research Associates.

Sunal, C. S., & Ridgway, K. W. (2007). Let's collaborate! [Special issue]. *Social Studies and the Young Learner, 19*(4).

Swan, K. O., & Hofer, M. (2008). Technology and social studies. In L. S. Levstik & C. A. Tyson (Eds.), *Handbook of research in social studies education* (pp. 307–326). New York: Routledge.

Switzer, T. (1986). Teaching sociology in K–12 classrooms. In S. Wronski & D. Bragaw (Eds.), *Social studies and social sciences: A 50-year perspective* (pp. 124–138). Washington, DC: National Council for the Social Studies.

Symcox, L. (2002). *Whose history? The struggle for national standards in American classrooms.* New York: Teachers College Press.

Taba, H. (1967). *Teachers' handbook for elementary social studies.* Palo Alto, CA: Addison-Wesley.

Thelan, H. (1960). *Education and the human quest.* New York: Harper & Row.

Thornton, S. J. (2008). Continuity and change in social studies curriculum. In L. S. Levstik & C. A. Tyson (Eds.), *Handbook of research in social studies education* (pp. 15–32). New York: Routledge.

Thornton, S. J., & Vukelich, R. (1988). Effects of children's understanding of time concepts on historical understanding. *Theory and Research in Social Education, 16,* 69–82.

Tibbett, T. (2004). Listen to learn: Using American music to teach language arts and social studies. San Francisco: Jossey-Bass.

Tierney, R. J., & Readance, J. E. (2005). *Reading strategies and practices: A compendium* (6th ed.). Boston: Allyn & Bacon.

Todd, R. H., & Delahunty, T. (2007). "A" is for aerial maps and art. *Social Studies and the Young Learner, 20*(2), 10–14.

Tomlinson, C. A. (2001). *How to differentiate instruction in mixed abilities classrooms* (2nd ed.). Alexandria, VA: Association for Supervision and Curriculum Development.

Tomlinson, C. A. (2003). *Fulfilling the promise of differentiated classrooms: Strategies and tools for responsive teaching.* Alexandria, VA: Association for Supervision and Curriculum Development.

Trifonoff, K. M. (1997). Introducing thematic maps in the primary grades. *Social Studies and the Young Learner, 11*(1), 17–22.

Tunnell, M. O., & Ammon, R. (1996). The story of ourselves: Fostering multiple historical perspectives. *Social Education, 60,* 212–215.

Turnbull, A., Turnbull, H. R., & Wehmeyer, M. L. (2009). *Exceptional lives: Special education in today's schools* (6th ed.). Upper Saddle River, NJ: Pearson.

Turner, T. N., & Hickey, G. M. (1991). Using radio tapes to teach about the past. *Social Studies and the Young Learner, 3*(4), 6–8.

Tye, K. E. (Ed.). (1990). *Global education.* Alexandria, VA: Association for Supervision and Curriculum Development.

Ukpokodu, O. (2006). Essential characteristics of a culturally conscientious classroom. *Social Studies and the Young Learner, 19*(2), 4–7.

Ullman, A. (2009). Welcome, citizen! Naturalization ceremonies that encourage service learning. *Social Studies and the Young Learner, 22*(2), 8–11.

VanFossen, P. J., & Berson, M. J. (Eds.). (2008). *The impact of technology on education for citizenship.* West Lafayette, IN: Purdue University Press.

VanFossen, P. J., & Nagel, P. (Eds.). (2010). Economics and higher order thinking. *Social Studies and the Young Learner* [Special issue], *22*(3).

Van Sledright, B. A. (2002a). Confronting history's interpretive paradox while teaching fifth graders to investigate the past. *American Educational Research Journal, 39,* 1089–1115.

Van Sledright, B. A. (2002b). *In search of America's past: Learning to read history in elementary school.* New York: Teachers College Press.

Van Sledright, B. A. (2004). What does it mean to think historically . . . and how do you teach it? *Social Education, 68,* 230–233.

Van't Hooft, M., & Anstadt, K. (2007). Got lemonade? Economics in the palm of your hand. In L. Bennett & M. J. Berson (Eds.), *Digital age: Technology-based K–12 lesson plans for social studies* (pp. 18–23). Silver Spring, MD: National Council for the Social Studies.

Vermette, P. J. (1998). *Making cooperative learning work: Student teams in K–12 classrooms.* Upper Saddle River, NJ: Merrill/Prentice Hall.

Virtue, D. C., & Vogler, K. E. (2009). Pairing folktales with textbooks and nonfiction in teaching about culture. *Social Studies and the Young Learner, 21*(3), 21–24.

Vygotsky, L. S. (1962). *Thought and language* (E. Hanfmann & G. Fakar, Trans.). Cambridge, MA: MIT Press. (Original work published 1934.)

Wade, R. C. (1993). Content analysis of social studies textbooks: A review of 10 years of research. *Theory and Research in Social Education, 21,* 232–256.

Wade, R. C. (1994). Community service-learning. *Social Studies and the Young Learner, 6* (3), 1–4.

Wade, R. C. (2008). Service learning. In L. S. Levstik & C. A. Tyson (Eds.), *Handbook of research in social studies education* (pp. 65–80). New York: Routledge.

Wade, R. C., & Everett, S. (1994). Civic participation in third-grade social studies textbooks. *Social Education, 58,* 308–311.

Walbert, K. (2004). How to do it: Oral history projects. *Social Studies and the Young Learner, 16*(4), pullout sections.

Wallace, B. (2005). Teaching thinking skills across the primary curriculum. London: David Fulton.

Walsh, H. M. (Ed.). (1992). Dealing with stereotypes and prejudices [Special issue]. *Social Studies and the Young Learner, 5*(2).

Waring, S. M., Santana, M., & Robinson, K. (2009). Revolutionary movies: Creating digital biographies in the fifth grade. *Social Studies and the Young Learner, 21*(4), 17–19.

Webeck, M. L., Black, M. S., Davis, O. L., & Field, S. (2002). Both sides of the classroom door: After 9–11, the many facets of teaching. *Social Studies and the Young Learner, 14*(3), 6–9.

Wentworth, D. R., & Schug, M. C. (1994). How to use an economic mystery in your history course. *Social Education, 58,* 10–12.

Westheimer, J., & Kahne, J. (2004). What kind of citizen? The politics of educating for democracy. *American Educational Research Journal, 41,* 237–269.

White, J. J. (1988). Searching for substantial knowledge in social studies texts. *Theory and Research in Social Education, 16,* 115–140.

White, J. J. (1989). Anthropology. In *Charting a course: Social studies for the 21st century* (pp. 31–36). Washington, DC: National Commission on Social Studies in the Schools.

White, W. E. (2010). Historic sites and your students. *Social Education, 74,* 74–75.

Wiggins, G. (1989). A true test: Toward more equitable assessment. *Phi Delta Kappan, 70,* 703–713.

Wiggins, G. (1992). Creating tests worth taking. *Educational Leadership, 49* (8), 26–33.

Wiggins, G. (1993). *Assessing student performance.* San Francisco: Jossey-Bass.

Wiggins, G. (1999). *Assessing student performance: Exploring the purpose and limits of testing.* San Francisco: Jossey-Bass.

Wiggins, G., & McTighe, J. (2006). *Understanding by design* (2nd ed.). Upper Saddle River, NJ: Pearson.

Wilen, W. W. (2004). Encouraging reticent students' participation in classroom discussions. *Social Education, 68,* 51–56.

Wilen, W. W., & Phillips, J. A. (1995). Teaching critical thinking: A metacognitive approach. *Social Education, 59,* 135–138.

Wilen, W. W., & White, J. J. (1991). Interaction and discourse in social studies classrooms. In J. P. Shaver (Ed.), *Handbook of research on social studies teaching and learning* (pp. 483–495). New York: Macmillan.

Wilkie, R. (Ed.). (1993). *Environmental education teacher resource handbook.* Milwood, NY: Kraus.

Willison, S., & Ruane, P. (1995). Promoting acceptance of diversity and service to others. *The Social Studies, 86,* 91–92.

Wilson, E. K., Rice, M. L., Bagley, W., & Rice, M. K. (2001). Virtual field trips and newsrooms: International technology into the classroom. *Social Education, 64,* 152–155.

Wilton, S. (1993). New biographies are "better than before." In M. Zarnowski & A. F. Gallagher (Eds.), *Children's literature and social studies: Selecting notable books in the classroom* (pp. 16–19). Washington, DC: National Council for the Social Studies.

Wineburg, S., & Martin, D. (2009). Tampering with history: Adapting primary sources for struggling readers. *Social Education, 73,* 212–216.

Wise, N., & Kon, J. H. (1990). Assessing geographic knowledge with sketch maps. *Journal of Geography, 89,* 123–129.

Wolfgang, C. H., & Kelsay, K. L. (1995). Discipline and the social studies classroom, Grades K–12. *The Social Studies, 86,* 175–182.

Wright, I. (1995). Making critical thinking possible: Options for teachers. *Social Education, 59,* 139–143.

Yell, M. M. (2002). Inquiry with an E-book: A natural strategy for social studies. *Social Education, 66,* 184–185.

Yell, M. M. (Ed.). (2008). Developing 21st century skills [Special issue]. *Social Education, 72*(7).

Yell, M. M., & Box, J. (2008). Embrace the future: NCSS and P21. *Social Education, 72,* 347–349.

Yopp, H. K., & Yopp, R. H. (1996). *Literature-based reading activities.* Boston: Allyn & Bacon.

Young, K. A. (1994). *Constructing buildings, bridges, and minds: Building an integrated curriculum through social studies.* Portsmouth, NH: Heinemann.

Young, T. A., & Vardell, S. (1993). Weaving readers' theater and nonfiction into the curriculum. *The Reading Teacher, 46,* 396–406.

Zarnowski, M. (1990). *Learning about biographies: A reading and writing approach for children.* Urbana, IL: National Council of Teachers of English.

Zarnowski, M., & Gallagher, A. F. (Eds.). (1993). *Children's literature and social studies: Selecting and using notable books in the classroom.* Washington, DC: National Council for the Social Studies.

Zarrillo, J. (1989). History and library books. *Social Studies and the Young Learner, 2*(2), 17–19.

Zarrillo, J. (1994). *Multicultural literature, multicultural teaching: Units for the elementary grades.* Fort Worth, TX: Harcourt Brace.

Zong, G., Wilson, A., & Quashiga, A. Y. (2008). Global education. In L. S. Levstik & C. A. Tyson (Eds.), *Handbook or research in social studies education* (pp. 197–216). New York: Routledge.

Zwiers, J. (2008). *Building academic language: essential practices for content classrooms, grades 5–12.* San Francisco: Jossey Bass.

Author Index

Subject Index

National Council for the Social Studies (NCSS), 3, 74,
        161, 195, 211, 225, 293, 301
    Ad Hoc committee on Ability grouping, 161
    Ad Hoc committee on Golbal Education, 315
    citizenship education, 5, 299
    data collection, 12
    diversity, 12
    integrated curriculum, 138
    Select Subcommittee, 239
    Task Force on Early Childhood/Elementary Social
        Studies, 19
    Task Force on Ethnic Studies Curriculum
        Guidelines, 226, 301
    Task Force on Revitalizing Citizenship
        Education, 5
    Task Force on Scope and Sequence, 19, 176
    Task Force on Standards for Teaching and Learning
        in the Social Studies, 4, 40
National Geography Standards, 46, 86, 189, 286, 294
National heritage, 255
National projects, on citizenship education, 230–233
National Standards for Civics and Government, 10, 86,
        225–226, 230–231, 234, 236, 244, 246
National Standards for History, 10, 71, 88, 145, 191,
        220, 255–256
*Native American Testimony: An Anthology of Indian
        and White Relations,* 125, 126
Native Hawaiians, 105, 106
News media, 321
New York Times 321
No Child Left Behind (NCLB), 9, 226
Nonwritten products, 73
Notes, 76
Novels, juvenile, 137
Number the Stars, 215

Oars, Sails, and Steam: A Picture Book of Ships, 60, 67
Objectives
    direct instruction, 36–37
Objectivity, 177
Observation, direct, 172
Ocean-Going Giants, 67
Online expeditions, 259, 264–265
Open-ended journal prompts, 42
Operators, 164
Oral activities, 77
Oral history, 125
    instructional units and, 38
Oral reports, 57, 77, 173

Osa's Pride, 329
Other Side, The, 329
Our Working World, 306
Outline maps, 287
Out of the Dust, 214
Ox-Cart Man, 141, 262, 267, 270–271

Pantomime, 59, 65, 99, 100, 141, 190, 270
Parent conferences, 90
Parker, Francis W., 6–7, 18, 131
Parthenon, The, 21, 32
Participation processes, 18. See also Student
        involvement
Participatory writing, 216
Patchwork Quilt, The, 314, 329
Peel, E. A., 253
Peer pressure, 312
People
    global education and, 318
    multicultural education and, 105, 121–122, 225
    social studies theme for, 11
Perceptual global education, 315–316
Peter's Chair, 94
Petitions, circulating, 238
Photographs, 21, 44, 57, 95, 99, 110, 143, 147
Physical anthropology, 300
Physical systems, 280
Piaget, Jean, 253, 276
Pictures, for inquiry learning and critical thinking,
        184–185
Pilgrims of Plymouth Colony, The, 186
Places, 53. See also Geography
Plan book grid, 31
Planning
    cooperative learning, 160
    group investigation, 173
Plants, 318–320
Playground rules, 241
Plays, 142
Pocahontas, 212,
Political campaigns, 218, 229, 233
Political candidates, 230
Political organization, anthropological study of,
        243, 300
Political parties, 238
Portfolios, student, 48, 72, 85, 88, 91
Positive interdependence, 158
Power, social studies theme for, 11
PowerPoint, 195–196, 217, 276, 290, 312, 320